Shapers of English Calvinism, 1660–1714

Shapers of English Calvinism, 1660–1714

Variety, Persistence, and Transformation

DEWEY D. WALLACE, JR.

OXFORD
UNIVERSITY PRESS

OXFORD
UNIVERSITY PRESS

Oxford University Press, Inc., publishes works that further
Oxford University's objective of excellence
in research, scholarship, and education.

Oxford   New York
Auckland   Cape Town   Dar es Salaam   Hong Kong   Karachi
Kuala Lumpur   Madrid   Melbourne   Mexico City   Nairobi
New Delhi   Shanghai   Taipei   Toronto

With offices in
Argentina   Austria   Brazil   Chile   Czech Republic   France   Greece
Guatemala   Hungary   Italy   Japan   Poland   Portugal   Singapore
South Korea   Switzerland   Thailand   Turkey   Ukraine   Vietnam

Copyright © 2011 by Oxford University Press, Inc.

Published by Oxford University Press, Inc.
198 Madison Avenue, New York, New York 10016

www.oup.com

Oxford is a registered trademark of Oxford University Press

Library of Congress Cataloging-in-Publication Data
Wallace, Dewey D.
    Shapers of English Calvinism, 1660-1714 : variety, persistence, and transformation / Dewey D.
Wallace, Jr.
        p.   cm.—(Oxford studies in historical theology)
    Includes bibliographical references (p.) and index.
    ISBN 978-0-19-974483-1 (hardcover : alk. paper)
1. England—Church history—17th century   2. England—Church history—18th
century   3. Calvinism—England—History—17th century.   4. Calvinism—England—History—
18th century.   5. Reformed Church—Doctrines—History—17th century.   6. Reformed
Church—Doctrines—History—18th century.   7. Theology—England—History—17th
century.   8. Theology—England—History—18th century.   I. Title.
    BR757.W34 2011
    284'.24109032—dc22   2010036755

1 3 5 7 9 8 6 4 2

Printed in the United States of America
on acid-free paper

For Robert G. Jones

And my other colleagues, past and present, at the George Washington University Department of Religion

Contents

Acknowledgments

A book that has been gestating for as long as this one accumulates a great many debts owed to those who helped me bring it to birth. The staffs of many libraries have been helpful as I pursued my research, including those of the British Library, the Lambeth Palace Library, the Library of the Warburg Institute, and Doctor Williams's Library, all in London, the Bodleian Library at Oxford University, the Firestone Library of Princeton University, the Speer Library of Princeton Theological Seminary, the Library of the Virginia Theological Seminary in Alexandria, Virginia, and in Washington, DC, the Folger Shakespeare Library, the Library of Congress, the American University Library, the Library of the Wesley Theological Seminary, and the Gelman Library of George Washington University. Particular acknowledgment is due to the library of Emmanuel College, Cambridge University, and to the late Frank Stubbings and Peter Jackson, who facilitated my use of the Peter Sterry manuscripts housed there. Thanks are also due to the University Facilitating Fund of George Washington University for Research Grants and to the National Endowment for the Humanities for a Travel to Collections Grant.

For encouragement and conversations regarding this project in its early stages I am indebted to Joseph W. Martin, Donald McKim, Rogers B. Miles, Ted Underwood, and the late Richard L. Greaves. Lunchtime conversations with two of my George Washington University colleagues, Alf Hiltebeitel and Harry E. Yeide, gave me an opportunity to clarify some of my ideas, even if they had to listen to a lot of matter remote from their own fields. Help with footnotes, bibliography, references, and perplexing questions came from Paul Duff, Jon Quitslund, William L. Fox, Paul Lim, Peter Thuesen, and Richard A. Muller. Ted Underwood responded helpfully to my queries about John Bunyan. Papers related to the subjects of this book were read at meetings of the American Society of Church History and commented on by Richard Greaves and Margo Todd, and I also received helpful comments from some who heard my presentation on Theophilus Gale at the Millersville Conference on Puritanism in Old and New England. An early version of the chapter on Peter Sterry was read and commented on by Patrick Cook and Grover Zinn. Later versions of chapters were read by Mark Noll, Paul Lim, and Michael McGiffert. And, far beyond the call of duty, the entire typescript was read by Dwight Bozeman. Thanks are also due to the two readers for Oxford University Press, whose suggestions have greatly improved the final version of this book. I am deeply appreciative of the assistance I have received from the staff at Oxford University Press, including Cynthia Read, Charlotte Steinhardt, Michael O'Connor, and Jennifer Rappaport. Allison Taylor helped me with computer-related questions and also with many tasks in the preparation of the final typescript. Help from all of these persons convinces me that the republic of letters is alive and well, and all of them have my deepest gratitude for their efforts in making this a better book, though, of course, I, not they, am responsible for whatever shortcomings remain.

A Note to Readers:

A word about quotations from (mostly) seventeenth-century texts will clarify my editorial practice: I have only modernized spelling, punctuation, capitalization, and abbreviations where it seemed needed for the sake of clarity—excessive change can detract from the tenor and vitality of the original texts.

Introduction

This book has arisen out of extensive reading in and reflection on the religious literature of the Restoration era and its aftermath in England, especially that of dissenting Protestants. The writers and thinkers considered here were late blooms on the Puritan plant and had their foundation in Calvinist piety and theology, including the one of them who conformed to the Church of England. They lived through a transitional phase of English Calvinism, in which certain strands of Calvinist thought were shaped in ways that had considerable influence on the future. What follows is an exposition and analysis of five representations of English Calvinist, or more accurately, Reformed spiritual and theological discourse in their social and cultural contexts during the era of the Restoration, the Glorious Revolution, and the reigns of William and Mary and Queen Anne. Each of these Calvinist thinkers and writers produced a rich and complex body of theological and spiritual works with the exception of Joseph Alleine, whose career was cut short by an untimely death, but about whose ministry an influential picture that amounted to a particular version of Calvinism was shaped. I have not presented a complete picture of these religious figures but have explored aspects and themes of their writings that merit further probing in light of some of the pressing questions raised in their times. But in no case have I done full justice to the range of their thinking, only calling attention to certain salient motifs. Rather, I have examined the challenges they encountered, the variety of Calvinist thinking they reflected, the persistence of older patterns of Calvinism among them, and their transforming reformulations. What follows are studies in five different English Calvinist moments or developments, based on individual religious writers in three cases and on group preoccupations in the remaining two cases. In each case they shaped and reshaped Calvinism, showing in the process its variety, persistence, and transformation. All five cases also represent theological or spiritual trajectories that long continued in British and American Protestant religiosity. They were also chosen because they defy stereotypes about Calvinism by being something Calvinists are not generally thought in their era to have been—mystics, purveyors of "ancient theology," natural theologians, Church of England conformists. This is less true of Joseph Alleine than the others, but even in his case the free offer of salvation that he proclaimed was increasingly detached from Calvinist predestinarianism, as in the later example of Methodism.

That Calvinism declined in England (and elsewhere) after 1660 has long been taken for granted. One of the chapters in Gerald R. Cragg's influential study *From Puritanism to the Age of Reason* was entitled "The Eclipse of Calvinism" and that has been a prevailing view of how Calvinism fared between the Restoration and the end of the reign of Queen Anne.[1] Taking into consideration the association of Calvinism with rebellion in the English civil wars, it is no wonder that many within the Church of England sought a new theological idiom, and even among Dissenters Calvinism underwent some attenuation after 1660. Christopher Hill was perhaps more specific when he remarked of Bunyan's time that one "sees the end of predestinarian theology as the major intellectual force it had been in the preceding century and a half."[2] But clichés about decline can be misleading, and the full story is more complicated than mere decline; it might be asked, for example, what aspects of it declined and among what groups? Calvinism was a powerful cultural force in early modern Europe, a cultural, experiential, and intellectual frame of reference that included doctrine, piety, attitudes, and life orientations and was far from an entirely spent force in the later seventeenth century. Calvinism meant not only the doctrine of predestination or a system of theology but also a certain cast of mind as well as theological approach and trajectory that has been represented in various ways down to the present by such diverse theologians as Friedrich Schleiermacher and Karl Barth. During the later seventeenth century and into the next in England there were persistences and creative transformations of Calvinism, and the present focus is on some of these continuations of the Reformed tradition. It is well known that the evangelical revivals of the eighteenth and nineteenth centuries breathed new life into a particular permutation of the Calvinist heritage.

There was considerable diversity in these Calvinist continuations. Variety had always been present in Reformed theology, as attested by the differences between the theologians of Geneva and Zurich from the beginning of the movement, the debates carried on by an international assembly of Reformed theologians at Dort, and the discussions sparked by the theological revisions of Moise Amyraux among the Huguenots or Johannes Cocceius among the Dutch. These and other differences within the Calvinist family were sometimes more than mere matters of nuance.

Many varieties of Reformed thinking were present in England in 1660, at the beginning of the Restoration era. Scholastic orthodoxy in a Reformed vein was one of them, and though it was more a theological method than a distinct school of theology, its greatest English representative in the era, John Owen, was one of the towering theologians of the Calvinist heritage. I have written about Owen elsewhere,[3] and several recent books have provided sophisticated studies of his thought.[4] Among the authors treated here, there is much that can be regarded as scholastic in the method and approach of John Howe, John Edwards, and Theophilus Gale, some of which will appear in succeeding chapters, although Reformed scholasticism as such is not a major focus of this study.

For all that most Calvinists decried it as heresy, much of what has been described as Antinomianism can be classified as another Calvinistic variety. There was a strong predestinarian component to Antinomian thinking, and other Calvinist emphases, such as the imputation of Christ's righteousness to believers, were central to the Antinomians. The controversies over Antinomianism that burst forth in late seventeenth-century England found many of the strictest Calvinists bordering on Antinomianism, or at least not particularly fearful of it.[5] Many of the strictly Calvinist Independents found the republication in 1690 of Tobias Crisp's *Christ Alone Exalted,* a work long reputed by many to be Antinomian, to be acceptable, but the more moderate Calvinists assailed it as Antinomian error. The spin-off of Hyper-Calvinism, which took special root among some Independents and Particular Baptists in the eighteenth century, was clearly related to strict Calvinism, particularly of those who fellow-traveled with Antinomianism in the 1690s.[6]

This book, however, focuses on other, and in some cases, less studied and less familiar Reformed variations, such as the mystical Calvinism of Peter Sterry, the combination of "ancient theology" and Calvinism in Theophilus Gale, the evangelical Calvinism of the circle gathered around Joseph Alleine, the natural theology of a group of moderate Calvinists associated with Richard Baxter, and the Church of England Calvinism of John Edwards. Four among these cases have in common that they are about Calvinists in relation to ways of thinking not easily fitted to Calvinism or at least not fitted to it at that time, as in the case of Church of England Calvinism. On the other hand, the evangelical Calvinism of Joseph Alleine is hardly a variety of Calvinism in which Reformed theology is joined to something not usually identified with it; but nonetheless it represents a distinct variety of Reformed discourse. It must of course be acknowledged that the practitioners of these types of Calvinism often overlapped with one another and shaded into one another. Variety is thus evident from the mere fact of the different directions into which Calvinism was taken by each of the individuals or groups examined but it must not be understood as referring to a complete difference of outlook.

The persistence of earlier patterns of theological thought and religious experience long after 1660 is also a striking feature of these thinkers. Even for those who were going in new directions, there was a Calvinist persistence that was foundational for the significant intellectual adaptations, reformulations, and transformations that were carried out, as an earlier regnant English Calvinism followed out some of its original impulses and produced a variety of religious expression. Calvinist Persistence is apparent from the way in which each operated out of a distinctly Calvinist core. None of the varieties examined in this book was altogether new: Gale pursued the theme of an ancient theology that had been followed by a few earlier Calvinists, though none perhaps worked it out with his thoroughness; Sterry was not the first Calvinist mystic, though few pushed mysticism as far as he; the evangelical Calvinism of Joseph Alleine and his circle was the continuation of a long and fairly consistent tradition of Puritan piety; there were precursors of a more moderate Calvinism long before Baxter, Bates, and Howe turned their attention to natural theology, Calvin himself having given much consideration to it; and John Edwards insisted that he was merely restating what had been the original theology of the Church of England.

But England after 1660 was undergoing profound intellectual and cultural changes that challenged older ways of thinking and acting, and the modifications, adaptations, and transformations made by English Calvinists will be described and analyzed in what follows. Reformulation within the Calvinist heritage is perhaps seen most clearly with the moderate Calvinism of Baxter's circle. Reacting to the new intellectual milieu in which they found themselves, they liberalized their Calvinist heritage in ways parallel to that of the Church of England Latitudinarians. Edwards likewise reacted to that milieu, certainly by challenging its departure from Calvinism, but also, upon investigation, by certain touches of the moderate Calvinist mood. He also illustrated some of the strains felt by a staunch Calvinist within the Church of England: his penchant for controversy comes out as he claims to be the true representative of the original English Reformation but felt marginalized within the established church and reacted to that feeling. Sterry also reacted to a new situation, especially the loss of power by one who had been close to it, at least in religious affairs, during the Cromwellian regime. His interaction with some of the more radical religious thinkers of the commonwealth era colored his reformulations as he turned from the collective eschatological hopes with which he bombarded his civil war audiences as a preacher to parliament to an inner spirituality in which eschatological hope was both collective through his universalism and individual, but not this-worldly, and his universalism can be regarded as a response to the incipient relativism of the age as well as an outgrowth of a mystic's overflowing charity. The reformulations of the Alleine circle are more subtle but can be found in an individualistic turn toward personal conversion and edification, not in the parish system of a national church but in the warm fellowship of the withdrawn conventicle. Gale, in formulating his ideas, reflected his awareness of the Platonic revival of his time, which he connected with the Augustinian Platonism of France's Jansenism as well as his awareness of the Cartesian philosophy. He clearly wanted to be a participant in the international republic of letters, reflecting the lure of some of its lore for him, particularly that of the "ancient theology."

The first chapter establishes context and challenges, sketching in a background for the advantage of those readers who come to this book with a general interest in the history of Calvinism rather than a thorough knowledge of seventeenth-century England. After characterizing Calvinism and Puritanism as well as some of their vicissitudes, it describes the ecclesiastical situation that was the context for these Calvinist thinkers and writers. The first chapter next turns to the intellectual challenges that confronted late seventeenth-century Calvinists, including a new understanding of rationality, the new science, scoffing irreligion, Deism, atheism, Socinianism, and increasing knowledge of other religions, with its attendant relativizing of truth.

The remaining chapters turn to the persons and groups who are the principal subjects of this book, beginning with Peter Sterry, the oldest of those examined here, and his Calvinist mysticism, and then proceeding to Theophilus Gale, perhaps the most old-fashioned of the group, and his Calvinist Hermeticism and version of the "ancient theology." The Calvinist evangelicalism of a circle that published and promoted books by and about Joseph Alleine comes next; Alleine was younger than all but Edwards, and his life was short, but his influence was established in the 1670s, as was also the case with Gale. The next to last chapter turns to a Calvinist version of natural theology adapted to an incipient age of reason through the efforts of Richard Baxter, William Bates, and John Howe. The final chapter presents in John Edwards a late example of Church of England Calvinism.

Each of the theological authors considered, several of whom were strikingly idiosyncratic, is interesting in his own right and proves an important point about later seventeenth-century English Calvinism on the eve of the Enlightenment; collectively they show a diversity of creative adaptations of the Calvinist impulse in a changing era. Each variety also adumbrates one of the paths taken in modern Christian thought and life. Most of them are also "writers of the second and third rank" of whom, Jacques Le Goff has said, may "tell us more about the regular currents of intellectual life" than thinkers of world-historical significance;[7] and while they are probably not among those whom Hans Frei had in mind when he declared that modern theology began in England at the end of the seventeenth century,[8] they represent paths to the modern as well as continuity with the past.

I

English Calvinism in a New Era

Before examining the religious thinkers and writers who are the principal subject of this book, it is important to clarify the meaning of Calvinism, relate it to the Puritan movement, place it in its English ecclesiastical context of conformity and Dissent, consider the intellectual world of the early English Enlightenment, and survey the challenges it faced in the later seventeenth century, including a changing definition of rationality, the rise of natural science, an awareness of other religions, scoffing irreligion, Deism, atheism, and Socinianism. This chapter thus provides the political, religious, and intellectual setting for those studied in the following chapters and seeks to clarify some of the problems on their cultural horizon to which they responded.

Calvinism

The English poet and literary critic Donald Davie, writing sympathetically about the literature of the English dissenting tradition, observed that "the term 'Calvinistic' is a catch-all bogey word, possessing, often enough, no strictly accountable meaning at all."[1] A study in the history of English Calvinism accordingly requires some attempt at defining Calvinism and some specification of what is meant by English Calvinism. As a term used in this book, "Calvinism" is shorthand for the Reformed tradition or Reformed theology, a distinct branch and theological school of Reformation Protestantism that emerged first among the Swiss and Rhineland reformers Ulrich Zwingli and Martin Bucer as an alternative to the Lutheran Reformation, with Calvin himself, oddly enough, a bit of a latecomer to the movement, even though providing it with its most generally recognizable name. But Calvinism can be a misleading term since Calvin was one among many theologians of the movement and belonged to the second generation of Protestant reformers, receiving much of his inspiration from Bucer. However, he has generally been regarded as the most important formulator of Reformed teaching, though he was never more than the first among equals in his relation to earlier and later theologians of this tradition.

Nonetheless, the term "Calvinism" has taken root and has the merit of suggesting an outlook that can be regarded as a powerful cultural impulse, a task only awkwardly fulfilled by references to the "Reformed tradition," which has the potential of being misunderstood as referring to Reformation Protestantism as a whole.[2] Discussing the term "Calvinism" in his essay "England and International Calvinism, 1558–1640," Patrick Collinson has outlined some of the problems involved in the use of the term at the same time that he concluded its use is unavoidable.[3] Accordingly, I will use the term "Calvinism" in what follows but also interchange it with the more accurate expressions Reformed theology and Reformed tradition, where it can be done without confusion or awkwardness.[4]

Another reason for using the term "Calvinism," especially in a book dealing with the later seventeenth century, is that by the second half of the seventeenth century "Calvinism" or variants of it such as "Calvinian" were widely used, and acceptable to those who identified themselves with the tradition. It was not always thus: in 1583 Walter Travers, who spoke for Elizabethan Presbyterianism and sparked the response of Richard Hooker, objected to the term; only "papists," he declared, "immortalized founders," as in such groups as Dominicans and Franciscans.[5] Thus the name "Calvinist" was not much used at first by insiders, but by opponents, in various English forms such as "Calvinian" or "Calvinistical." Only after the middle of the seventeenth century did it come to be widely accepted within the Reformed tradition, and then it was still used sparingly, for they considered themselves as having reformed the church and its theology in accordance with scriptural and early Christian norms. Only gradually did they accept the term "Calvinist" as applying to themselves, and even then seemed to think it somewhat limiting, as they were never committed to slavishly following Calvin or any other nonbiblical writer. At the sectarian edge of English Calvinism even in the later seventeenth century, John Bunyan disavowed following Calvin, insisting that he was merely following scripture.[6]

In fact, it is somewhat surprising how seldom English Calvinists cited or discussed Calvin. However, sixteenth- and seventeenth-century writers often only cited by name much earlier thinkers—there persisted the notion that "authors" were figures of the remote past who could be cited as authoritative precedents in an argument more effectively than contemporaries or those of the recent past. Ancient classical authors are often cited by name, as are patristic authors and even medieval "doctors." Later Reformed theologians often depended, frequently without citation, on their Calvinist contemporaries rather than Calvin in theological argumentation because these later authors were more precise and up-to-date than he in formulating theological refinements of the sort that had become useful in disputation with theological opponents. Moreover, seventeenth-century theologians did not engage in theology by discussing fellow theologians and then explicitly refining or modifying the views of predecessors in their tradition, citations to others appearing mainly when precedents for a point were being amassed. Theology was an exercise in the definition of timeless truths in which discussion of particular thinkers was not generally relevant—unless they were opponents, who were then cited in profusion. And no doubt another reason for a certain reticence with regard to "Calvinism" was that it had become a term of reproach for its enemies, exemplified in John Milton's statement that "the Calvinist is taxed with Predestination, and to make God the Author of sin,"[7] which might be prudently avoided by its supporters. But it is clear that when Calvin's teachings or those associated with Calvinism were attacked these later Reformed theologians knew that they were under attack and mobilized for action. And Calvin was certainly not forgotten in England where the publication of his writings, both in the original Latin or in translation, proceeded apace, with dozens of editions and reprints.

The authors studied in the present book vary in their comfort with and use of the term "Calvinist." The last chapter will examine the reasons why the sole conformist to the Church of England examined extensively in this book, John Edwards, was the one who most commonly and aggressively, even defiantly, chose to use the term. Richard Baxter, for example, was somewhat guarded about its use, though he did include Calvin (and not Luther) among the rather long list of those with whom he hoped to converse in heaven, as he cleared up various points of theology and practice during his "everlasting rest." Theophilus Gale was comfortable with the term as a self-designation, while Joseph Alleine in his published writings seems only to have used it once. The range expressed in references to Calvin and Calvinism by English authors is broad: William Ames is typical in referring to Calvin as one of the best interpreters of scripture, Samuel Lee honored him as "judicious Calvin," and Thomas Jollie, defending his position on admittance to the Lord's Supper, cited Calvin as a precedent for his view. In the voluminous writings of John Owen, Calvin is cited several dozen times, a little less than Cicero and much less than St. Augustine or Tertullian, and decidedly less than opponents such as Socinus and Robert Bellarmine.[8]

Reformed or Calvinist theology was characterized by certain distinctive doctrines and emphases. Many of the earliest references to "Calvinism" in the wider European context meant by it the rejection of the real presence of Christ in the Eucharist as that was understood by both Lutherans (who were apparently the first to use the term "Calvinists") and Catholics and the teaching of a more spiritual or symbolic presence in its place.[9] In addition to this, the Swiss Reformers had from the beginning of the Reformed tradition placed greater emphasis on the place of law and commandment in the Christian life than had the Lutherans, an emphasis eventually formalized in the Reformed notion of a third use of the law, whereby in addition to restraining evildoers and convicting of sin the law also served to guide believers. This third use of the law was in turn related to the Reformed emphasis on believers coming to salvation not only through justification but also through their sanctification which was seen not as just the result but the purpose of God's predestination of the elect. Christian law, as in the Mosaic commandments and the teaching of Christ, was regarded as giving direction to the sanctified life without compromising its character as a gift of grace; thus the Imitation of Christ, rooted in late medieval piety and found by Calvin in Bernard of Clairvaux as well as in Erasmian Christian humanists, played a role in Reformed thinking. The Reformed tradition also pushed church reform to a farther point, in accordance with biblical precedent, than had the Lutheran Reformation, and sought to shape a more thoroughly Christian social order. Reformed Biblicism with its concomitant urge to further reformation had great resonance in the later generations of the Protestant Reformation. In social and ecclesiastical context, such emphasis on law, order, and discipline can be understood as a reaction to some of the possible radical implications of Luther's declarations about Christian freedom, implications which threatened to undermine the stability and social utility of the Reformation cause.

The extent to which later Calvinists were faithful to Calvin has been a matter of considerable argument. Calvin wrote his theology in the context of the excitement of the striking insights of the early Reformation, and a later Reformed scholasticism developed that was methodologically at some remove from Calvin and sometimes less flexible in its formulations. Nonetheless, Reformed theology was a living tradition and not just the theology of Calvin, so that development, both as the unpacking of the implications of the early Reformed theologians, including Calvin, and as the need to adapt the Reformed outlook to new conditions and challenges, was inevitable.[10] Thus Calvinism came to stand for a position that emphasized the doctrinal points enshrined confessionally in the most international of the Reformed statements of faith, the Canons and Decrees of the Synod of Dort of 1618. And while the decrees of Dort as a definer of Calvinism can be exaggerated, insofar as there were many strands of Reformed theology, this doctrinal statement articulated what came to be known as the "five points" of Calvinism: unconditional election (predestination), total depravity, limited atonement, irresistible grace, and perseverance of the saints, that is the indefectibility of the elect—what some later Calvinists called "once saved, always saved." But these points were a kind of carapace surrounding and protecting the softer body of Reformed religiosity and teaching, which consisted of an overwhelming sense of divine sovereignty and of the pure gratuitousness of the saving grace of God, both of which were soteriological in focus.

English Calvinism

This book, however, is not about Calvinism generally but about English Calvinists. Although English Calvinists felt themselves to be participants in an international movement that included Scottish, Swiss, French, Dutch, Hungarian, and many German Protestants,[11] English Calvinism had a very distinctive history and developed some particular traits of its own which were to be influential in the larger Reformed world.

Though it sounds oxymoronic, English Calvinism preceded Calvin insofar as the Swiss and Rhineland theology associated with Zurich, Basel, and Strasbourg was a prime influence on England's earliest reformers from Tyndale onward, very few of whom accepted Luther's ideas about the Eucharistic presence or his views on the place of law in the Christian life. This of course underlines the usefulness, especially in earlier periods, of referring to Reformed rather than Calvinist theology. Such a prime mover of English Protestantism as Thomas Cranmer underwent a steady development toward Reformed rather than Lutheran Protestantism, a development that had reached maturity in the reign of Edward VI, a reign which saw the triumph of these views in the Church of England, abetted by the presence in the universities of the island nation of such Reformed luminaries as Martin Bucer (Cambridge) and Peter Martyr Vermigli (Oxford).[12]

After the interlude of Catholic restoration under Queen Mary and during the reign of Elizabeth I, Reformed theology was the prevailing outlook of the Church of England. It is generally conceded that this Calvinist hegemony persisted until challenged by King Charles I and Archbishop of Canterbury William Laud, whose program for the Church of England sought to supplant Calvinism with a more conservative Protestantism that had much in common with Lutheranism, especially in its focus on the sacraments and downplaying of such tenets of Calvinism as unconditional predestination. By analogy with the Dutch movement, this was called "Arminianism" by Calvinist opponents. This "Laudian" turn in the Church of England became the occasion for the resurfacing in the Church of England of much traditional ceremony and older notions of Episcopal authority.[13] Feared by many in England as preparation for a return to "popery," this "Laudianism" begot fierce opposition that played a role in the coming of civil war and the overthrow of the monarchy. During the era of civil war and Interregnum, Calvinism returned to its former prominence in a greatly altered national church but also had to compete, in a newly freed religious atmosphere, with a variety of sectarian ideas inimical to it. With the Restoration of the monarchy in 1660, Calvinism passed under a cloud in the established church because of its seeming involvement in the attack upon monarchy and its connection with a discredited Puritan ecclesiastical opposition but hardly disappeared. Although earlier the prevailing outlook of English Protestants, Calvin and Calvinism became for many objects of obloquy and hostility in the generations after 1660. David Field has described this rejection of Calvinism as "the single most important feature on the theological landscape of England in the later seventeenth century."[14]

Calvinist Scholasticism

During the Elizabethan and early Stuart periods, English Calvinism underwent some significant changes, which were related to developments in the Reformed churches elsewhere. One of these developments was the emergence of a theological scholasticism, and Richard Baxter, musing on his youth and education, provides insight into its appeal and suggests its need. "In order to the knowledge of divinity," Baxter wrote, "my inclination was most to logic and metaphysics . . . these had my labour and delight, which occasioned me . . . to plunge myself . . . into the study of controversies, and to read all the Schoolmen I could get; for next practical divinity, no books so suited with my disposition as Aquinas, Scotus, Durandus, Ockam and their disciples; because I thought they narrowly searched after truth and brought things out of the darkness of confusion; for I could never from my first studies endure confusion."[15] The shaping of a Protestant scholasticism emerged from a variety of imperatives in the Protestant world, perhaps foremost of which was the need for a more systematic statement and thorough articulation of doctrine, catalyzed both by the polemical desideratum of refuting Roman, Lutheran, and other opponents, and by the importance of presenting Reformed doctrine in a way appropriate for teaching it to others, particularly in the universities (scholasticism in this era still retained something of its original meaning of academic discourse). Once the need for this kind of theological activity was felt, it was natural that it should increasingly draw upon medieval theological resources to find language, method, and structure for a more precise articulation of doctrine. But the medieval Catholic scholastic tradition, which had been excoriated by Protestants as unbiblical could hardly be borrowed wholesale; it was "mediated and modified" by such Reformed theologians attuned to the scholastic mode as Peter Martyr Vermigli, Jerome Zanchi, Theodore Beza, and Zacharias Ursinus. Such a development also required some attention to delineating the respective spheres and resolving the disagreements between theology and philosophy, but it was especially important as a method which Protestant theologians thought could be usefully put to the service of Reformed theology without entailing the unprofitable quibbling and unedifying speculation for which its humanist critics and the Reformers had assailed it.[16] In fact, the Protestant scholasticism of the seventeenth century and earlier mingled elements of Renaissance humanist rhetoric with their scholasticism to such a degree that the conventional opposition of humanist and scholastic does not apply to their approach. This inclusion of humanist method and insight in the scholastic enterprise was exemplified not only by the use of the rhetorical practice of breaking texts down into their topics (or loci) in order to provide orderly exposition of their content but also by the infusion of scholastic theological discussion with philological analysis and contextualized discussion of biblical and other texts that had been such a signal achievement of the Christian humanism of the Renaissance. These approaches can be seen in the enormous output of Reformed biblical scholarship produced during the seventeenth century.[17]

Logical Method

In the passage of Baxter's autobiographical *Reliquiae Baxterianae* already cited, Baxter added that "distinction and method seemed to me of that necessity, that without them I could not be said to know; and the disputes which forsook them or abused them seem but as incoherent dreams."[18] Distinction and method meant logic, and for a system of logic, the western intellectual tradition had long built upon that of Aristotle, whose logical rules and vocabulary suffused medieval scholasticism and carried over into the Protestant version, in spite of Luther's invective against him as a "rascally heathen."[19] But Aristotelian logic and the devices of medieval scholasticism proved to be too deeply embedded in university education as a tool of instruction and a frame of knowledge, and too helpful in clarifying theological complexities, even in Protestant countries, to be easily dislodged. In any case, it was primarily a method. A version of Aristotle adapted to Protestant uses had been mediated through such Italian Protestants familiar with Thomas Aquinas as Vermigli and Zanchi, and was cultivated by Calvin's Genevan successor, Theodore Beza. Both Vermigli and Zanchi mediated the renewed and revised Aristotelianism of Renaissance Italy, especially connected with Pietro Pomponazzi and Padua.[20]

Also attractive to Reformed theologians and an aspect of Reformed scholasticism was the new logic of Petrus Ramus, who, in his process of developing another method for the articulation of theology and of all knowledge, had assailed Aristotle. Ramus had the cachet for the Reformed of being one of the martyrs of the St. Bartholomew's Day massacre of Protestants at Paris in 1572. Baxter, expressing his desire to escape confusion, declared that "I never thought I understood any thing till I could anatomise it and see the parts distinctly, and the conjunction of the parts as they make up the whole."[21] Such a remark sums up exactly why seventeenth-century thinkers were drawn to Ramist logic, for it articulated the unity and diversity of all knowledge of things human and divine by breaking wholes into parts and defining parts through their bifurcation or by their opposites—a system of clarification by classification which was ideal for instruction and memorization. As such, its popularity "lay in its pedagogical power,"[22] and the Calvinist project, going back to an emphasis in Calvin, was certainly one of instruction in faith.[23] William Perkins and William Ames were two English Reformed theologians in the Elizabethan and early Stuart period who employed Ramist method (though without abandoning the use of Aristotelian categories) and who had international influence as participants in the shaping of Calvinist scholasticism. Perkins, a mainstream Reformed theologian in the Elizabethan Church of England not on record for nonconformity, had enormous influence on later Puritans. Ames, whose militant Puritanism and Congregationalist ecclesiology drove him into exile, was almost equally important in the codification of English scholastic Calvinism.[24]

Federal Theology

A second development in English Calvinist thought, also international in its scope, was the rising importance of federal theology. Federal theology built upon the covenant theology of the Reformers, especially that of Heinrich Bullinger, Zwingli's successor at Zurich, and also of Calvin. For Bullinger, God had made only one covenant with humanity, the covenant of grace, known by anticipation in the times of the Old Testament and by remembrance after the coming of Christ. For Calvin too there was but one covenant, that of Grace, but he stressed its testamentary character whereas Bullinger spoke of it as more conditional, although for both the covenant was the means in a history of salvation by which God unfolded his purposes. At the end of the sixteenth century, the Heidelberg Reformed theologians Zacharias Ursinus, Caspar Olevianus, and Franciscus Junius shaped the idea of a covenant of works distinct from and preceding the covenant of grace. Important English Calvinists, beginning with Dudley Fenner and including many later Puritans, adopted this double covenant federal theology with its covenant of works made with Adam, the federal head of humanity, to be followed, after the fall of Adam, with the covenant of grace, which was anticipated in Moses and fulfilled in Christ, the federal head of redeemed humanity.[25] This federal theology was not only a pedagogically useful and biblically warranted scheme for organizing theology but also "a useful vehicle of the gospel message,"[26] closely related to the flowering of Calvinist piety.

Calvinist Practical Theology

Encouragement of the devout life and the articulation of a practical theology concerning it was a third development in the formation of Calvinism in the years after the Reformation that had special resonance in English Calvinism, rendering it an important influence on the rest of the Reformed world. Richard Baxter may have loved the order and method of scholastic authors, and multiplied scholastic-like distinctions in his writings, but nonetheless he rued that he had in his youth been too eager to involve himself in controversy and find "delight" in "scholastic writings"; more important was the plain and straightforward explication of the "fundamentals" of piety and doctrine, so that others might be edified.[27] Medieval theologians had disputed whether theology was primarily a practical or speculative science, with the Franciscans, such as Duns Scotus, choosing the first alternative and the Dominicans, following Thomas Aquinas, the second. Those who saw theology as a speculative science gave primacy to intellect over will, and the opposite was the case with those who chose the alternative view. Reformed theologians, even when they argued that theology was a mixture of the theoretical and the practical, tended to see it as more practical than theoretical and speculative. Ames, for example, defined theology as the doctrine "of living to God." Another source of the practical emphasis in Reformed thinking was its Erasmian and Christian humanist roots, so important in the formation of Calvin's outlook: Erasmus decried speculative theology in the interest of practical edification, and Calvin considered theology to be instruction in Christian living, sharing some of the Erasmian resistance to mere speculation.[28]

English Calvinist authors probed the nature of Christian living with an insistence, thoroughness, and degree of introspection that was to make them pacesetters in the Reformed world in this regard. As a consequence, they produced an enormous literature on the Christian life, much of which was translated into other languages. This literature concerned itself with moral duties, the morphology of the Christian life, and above all with the question of assurance: what were the evidences that one was in a state of grace and among the elect? Books and sermons that encouraged self-examination and analyzed cases of conscience played a key role in this development.

In all of this, English Calvinists were part of a wider devotional and disciplinary movement in the post-Reformation Christianity of Western Europe in the seventeenth century that was related to the process of confessionalization as Catholics, Lutherans, and Reformed alike stressed the need for an orderly Christian society.[29] But English Calvinist authors stood out for their contributions of this sort: continental Reformed churches relied extensively on the translation of English Calvinist works for their supply of devotional literature, while, as Philip Benedict has shown, the French Huguenots, striving to uphold their faith in the face of pressures to return to Rome, showed relatively little interest in the probing self-examination of this literature, preferring doctrinal treatises useful in stiffening Protestant loyalty.[30]

All of these developments, logical method, whether Aristotelian or Ramist, scholastic theology, federal theology (itself often quite scholastic), and practical theology, which was sometimes developed with scholastic precision, were in English Calvinism and the wider Reformed world alike aspects of that process of consolidating the Reformation which occurred after the first several generations of Reformation upheaval. The creative and innovative insights and drastic ecclesiastical changes of the earlier period needed time to be absorbed, systematized, schematized, formalized, and defended, as well as probed to elicit their implications. Seventeenth-century intellectual life thus came to be characterized by consolidation, as the need for stability followed the intellectual disruptions of Renaissance and Reformation.[31] The exciting and startling insights of the Protestant Reformation required codification and institutionalization if they were to have staying power;[32] and this codification and institutionalization was an aspect of confessionalization, as Reformed, Lutherans, and Roman Catholics each established boundaries. Theologically this took the shape not just of catechisms and confessions of faith but also of enormous logically worked out systems of theology, countless published guides for the

Christian life, and massive works of classical, biblical, and patristic scholarship. This last was a late phase of the textual and historical scholarship of Renaissance Christian humanism, represented in the Protestant world by the erudition of such men as Isaac Casaubon and Joseph Scaliger—and Theophilus Gale, as will appear in chapter 3.

It has already appeared in this chapter that Reformed theology was the regnant point of view in the Church of England as a whole in the Elizabethan and early Stuart periods, and there is much about even late Stuart Church of England religious writers that puts them in the Reformed (as opposed to the Lutheran) camp. Nonetheless, the most ardent Calvinist thinkers were often persons who were sometimes in trouble for nonconformity with regard to some of the liturgical and ecclesiastical patterns of the national church. During his tenure as archbishop of Canterbury, Laud enlarged his attack on nonconformity by also seeking to identify Puritan dissidents particularly with Calvinist theology. Yet again on the defensive after the restoration of the monarchy in 1660, Calvinism came to be especially associated with those designated Dissenters, the offspring of the earlier Puritan nonconformists.

Puritanism

English Calvinism after 1660 was not exclusively Puritan, and was still a significant presence in the established church, but Calvinist theology had been a widespread and dominant element in the Puritan movement and cause, and continued as the main theological current among descendants of the Puritan impulse. Caveats have been raised about the appropriateness of the term "Puritan," especially after 1660, since so much of what it commonly conveys was characteristic of the Elizabethan and early Stuart Church of England prior to the efforts of Laud and his allies to reconstruct it along more traditional lines. However, the term was widely used in the seventeenth century and though at first mostly used by opponents in scorn, those designated Puritans preferring to refer to themselves as "the godly," the name was eventually worn as a badge of honor.[33] However, acknowledging that the term was used at the time (unlike, for example, "Anglicanism"), that general categories of the sort are inevitable in trying to write history, and that there were some distinctive things about those called Puritans after all, the term has come back into favor, as attested by the remark of a recent scholar that "without 'puritanism' (or some synonymous category) we cannot begin to explain the tumultuous political and cultural world of Tudor-Stuart England," or New England, one might add.[34]

For present purposes, even though this book is more about Calvinism than Puritanism, the use of the term has proved unavoidable, and so a rough definition may be in order. A place to start might be with such a minimalist definition as to call it a movement for further reform of the Church of England that sometimes burst the bounds of that institution, which began in the reign of Elizabeth and persisted past the middle of the seventeenth century in England. It had roots in the more radical Protestantism of the Henrician and Edwardian years, and its legacy in the religious and cultural life of England and America long persisted. Its reforming impulse took a number of forms, including efforts to change the liturgy and polity of the Church of England, to establish within church and nation a more earnest and disciplined Christian life, and to preserve a Reformed piety and theology in the established church. And the thrust toward godliness was surely at the heart of the definition of what it was to be a Puritan. But neither Puritanism nor Calvinism should be treated as monolithic.

There is some question as to the terminus ad quem beyond which the term "Puritan" should no longer be used. In general, after 1660, when for the most part Puritans could no longer expect a reform of the Church of England along the lines they desired, the preferred term has been "Dissenter," to indicate their dissent from various aspects of the national church and their status as outsiders to it. However, these Dissenters had so much continuity with the earlier movement that "Puritanism" sometimes suits a context better than "Dissenter." Bunyan revealingly said that the word Puritan was what "the godly were called in times past."[35] Granted the continuity from Puritan to Dissenter, I will use both terms in discussing the Calvinism of those Protestants outside the Church of England after 1660.

The Restoration Context: Conformists and Dissenters

The various shapings of Calvinism carried out by the thinkers and writers who are the subjects of this book were not only affected by a Puritan past and earlier English Calvinist developments which they variously incorporated into their thinking or modified but also by the time and place in which they found themselves: England after the Restoration of the monarchy in 1660 through the Toleration Act of 1689 up to the end of the reign of Queen Anne in 1714. With the Restoration of the monarchy in the person of Charles II in 1660, Calvinists, many of them, especially the most voluble, now Dissenters from the Church of England, were in a distinctly new situation.

The restoration of the monarchy seemed a resolution of the problems and turbulence of the era of civil war and the Interregnum of Oliver Cromwell's rule.

During those two decades of the 1640s and 1650s, the radical potential of the Puritan agitation was disclosed by the execution of Charles I and the growth of sectarianism, and those loyal to an Episcopal Church and faithful to *The Book of Common Prayer* in reaction strengthened and accentuated the anti-Puritan and anti-Calvinist trends associated with the Laudian program, although they failed after 1660 to restore the full ecclesiastical power in England of the years of Caroline and Laudian hegemony. The resolution, however, was no more than superficial: Restoration England was a deeply divided society and strong currents ran against those who sought to create a more inclusive established church or allow greater religious toleration. Thus the religious divisions which had been a key factor in the political life of England before the civil war and Interregnum continued to disrupt the nation after the Restoration: according to Mark Goldie, during the Restoration "the predominant language of politics was overwhelmingly the language of religious parties and civil war wounds." The chronicling of the wounds of war as a tactic in the skirmishing of religious parties persisted well beyond the Restoration era and into the next century.[36]

The religious and theological context of the Restoration era and its aftermath is framed by the Act of Uniformity in 1662 and the death of Queen Anne in 1714. The Toleration Act of 1689 provides a midpoint to the era, although it was only with the Hanoverian succession in 1714 that Dissenters felt really free from the menace of persecution. In short, Restoration England was a persecuting society; persecution began with "the triumphant Anglican crackdown of 1662"[37] and only ended with an at best grudging toleration in 1689, after which Protestant Dissenters still felt threatened for another generation. And though this persecution came by fits and starts, it always loomed over dissenting heads. The legal basis for persecution was established in a series of acts passed by Parliament collectively known as the Clarendon Code, since Edward Hyde, Lord Clarendon was then Lord Chancellor. These acts were not only payback for the years of Cromwellian repression of "prelacy" but also an expression of the fears of a reestablished monarchy and especially of a church establishment that Puritan sedition might rise again. First was the Corporation Act of 1661, which required municipal officials to receive the sacrament of the Lord's Supper using the rite of *The Book of Common Prayer,* effectively excluding from office those who objected to that liturgy as containing unreformed and superstitious elements. The Act of Uniformity (1662) required that all ministers, schoolmasters, and university incumbents take an oath attesting their acceptance of everything included in *The Book of Common Prayer* and their agreement to use it for all services of the church. Any who wanted to continue in the ministry of the Church of England but had not been ordained by bishops would have to receive Episcopal re-ordination. With the replacement of intruded Puritan incumbents by their earlier possessors beginning in 1660 and the ejection of those who would not accept the Act of Uniformity in 1662, something approaching two thousand clergy of Puritan sympathy, overwhelmingly Calvinist, left or were expelled from the ministry of the Church of England. The Conventicle Act of 1664 fined anyone worshipping outside the established church, including any household meetings that included more than four persons not of that household. It was renewed in 1670 with stiffer penalties. The Five Mile Act of 1665 forbade nonconformist clergy from coming within five miles of their former pastoral charges, thereby distancing them from their erstwhile flocks. The enforcement of these acts differed from place to place, and waxed and waned, often in relationship to the flaring up of fear of "popery," at which times persecution shifted elsewhere and Dissenters seemed at least temporary allies of conformists—this was briefly the case during the excitement in 1678 over the putative "popish plot." Conformist and nonconformist alike joined in the general fear of Rome, perhaps the chief bond of all English Protestants. In 1672 a brief "Indulgence," allowing Dissenters to hold meetings that were licensed with the government, provided some respite from the pressures of persecution. A theoretical case for persecution was meanwhile mounted by conformists and even many of those regarded as liberal-minded Latitudinarians accepted its premises and conclusions. And when toleration did come with the act of 1689, it was not particularly generous.[38]

Some Dissenters, usually those designated Presbyterians, yearned for inclusion within a broader Church of England and were suspicious of the implications of a broad toleration, fearing the unleashing of sectarian excess. These Presbyterians did not for the most part advocate a full Presbyterian system on the Scottish model but did insist upon the validity of ordination by presbyters and believed in the usefulness of ministerial associations. Many, including Richard Baxter, wanted a "reduced episcopacy" or "primitive episcopacy" such as had been proposed by Archbishop James Ussher of Armagh in Ireland, an episcopacy without dictatorial bishops lording it over the general body of clergy, and which allowed for ministerial associations with which bishops would consult. Baxter and those of his party also had no objection in principle to a liturgy or set form of prayer.[39] These Presbyterians were also usually less rigid in their Calvinism than the Independents, or Congregationalist Dissenters, and thus somewhat less alarmed about theological tendencies in the Church of England than were other Dissenters. Richard Baxter claimed that the "Presbyterians" were not a party at all, but simply "the greatest number of the godly ministers and people throughout England," those spiritually serious persons who had earlier been called "Puritans" but who had not joined themselves to a sect such as the Independents.[40] To Baxter, these Presbyterians were the generality of those who emphasized preaching and cultivated the spiritual life. Baxter gradually emerged as a leader of this group, but John Howe, William Bates, and Thomas Manton were also important. Later Daniel Williams (1643–1716) assumed their leadership. This group repeatedly tried to work out a scheme for their "comprehension" within a more broadly conceived Church of England, but these efforts came to naught.[41]

These Presbyterians had friends in and connections with the established church, sometimes worshipping in the parishes of the Church of England and receiving communion therein. Often they worked cooperatively with conformists who either sympathized with Dissent or were somewhat reluctant conformists such as Edward Reynolds or John Conant. In some local settings, the line between conformist and nonconformist was blurry, straddled by the phenomena of partial conformity and reluctant nonconformity. Many Presbyterians avoided separate meetings during the Sunday morning services of the established church and thought of their private meetings as supplementing the spiritual diet of the Church of England. Among the laity were those who found spiritual nourishment in both camps, and moderate Dissenters recognized the godliness of some parish incumbents.[42] Edmund Trench, for example, claimed that he only held meetings for those who were "ill" provided for in the established church, and felt that the "more conformable" found no fault with his moderate course; he was troubled by those Dissenters "who avoided all Communion with the Parish-Churches." In 1686 he found himself wondering if his "scruples" against conforming were warranted.[43] Such Presbyterian Dissenters often agonized over the decision not to conform and were slow to blame others who did.[44] Thus in spite of a sometimes heated rhetoric of opposition, the boundary between Presbyterian nonconformist and conformist was often porous. The heated rhetoric was sometimes an effort by the "high flyers" within the Church of England to guard the border against Dissent and of more radical Dissenters to obviate defections to the established church.

The boundary between these Presbyterians and the Independents was also porous, more porous in fact than that between the Presbyterians and the established Church, Baxter describing the Independents as a group "who are for the most part serious godly people," although he thought among them were those "addicted to separations and divisions, their zeal being greater than their knowledge."[45] Baxter especially feared that the Independents were too lenient with regard to Antinomian error, while many Independents considered Baxter to be too close to Arminian works righteousness in his theology. But whatever their zeal, there were many among the leaders of Independency who had more knowledge than Baxter, such as the learned theologians and scholars John Owen, Thomas Goodwin, and Theophilus Gale. These Independents included leading figures from the Cromwellian church establishment and were Congregationalist in their polity, striving to gather pure congregations of the elect in which members could give testimony to an experience of conversion. Among the staunchest of Calvinists, the Independents favored a general toleration of doctrinally orthodox Protestants outside of the Church of England, and no longer sought inclusion in the state church. But Presbyterians and Independents shared a commitment to rigorous yet warmhearted piety and Reformed theology. Granted this commonality, and the waning of Presbyterian hopes for inclusion in the established church, the two groups labored to bring about a closer union through organizations such as the Pinners' Hall morning lecture founded in 1672, the common fund to support the education of ministerial candidates established in 1690, and the "happy union" of 1691, but all of these efforts foundered over Presbyterian fears of lurking Antinomianism and Independent fears of creeping Arminianism.[46]

The Presbyterians in distinction from the Independents regarded the parishes of the established churches as in principle a wider opportunity for the nurture of souls and tended to administer baptism and the Lord's Supper to a wider assembly of people than the Independents. Thus the Presbyterians, however amorphous the designation, desired not only comprehension within the established church but also closer working relations with other evangelical Dissenters; but, in short, they cared less about the fellowship of a pure congregation than did the Independents and more about the importance of individual conversion and the disciplined spiritual life as the old Puritans had defined and pursued them than did many of the conformists to the Church of England.

The Baptists, committed like the Congregationalists to an ecclesiology precluding inclusion in the parish system of a state church, sought only toleration outside the establishment. And while some of them, known as General Baptists, had an Arminian theology, the greatest number were strict Calvinists; indeed, among these so-called Particular Baptists (so-called for teaching the predestination of particular persons) one could find some of the most rigid Calvinists of all.[47]

But whether moderate or radical Dissenters, all of these groups outside the established church had the reality of separatism forced upon them even if, like the Presbyterians, they rejected it in theory, and whether they thought of themselves as separatists or not. And that seemed to spell the end of an earlier Puritan hope and agenda for reshaping a national church. For those who had been in power in the Cromwellian years, this must have been especially galling, and sometimes the revolutionary potential of these restless souls became actual in agitation and plotting against the government. Such activity peaked with the rebellion that broke out connected with the Duke of Monmouth's challenge to the accession of the Catholic James II to the throne in 1685. As respectable a dissenting minister as the Presbyterian John Hickes paid with his life for involvement in the uprising, and the Independent theologian John Owen was questioned by the government in the wake of the Rye House plot of 1682. Owen's sometime associate, Robert Ferguson, a notorious plotter, fled England after the failure of the Rye House Plot, in which he had been engaged, and returned as a chaplain to the rebel Duke of Monmouth in 1685; once again he fled safely to the continent after its failure. Richard Baxter, who had no involvement in the Duke's uprising, was in its aftermath tried and imprisoned for libeling the Church of England.[48]

When toleration did come in 1689, it exempted Trinitarian Protestant Dissenters from the penal legislation of the Clarendon Code and other acts without repealing these acts, allowing them freedom of worship if they registered their meeting-places and their ministers swore an oath of loyalty. But the doors of dissenting meetinghouses could not be locked or barred during services; tithes to the established church still had to be paid by Dissenters; and it did not remove the civil disabilities of Dissenters, who could still not receive degrees from the two universities or hold public office, although in the latter case if they were willing to receive communion in the Church of England, thus practicing what was dubbed "occasional conformity," they might hold office. But even this much toleration was distasteful to a large swath of Church of England opinion, rendering its provisions precarious for at least another generation. Toleration was, however, welcome to King William III, who would have liked an even more generous act, Reformed Dutch Protestant that he was, and to many others in England who saw it as a reward to the Dissenters for their loyalty and support in the revolution of 1688. During the reign of Queen Anne, whose ecclesiastical policy was often shaped by Tories, however, its protections seemed endangered, as in the cases of the Sachaverell riots of 1710, in which dissenting meetinghouses in London were burned by mobs, or the Schism Act of 1714, which forbade the Dissenters from operating schools, and thus struck at their system for educating a new generation of ministers. But with the death of Queen Anne and the succession of the Hanoverian Lutheran George I, and the need for unity against the Jacobite rising of 1715, the threat to the Dissenters receded, and harmony between Church and Dissent grew.[49]

Ejection, indulgence, and toleration also helped create a more denominational pattern. While the Church of England was still an established church, it was no longer a national church, having lost its monopoly. Presbyterians of a later generation such as Daniel Williams, Samuel Annesley, and Thomas Watson, broke with Baxter, who had tried as late as 1689 to revive an earlier scheme for a reduced episcopacy, in abandoning hopes for inclusion in the established church.[50] A more comprehensive establishment might have emerged instead of the Toleration Act, as it had many supporters both in and out of the Church of England at the time, including apparently both Queen Mary and Archbishop John Tillotson, as John Howe mused upon both their deaths within a month of each other in 1694,[51] but the fact that it did not was a further impetus to denominationalism, insofar as such a large body of respectable Dissenters as the Presbyterians were finally forced to face the permanence of their separate existence.[52]

In Restoration and later England, in spite of a porous boundary, there were the distinct religious communities of the Church of England and Dissent. With the purging of the Puritans by the Act of Uniformity, the Church presented a different profile, as a new Anglicanism, or perhaps Anglicanism itself, was constructed. This identity, sharpened by the experience of being out of power during the Cromwellian Interregnum, was built on the foundations of Laud and the Caroline Divines, and resulted in a church, in the words of John Spurr, "with a distinct doctrinal, ecclesiological and spiritual identity." This Anglicanism centered in liturgy and Episcopal authority, and was increasingly Arminian and anti-Calvinist, though still distinctly Reformed in its Eucharistic theology and many other matters. Within the established church the Laudian perspective continued to thrive among those who were particularly adamant against any compromise with Dissenters and who, after the Glorious Revolution of 1688 might be dubbed "High Churchmen." Another segment of clergy in the Church of England who grew to importance during the period were those designated "Latitudinarians" who sought to focus on central Christian truths and moral duties and set aside some of the more abstruse and controversial points of doctrine, among which they included many teachings dear to Calvinists, joining with the descendants of Laud in this respect if not with regard to their punctiliousness in matters of ritual.[53] But there persisted within the Church of England a sometimes embattled Calvinist strain, exemplified both in piety and theology, a subject that will be considered more fully in the last chapter. The restored Church of England, however, never regained the political authority it had possessed in the days of Laud and Charles I; it was a diminished establishment with a weaker monopoly than it had maintained before.[54]

The dissenting religious community, especially the more orthodox and Calvinist part of it, made up chiefly of the Presbyterians, Independents, and some of the Particular Baptists, developed a fairly homogenized culture of the conventicle or gathered community that was centered on warm and edifying fellowship within their congregations, "walking together" in the ways of the Lord and eschewing worldliness. They could enforce within the confines of these congregations a degree of voluntary discipline unworkable in a parish system and enjoy the long sermons of "affectionate" pastors who supplemented their sermons with a steady diet of spiritual discourse and exhortation in more personal settings. Within these congregations the leading lay persons were increasingly drawn from merchants and the middling sort rather than from members of the gentry of Puritan sympathies, for whom Dissent meant exclusion from political involvement.[55]

The intellectual weight and reputation of such Dissenters as John Owen, Samuel Lee, Theophilus Gale, William Bates, and John Howe meant that some of the best scholarship and theological inquiry of the time flowed from dissenting pens. The dissenting academies which provided education for those to whom the universities were closed became centers of a more innovative and modern education than was often to be found in the older academic institutions. Academies under the leadership of Thomas Doolittle, Charles Morton, Theophilus Gale, and Thomas Rowe, all in or near London, were particularly notable.

Within these limits, dissenting Calvinists shaped a vibrant culture built around shared memories and hopes. Mass gatherings at funerals were one way they celebrated these memories and hopes at the same time that they mourned the passing of great leaders of their Israel. Sharon Achinstein has called attention to the role that these funerals, especially of prominent ministers and lay magnates, played in dissenting culture: they were occasions for community renewal, as the past was remembered; they even functioned as "opposition acts" in which Dissenters could publicly flex their muscles.[56]

This dissenting culture was also creative in the realm of imaginative literature. Psalm paraphrases and hymns were produced by the Calvinistic Baptist Benjamin Keach, who also wrote allegories like the better known John Bunyan. Bunyan and John Milton, the latter of whom was too individualistic and independent-minded to participate in dissenting congregational life, gave special luster to dissenting literature. In a later generation Elizabeth Rowe, Daniel Defoe, and Isaac Watts continued this dissenting literary productivity. As N. H. Keeble has observed, "Far from denigrating literary composition and the exercise of the imagination, nonconformity welcomed them as the natural and inevitable expression of the graciously inspired and heart-felt experience of faith. . . ."[57]

The Dawning of an Age of Enlightenment

The emergence of a new intellectual world that challenged many of the traditional religious assumptions of an earlier time was particularly relevant to the shaping of English Calvinism during the Restoration and its immediate aftermath and many studies of the period have concluded it was a watershed in the transition of England into a more modern world. For example, a book by Gerald R. Cragg, published in 1950, bears the title *From Puritanism to the Age of Reason: A Study in the Changes in Religious Thought Within the Church of England, 1660–1700*. Another declared confidently that "there is no doubt that something of immense significance happened in the minds of the thinking minority of Englishmen somewhere about the middle of the seventeenth century."[58] Some older treatments of the European Enlightenment as a whole, such as that of Paul Hazard, found the Enlightenment already dawning by 1685, with the first generation laying the foundations for its central ideas; the recent work of Jonathan Israel emphasizes the impact on late seventeenth-century culture of the large volume of radical books that flowed from European presses after 1650, the importance of the ideas of Baruch Spinoza in this radicalism, and the systematic nature of this concerted attack on traditional religion.[59]

However, with regard to England during this period, the assertion of the emergence of new strains of thought inimical to traditional religious views needs to be modified with the emphatic reservation that much of the traditional religious outlook continued into the post-1660 world and that the intellectual history of the era has often been dominated by the "Whiggish" anachronism of reading the era in the light of later developments. Barbara Shapiro has cautioned that seventeenth-century intellectual life should be discussed as "a distinctive intellectual culture" concerned with its own problems.[60] Several other treatments of the thought of the Church of England in the later seventeenth century have warned against reading the theology of its Latitudinarian wing as somehow the beginning of a slippery slope toward modern rationalism: W. M. Spellman has shown how orthodox on traditional doctrinal points the Latitudinarian theologians were and how misleading it is to consider them merely as a way station to something dubbed more modern; and John Spurr has portrayed a Restoration Anglican theology and piety that were coherent and traditional but in which also "Anglican rationalism" "could pursue 'enlightened' goals within, rather than in opposition to, organized religion and piety."[61] John Gascoigne has pointed to the role of Cambridge University during the Enlightenment in absorbing various Enlightenment ideas into English life instead of letting them become subversive.[62] J. C. D. Clark, perhaps with some exaggeration, has insisted that there are important respects in which an intellectual and cultural old regime persisted and even dominated throughout the eighteenth century in England, with theological and ecclesiastical matters still a major concern of elites. He also cautions against treating religious heterodoxy as secularizing and necessarily modern.[63] Unorthodox opinions have, after all, been a constant in the Christian story. J. G. A. Pococke has noted the difficulty of speaking of an English Enlightenment because of the absence of radical "philosophes" in

England until the "Philosophic Radicals" of a much later period; there were no such radicals because there was no occasion for them—"no *infame* to be crushed" in a society that was Erastian, Whig, and Protestant.[64]

All this is not to deny an early English Enlightenment but to modify some of the claims about and characterizations of it. What is required is a more modest conceptualization of the English Enlightenment. Michael Winship, in what he admits to be an imprecise definition, uses the term "early Enlightenment" in England to refer to "the Restoration campaign against enthusiasm, shading imperceptibly into the normative cultural values of Addisonian England," and emphasizes the way in which a new science discounted providential interventions.[65] Henry F. May has also emphasized the importance of a "moderate Enlightenment" for England and the American colonies, in which a liberalized Protestantism and Enlightenment reason marched hand in hand.[66] In any case, an early English Enlightenment, moderate, often clerical, with impact on both the established church and the Dissenters, was an important part of the context in which the Calvinist writers considered in this book engaged in theological reflection; but the subversive ideas of a more radical Enlightenment unleashed during this period which also impinged upon the Calvinists thinkers considered here must not be overlooked. Moderate or radical, it is clear enough that there was much that was religiously unsettling in the intellectual life of England in the first generations after 1660.

New ideas that were disturbing and challenging for conventional religion were disseminated in this era through an international exchange of ideas and learning that has been characterized as a "republic of letters" (or as John Locke dubbed it, "the commonwealth of learning") which transcended national and confessional boundaries and helped create a broad public sphere of discourse in which newer and profoundly controversial intellectual initiatives vied for attention alongside of older ways of thinking. In this republic of letters, older forms of scholastic learning built on unified systems of logically articulated knowledge (Ramist and Aristotelian), the humanist heritage of the rhetoric and literature of the ancient Graeco-Roman world (including skeptical authors, such as Democritus or Lucretius), and new departures in philosophy, natural science, and heterodox theology all jostled for attention, while intellectual strands which a later era would distinguish from each other as philosophy, theology, belles lettres, and natural science were treated as a package. Looming over this republic of letters was a ceiling of traditional Christian commitment, but cracks were beginning to appear in it, abetted by the philosophy of Descartes and by Huguenot exiles in the Netherlands such as Pierre Bayle, whose influential encyclopedia gave more space to his article on Spinoza than to anything else; Bayle began to explore radical options. The late seventeenth-century republic of letters offered more choices and less certainty than the preceding age.[67] Among those considered in this book, Theophilus Gale and John Edwards were more particularly engaged with this republic of letters.

A greater freedom to publish books of unconventional opinion, especially in England and the Netherlands, was another factor in the intellectual ferment of the time. Press censorship by the crown in England had been in place since the time of Henry VIII, but during the years of civil war and Interregnum a surprising degree of press freedom accompanied unsettled times; parliamentary efforts to restrict this openness famously called forth John Milton's defense of freedom of publication in 1644. The Licensing Act of 1662 was especially directed at books that questioned monarchical authority; it required that all books be entered at Stationers' Hall and then approved by appropriate readers before a license was issued. In 1694 this act lapsed and was neither renewed nor replaced with another, so that thereafter English publishing was remarkably free.[68] After the Toleration Act of 1689, there was an increase in the publication of unorthodox books, in spite of a parliamentary Blasphemy Act in 1689.[69] In the Netherlands, where more books were published in the seventeenth century than anywhere else in Europe, a large number of books that expressed unconventional and radical ideas in many different fields came out, including natural science and theology.[70]

Among the frequently raised aspects of later seventeenth-century culture in Restoration England that were religiously unsettling were the demand for greater rationality, new discoveries in science (or "natural philosophy"), awareness of other religions, scoffing at religion, denial of such a central pillar of orthodox Christianity as the doctrine of the Trinity (often referred to at the time by a kind of shorthand as "Socinianism"), Deism, and atheism.

Reason

Discussions of the Enlightenment often describe the late seventeenth century in Western Europe as an era of incipient rationalism, with "reason" claimed as the primary criterion for truth. The assertions of many of the persons who are considered typical Enlightenment figures that they were especially rational were of course self-serving. That which counts as reasonable in any given time or place is largely determined by cultural context. "Reason" is a slippery term, and one must beware of taking claims to pure rationality at face value. Carl Becker, in an older but still classic study of the Enlightenment, claimed that the main principles of Enlightenment thought were but new dogmas based on faith, the "philosophes" having torn down an earlier "city of God" only to rebuild it, in Becker's metaphor, with more "up-to-date materials."[71] Medieval Catholic scholasticism was a highly rational enterprise, and many of its representatives conceded a great deal to the role of reason in religious discourse. As already seen, reason and logic, whether Aristotelian or Ramist, came to play a significant role in Protestant scholasticism as well. "Reason" in this era also had its sectarian uses: Church of England conformists, especially those of more liberal or Latitudinarian outlook, belabored Dissenters as irrational fanatics, and Dissenters said the same of sectarian extremists.[72]

John Owen, most prominent of the English Calvinist scholastic theologians of the last half of the seventeenth century, in debate with the Roman Catholic and Franciscan John Vincent Cane (or Canes) in 1662, found himself a defender of reason's competence against his opponent's fideist claim in *Fiat Lux* that apart from the papal chair as arbitrator and acceptance of timeworn customary views, there was no way to decide between conflicting religious claims, granted the weakness of human reasoning. England, claimed Cane, was in a "maze" with a variety of conflicting religious sects and opinions based on the Bible, which was too obscure and liable to misinterpretation to help.[73] Owen's reply focused on the clarity of scripture and the competence of reason: "If our author can persuade us first to throw away our Bibles, and then to lay aside the use of our reason, I suppose there is no doubt but we shall become Roman Catholics." It is scripture, Owen continued, that makes us Christians, and reason that makes us "men."[74] In a second reply to *Fiat Lux*, Owen argued that it would deny our humanity to claim that we should not use our reason to understand the meaning of those propositions by which "the truths of religion are represented to us"; for the religion we profess is "highly rational," so that even the most mysterious articles of it "are proposed unto our belief on grounds of the most unquestionable reason." "Trifling instances" of human abuse of reason in thinking about God should not deter us from the exercise of that reason which is God's gift that made us human.[75] In short, traditional Calvinist theologians could appeal to reason although they spoke also of its limitations. "Reason" was not just the plaything of advanced thinkers.

But new emphases in understanding reason did appear in mid-seventeenth-century England, and one of these is to be found in the revival of Platonism (or Neoplatonism) among those dubbed the Cambridge Platonists. This Platonic revival long colored what was meant by reason in the discourse of the time. Platonism seemed to many a "religion-friendly" way of thinking, and the Cambridge Platonists described reason as "the candle of the Lord," in the familiar cliché. For them, reason was an innate faculty by which divine truth as well as other truths could be intuited, and knowledge of God was innate to human beings—as with St. Augustine, it was a kind of divine illumination, "semi-mystical" in character. Reason was thus the highest human faculty, a faculty which was capable of knowing something of the divine mind, to which it was akin. The leading Platonists such as Henry More had remained in their university posts during the Cromwellian years but generally conformed at the Restoration. But there were Calvinist thinkers (Theophilus Gale, Peter Sterry, John Howe, and John Edwards, four of the subjects of this book, being prime examples) whose theological reflections were much indebted to Platonism.[76]

Some of the Cambridge Platonists were at first taken with the ideas of Descartes, which spread into England in the 1640s, sympathizing with it as akin to Platonism and impressed with its version of the ontological argument for proving the existence of God, but later recoiled from its dangers, especially from its dualism of mind and matter and its materialistic physics.[77] The logical method associated with Descartes emphasized mathematical exactitude, logically airtight propositions, and clear and distinct ideas. It regarded the physical world as a machine, explaining things in the world through bodily extension, number, and motion rather than in the teleological manner of Aristotelian-based scholasticism or as reflections of the divine mind as with the Platonists. Cartesianism eventually found its way into the universities (in Holland as early as the 1650s, Cambridge by the end of the century), demolishing the older Aristotelian logic that had so long dominated them, and in doing so broke up much of the intellectual consensus shaped earlier in the century by over-throwing the study of texts as the principal means of finding truth.[78] By the later seventeenth century, the dissenting academies had succumbed to the Cartesian approach, the academy of Thomas Rowe having adopted the use of handbooks presenting Cartesian method alongside of the writings of such High Calvinists as John Owen and Thomas Goodwin.[79] Cartesian philosophy became dominant in the Reformed stronghold of the Genevan Academy by the last decades of the seventeenth century and was wielded there as a counter to rising skepticism. But notwithstanding its possible use in defending Christianity, Cartesianism spread a mechanical philosophy that by the end of the century was giving rise to ideas and movements that undermined traditional religion.[80]

Thus in the Restoration era and later, a diverse group of thinkers thought of themselves as eminently rational as they drew upon various ways of thinking understood by them to be based upon reason in its truest sense. Often, indebted to Descartes and others, this meant "lucidity and common sense, not Scholastic obscurities,"[81] but there also emerged a distinct "edge" to the meaning of reason in this era that was more worrisome: reason as the use of a more critical human intelligence and new standards as to what constituted proof to dismantle conventional and accepted views. Rejecting Becker's interpretation of the

Enlightenment, Peter Gay has stressed this meaning for "reason" in that era.[82] Reason was ceasing to mean primarily logic and the mental power to reduce ideas and things to order, and was coming to mean the critique of traditional ideas and institutions and the demand for accessible evidence as necessary for proof. It was a skeptical "tool of inquiry" for the investigation of empirical data not for the elucidation of a priori truths. Skepticism about what can be known had been a commonplace of Renaissance rhetoric, and fideists such as John Cane, building upon the skepticism of Montaigne and his disciples, used skeptical reason to dismantle reason in defense of Catholic truth, but now these antireason reasoners were hoist on their own petards, as Owen had argued in his quarrel with Cane, and as many defenders of religious truth were coming to realize. Now Platonism might no longer seem reasonable, as in Samuel Parker's attack upon it in 1677.[83] Thus reason moved beyond its uses in the logical deduction of truth and in the destruction of false views that stood in the way of accepting revelation, and was coming to bear more destructive implications. In this regard, the impact of Cartesianism can be seen as a radical watershed in European ideas.[84]

Natural Science

The emphatic affirmation of reason intersected with an interest in natural science, or what was more typically called at the time "natural philosophy." During the Restoration, many of those who promoted the importance of evidence and critical thinking in reasoning not unexpectedly evinced interest in natural science. This scientific interest followed two trajectories, the empirical and classificatory one looking back to the program of Francis Bacon, and the more mathematical one, interested in quantifiable measurement and general laws of nature. Reliance on observation and experiment for the testing of what counted as knowledge and mistrust of authorities were keynotes of this new scientific method, the results of which could be seen in the great advances in chemistry made by Robert Boyle, and in physics by Isaac Newton, whose *Principia* was published in 1687. This new science was an important factor in the overthrow of Aristotelianism in the universities in the later seventeenth century, as it showed that Aristotelian natural science was mistaken in both method and conclusions.[85]

In England the scientific world was very much a clerical one, the Royal Society for the Advancement of Science, which had been founded in 1660, and chartered in 1662, having a large number of Church of England clergy among its first members (fifty-three were elected to the society between 1663 and 1687).

These clergy have been dubbed "the scientific divines," and have been studied not only for their place in the history of science but because of their theological reflections on the implications of new scientific discoveries.[86] One of the foremost among them was John Wilkins, who had ties with the Puritan world of Cromwellian Oxford but conformed at the Restoration and eventually became a bishop. He turned Wadham College at Oxford into a center of interest and study in natural philosophy.[87] Robert Boyle, though a layman, had firm religious commitments, as evidenced by his treatise on biblical interpretation, promotion of Bible translation, opposition to Socinians and atheists, and bequest to establish a lectureship in defense of revelation against skeptics.[88] Puritanism has been given some credit in the rise of modern natural science, so it should not be surprising that there was considerable interest in the new science among Dissenters.[89] Natural philosophy received considerable attention in some of the dissenting academies; that of Charles Morton, for example, conducted between 1675–1685 at Newington Green before Morton departed for New England, had a laboratory equipped with air pumps, thermometers, and various mathematical instruments. Morton emphasized the importance of observation and measurement in natural philosophy and of the use of the telescope and microscope.[90]

There is relatively little evidence that the new science was experienced generally as a challenge to religion in Restoration England. For the scientific divines, Dissenter or Church of England, natural philosophy, by showing the order and regularity of the universe, provided evidence for the belief that God had designed an orderly and purposeful world. But if not a widely acknowledged challenge to religion, the new science emphasized new ways of thinking about evidence which had implications for the theological enterprise, including the conclusion that knowledge was not necessarily certainty. Perhaps Jonathan Israel states the challenge with appropriate care in his remark that the new science of Galileo and Descartes "added many fresh complications for theologians."[91] In any case, the new science was an important part of the intellectual context within which Calvinist and other thinkers operated.

Religions

In later seventeenth-century England, "religion" was a word which came to be used in a new way that had implications and supplied context for Restoration theology. This word gradually shifted its meaning from referring to a distinct way of life or to piety (here the word had overtones from its medieval meaning connecting it with monastic life and rule) to referring to a general phenomenon of human experience and culture under which could be subsumed a number of specific groups. Henry Smith, noted late Elizabethan and Jacobean preacher, divided religion into that of the Gentiles (meaning ancient and perhaps modern worship of many gods, dubbed by some "Gentilism"), Judaism, Christianity, and the false religion of "Mahomet." This reflected and familiarized a fairly standard typology.[92] This shift in the meaning of religion in the intellectual life of post-1660 Britain signaled a change in how people thought about Christianity, regarding it increasingly as a viewpoint rather than a tissue of rites, beliefs, and behaviors. This intellectualizing of Christianity as a "religion" established a kind of distance from it, rendering it something examined from the outside, and insistently raised the question of its truth and the evidence for it. C. John Sommerville has seen the seeds of secularization in this shift, arguing that religion, which had been a "religious culture," a pattern of rites and assumptions tied to all other aspects of life, became segmented as a "religious faith," a set of beliefs differentiated from other parts of human activity. As a consequence of religion becoming so explicitly things believed or held to be true, it became more amenable to doubt and rejection and more in need of rational defense.[93] "Religion" was becoming an impersonal and objective term, designating an object for investigation that could be theorized about in a general way, and from a critical or hostile perspective as well as a friendly one. The skeptical hostility about religion expressed by ancient authors was revived, including the notion, going back to Democritus and Lucretius, that religion arose from ignorant fear or resulted from imposture.[94] From the middle of the seventeenth century onward, there appeared in England and elsewhere a number of treatises that constituted a kind of early comparative religion, attempting on the one hand to formulate a chronology and taxonomy of religion and on the other either to defend or undermine Christian belief. More sympathetically, religion understood as chiefly things believed and something objectified might be reduced to a few common notions, as with Lord Herbert of Cherbury.[95] The Cambridge Platonists so emphasized natural religion that it enabled them to discuss the "religions" sympathetically, and even to speculate that the virtuous pagans would be saved, a view that even the more Calvinistic among them, such as Nathaniel Culverwell, accepted, as, we shall see, did Peter Sterry.[96]

Yet a third implication was that one could think about Christianity within a frame that included a number of different religious options. When John Bunyan worried that perhaps the Turks had their scripture to prove Mohammad the Savior just as Christians had theirs, he was adumbrating the problem of relativism that has dogged modernity.[97] No doubt such skeptical thoughts had been expressed by those who haunted taverns long before and was reflected in the radical thoughts of such as the Ranters during the Commonwealth; but it was also creeping into the high cultural discourse of such as Montaigne and Pascal. Montaigne had famously noted in his essay "Of Cannibals" that some otherwise decent people ate other folks while elsewhere this was thought improper, and Pascal in his *Pensées* worried repeatedly that what counted for truth seemed to change when one crossed national borders. Relativism in morals and belief thus appeared in the seventeenth century and could not help but color some of the theological reflection of the era. Baxter worried about it but was willing to concede that "I am not so much inclined to pass a peremptory sentence of damnation upon all that never heard of Christ, having some more reason than I knew of before to think that God's dealing with such is much unknown to us," a sentiment that he then turned into an exhortation by stating that "the ungodly here among us Christians are in a far worse case" than those who had not heard of Christ.[98]

Isabel Rivers has commented of this period that "the most important question that concerned the freethinkers was the nature of religion, particularly its historical development, its influence on and manipulation by human beings, and its future, if any."[99] In thinking about other religions, the freethinker Henry Stubbe concluded in *An Account of the Rise and Progress of Mahometanism and a Vindication of Him and His Religion from the Calumnies of Christians,* which was never published but distributed in manuscript, that the prophet's religion consisted of a few simple religious propositions that were based on reason alone.[100]

Deism

The notion that true religion consisted of a few plain propositions based on reason had been abroad in England for awhile by the time Stubbe wrote and is often traced to Lord Herbert of Cherbury, whose attempt to present a more favorable kind of "Gentilism," which he thought consisted of the common religious ideas of mankind, such as the existence of God and the rewards of an afterlife for the virtuous, seemed to suggest the possibility of a pure and universal religion even without revelation (although Herbert himself did not explicitly deny revelation). Such a view of a few simple religious truths based on reason and rejecting revelation was beginning to be dubbed "Deism."

Charles Blount (1654–1693), who considered himself a follower of Lord Herbert, is sometimes called the first English Deist, but his focus was more on the corruption of religion by priestcraft than on Lord Herbert's common beliefs.[101] This was not an altogether new idea, having appeared in some of the skeptics of antiquity. Calvin had mentioned this view, and so had Robert Burton earlier in the seventeenth century, who commented that some reasoned that religion came from the "imposture and knavery of priests."[102] In fact, Protestants had sometimes applied the priestcraft argument against Roman Catholicism, and one English anti-Deist author attributed the rise of Deism in England to English youth traveling in lands where they beheld the "Idolatry and Superstition of the Roman Religion" and realized that it was simply created by priests for their own profit and power, and then wrongly made it a general truth about religion.[103] Another English author at the end of the seventeenth century used the priestcraft theory of religious origins against pagans, Roman Catholicism, and much else, but excepted from it rational Christians such as his admired Archbishop John Tillotson.[104]

Deists of course could wield this deconstructive weapon against Christianity as a whole, and did so. The combination of the priestcraft theory of religious origins and the common notions of rational religion available without revelation constituted the essence of the Deist challenge. John Toland, who claimed to be following John Locke, though Locke denied the parentage, continued the Deist trajectory with his *Christianity Not Mysterious* (1696), in which he argued that Christianity, insofar as it was true, was constituted of simple truths rationally discerned, and that there was nothing in it above reason, denying that any essential truth was unknowable to reason. The simple truth taught by Jesus, he asserted, had many "fooleries" added to it and excused as mysteries, thereby enhancing the power of the clergy—whereas the human mind can only properly assent to "clear perceptions."[105]

Many replied to this Deist challenge, and among the Calvinist thinkers considered in this book, Baxter made reference to the folly of Deism,[106] but it was Edwards who was most troubled by Deism. The poet John Dryden, then still a son of the Church of England, asserted that the so-called Deist

> "truths are not the product of thy mind, but dropp'd from heaven . . .
> Reveal'd Religion first inform'd thy sight,
> And Reason saw not, till Faith sprung the Light."

One other early rejoinder to the Deist menace came from Edward Stillingfleet, who became bishop of Worcester in 1689. In 1677 he penned *A Letter to a Deist,* which he wrote to satisfy a person who believed in God and providence, but "expressed a mean Esteem of the Scriptures, and the Christian Religion," which Stillingfleet identified as a common theme "among the scepticks of this Age." He complimented his correspondent for writing with civility, and not "Raillery and Buffonery," before he unfolded his serious arguments against the Deist position.[107]

Scoffing and "Enthusiasm"

In some cases Deism may have been a cover for those, who, in their scorn for religion, meant more than they said. In 1696, William Stephens, long a country vicar before becoming Archdeacon of Sutton, published *An Account of the Growth of Deism in England,* in which he clearly defined Deism as a denial of all revelation, and acknowledged that some persons of "probity" held such ideas, perhaps driven to it by the "Idolatry and Superstition of the Roman Religion," and the high-handedness of Protestant "High Priests" such as William Laud and Scottish "Presbytery," but also declared that many who called themselves Deists were really no more than skeptics, readers of Hobbes and Spinoza, who ridiculed miracles and revelation.[108] It has been noted that "bitterness toward a scoffing world was a prominent feature of popular religious literature" in the later seventeenth century, and John Redwood has claimed that the period 1650–1750 was an "age of ridicule" and that this ridicule "did far more harm to the Christian defenses than did the onslaught of reason and nature."[109]

Scoffing at religion should be taken seriously as a strategy of revolutionaries and freethinkers. Ridicule has always been a potent instrument of demystification, as was already recognized in the seventeenth century when Francis Bacon observed that scoffing "doth little by little deface the reverence for religion."[110] It was also an instrument that could be wielded by persons of all stations of life. Revolutionaries understandably subject hated old regimes to ridicule in the attempt to bring them down, and in the history of Protestantism the potency of ridicule can be seen especially in the early years of the Reformation. Later, as more disciplined Christian societies were being shaped by Protestants after the destructive phase had passed, there was less encouragement of ridicule. But ridicule of "popish" superstition remained an acceptable outlet in Protestant culture.

The Puritans in England had often been the butt of ridicule and their literature is filled with rebuke and repudiation against those who scoff at the "godly." This became a major theme of Puritan discourse as early as the 1580s and long continued.[111] Proudly bearing such jeers and scoffs was an important element in the building of a sense of distinctiveness and a definer of the godly. John Winthrop thought that the scorn of the ungodly should be taken by the godly as warrant that they were on the right path.[112] In the Cromwellian years those who had been the butt of such scoffs had the power to retaliate upon scoffers: a directive for the removal of scandalous ministers included in the definition of scandal those who reviled the godly.[113] During the Restoration these scoffs had added sting: the tables had been turned, and the godly, as will be seen in the career of Joseph Alleine, in addition to being persecuted with fines and imprisonment, were reviled, and that after many of them had enjoyed positions of power and prominence. The scorn directed at Dissenters as vicious rebels in Samuel Butler's *Hudibras* provided laughter for polite society at the same time that it warned of the menace of these progeny of rebellious Puritans.

Butler charged the Puritans and Dissenters with claiming that their ideas came from the "new light" they had received, a claim widely reviled as "enthusiasm."[114] J. G. A. Pococke has called attention to "the great campaign against enthusiasm" of "post-Puritan England."[115] Enthusiasm was associated with religiously motivated disorder of the kind that Royalists blamed for the civil war and the execution of the king. Generally the term came to bear a meaning much like that later assigned to "fanaticism." Henry More's *Enthusiasmus Triumphatus* was an early anatomy of enthusiasm, written in the 1650s but not published until 1662. More, one of the Cambridge Platonists, carefully excepted a true piety that might even be called "ecstatic" from enthusiasm and did not mention Puritans among the enthusiasts, directing his book mainly against dabblers in alchemy and magic, such as the followers of Paracelsus, but in his treatment of it as arising from the mental disorder of melancholy and as domination by fixed but delusionary ideas (for example, a nobleman who thought he was made of glass, or a woman who thought she was a cat and pounced on mice), he helped set the stage for an antienthusiast campaign. Tracing it to Simon Magus and Montanus in ancient times, the contemporary religious sects he described by this term were the Anabaptists and Quakers.[116]

But "enthusiasm" also carried specific theological meaning, in particular the claim that enthusiasts thought themselves, in More's term, "inspired," and capable of revealing new truths, to which More replied that the Holy Spirit acted only in a manner in accord with the highest rationality.[117] Understood as such, "enthusiasm" had been used by the Puritans themselves against those who relied on private revelations and reduced religion to a spiritism in which the indwelling of the Holy Spirit and its guidance of believers into new truths was the principal tenet. English and New English Puritans had detected enthusiasm in this sense in the teachings of Antinomians such as Anne Hutchinson, and conformist and nonconformist alike agreed that the Quakers and before them the Familists were prime examples of this error.

Nonetheless, it was "enthusiasm" as the fanaticism of claiming direct and private access to God with which conformists charged Dissenters, in spite of the fact that as Calvinists they rejected the notion of extra-scriptural revelation, which they thought was not implied by their belief in the gracious and renewing indwelling of the Holy Spirit in believers. Often this charge of "enthusiasm" was phrased in terms of "prophecy" so that Dissenters could be put down as like the fanatics of Reformation Munster or assimilated to Familists and Quakers.[118]

Occasionally, the Dissenters made themselves vulnerable to the charge of enthusiasm, as in the case of Richard Dugdale, the Surrey demoniac, who had voided large stones and vomited nails. Several respectable Dissenters, including Thomas Jollie and John Carrington, attempted and finally carried out a successful exorcism of Dugdale during 1689–1690, publishing a description of the occurrence in 1697. This exorcism they thought would not only bring attention to the spiritual power of the dissenting interest but would be an empirical vindication of the reality of the spiritual world of the sort which such scientific divines as Joseph Glanvill, an early member of the Royal Society, would appreciate (Glanvill had asked miners to report any signs they found of demons in the bowels of the earth). With the publication of this description of their exorcism of Dugdale, the anti-Dissenters had their chance. Zachary Taylor, a church of England incumbent, responded in 1698 with *Popery, Superstition, Ignorance, and Knavery . . . very fully proved upon the Dissenters that were concerned in the Surrey Imposture*. In this brief tract, Taylor charged the Dissenters with both hypocrisy and enthusiasm, whipping persons into a frenzy that resulted in "much whoring" and "many bastards" by their "forgeries" and "Rhapsody of Superstition." Taylor reminded his readers that these were the people who beheaded the royal martyr and more recently acted as tools of the papist James II. These Dissenters says Taylor, should abandon their "fanatick prayers" and accept governance by their lawful rulers in the established church.[119] Jollie replied to Taylor and Taylor responded with another diatribe against Dissent,[120] but damage had been done to the dissenting cause.[121]

George Trosse, who turned from a sinful life to become a Presbyterian minister later in the century, reported in his autobiography that before his conversion he "derided" the Holy Spirit, presumably by mocking the godly as "enthusiasts" on account of their language about the indwelling of the Spirit, and this may be what he meant when he feared he had committed the unpardonable sin against the Holy Ghost. This scoffing and railing against enthusiasm was a sign of the severe social strains of Restoration England and the hostility directed against Dissenters at that time. The Dissenters took this derision seriously as threatening, portending danger. Trosse counted it as one of his greatest sins that he had once been an enemy of "Puritans," a "great reproacher of strict professors," who "jeered at godliness" and scorned those who worshipped God strictly with "sarcastical language." So repentant was he for his earlier reviling of godly ministers that he apologized to several of them.[122] That reviling of Puritans could have political overtones is also evident from Trosse's revealing account, when he says that during his period as a scoffer he reviled Oliver Cromwell. Puritan authors also struck back: Milton, in *Paradise Lost*, says of the rebel angels that they "stood scoffing" at God and the loyal angels;

and Benjamin Keach, dissenting Particular Baptist, was sure that the wrath of God would burn up "all the proud and haughty ones" who rely on a religion of nature and "despise and ridicule the holy Gospel."[123] In an allegory Keach introduces the characters "Scoffer" and "Scornfull," who tell the character "Godliness" that they cannot endure him after he has upbraided them for their sins, adding that they will repent "later" since they now want to enjoy "liberty for the flesh"; then they swore "Damn him," jeering and lolling "their tongues at Godliness."[124] Bunyan's depiction in *Pilgrim's Progress* of Vanity Fair and the incidents occurring there highlighted the wickedness of scoffers; Bunyan pictured the tables turned on scoffers at the judgment day.[125] Baxter called attention to the collapse of a gallery in a Dublin playhouse in which several were killed and many injured, noting that the play being performed was Ben Jonson's *Bartholomew Fair,* which Baxter called "a play in scorn of godliness."[126] Clearly the charge of enthusiasm and the scoffs of persons in the established church directed against the Dissenters stung.

In 1674 a brief, anonymous treatise entitled *The Vanity of Scoffing: Or A Letter to a Witty Gentleman, Evidently Shewing the Great Weakness and Unreasonableness of Scoffing at the Christian's Faith* was published in London. Its author, Clement Ellis, was a Nottinghamshire rector, who had remained a college fellow at Queen's, Oxford, until the Restoration, when he welcomed the King with the publication of some congratulatory verse followed a year later by a sermon praising the King's return.[127] Royalist that he was, he blamed religious scoffing on the Dissenters, whose forebears, out of misguided zeal, "have made bold to murder kings and fire kingdoms," thus undermining true religion by their counterfeit religion of rebellion. Ellis addressed his treatise to someone whom he presumably knew but does not name and expressed surprise that a person of good education and devout parents would take pleasure in scoffing at religion. Ellis identified a specific scoff, that there is no certainty of an afterlife and so one should enjoy the present life and live "as merrily" as one can, letting "fools that dance after the pipe of a company of cheating Priests please themselves with the fond hopes of a new life and Heaven after they are dead," all this being accompanied by "various oaths." Ellis added that it was currently "modish" to pronounce believers in Christianity to be fools, and to deny God, the afterlife, and the soul. Christianity itself was becoming a butt of ridicule to the witty.

The *Vanity of Scoffing* offered a critique of scoffers that developed several points. First, and rhetorically, believers will not to be "hectored" out of their faith with "some dazzling flashes of this new-fashioned wit, and a thunder-clap of oaths." Those who talked this way degraded themselves to the level of beasts. Then Ellis argued that, echoing Pascal's wager, believing in Christianity is the "safer" option, for there is more to lose (eternity in heaven) by not believing than by believing (pleasures in this world). Next came the argument that if all believed as the scoffers did, there would be no public order, the world being bad enough when people believe in hell; imagine how bad it would be if the fear of hell were removed! Then no man could sleep for fear his wife or child would "cut his throat." Next came an argument from self-interest: if there is no public order, the scoffers, presumably persons of means and prominence, can no longer count on a social stability that is in their own best interests. Christianity, whether its truth be certain or uncertain, is "very serviceable to the world: it doth much good, and hurt it can do none." Further, the author thinks that it is precisely the fear of hell which leads to such scoffing, as scoffers "swill" themselves "in all carnal jollities" in order to free themselves "from the terrors of a future Hell." Finally, such scoffing at the Christian faith is not the result of reason, but of lust, an excuse for uncontrolled behavior. This treatise on scoffing turns from this set of arguments to another: Christianity is not the morose joy-killing thing that the scoffers suppose. Rather, it does not "abridge our selves in any honest comfort or delight," but only causes us to abstain from what is hurtful.[128]

This broader Christian worry about scoffing and its consequences was echoed by the conformist Glanvill who declared that scoffing at religion was the last refuge of Christianity's enemies:

> And therefore others, and the most, go an easier way, and fight
> against Religion By scoffing and buffoonery: This is the game the
> Devil seems to be playing in the present Age. He hath tried the
> power and rage of the mighty; and the wit, and knowledge of the
> learned; but these have not succeeded for the destruction of Religion.
> And therefore now he is making an experiment by an other sort of
> enemies, and sets the Apes, and Drollers upon it. And certainly there
> was never any other Age, in which sacred and serious things have
> been so rudely, and impudently assaulted by the prophane abuses of
> Jesters, and Buffoons, who have been the contempt of all wise Times,
> but are the darlings, and wits of these.[129]

Thus the protestation against scoffers had migrated from a Puritan and Dissenter device used against the putative impiety of scorners in the established church to a weapon, available to both conformist and nonconformist, wielded in the defense of Christian faith against the irreligious. Church of England anti-scoffers, as the remarks of Ellis make clear, had in mind persons of prominence, who must be made to see the usefulness of Christianity for social stability. The Christian life is not costly but pleasant, contrary to the opinion of pleasure-seeking scoffers. Many of these arguments against irreligious scoffers were to be echoed, with greater wit and irony, in Jonathan Swift's "Essay on the Abolition of Christianity," which also reflected Swift's concern about the ridiculing of the clergy, apparently a sport of the irreligious. In 1699 Church of England bishop White Kennett declared that "contempt of the clergy is the sin and shame of this latter age."[130] The menace and impiety of scoffing not just at dissenting enthusiasm but at Christianity generally, hung over the work of the Calvinist writers treated in this book, and could be a catalyst for their theological books and discourse. As Lord Halifax remarked, "The world is grown saucy, and expecteth reasons."[131]

Atheism

William Stephens declared that the scoffers who pretended to be Deists were nothing more than "meer Sceptics, and practical Atheists."[132] Bunyan put a character "Atheist" into his *Pilgrim's Progress*, who laughs at those so deluded as to believe that there really is a "heavenly city." Clement Ellis also raised the specter of atheism in this connection. The scoffers, he said, do not want to be accounted atheists, and yet they are clearly on a path leading there if they have not arrived already.[133] Long before Ellis, Francis Bacon and Thomas Fuller had argued that scoffing led to atheism.[134] That scoffing might lead to atheism rather than exemplify it is a significant way of putting it: for atheism suggested to sixteenth- and seventeenth-century persons an "iconoclastic attitude towards religion."[135]

George Trosse confessed to both scoffing and atheism before his conversion; his posthumous autobiography, not published until 1714, but written in 1692, describing his pre-conversion state in the 1640s and 1650s, discloses an interesting intersection of the two evils that confirms Ellis's view on the matter. Of the period before his conversion, when he jeered at the godly, he continually refers to himself as an atheist: he was "a profane atheist," a "very atheist," and elsewhere "a perfect atheist." Sinning "confirmed" him in his atheism and so he was "living in atheism." Sometimes he qualified himself as a "practical atheist," engaged in "a practical denying of God," by which he meant denying God in practice, without ever saying he disbelieved in God's existence. Nor did his atheism prevent him from favoring and attending Church of England services and acting as though devout, though all along godless. Thus atheism was very much for him a way of life and not a viewpoint, and it was associated with scoffing at the strict religion of the hotter sort of Protestants. In one of his references to his former atheism, he contrasted it, not with belief in God, but with orthodoxy. That he could use the term in this fashion writing as late as 1692 is of some interest. He particularly called attention to incidents in which he ignored or rejected the obvious lessons of divine providence as examples of atheism, suggesting that this failure to recognize God's work in the world through providential signs was an important aspect of atheism, perhaps even the principal definer of what it was.[136]

Clearly the term "atheism" was ambiguous in the seventeenth century. Does it mean irreligion as it did for Trosse, or an outright denial of God's existence? Several generations ago Lucien Febvre argued that atheism in the modern sense was nearly an intellectual impossibility in the sixteenth century, and that the putative discovery of atheism in much earlier times was a highly anachronistic exercise in which some modern intellectuals engaged, convinced as they were that persons of a truly atheistic sensibility must have existed in earlier times and that such skeptics played clever games of indirection and subterfuge in order to hide the real meaning of their words. Along the same lines, Richard Popkin has argued that many figures in the seventeenth century, such as Descartes, who had been taken as implicit atheists and anti-Christians were not, and must be understood at face value in their professions of religious belief. A similar discussion has revolved around the meaning of Thomas Hobbes in seventeenth-century England and the Huguenot exile Pierre Bayle in the Netherlands—were they eccentric Calvinists or outright skeptics? Hobbes's denial of immaterial spirits was generally taken for atheism at the time but is of a piece with his biblically supported mortalism; Bayle's real religious convictions remain a mystery; but it is clear that he raised a point surprising to his era: that atheism could be sincere, and not necessarily an excuse for immorality—the atheist might even be a moral person.[137]

Most of the references to atheists and atheism in seventeenth-century England appear to designate not an intellectual conviction but a way of life, and that as late in the century as when Ellis and Trosse wrote. This was sometimes distinguished as "practical atheism" rather than the speculative kind.[138] Perhaps a good modern synonym would be "godlessness," with its implication not of intellectual conviction so much as of lifestyle. And as with "godless," atheist denoted a blasphemer and served as a fairly broad term of abuse. Atheism and irreligion are coupled and refer to living and acting as though there were no God, or thinking that God is unconcerned with what humans do, thereby denying providence, a notion having some connection to the Renaissance revival of Epicurean skepticism.[139] When the Puritan stalwart George Gifford of Malden in Essex, late in the sixteenth century introduced into a lively dialogue a character named "Atheos," he is not at all a disbeliever in the existence of God, but a person who carelessly and thoughtlessly thinks that he can live as he lists and perhaps repent at the last moment, or in any case that a rigorous and strictly disciplined life is not incumbent upon Christians but is too unrealistic for ordinary mortals.[140] "Atheos" had already appeared in John Lyly's *Euphues* in 1578 and was perhaps a character in the literature of the time.[141] The published sermon by Henry ("Silver-tongued") Smith that first appeared in 1593 and was reprinted eleven times before 1640, *God's Arrow Against Atheists*, tends to assimilate atheism to godlessness, and thought even the references of the ancients to atheism was because godlessness was odious even to virtuous pagans. Atheism, if it denies God, does so because that allows "more libertie of sinning."[142] Lord Herbert thought atheism was really just irreligion; true atheism was something so mad that he doubted it had ever really existed.[143] Yet Robert Burton thought in 1621 that "loose Atheisticall spirits are too predominant in all Kingdoms," no doubt because he too was thinking of it as irreligion.[144] In New England, Anne Hutchinson referred to the "atheism of her heart" in a prayer.[145] Milton in *Paradise Lost*, writing during the Restoration, in his description of the war in heaven calls Satan and his allies "the atheist crew," but clearly these rebels against God do not deny the divine existence. And elsewhere Milton refers to the beautiful women of the race descended from Cain, who live in the "tents of wickedness," as "fair Atheists."[146]

Sometimes atheism as godlessness received a political twist: in an Elizabethan reference to atheism, Roger Ascham describes Machiavellians as atheists, and the Italian comes up with some frequency in discussions of atheists and the irreligious. The atheist villain in the Jacobean drama *The Atheist's Tragedie* is a political Machiavellian, scheming without conscience to gain wealth and position.[147] Robert Burton makes this more explicit: one form of atheism, he says, is that of "Herodian temporizing States-men" who make a hypocritical "show" of religion to gain power.[148] Atheism thus is tantamount to impiety and irreligion, and this fits Clement Ellis's argument that the gentleman whom he has warned against scoffing is on the slippery slope to atheism, not already there, as well as Glanvill's assertion that the irreligious scoff because they cannot get rid of religion by reason.

Some seventeenth-century authors treated atheism as the result of mental disorder, of which their scoffing was a symptom. Two examples of this approach were those of Robert Burton, in his exhaustive *Anatomy of Melancholy* (1621), and Henry More, in *An Antidote against Atheisme* (1653). Citing Phillip Melanchthon's opinion that atheism was a "poisoned melancholy," Burton treats it as such, calling it "a brutish passion."[149] More considered atheism a mental disorder because it was irrational to disbelieve in God in the face of all the evidence for the divine existence from nature and providence, and thought it resulted from "fancy" and was akin to "enthusiasm."[150] Similarly, Ralph Cudworth called atheism a "Blind and Irrational Impulse."[151]

But Ellis's and Glanvill's arguments do suggest that they are aware of intellectual atheism which denied God's existence altogether. Nor can Descartes, Hobbes, and especially Spinoza be excluded from the sources, or at least occasions, of this speculative atheism. Descartes was no atheist but argued for God's existence; nonetheless his dualism and mechanism, and especially his method of systematic doubt raised for some the possibility of intellectual atheism. A misunderstanding or not, it has been claimed that Hobbes provided "the main theoretical basis for Restoration atheism," and it is clear that contemporaries denounced him as atheistic. And Spinoza's combination of naturalism, materialism, and empiricism was taken by all his contemporaries, including sympathizers, as atheism.[152]

Another basis for atheist opinion is to be found in the revival of ancient classical authors, especially the Epicureans; as was imagined in an antiatheist publication of 1706, atheists proclaim that since Diagoras, Epicurus, Lucian, and others have been atheists, we "may safely be so."[153] It has also been claimed that in England, the appearance of irreligion and atheism was a consequence of the religious extremism of the civil war years, when many unconventional ideas were voiced.[154] When Bunyan made reference to the possibility of a real atheism of denying God's existence, it probably reflected his familiarity with the religious and irreligious discourse of the civil war years. It has been claimed that the Interregnum radicals known as Ranters denied God's existence, and that Bunyan's "Mr Badman" in his allegory *The Life and Death of Mr Badman* was a Ranter. That Bunyan had contact with Ranters in his early religious searching is well known.[155] Thus David Wootton's remark that in the period from 1680 to 1715 there was "a take-off point for irreligious speculation,"[156] including the denial of God's existence, seems about right; thus by the last generation of the seventeenth century in England, defenders of religion were confronted by not just the prevalence of irreligion but the appearance of outright denial of God's existence.

Not that this speculative atheism was altogether new. Calvin referred to atheists who seem to be real deniers of a divine existence. The Church of England bishop Martin Fotherby in a 1622 book divided atheists into those who entirely denied God's existence and those who professed to believe in God but either renounced him in their hearts or denied him by their evil deeds.[157] Francis Bacon's essay "Of Atheism," after sounding some of the familiar thoughts about it as godlessness, also used the term to refer to those "that deny a God," which he considered "contemplative" atheism, in contrast to the practical variety. Such denial of God he thought very rare, and he connected it, as so many authors of the time did, to classical authors more than contemporaries, naming Democritus and Epicurus.[158] Hugo Grotius maintained that it was enough to refute these ancient atheists since the contemporary ones have merely revived their arguments.[159] Atheism as denial of the reality of spiritual beings particularly exercised the Cambridge Platonists and was a viewpoint often described as "Saducism,"[160] after the ancient Jewish party that denied the afterlife. The title of Henry More's *An Antidote Against Atheism or an Appeal to the Natural Faculties of the Minde of Man, whether there be not a God*, published in 1653, suggested an understanding closer to the modern about the meaning of the term. Cudworth's *True Intellectual System* (1678) argued against those who denied God's existence altogether, whom he called "philosophical atheists."[161] Many of these thinkers thought that reason was on the side of belief in God, Gilbert Burnet, for example, arguing that the Catholic fideist argument against the capacities of reason that John Owen had refuted in Vincent Canes, led to atheism.[162] Richard Baxter used the term "atheist" for a real denial of the divine existence.[163] Another Dissenter during the Restoration, John Bunyan, also referred to "atheism" as though he meant by it such a denial.[164] In New England, Anne Bradstreet felt tempted to doubt God's existence.[165] The Boyle Lectureship, established in 1691, was aimed against atheism as denial of God as well as against "Theists" (a term sometimes used in place of Deists), and other religions.[166] As will appear later, Restoration Calvinists worried about atheists of both the practical and speculative sort.

Socinianism

Deism, scoffing, and atheism constituted a full agenda for refutation by late seventeenth-century and early eighteenth-century English Christian theologians, but there was also an insidious challenge to orthodox belief from another direction, which claimed to be true biblical Christianity, that of Socinianism. It was a major worry of both Church of England and dissenting divines. The charge of Socinianism could be used loosely in the period, just as with atheism or Deism, but there were differences: Socinians did not scoff at religion and they believed in divine revelation in scripture, though denying that those who claimed to be orthodox had properly interpreted it. As used by many Church of England writers it had the principal meaning of denying the doctrines of the ancient creeds concerning the Trinity and the two natures of Christ. More strictly Calvinist authors attached additional meanings to it, particularly the denial of the atoning death of Christ as a satisfaction of God's just wrath toward sinners and the imputation of Christ's righteousness to believers in salvation. Instead, Calvinist theologians saw it as a mere moralism which denied salvation by grace. Socinians also denied the doctrine of original sin. But there may have been even more to Socinianism, as its rejection of "mysteries" that could not be warranted before the bar of reason has been claimed as a major source of English radicalism, political and religious, throughout the later seventeenth and the eighteenth centuries. With its rejection of mysteries it blended with Deism.[167]

Socinianism was a species of radical reformation anti-Trinitarianism that had arisen in Italy and taken root in Poland, from which came the *Racovian Catechism,* a summary of Socinian teaching that was published in a Latin version in England in 1609, causing such alarm that the offending catechism was publicly burnt in 1614, just two years after the last English burnings for heresy, those of Bartholomew Legate and Edward Wightman, punished as Arian deniers of the Trinity. "Arian" in these cases was an imprecise term: Legate had claimed that Jesus was a mere man and that no true church existed on earth (the later "Seeker" principle); Wightman had proclaimed himself to be the Holy Spirit. In the 1640s the Puritan radical John Goodwin and the liberal-minded conformist William Chillingworth were both accused of Socinianism. But the clearest early example of an English Socinian who denied the Trinity was Oxford-educated John Biddle, whose writings, along with the *Racovian Catechism,* were turned over to John Owen by the council of state for refutation in 1652. Thomas Firmin (1632–1697), a wealthy philanthropist, was one of the most explicit anti-Trinitarians of the later seventeenth century. He had known and been influenced by Biddle, and was involved in the publication of anti-Trinitarian tracts, including several by Stephen Nye, who in 1687 was one of the first to use the term "Unitarian" for his beliefs. Early in the eighteenth century, some in the Church of England, including Samuel Clarke, William Whiston, and Daniel Whitby, rejecting the Athanasian Creed, maintained the subordination of the divine Christ to God the Father, a view less extreme than that of the Socinians and at the time described as Arian;[168] eventually some among the Dissenters joined them, such as the English Presbyterian John Emlyn. Isaac Newton was also an Arian.

The outcry against Socinians during the Restoration and into the eighteenth century that came from Dissenter and Church of England alike was massive. John Owen directed much of his later theological work against Socinianism, and so did John Edwards, as will be seen in the last chapter. Among conformists, Bishop Edward Stillingfleet and the English Jonathan Edwards, long-time Principal of Jesus College, Oxford, were notable anti-Socinian authors. In New England Cotton Mather rejoiced in 1700 that there was not a single Socinian in New England;[169] later he feared they were lurking in Rhode Island. The Toleration Act of 1689 explicitly excluded deniers of the Trinity from those to be granted toleration. But defending the doctrine of the Trinity in a context in which religious mysteries were under attack and rationality defined as possession of clear and distinct ideas was difficult.

In the period from 1660 to 1714, English Calvinist thinkers, many of them Dissenters, but including some clergy of the Church of England, worked out their responses to the cultural and intellectual challenges of their times within the parameters of Reformed theology, in the contexts of an international world of learned discourse and a troubled ecclesiastical framework. With this background as context and challenge, the remaining chapters will explore examples of these responses.

2

Peter Sterry

Calvinist Mystic

Peter Sterry was an enigmatic and eccentric figure who variously baffled and outraged his contemporaries. Richard Baxter, who eventually came to admire Sterry's piety and irenicism, earlier coupled Sterry with Sterry's friend Henry Vane the Younger, who had briefly been the governor of the Massachusetts Bay Colony where he was implicated in Antinomian heresy, remarking of them in a noteworthy pun that "vanity and sterility" were joined in these two writers.[1] The Oxford antiquarian Anthony Wood, who rarely gave quarter to anyone he thought tainted with Puritanism, was even less sympathetic; he called Sterry a "high-flown blasphemer." Another critic was Robert Baillie, a Scottish Presbyterian alarmed about heresy, who placed Sterry with a "malificient crew" that included "blind Milton," another friend of Sterry, declaring that the justice of God had brought them both down.[2] Later times were to be less harsh: the nineteenth-century Anglican broad church theologian Frederick Denison Maurice admired Sterry as "a very profound thinker," and T. S. Eliot praised him for nobility of spirit and majesty of language.[3]

Born in 1613, Peter Sterry was the oldest of the main subjects of this book (though only two years older than Baxter). He rose to prominence as a preacher to parliament in the 1640s and as an adviser to Oliver Cromwell in the 1650s. However, that earlier part of his story is not the focus of this chapter but rather his outlook as it found expression in posthumous publications that came out between 1675 and 1710 and in letters and manuscripts that circulated among his associates, some of which have been published in the twentieth century. It was through this material that Sterry's thought related to the religious and intellectual currents of Restoration England. However, it is not the purpose of this chapter to present a complete picture of Sterry as a theologian and religious writer but to focus on the mystical strain in his thought and the way in which he continued, developed, and transformed the mystical elements that had already appeared in the Calvinist or Reformed tradition. There is much about Peter Sterry to suggest that he should be enrolled in the company of Christian mystics. Nor was he unique or an aberration in this regard: examination of Sterry brings into focus the mystical strain present in many Puritans and other Calvinists. Thus, after some description of Sterry's career, this chapter will examine him as a Puritan, Calvinist, and mystic, whose mysticism was rooted in his Puritan piety and Calvinist theology.

Both their friends and critics have agreed that Puritans and Calvinists were not hospitable to mysticism.[4] Many friends of the Puritans have been pleased with the thought that they were not mystics, since for them mysticism compromises the evangelical message of the Reformation and blurs the distinction between the gospel and other religions.[5] Others, often influenced by the late nineteenth-century German theologian Albrecht Ritschl, consider mysticism inimical to Protestantism, the importation into it of Catholic elements that undermine its ethical focus. Ritschl's disciple Adolf Harnack sneered at mysticism as "faded rationalism." Max Weber commented that while a mystical union might have survived in Lutheran piety, Calvinists were too activist to be mystical. On the other hand, Ernst Troeltsch argued that mysticism was an alien importation into Calvinism from "sect Christianity," to which some Puritan radicals succumbed. This is perhaps closer to the mark in Sterry's case at least but overlooks the mysticism of more mainstream Puritan figures than Sterry. But Troeltsch thought mysticism too "impractical" to appeal generally to "Calvinistic peoples."[6] Yet others with a "Catholic" sensibility, Roman or Anglo-Catholic, and perhaps more likely the latter than the former, associate Puritans and Calvinists with a narrow and unlovely piety that fits ill with mysticism, which they deem the highest realization of pure religion. They tend to think that the mysticism found in Puritan authors was a faded borrowing from medieval Catholic writers.[7]

There has, however, recently been a shift toward the recognition of mystical elements and mystical potential in the Protestant Reformation and the Protestant tradition. Summarizing some of this scholarship and his own investigations, Bernard McGinn recognizes the concept of union with Christ in both Luther and Calvin as having mystical aspects and asserts that "a mystical element played a role in classic Reformation theology." A similar conclusion about Calvin has been reached by a scholar who has investigated the relationship of that reformer with the twelfth-century spiritual writer Bernard of Clairvaux. If this is the case, it would be unnecessary to regard later Protestant mystics as chiefly inspired by medieval Catholic mysticism and as departing from their Reformation heritage; rather they were developing what was in that Reformation heritage. These authors also see the Reformation heritage as having continuity with aspects of medieval mysticism, and so it is not surprising that this would also be true of Puritan spiritual writers.[8]

In any case, the general literature on mysticism has paid relatively little attention to Puritans, and even scholars of Puritanism have often been sufficiently intimidated by this consensus about an antimystical Puritanism to have carefully qualified what they say about the mystical strains within Puritanism. There has even been reluctance among some of those who have studied Sterry to call him outright a mystic; for example, Vivian de Sola Pinto, a modern editor of some of Sterry's writings, declared that "it is not easy to determine whether we can correctly describe Sterry as a mystic," though he proceeded to give good reasons why he might be.[9] Few have bucked this consensus, but Jerald Brauer, Gordon Wakefield, Geoffrey F. Nutall, Charles Hambrick-Stowe, Janice Knight, and Belden Lane have accepted the notion of a Puritan mysticism, Knight writing of a "passionate mysticism" to be found in certain New England Puritans, and Lane declaring that the Puritans had "a passion for personal intimacy with God, the *unio mystica,* a vision of God transfixing their hearts and minds with a beauty they could not withstand."[10] N. I. Matar, a literary scholar who has authored many articles on Sterry as well as edited a volume drawn largely from Sterry's unpublished manuscripts, describes him without hesitation as a mystic, though this point is not the focus of his work on Sterry. D. P. Walker forthrightly calls Sterry "a genuine mystic."[11]

Sterry's Career and Puritanism

Peter Sterry, the son of Anthony Sterry, a cooper, was born in 1613 and baptized at St. Olave's Southwark, on September 19, 1613. As his life unfolded, there were many connections to Puritans and the Puritan movement.[12] He was educated at Emmanuel College, Cambridge, as were so many Puritan leaders, entering it in October 1629, receiving the B.A. in 1633, and an M.A. and a fellowship in 1637. While there, his prayers and discourses were said to have been an inspiration to others, the kind of remark commonly made about devout Puritans.[13] He left the college soon after receiving his degree, and beginning in 1638 served as a chaplain to Robert Greville, Lord Brooke, opponent of episcopacy, lay stalwart of the Puritan movement who had been interested in New England settlement, and parliamentary general who was killed in the civil war in 1643. Named to the Westminster Assembly, Sterry identified himself with the Independent dissenting Brethren, though he spoke little. He preached to the Parliament, striking a millenarian note, and encouraging those opposed to the monarchy.[14] After the King's execution, Sterry became a preacher to the Council of State. When Oliver Cromwell became Lord Protector, he appointed Sterry one of his chaplains, and Sterry moved into lodgings at Whitehall. Along with John Owen, Nicholas Lockyer, and Joseph Caryl, he was one of the Congregationalists or Independents upon whom Cromwell frequently relied for advice in religious matters. For example, Sterry, Owen, and Caryl were appointed to examine a book published in 1653 by the Independent minister Nathaniel Holmes, *The Resurrection Revealed,* upon which they reported favorably. He joined Philip Nye, Thomas Goodwin, and John Milton in inventorying various records and papers. A sermon preached to the House of Commons on November 5, 1651, asserted "Independency" against the "fleshly principle" characteristic of both "Romish-Papacy" and "Scottish-Presbytery." He was a propagandist for the Cromwellian regime, whose encomia for Cromwell, especially after the Lord Protector's death, were effusive, earning him enmity from royalists. Particularly offensive to royalists was Sterry's prayer, as reported by the hostile Gilbert Burnet, that he had asked God to make Oliver Cromwell's son Richard, who succeeded him, "the brightness of the father's glory."[15]

After Cromwell's death in 1658, Sterry became a chaplain to Philip Sidney, Viscount Lisle, who had been a member of both the short and long parliaments and was a member of the Council of State under both Cromwells. In 1677, with the death of his father, Sidney became Earl of Leicester. Sidney lived on an expansive estate at West Sheen near Richmond, south of London, and there Sterry, and eventually Sterry's pupils, joined him. Because of his ties to some of the regicides, the first months after the Restoration of Charles II were perilous times for Sterry. However, in November 1660, he received a pardon from Charles II. Eventually he began to preach to dissenting audiences in and around London, and operated an informal academy and became a spiritual adviser to his own family, the Sidney family and some of their visitors, and the pupils who had gathered to study with him at West Sheen. Because of their sense of spiritual connection with one another, Sterry dubbed this group "the lovely society"; his inspiration for such a retired community came from the French romance *Astrea,* by Honore D'Urfe, which depicted a small community of Druids in fifth-century Gaul—Adamas, the name of the community's leader in D'Urfe's fictional account, was adopted by Sterry in some of his correspondence.[16]

He maintained ties with other Dissenters, joining John Owen, Philip Nye, and William Bates in a joint lecture in Hackney in 1669.[17] Sterry took out a license to preach at three places in Hackney and London under the 1672 Act of Indulgence[18] but died later that year, on November 19. He was buried at Little St. Helen's, Bishopsgate.

Apart from a few sermons, Sterry's published works were posthumous, brought out by admirers. His son Joseph and daughter Frances helped gather some of his manuscripts for publication, and an anonymous friend, perhaps Jeremiah White, gathered the different parts of his *A Discourse on the Freedom of the Will*, which was published in 1675. White, who had also been a chaplain to Cromwell and was singled out for denunciation as a republican radical by Tory propagandists as late as the 1690s, was a member of Sterry's circle of friends, shared many of his ideas, and published other Sterry manuscripts. These were brought out, the first with a preface by White, and the second prefaced by Joshua Sprigg, a dissenting minister whom Baxter dubbed the chief of Sterry's disciples and who said that he had gathered them from various persons, as *The Rise, Race, and Royalty of God in the Soul of Man* in 1683 and *The Appearance of God to Man in the Gospel* in 1710.[19] Other writings of Sterry remained in manuscript, circulating for awhile among his pupils and friends, and, after being taken to Australia and brought back, were placed in the library of Emmanuel College, Cambridge.[20]

Sterry and the Radical Puritans

Sterry was generally considered one of the Independents, as were White and Sprigg—Anthony Wood called him a "notorious Independent"—and it was with them that he was principally associated in the Westminster Assembly and as a chaplain and adviser to Cromwell, though perhaps his eccentricity and impracticality rendered him a less important adviser than John Owen, Philip Nye, and Thomas Goodwin.[21] But Cromwell thought that Sterry was an appropriate person, presumably because of his radical millenarianism, to help reconcile the Fifth Monarchists to the government, as exemplified in Sterry's conference with Christopher Feake, whom he exhorted, apparently fruitlessly, to reconcile with the Cromwellian regime.[22] He was also a bridge for the government to the more radical Welsh Independents, such as Vavasor Powell.[23] Sterry's radical credentials probably also made him seem an appropriate person for the refutation of the Ranters.[24]

Sterry's advocacy of toleration also connected him to Puritan radicals, and went beyond the view of many Independents who advocated only a limited toleration for godly persons who might differ on matters of rite and doctrine; Sterry called in question the very certainty with which all sides maintained their positions, since all sides might have access to some part of the truth: the devout, he thought, should be aware that in different circumstances one might have had different views. One should avoid "bitter zeal," because "often . . . two opposed parties have something on each side, excellently good." Thus it is "the vanity of poor Men to fight one with another, and kill one another, for their differences in Opinions."[25] This is certainly at a considerable remove from the position of such a leading conservative Independent as John Owen who favored some religious toleration;[26] it is not merely a plea for legal toleration, but for Christians to bear with and have fellowship with one another in spite of major theological differences.

Cromwell, aware of Sterry's tolerant views, and favoring the return of Jews to England, considered Sterry a supporter of the petition of the Dutch Jew Menasseh Ben Israel concerning the permission for Jews to return to England. Some of the sectarians and radical Puritans were eager for the return of the Jews, not least in relation to their beliefs about the fulfillment of prophecy and their eschatological hopes.[27]

Sterry's discussion of law, echoing some of Luther's language in declaring that the law brought "a servility and Bondage upon the Spirits of Men," also connected him to the radical edge of the Puritan movement. This similarity to Luther and language about law suggests some affinity especially with those radical writers on the Puritan margins who leaned in an Antinomian direction, such as those identified by Dwight Bozeman as representing a backlash against "the precisianist strain" of Puritan discipline and by David Como as constituting an Antinomian "underground"; but in Como's distinction, Sterry would clearly have been close to the "imputative" Antinomians who emphasized grace rather than the "perfectionist" Antinomians. Sterry rebuked the perfectionist Antinomian conclusion of the Ranters that persons were free to do all things and that there is no sin.[28] However, the seeker William Erbery considered Sterry to be closer to understanding the godly new world of the saints than the other preachers connected to Parliament and the army, although Erbery thought Sterry had not yet arrived at the full truth.[29] Many of these religious radicals on the fringe of Puritanism, such as John Everarde, also evinced mystical traits in their thinking.[30]

Sterry was on the cusp between the more radical Independents and the yet more radical mystically inclined sectarians and free spirits. He is thus to be distinguished from the mainstream of disciplinary Puritans, whose approach, it will appear in a later chapter, persisted in the piety of Joseph Alleine and Baxter. This, along with Baxter's well-known dislike for the army radicals of the

1640s would explain Baxter's distaste for Sterry when he coupled him with Sir Henry Vane, who had supported the Massachusetts Antinomians. Indeed, Vane, friend of Sterry, was a leading figure among these proponents of a "free grace" that repudiated much of the disciplinary tradition of mainstream Puritanism. David Como has recently drawn a picture of a radical Puritanism that mingled Antinomian, occult, and mystical motifs of varying unorthodoxy and spoke unguardedly of the ecstatic joys of the state of grace suggestive of Sterry, although Sterry also sought to rein in such impulses.[31]

Sterry's most notable connection to radicalism, however, is to be found in posthumous publications and especially in unpublished manuscripts, which reveal him to have adopted a doctrine of universal salvation or apokatastasis, the restoration of all things to their original state of unity with God, even the fallen angels. Ultimately, then, "the Son of God will be brought forth in the whole creation," and "each particular Creature" by union with Christ, will return to its state "before they descended into this shadowy Image" of earthly existence. God's love will pursue souls until "all return to their Original." The whole world lives, dies, and rises with Christ. But for the damned, as opposed to believers, there would be a period of mental suffering in which God's "strange work," his love in the form of wrath, burns away all sin. For Sterry, in Christ all sins were pardoned and eventually the whole creation set free from bondage.[32] Sterry aimed in this way to bring together the absolute sovereignty and absolute goodness of God.[33] *A Letter of Resolution Concerning Origen and the Chief of his Opinions*, calling attention to the universalism of that early Christian writer, who was a favorite of the Cambridge Platonists, was published in 1661; it may have been by George Rust, who had been a fellow of Christ's College, Cambridge, and was associated with the Cambridge Platonists and so would have been known to Sterry. The Cambridge Platonist Henry More, an enthusiast for Origen, gave consideration to the idea of apokatastasis.[34]

This universalism was also affirmed by Sterry's follower Jeremiah White in his *The Restoration of All Things*, published in 1712. White, who claimed that Sterry had confirmed that he was a universalist on his deathbed, also said that he had learned his universalism from Sterry. But White's universalism was more explicit and made more public than Sterry's.[35]

Sterry's Calvinism

Sterry was a Puritan and an Independent, but his universalism clearly places him on the radical edge of those movements. And although there is much about the radical edge of Puritan Dissenters in the later seventeenth century that connects them to "the phenomena of the Pre-Enlightenment,"[36] Sterry's universalism was distinctly of a Calvinist sort, entailing a universal election, and rejecting anything remotely smacking of Arminian free will. The strongest evidence of Sterry's Calvinist predestinarianism is to be found in his treatise on *The Freedom of the Will*, which Baxter thought so extreme in its determinism as to be classed with the views of William Twisse, a highly reputed Calvinist theologian of supralapsarian views who had been prolocutor of the Westminster Assembly and who worried that the doctrine of reprobation was being neglected. Other aspects of Sterry's thought also line him up with the Calvinist theologians of his time: the Reformed scheme of the order of salvation proceeding from election through calling, justification, and sanctification to glorification is a central presupposition for much of his thought; like many high Calvinists (John Owen, for example) he understood Christ in his atoning death to have suffered the agony of abandonment by God the Father, Christ becoming sin, wrath, and a curse for the sake of humankind; and although the covenant theme is not prominent in Sterry's writings, where he does mention it, he presupposes the double covenant federal theology characteristic of high Calvinists. And most emphatically, as theologian and spiritual writer, he stressed grace as irresistible and as the sole cause of redemption.[37]

Sterry's Mysticism: Neoplatonism

Thus Sterry may be reasonably identified as a Puritan and Calvinist; what is the evidence for his mysticism? Mysticism is, if anything, a more slippery category than Puritanism, so some consideration of its meaning as used here is in order. Universalizing theories of mysticism have treated mysticism as a union of the soul with ultimate reality and correspondingly have found it above all in certain religious traditions of Asia, with Christianity providing fellow travelers such as Meister Eckhart in the fourteenth century. One can find passages in Puritan spiritual writing that fit such a definition, but not many. However, in his study of Christian mysticism, Bernard McGinn, emphasizing that mysticism must be understood in historical context and in connection with particular historical religions, thinks that a focus on unitive mysticism of that type would make mysticism a rare phenomenon in Christianity and prefers to describe Christian mysticism as beliefs and practices related to a consciousness of "the immediate or direct presence of God." It is this that is the claim of most Christian mystical texts. And McGinn further observes that the historian has access to mystical texts and their mystical language, not to mystical states and experiences. These judgments strike me as persuasive and for present purposes will be taken as normative in this depiction of Sterry as a mystical writer, even though the theme of mystical union does make some appearance in his thought.[38]

McGinn also calls attention to the fact that in the Christian mystical tradition one may expect to find many references to "Plato, Philo, Plotinus, and Proclus."[39] Since one is known by the company kept, Sterry's citations provide insight into the cast of his thought and show him to have been reading authors connected to the Platonic (or more accurately, Neoplatonic) tradition that nourished mysticism. Plato, Plotinus and Proclus (if not Philo) are frequently cited; citations to "Orpheus," Pythagoras, Parmenides, and Plutarch appear, all names associated in one way or another with the mystical and Platonic traditions from antiquity. Among Sterry's manuscripts are extensive extracts copied from Plutarch, Porphyry, and Maximus of Tyre, the first of whom was associated with knowledge of ancient mystery rites while the latter two considered themselves followers of Plato. As for ancient and medieval Christian authors of interest to mystics, Sterry cited Gregory of Nyssa, Augustine, Boethius, Dionysios the Areopagite, Thomas Aquinas, and Nicholas of Cusa. A partial list of his books included a volume of Origen. Jewish mysticism is represented by references to the "Cabala." There are also references to Renaissance Platonists of mystical bent such as Marsiglio Ficino, Leo Hebraeus, and Tommaso Campanella and to the Cambridge Platonists Ralph Cudworth and Henry More.[40]

Sterry had close ties to the circle of the Cambridge Platonists, especially to Benjamin Whichcote, who preached Sterry's funeral sermon. Whichcote had arrived at Emmanuel College three years before Sterry, and they seem to have influenced each other. John Smith, another of the Cambridge Platonists, had also arrived at Emmanuel before Sterry; two others associated with the group, Nathaniel Culverwell and Ralph Cudworth, arrived before Sterry left the college. Some historians of the movement have considered Sterry a member of the group.[41] And while the Cambridge group tended to abandon the stricter Calvinism of their background, Culverwell certainly remained, like Sterry, an anti-Arminian Calvinist as well as a Platonist.[42] The combination of Calvinism and Platonism was far from unusual in the later seventeenth century in England. As will be seen in later chapters, Theophilus Gale was thoroughly imbued with the Platonic outlook, albeit in his own revised version, and John Howe and John Edwards were also thinkers deeply influenced by Platonism. To these Reformed thinkers, Plato seemed a "religion-friendly" philosopher who supported the reality of the spiritual and the ideal as well as such specific truths as the immortality of the soul. The connection of Calvinism and Platonism can be argued to have gone back to Calvin himself.[43]

Sterry was thought by a contemporary to have been one of the first to have made "a public profession of Platonism" at Cambridge and was a fellow student of Whichcote and later chaplain to Robert Greville, Lord Brooke, whose *The Nature of Truth* (1640) was perhaps the first book espousing Platonism to come from the Cambridge circle of Platonists. There is reason to believe that Sterry had a significant role in this publication and may have been responsible for some of its language.[44] Certainly Sterry's writings are deeply tinctured with Platonism, or more precisely, Neoplatonism. According to Sterry all things had come from the supreme God by emanations and formed a hierarchy from God down to the most shadowy being. The physical world was "a land of Shadowes only and Dreames."[45] But these shadows are shadows of a higher realm of ideas and, in Sterry's cosmic Christology, Christ is the unity of all things and their image. In Christ all things have preexistence, for Christ stands in a "Middle State" between God's oneness and the creation's variety, "comprehending the whole creation eminently in himself, before it have a subsistence in it self." Christ is thus the way "by which the Creation cometh forth from God," being thus the image of the invisible God. As such, Christ is the divine word and "Divine Understanding," in which all variety is one as he is one with the Father. Thus Christ is "the Treasury of all ideas" and the "Head and Pattern" of all creation. He is also in the creation as a divine seed in creation's "shadowy Image," and as the "seminal Virtue which puts forth it self through the whole Creation." Furthermore, the shadowy realm is emblematic of that higher spiritual realm which is in and through Christ. Adumbrations of this cosmic Christology appear as early as his sermon *The Clouds on Which Christ Comes*, preached in 1647 and published in 1648. D. P. Walker has described these ideas as an "amalgam of Pauline Christology and Neoplatonic emanationism."[46]

Shadowy the natural world might be, but Sterry was very much taken with the beauty of it, which he often described effusively and took to be a reflection of the divine beauty. A poem left in manuscript praises the beauty of the sun, sky, trees, and the "flowery carpet" of "perfumed fields."[47] Nonetheless, souls, which Sterry thought preexistent, following Platonism and Origen, are cast as "fugitives" into this shadowy world by both creation and the fall, lose their memory of a former state, and are deadened to higher spiritual realities until the spiritual (and Christological) seed within is awakened and drawn to its source.[48] For Sterry, eventually all souls will return to the ultimate spiritual reality from which they have come. Evil and sin are privation of the good and have arisen from the "Nothingnes & Emptiness of the Creature" and will eventually lapse into "nothingness." If sin were a positive thing, God could not be acquitted of being its author.[49] Thus in Sterry's Neoplatonic Christianity, all things come forth from God but also return to him, reminiscent of that ancient Christian universalist, Origen of Alexandria, with whom, as already seen, Sterry was familiar. Sterry's view of evil as the privation of good is also ultimately Neoplatonic as well as rooted in Augustinianism. This notion had of course reappeared with frequency in the centuries between Augustine and Sterry.

Other Neoplatonic commonplaces can also be found in Sterry's writings, such as truth as conformity to the heavenly ideas and the plenitude of being. The first of these had epistemological significance, since knowledge came from grasping the ideal essences of things. Explaining the latter, Sterry says that "the Variety from its highest state extends it self to the most remote distance, by even and united steps, that all the distances be full."[50]

Christian mystical spirituality which had come down from antiquity was deeply imbued with Neoplatonism, but it also included traces and elements of Stoic thought, and there are references in Sterry to some of the ancient Stoics, especially to Seneca, a Roman writer in great favor with Renaissance thinkers and widely cited by Puritans before Sterry.[51] In some of the passages in which Sterry describes the religious life, he develops themes close to the ancient Stoic ideal of *apatheia,* and does so in relation to a Neoplatonic framework: if the world of our experience is one of shadows, then, one should "live unconcerned with this world," in which nothing is real. One should pass through "all estates with a perfect indifference of Spirit, in a constant calm," recognizing no difference between grief and joy, or between having wealth and family or not having them.[52] With this Neoplatonic metaphysical scheme and its Stoic accompaniments, Sterry lays the groundwork for his mysticism.

Sterry's Mystical Imagery

Many of the images and themes characteristic of Sterry's writing are among those that have commonly appeared in Christian mystical literature, even though Sterry sometimes gives his own twist to them. For example, the spiritual life as a ladder of ascent to God, based on the biblical story of Jacob's ladder, is a frequent motif of Christian mystical literature and is employed by Sterry. Augustine used the ladder as an allegory of the path to God, and John Climacus, the seventh-century Greek Christian author of the *The Ladder of Divine Ascent,* divided the ascent to Christ into thirty steps, corresponding to the years of the earthly life of Christ. *The Rule of St. Benedict* in the sixth-century Latin West used the image of Jacob's ladder to suggest the soul's upward climb out of this life and toward God through steps of humility and discipline. Gregory the Great in the same century connected the ladder to mystical contemplation, and notably the thirteenth-century Franciscan Bonaventure built a famous treatise around the mind's road to God based on the ladder which he broke down into steps of mystical ascent. The English mystic Walter Hilton's *The Ladder of Perfection* continued this mystical use of the ladder image. Neoplatonic mysticism had imagined the soul moving upward toward its fulfillment in the higher reality of the "One"; blended with Christian mysticism since ancient times and revived in the Renaissance Platonism of fifteenth-century Florence and of the Cambridge Platonists, it cannot have been far from Sterry's mind. In his profusion of images, Sterry describes the person of Christ as "a mystical ladder" and says that Jacob's ladder is within the believer, joining heaven and earth, making it a description of the path to God. Elsewhere Sterry calls Jacob's ladder a type of the "ranks and degrees of being," and "mystical steps" in the "scale of Divine Harmony" in an image redolent of the Neoplatonic *scala mundi*, a motif with the Cambridge Platonists. Thus for Sterry the ladder represents both the soul's spiritual ascent and the gradations of being traversed in such an ascent. But it is also "a Mystical Ladder of Divine Loves reaching from Heaven, to Earth," a use of the image suggesting Sterry's very Protestant sense of the path to God being initially a path of God's gracious descent to the lower realm to bring about the redemption of humankind.[53] Another image common in Christian mystical literature used by Sterry is that of Moses in the presence of God on Mount Sinai, where he saw God "face to face."[54] This mystical motif is particularly associated with the fourth-century Gregory of Nyssa's *Life of Moses*.

The image and motif of mystical experience as light and illumination, common in the medieval mystical tradition, with the sun and fire as special symbols of this, is frequent in Sterry. God is light, asserted Sterry, and the appearance of God in nature is like so many "candle-lights," shining here below. But God in the gospel is "a burning and shining light," a "free light," shining through all things and making them transparent (the law, as contrasted with the gospel as sunlight, is but "star-light"). Christ "shining in our spirits" is a "divine light" enabling persons to see "divine things."

Reason too is a light, even in fallen humanity, an image that was utilized by the Cambridge Platonists, famously as "the candle of the Lord," though an inferior one to the light of spirit (Sterry distinguished reason and spirit, and regarded spirit as superior). Sterry spoke highly of human reason as the noblest power of the soul, a power that imitates the divine nature. Philosophy represents the "perfection of our reason," and natural theology using philosophy can teach us about such spiritual substances as God, angels, and souls, though it needs to be supplemented by the divine illumination of revelation for a fuller knowledge of these things. Sterry, also, in Platonic fashion, claimed that reason can show the unity of all things and referred to the beauty of logic.[55] Clearly, he would not have sympathized with the current fideist argument that, as seen in the first chapter, had been rebutted by Owen, though Sterry also acknowledged the limitations of reason: reason had betrayed humankind in Eden, and in a sermon preached before Parliament in 1656 he insisted that those truly capable of using the light of reason are spiritual persons, persons of faith. The unspiritual are also the unreasonable, because their reason is defiled by "the prince of darkness and a principle of Corruption inwardly," as for them "carnal interests" interpose between the light of their minds and the light of God. Thus the divine light is eclipsed so that they cannot judge rightly regarding the testimony to truth which "the light of Nature inwardly gives," and instead "deny it according to their fleshly lusts, and ends." The result of this, Sterry contended, was "a stupid Atheisticalness," revealing his awareness of that issue of the time, and suggesting that he understood atheism as a kind of senseless disregard of truth obvious to a properly exercised and illuminated mind. Sterry also argued that human idolatry, a failure to recognize the unity of God, was near to atheism: "He that makes many Gods, makes none."[56] But in his strictures on the limitations of reason, Sterry's strong Calvinism, coupled with his Platonism, renders him a somewhat more complex thinker than the main group of Cambridge Platonists.[57] However, like them, Sterry was drawing on a more Platonic and traditional view of reason than was increasingly becoming current among those following Descartes.

There is among the Sterry manuscripts a brief item entitled "Of Ye Sun" which declares that the sun is a "figure" of the human soul with its capacity to see God, and corresponding to it, as a kind of antitype, is "the Eternall Word, our glorified Jesus," in whom, as has already been seen, are contained all the ideas and forms of things. The soul, figured as the sun, has light by which to see all that is contained in the eternal word. But the sun is also a figure of God's unity, for that unity is the "Eternal Sun, from which alone all the Divine beams, and Sacred Lights of Truth flow thro' all Understandings, all natures, all Orders of Things, from the highest to the lowest."[58] Fire, like the Sun, is another related image for Sterry. There is both the fire of the ascending flame of the soul reaching toward God and the fire of the condescending love of God that purifies believers. In one of his published sermons sun and fire are to Sterry images of heaven.[59]

Not only has light been an image in the Christian mystical tradition but also darkness, and this image too looms large in Sterry's writing. Some passages in Sterry dealing with darkness are suggestive of the mystical theme of the soul's dark night, as when he cries out that "in a long, and darke night, when all things are husht up in the sleepe of death round about mee, I watch, and waite for the Morning, and Day-spring of thy face, o my God." This spiritual anxiety is relieved when he sees the glimmerings of light as the dawning of God upon him.[60] But darkness is not just an image for a phase of the spiritual life for Sterry, it is also central to the metaphysic underlying his mysticism. For it is part of the mystery of God that he hides his glory under a veil in the world. The world of matter and of the body is darkness. This is the mystery of the fall, the law, the "letter" (as opposed to the spirit), the disharmony that its breach brought into the world, of death, suffering, and hell, and of that paradise which had a serpent in it. Indeed, the whole creation had its root in darkness, God having commanded the light to shine forth out of darkness and chaos. By the fall humankind darkened the light of God's image which "lay buried under the Ruines" of the soul, though one might catch "some Glimpses" of God's beauty. The law given at Sinai was "a shadow" that hid and veiled the truth in darkness even as it adumbrated it in figures; and yet the law was the gospel of "eternal love vailed," a love that will shine forth when the veil is removed. The "letter," like the law, "casts a Vail upon the face of God." Disharmony is the work of the devil, who is disharmony itself, and "every Sin must at last bring forth a Devil." Suffering and death are also but a veil, removing us from "Place and Time," which are "the chains of the darkness of this world"; so the believer should "Kisse death as a lovely bride." Even hell is but God's "strange work," in which he estranges himself from himself, bringing forth his works "in contraries; Light and Darkness; Good and Evil."[61]

In a sermon preached in 1656 and published the next year, Sterry distinguished between the right and left hands of God, and this distinction lurks in the background of many passages in his writings. God's left hand is his strange work and his wrath; and it is, as he says elsewhere, a work of contrariety, and is manifested in law, the "letter," sin, death and hell; but it is actually only a disguise for his proper work, that of his right hand, at which Christ sits, which is love, joy and glory, which the saints in beatitude shall see in its true character.[62] Ultimately then, for Sterry God's wrath is but God's love disguised, and on that basis he developed a theodicy: "God sees the saddest, the bloodiest Tragedies, that are acted by Man or Devils: yet he sees them with pleasure, because he sees them in his own light. By this light he sees the Power, Wisdom, Goodness, Glory, working in every Object." And so he exhorts his readers to "no more call any thing by those afflicting Names of Death, Sorrow, Loss, or Pain" but to "see in every thing a Joy unutterable." When the work of God's wrath shall be seen as part of a complete divine design it will be seen as a triumph of divine love.[63]

Related to light and darkness is Sterry's use of the image of the eye: besides the natural eye of reason (understood as already seen in Neoplatonic fashion) there is in humans the divine eye, "a Divine Principle or Faculty of seeing Things" and a "Power of Knowing," even of knowing God, which is closed between the fall and the regeneration of a soul, being awakened by Christ as "a Sun beame beating with a strong Light upon the Naturall Eye." What the spiritual eye can see of divine things, however, depends on growing in holiness, for holiness, Sterry says, is an "eye salve" enabling us better to see God. This image of an inner spiritual eye in the soul becomes in other places a spiritual seed or a divine spark, the latter of course also an image of light. From the spiritual spark in souls there "springs up a Light, which leads them into ye Depths of the Godheade."[64]

For the spiritual eye truly to see, there must be some retreat into quiet and prayer. He recommends in a letter of spiritual advice that one should be, before God, "wholly silent, obedient, and Resigned." For this, it is necessary to retire into the seed of God within oneself, or, as he puts it elsewhere, "Retire your self into your Chamber, in which the candle of the Lord shines, that is, into your Spirit, as it hath the Spirit of God. There wait quietly:

> Let God be God; I am at Rest
> Divinely sleeping on His Brest.[65]

But Sterry speaks of prayer as well as of quiet contemplation. Prayer is the Christian's soul, the form of his life with God. It is "the Breath in the Nostrils of the Spiritual Man, while he is cloth'd with an Earthly Body."[66]

Sensuous Imagery

Sensuous and body imagery has been a frequent accompaniment of mystical writings, and appears often in Sterry. Thus smelling and tasting become spiritual metaphors: in a manuscript letter, Sterry advises his son Peter to "perfume" himself with the "sweete Odours" of the love of Christ and to taste of Christ. The Lord's Supper is called a feast of the "Flesh of Christ." In another passage, not explicitly Eucharistic, though clearly echoing that language, Sterry speaks of eating Christ, and of "How pleasant is the Taste and Relish of him upon our Palates? How rightly doth he go down, answering and satisfying all our Appetites," and passing into all parts of those who believe in him and take him as "their Heavenly Bread and Wine." The earlier Puritan mystical author Francis Rous declared that the taste of Christ "hath distasted all the taste of the creatures." A pleasant garden is another image of mystical experience, and he speaks of being led into the "Garden of Christ" where one may "feed upon his Spices." This garden replicates the original Garden of Eden, when all of creation was a garden, and all was close to God.[67]

In a letter to his daughter, sensuous imagery of many kinds centers on the garden, which is "the Spirituall Image of Jesus Christ in us, and in every Creature."

There perfumes are to be smelled, the pure water of eternity and the fruit of divine pleasures tasted, and Christ as the beloved met.[68] Meeting the beloved introduces erotic and earthly love as an image of mystical experience; perhaps no image has been as frequent and universal in mystical literature. A profusion of erotic images come tumbling out of Sterry's prose: he exhorts the believer to see himself "on thy Marriage-day with thy Husband, Jesus"; there are the kisses of Christ upon the lips of the believer (the lips of Christ refer to the "naked Person of Christ in Glory"), the embraces of the savior, lying in the bosom of Christ, Christ as the "wife of our youth," the ravishing love and beauty of Christ, "the Bed of Divine Loves," the "Wine of Love," "mysterious Love-sport," "Divine Love-play," "ravishing contrivances," "breathings" of love, and many references to the mystical marriage of the soul to God and Christ. Death comes as the consummation of the love of this mystical marriage, leading to a better life, as Sterry uses the image of sexual consummation as death common in the love poetry of his time.[69] And commenting on a Genesis story he writes, "As Jacob laid the peeled Rods before the Ewes at watering: So Jesus Christ sets his various, and naked Excellencies before the Soul, when she is big with Desires."[70]

Much of this imagery comes from the biblical Canticles, or Song of Solomon, a book that, interpreted allegorically, had long nourished Christian mystical speculations. Calvin, who had opposed Sebastian Castellio for claiming that the book was ancient Hebrew love poetry, authorized for the Reformed the notion that the book was an allegory of Christian spirituality. Its use in explicating the spiritual life had much precedent among those considered important in the development of Puritan spirituality: George Gifford had published *Fifteene Sermons upon the Song of Solomon* in 1598; Henry Ainsworth had commented on the book in a publication of 1622; in 1639 Richard Sibbes authored *Bowels opened; or a discovery of the neere and deer love, union and communion betwixt Christ and the Church, and consequently betwixt him and every believing soule,* based on the fourth through the sixth chapters of Canticles, realizing, as his biographer notes, that its sensual language "was a powerful metaphor for the love between God and the soul"; in 1631 Francis Rous had published *The Mysticall Marriage: Or Experimental Discoveries of the Heavenly Marriage between the Soule and her Saviour,* which extensively drew on the imagery of this biblical book, and in another book Rous shows familiarity with the famous sermons on Canticles preached in the twelfth century by Bernard of Clairvaux. The mystical Scottish Puritan Samuel Rutherford showed considerable interest in the book. The diarist John Evelyn particularly associated preoccupation with Canticles with Puritans; having attended a sermon on October 12, 1656, he noted in his diary that "our Preacher is againe in the Canticles (as these halfe Independents & Presbyters delighted to be." There were many verse paraphrases of the book in English, such as those by Edmund Spenser, Philip Sidney, and Thomas Middleton, and more to the point, by such Puritan stalwarts as Dudley Fenner and Arthur Hildersham.[71] The book's popularity with dissenting spiritual writers continued among Sterry's contemporaries, as exemplified by James Durham's posthumously published *Clavis Cantici* (1668) and Thomas Vincent's *Christ the Best Husband* (1672). Durham's book was prefaced by John Owen, who described the Song of Solomon as an allegory of the mystical communion between Christ and his church and between Christ and every believer's soul.[72] A recent study has found extensive use of the imagery of Canticles by the Restoration Baptist poets John Reeve and Benjamin Keach.[73] Extensive American Puritan engagement with the Song of Solomon and the prevalence of the image of marital intimacy for the spiritual life has been noted for New England as well and persisted there to the end of the seventeenth century; the New England poet Edward Taylor and later Jonathan Edwards were drawn to its imagery in explicating the spiritual life.[74] Attention has also been drawn to the widespread use of bodily passion as a metaphor of the spiritual life in seventeenth-century English devotional poetry generally, noting it in the verse of Church of England conformists John Donne and George Herbert; but after the Restoration the use of such language in preaching was criticized by conformists as Puritan fanaticism and "enthusiasm." By the eighteenth century, the Dissenter Isaac Watts was embarrassed by the preoccupation with the Song of Solomon of earlier generations of Puritans and Dissenters.[75]

Sterry drew extensively on the imagery of the Song of Solomon and wrote a verse paraphrase of it which remained in manuscript at his death. Also, among his posthumous publications was a sermon on Psalm 45, which, like the Song of Solomon, he treated as about the marriage of Solomon and the daughter of Pharaoh, and interpreted as a "type of the Mystical Espousals" and "Marriage-Union" between Christ and the soul sung by the friends of the bridegroom, whom he thought were angels. According to Sterry this "type" contained the "whole mystery of the gospel."[76]

Clearly, erotic language and a fondness for the Song of Solomon in explicating the spiritual life and describing mystical experience were characteristic of many Puritan and Calvinist writers. The erotic motifs drawn from Canticles had with Protestant writers a special aspect which was not missed by the Puritans: married sexuality was an image of the mystical life which was not only a type or an allegory but also an experienced example of "the improving of the creatures," a phrase used by Puritan devotional writers to describe the finding of spiritual meanings in everyday life. In this case conjugal union in marriage reminded married believers of a higher and entirely spiritual union. Protestant and Puritan authors did not need to read the Song of Solomon as purely allegory but could understand it as a literal account of married love that allegorically also referred to the higher love between the soul and Christ. Thus was marriage not only a type of mystical union but was sanctified by virtue of its typological significance. Sterry made the most of this analogy between married love and spiritual love and set it in the context of his own married life.

Sterry recommended that those who were married were to see their marriages as analogous to the mystical marriage of God and the soul.[77] In correspondence with his wife Frances, Sterry described spiritual experience in sensuous terms. In these letters to his wife, who is addressed in one of them as "My Dearest Love, and most truly sweetest of all earthly Sweets," he frequently refers to Canticles, in one case comparing himself and Frances to Solomon and his Shulammite. In another letter he expatiated at length on the mutual love of the soul and God, and then tells her how much he ardently desires "to bee with you . . . to walk, talk, sleep together, and enjoy each other."[78]

It is clear in Sterry that Puritan mysticism was not solitary and withdrawn, but was lived out in family and community and in this way it differed from Christian mysticism that was solitary and celibate.[79] The community of spiritual experience for Sterry was neither a parish church nor a dissenting congregation (though had the times allowed it, it might have been that) but a fellowship consisting of his family, his pupils, and the other members of the "Lovely Society," and it also radiated outward to persons with whom he corresponded. Ultimately, this was for him a kind of congregation, spiritual fellowship with others being the sine qua non of what other Congregationalists besides Sterry considered the ideal church.

Familial love is illustrated in correspondence with his daughter Frances, by then married and living elsewhere, and his son Peter, and utilized sensuous language in portraying this love. To his daughter he speaks of her spiritual closeness to both himself and his wife, and of their sense of her closeness, as they share in the fountain of the God who loved them. "Your Mother and I believe we meet you often, and see your face shining, and smell your perfumes." Elsewhere he speaks of the daughter as perfumed with the "Odours, & Oyntments of Divine Loves & Joys & Grace, like a Queene on her Marriage Day." He recommended that his daughter "triumph" over the storms of life in the "Embraces of your Heavenly Lover."[80] With their son Peter it was a different matter, for he fell among bad companions, figuratively wounding his parents (having thrust "stinking poniards into their hearts, as often as you are making merry with companions; and drinking their blood in your cups together with your wine"), and had to be warned not to "return to your former Vomit" and to avoid the "Strange Woman," upon whom he had apparently wasted money. But Sterry remained with the same image, moving from the embrace of harlots to the embrace of Christ: "O yet fall into ye embraces of his Love," he tells Peter, for he (Peter) is the bride of Christ, and Christ is in him as a seed, "a living diamond" being at the center of his soul. He also reminded Peter of Christ as mother, referring to the "Bosom of your Mother, where you hang like a precious jewell, where you lie by the sides of those pleasant fountains of milk and honey, ye full breasts of ye Godhead."[81] Correspondence with friends can be the occasion for similar language. Writing to Morgan Llwyd, Sterry refers to his "Communion with my Bridegroome in you," which, he tells Llwyd is an "Enjoying you in Him."[82]

The angels sang of love at the marriage of Solomon and his bride in Canticles, and the theme of God as love is both a theological point for Sterry and a spiritual truth, adumbrated in earthly love. He defines God as "Love it self, in an abstracted eternal Divine Essence and Substance, pure Love altogether unmixt." This love of God runs through all of God's work, as God "letteth down all Love out of himself, and taketh it into himself again," uniting all "into one Master-piece of Divine Love." All that has being is God's "Immortal Love sporting with itself in manifold lovely shapes, in which it endlessly figureth all the innumerable Forms of loveliness, with all its Lights and Shades; and acteth all the innumerable Parts of Love in all its Mysterious Obscurings and Outshinings, its Captivities and its Triumphs, its Crucifyings and its Crownings." Those who love God ascend to him as a flame of love, seeing the tracks of his love in creation and revelation.[83] Indeed, the human will is only truly free as it is inclined by love toward God, its object, by a kind of attraction of similitude, as love for God draws one to God. Love is a union of the lover and the beloved.[84] This language about ascending to God as a flame of love and the attraction of similitude is redolent of Neoplatonic and Augustinian mysticism. For Sterry God's love seems to take precedence over all the other divine attributes, and he thought that this supreme truth about God as love had been particularly brought back by Paul from the "third heaven," that passage in II Corinthians (12:2–4) having long provided a warrant for visionary and mystical experiences in Christian spirituality. Of course, this precedence of love over other divine attributes is clearly a root of Sterry's universalism.[85]

Mystical Unity and Union

It is a commonplace of the discussions of mysticism that the mystic finds unity in all the variety of being, and Sterry's discussion of love clearly reaches that point. "When we understand the whole nature of things," says Sterry, we realize that all variety is swallowed up in a higher unity, which is diffused through all the variety.[86] That the variety of experience reduces to a unity in the experience of God is a theme frequently repeated by Sterry. This unity of all things is a unity in love and therefore is a grand harmony, which Sterry expands by using the Platonic notion of the music of the spheres, which results from God's tuning both the visible and invisible world "to a happy harmony." It is also the harmony of the persons of the Trinity, and thus "The whole Frame of things from the beginning to the Ende is one melodious Consort of the most excellent Musicke."[87]

The love of which the friends/angels sang was not only the unity of all things, but more particularly the unity of the soul and God. Union, according to Sterry, is an aspect of love. When the soul loves God in loving itself, in a true self-love, he says, God and the self are one.[88] Sterry expressed this oneness through images, such as that of the soul drawn to God like iron to a lodestone.[89] This oneness of God and the soul comes by a kind of deification: the Holy Spirit, he says, echoing II Peter 1:4, makes believers "Partakers of the Divine Nature."[90] Elsewhere Sterry explained this union as taking place in three stages: the first is the "shadowy" stage, when a person awakens to the reality of a mutual union of God and souls by virtue of souls being the creation of God; next is the "wrathful," in which "Man in the state of sin and in hell is united to God in his Wrathful Shape," an example of God's left hand; the third is the "Love Appearance," when God is decked as a bridegroom for a mystical marriage and a "spiritual union between himself and Man." In this discussion he concludes, "Thus you see it is easy for God to bring you into a Glorious Union and Communion with himself," for "Tis but a Discovery of that, which is already in you."[91] In yet another place he outlines a "threefold union," of sense, affection, and substance. The union of sense is when the divine loveliness shines upon the mind and imprints "a lasting and lovely Image of itself," a sense of "its Sweetness, Desirableness and Excellency." The union of affection follows this, as "the Sight of the Divine Beauty sown into the heart" springs up in the understanding and "burneth out in the Will" and affections with great fervour "until it meet with the beloved Object, the Image of whose Amiableness it hath seen in itself." In the union of substances, the soul is transported outside of itself and of all that pertains to creatures "upon Spiritual Wings" and "into the Bosom of this pure Eternal Beauty."[92]

This unity of all things and unity of God and the soul is also a unity in Trinity. For Sterry, as for much of Christian mystical reflection, there is great interest in the doctrine of the Trinity as a way of casting mutuality and reciprocity and diversity in unity into the very nature of the Godhead: "The Radical [i.e., root], and Original Unity is that of the Blessed Persons in the Trinity" and the human being, made in the image of God is also a trinity (as Augustine had long before maintained).[93] God as Trinity means that "God is not a Solitary Unity," but a "unity richly replenish'd, and Eternally entertain'd with a Variety,"[94] which includes all that is, since the second person of the Trinity includes within himself all the exemplars of creation. Since God is love, the inner life of the Trinity is in its "essence" love, in which are joined the lover, the beloved, and the "Love-Knot;" they enjoy "mysterious embraces," the Trinity "possessing and enjoying itself" in its "mutual Activities."[95] The Trinity as love is a "Fountain of Love," gushing forth as "a Pattern of Marriage," by which souls return to their divine source. The unity of God is also an exemplar of the union of the soul with God.[96] The Trinity is thus a focus for mystical contemplation: What "Volumes of Mystery, of Glory, of Ravishing Pleasures doth this Truth of ye Trinity write upon those Hearts to which it is pleased to appeare in any Thing of its owne Light?" This is a foretaste of heaven, where saints will see and know all things mirrored in the Trinity.[97] Here Trinity and heavenly mindedness intersect. It is in this context that a reference by Sterry to the Socinians is relevant: the Socinians, he declared, are mistaken in limiting us to what reason can see, and thus Sterry's objection to them was rooted in his spiritual outlook which found fulfillment in a dynamic God within whom were interpersonal relationships rich in mystical implications. Whether he often had the Socinians in mind or not, Sterry's thought is Trinitarian through and through: at many points in his writings, sometimes where it is surprising, Sterry commented on the Trinity—the impression grows that the doctrine of the Trinity was a central part of his theological reflections.

In his speculations on the Trinity, Sterry presupposed an ancient theology in which there had been from time immemorial glimmers of the Trinity, citing Pythagoras, Proclus, and Parmenides in this connection as well as persons nearer his own time such as Nicholas of Cusa and Marsiglio Ficino. But for him ancient theology was a kind of implicit received wisdom, which could be drawn upon as needed; he did not systematize or schematize it as did Theophilus Gale, as the next chapter will disclose. Nor did he, like Gale, give all credit to an original revelation to the Jews. Sterry acknowledged "glances" of truth to be found in the poets and philosophers. And his interest in poetry was not just in the ancients (he quoted Homer and Virgil), but also in those of his own time: he referred to Spenser, Donne, Herbert and Tasso in his works, and is credited with owning something authored by Shakespeare.[98]

The unity that Sterry felt connected the soul to God and the persons of the Trinity to one another was also to be found in the connections between humans and angels. Angels were important to Sterry, and were mentioned frequently in his writings. One of the common motifs of Puritan spirituality was what spiritual writers termed "heavenly mindedness," by which was meant a foretaste of beatitude that was described as a mystical contemplation and experienced as an awareness of the divine presence. Richard Baxter wrote a major work on this, *The Saints' Everlasting Rest,* and as chapter 4 of this book will discuss, presented Joseph Alleine as an exemplar of it. For Sterry, heavenly mindedness took the particular form of seeing oneself as encompassed by angels, in their songs and dances. He also envisioned angels who "stretch their glorious wings full of eyes round about you on every side to be your guard" in this life. Sterry writes as though he felt very familiar with Angels, and much aware of them.[99] As for their dancing, Sterry envisaged the redeemed soul in beatitude engaging in a "mystical dance" "round the Throne of her King," and commented that it was only the "grossness" of our bodies which shut out the heavenly light and hindered us, even in this life, from dancing around God's throne![100] Such a reflection certainly reflects a mystical heavenly mindedness. Somewhat later, Cotton Mather in his diary recorded visions of angels and opined that angels abetted the spiritual ecstasies of the mystical relationship of the soul with God.[101]

Mystics are often accused of blurring distinctions in their emphasis on a unifying kind of religious experience, and this is perhaps the ultimate basis for Sterry's tolerant outlook. As seen earlier, Sterry warned against "bitter zeal," observing that often both sides in a controversy have something good to say— had circumstances been different one might oneself have another point of view. One should look for the good in others and be conscious of the evil in oneself. In an exegesis of Ecclesiastes 7:16, posthumously published, Sterry warned against placing "too much weight" upon opinions and "outward forms"; our "notions" are but "broken things," "Bits of Spiritual Truth," and the "outside and dross" of an inner truth rather than the truth itself. "It is impossible for us to have a full View of the Whole Face of Truth." It is in remarks of this kind that we sense the mystical root of Sterry's tolerant outlook, as the personal experience of God trumps doctrinal niceties. Persons should not fight and kill for opinions, especially since "both may possess the same Truth and the same Treasure."[102]

So far little attention has been given to form and style in the mystical writings of Peter Sterry. Perhaps enough has been cited to suggest the emotional effusiveness of his prose, and also its allusive character. Vivian de Sola Pinto, who was interested in Sterry as a stylist, thought that his prose was very much like the poetry of such contemporaries of Sterry as George Herbert, Henry Vaughan, and Thomas Traherne, and commented that characteristically in his writings Sterry crystallized his thoughts in a "short prose poem or meditation consisting of a vivid presentation of one or more images followed by an interpretation in a spiritual or religious sense, or conversely the enunciation of a spiritual truth followed by imagery that illustrates and embodies it."[103] Sterry's contemporary Baxter, however, faulted him for a style in which "clear conceptions" are "drowned, buried, or lost" in "allegories" and "a torrent of ambiguous Metaphors." For Baxter, the barbarities of the medieval scholastics were preferable to the "equivocations" of Sterry's writings.[104] In spite of Baxter, Sterry's style had some continuity with earlier Puritan authors, such as Richard Sibbes, John Cotton, and John Davenport, whose preachments, Janice Knight has argued, "trade on incantation, hovering over single words or verses of scripture," favoring "affect over logic, sensibility over meaning, sometimes even sound over sense."[105]

Often Sterry allegorized scriptural texts, and this penchant is related to his mysticism. Richard Kieckhefer has observed that "whatever else mystical piety may be, it is also a mode of reading, a strategy for breaking open the mysteries of the sacred text and finding its allegorical or mystical significance."[106] Sterry allegorized scripture and the pagan classics. This is apparent in his treatment of Canticles, which approaches full-blown allegory. But for Sterry and other Protestant authors who allegorized that biblical book, interpretation of it as allegory was based on their assumption that it was written as an allegory as well as a literal story so that their interpretation accorded with its intended meaning. Other biblical passages were allegorized, or perhaps more precisely, typologized, by Sterry, for example the pot of manna and budding rod of Aaron which were contained in the Ark of the Covenant: the pot of manna he interpreted as the hidden seed of Jesus, running through the wilderness of this creation in the state of fallenness, and the rod of Aaron as Jesus in the state of the glory of the gospel.[107] According to Sterry, scripture is veiled to us until God the Father sends forth the Holy Spirit as a spirit of wisdom.[108] But such a notion of scripture as "veiled" takes a step beyond the Calvinist commonplace that the witness of the Holy Spirit authenticated and interpreted scripture for the believer. The tendency to allegorize also connects Sterry to the radicals who flourished on the edges of Interregnum Puritanism.

Sometimes Sterry himself wrote allegory, especially when dealing with motifs drawn from pre-Christian lore. One of his manuscripts features Apollo as a figure of Christ in his allegorizing of a story drawn from Ovid. Another is a poetic allegory of mystical experience in the form of a dialogue between Amasis the nymph and the Druid Adamas. Sterry's "lovely society" was based on his imaginary reconstruction of a Druid community, partly borrowed as already pointed out, from *Astrea*, by Honore D'Urfe, with himself as "Adamas" and his wife as "Amasis." Some proponents of ancient theology had seen the Druids as bearers of that tradition. In other writings such mythological personages as Orpheus and Semele appeared as allegories of spiritual truths: Orpheus the musician represented an attractive harmony, a theme related to his emphasis on unity, and Semele, who, according to Sterry, "had the chief God for her Lover," was a natural choice for him.[109] Sterry thought that the ancient pagan authors had "Mysteries wrapt up in all their Fables" that "darkly pointed at Jesus Christ."[110] In a letter to his wife, Sterry described and then allegorized a painting, so far unidentified, of a valley with fountains and palm trees, and swans with cupids riding upon them.[111]

Calvinist Mystic

It would appear then, that Peter Sterry, Puritan and Calvinist, was a mystic, sharing much with the Christian mystical tradition as a whole and even with non-Christian mystics. But in what sense was he a Calvinist mystic? Was he an isolated representative of some perennial phenomenon of mysticism set down in a Puritan and Calvinist context, or was his mysticism tied to or a product of his Puritan and Calvinist provenance? It is the present contention that Sterry was not a maverick mystic among the Calvinist Puritans, nor even a mystic who poured such mystical language as it might bear into his Calvinist and Puritan heritage, but a mystic whose mysticism was rooted in his Calvinist theology and piety. Insofar as in no religious tradition is it the case that everyone becomes a mystic, and even though the Puritans tended to democratize spiritual experience, it is clear that some Puritans did exemplify the recurring traits of Christian mystical experience and did so in relation to a tendency within Puritan Calvinism. And there is plenty of evidence to suggest that within the world of Puritan piety certain individuals were thought to be more spiritually adept than others, and accordingly models for others to emulate.[112]

Sterry's Calvinist mysticism can be seen as a focused variant of Puritan spirituality that brought to fruition the mystical potential of many elements in that spirituality, and although it can hardly be claimed that he was the first to do this, he did it with an unusual thoroughness so that it permeated his entire outlook and in such a manner that it transformed his persisting Calvinism. But many mainstream Puritans such as William Ames, Richard Sibbes, John Preston, Francis Rous, Samuel Rutherford, Thomas Goodwin, and even the extremely sober John Owen exhibited a mystical piety in their writings.[113] Rous even spoke of "mysticall Divinity."[114] Puritan radicals, such as the Welsh Vavasor Powell, Walter Cradock, and Morgan Llwyd, were other mystics within the Puritan movement.[115] Isolated individuals such as John Everard and many Quaker leaders were mystics inspired by tendencies within the Puritan impulse, especially the focus on the indwelling of the Holy Spirit in believers, who moved outside of Calvinism altogether.[116] And it was especially in the freer atmosphere of the Interregnum period that these mystical tendencies flourished.

Among the aspects of Sterry's mysticism already examined much was shared with earlier and contemporary Puritan spiritual writers as well as with the broader stream of Christian mysticism. Other aspects, such as Sterry's sense of marriage, family, and community fellowship in the spiritual life, were broadly Protestant. A number of the points central to high Calvinist theology and spirituality, such as the union of the soul with Christ, the new birth, election, substitutionary atonement, and the imputation of Christ's righteousness to elect believers, were treated by Sterry in a way that explored and exploited their implications for mystical piety. It is surprising that these doctrines have been so little examined for their mystical potential: predestination, for example, leaves the soul naked before the dominating God, stripped bare of all its claims;[117] union with Christ introduces a language of union which invites mystical explication; and the substitutionary atonement and imputed righteousness identify the believer with God in Christ, with openings to rich embroidery in mystical piety. Sterry made the most of the mystical potential in these themes of Calvinist theology.

The union of the soul with Christ is for Sterry certainly a mystical union, described, as already seen, through the allegorization of the erotic imagery of the Song of Solomon. Some have argued that the Protestant sense of union with Christ is not to be confused with the language of mystics, who see the soul united to God. But granted Sterry's thoroughly Trinitarian perspective, and his ubiquitous language of espousal to Christ and God, I find this argument unconvincing. Some standard Calvinist theologians, such as William Ames, referred to union with God, as Sterry does occasionally,[118] though union with Christ was the more common expression among Puritan spiritual writers, and that this was a "mystical union" appears in the works of Francis Rous and John Owen.[119] Medieval Christian mystics also spoke of union with Christ. For Sterry, the soul of the believer and Christ are united by the Holy Spirit into one spirit, love driving the unresting soul on to the "possessing of Christ" until the soul is at rest, "inwardly united to him."[120] This union is a foretaste of beatitude, and thus one has returned again to the theme of heavenly mindedness: "A believer is ever in Heaven, and hath heaven in Himself"; we "carry a heaven with all its Inhabitants about with us now," he says in a letter to his daughter.[121]

Puritan spiritual writers wrote much on the new birth and its necessity for salvation, but it had a special mystical implication for Sterry. He described the new birth as that point when the "seed of God" is sown in the soul, and the soul "is new-born into the Divine Nature."[122] With its echoes of God in the soul and the soul's divinization, his language about the new birth is rich in mystical implication.

One can hardly exaggerate the importance of the atonement for Sterry, as he returned to it again and again as the climax in the divine design for redemption. The atonement effects the restoration of an original unity, since it reconciles all things on earth and in heaven (Sterry maintained that Christ died for all, but, in his universalism, effectively so; he is no Arminian, basing election on foreseen faith). In Sterry's high Calvinist version of the atonement, Christ is made sin and a curse for the sake of the redeemed, and his sufferings are maximized as he enters into the dark night of the soul for the redeemed: "He is devoted by the most solemn, most sacred Curses, to bear the weight of all Guilt, to satisfie the Divine Justice, to sustain the Divine Wrath to the utmost." Sterry adds that in Christ on the cross God "in his own Person" is "divided from himself by the force and fury of an unexpected wrath," suffering the torments of eternity, experiencing "Desertion on the Cross" in which Christ becomes "the abominable, execrable, detestable thing in the Eyes of God." Thus on the cross is Christ's heart "broken." Sterry's language at this point is extreme: God himself felt in his own person in our nature the "height of suffering," suggesting a suffering God. But through this, death is swallowed up, the "shadowy Image" dissolved, and all contrariety overcome, and variety returns to unity, as reconciliation is effected and harmony restored. This Sterry called "the Spiritual Sense" of Christ's sufferings and death, in which Christ stands as "the only and the universal Sinner, yet without Sin." Thus even in its sinfulness Christ is united to humankind, and Sterry spoke much of the imputation of the righteousness of Christ, the sinless sinner, to the elect. Sterry enjoined the believer to "See yourselfe ever in this glasse of the Saviour's Glorified Person." For by "the eye of faith" believers can see themselves "already perfect in the Father and in Christ above, as also the Father and Christ living in us." Thus do atonement and imputation receive a mystical twist in Sterry's theology.[123] Both the atonement as the abandonment of Christ in his crucifixion to divine wrath and a strict view of the believer's righteousness as being only the imputed righteousness of Christ are commonplaces that can be found in such high Calvinist theologians as John Owen or Thomas Goodwin. Often the refutations of Socinianism in the later seventeenth century focused on the atonement more than the Trinity, insofar as Socinians denied all suggestion of the death of Christ as satisfaction of divine wrath or a substitution of Christ for the believer. This is the case with much that John Owen wrote against the Socinians. Sterry's treatment of the Socinians, like his many recurrences to the Trinity, set him, like other strict Calvinists, at a great distance from them.

Sterry also gave mystical purport to the doctrine of predestination. For him predestination is entirely an act of God's love, and thus of his essential nature. Persons are elected because Christ "falleth in love" with them. Since God's will is God's love (in making this point Aquinas is cited) and the human will renovated by the grace of God's electing love is united to God as the good it loves, the elect are inevitably drawn to God by a kind of voluntary necessity, liberty and necessity becoming one (the only real liberty being the liberty of harmony), although in a few places Sterry speaks of God's gracious love as entirely "without the conjunction of Free-Will" in humans. The election of a soul is thus a ravishing of that soul: "The free will, of which wee speake in Man, is plainely contradictory to ye freedome of ye Eternal Wisedome, & Will in ye Divine Nature: consequentially, to ye Whole Beauty, & Sweetnes of ye Evangelicall Mystery. Where are ye Ravishing pleasures of an Undeserved, Unexpected, Irresistible Love, if this Love bee subject to ye Indifferent Receptions, or Refusalls of my Will?" One is thus not surprised that Sterry finds Canticles relevant to his exposition of election. Furthermore, Sterry proceeded to a complete determinism of love: since harmony is ultimately the truth of all things, when we understand "the whole nature of things, from the greatest to the least parts and motions of it to be determined," we understand that this is "the work of Divine Love" as "the highest Unity, containing all Variety Originally in it self, sending it forth from it self, and diffusing it self through all."[124]

Unfolding from electing love is the "golden chaine" (a metaphor made commonplace by William Perkins) of the order of salvation, each link of which is a stage in the uniting of the soul to God in Christ. This order is a descending ladder of gracious love by which the soul ascends back to its source. Thus justification "actuates" election and espouses the soul to Christ; adoption is the "forming of Christ in the Soul" and the discovery of eternity in it; sanctification is "as the estate, which Woman hath by marriage" and is an anointing with oil, in which the anointing God and the anointed saint are made one; glorification is that eternal life which is "the whole Work of God upon the Souls of the Elect from the beginning to the End; the Divine Life begun in Grace on Earth, completed in Glory in heaven."[125] The whole order of salvation results from God's "Preventing Love" (love that comes before) which is a "Golden Chain" drawing humankind to God; thus "the whole of our Redemption, salvation, glorification in the entire circle of it from the beginning to the end, is the work of God for us, and in us," beginning in "Eternity from the heart of the Father," going forth through "the heart of Christ," and coming down into human hearts, carrying those hearts once again through Christ and back into eternity. God the Father thus "contrives and establishes the whole way of Beauty & blessedness from the beginning to the End as the most perfect designe of the most perfect Love," while God the Son "becomes our Loveliness, which offers itself up for us, which presents itself in our stead."[126]

Behind this work of God in believers is very clearly God's loving and irresistible grace, the grace of God "being the fountain of Love." Indeed, "Grace is the name of Love in its Freedom, Sweetness, and Fullness," another indication that for Sterry love is the prime attribute of God.

It is interesting to note that with regard to the theology of grace, Sterry, like Theophilus Gale, whom it is possible he had read on this matter, had discovered allies in the Roman Catholic Jansenists in France. In one of his unpublished manuscripts there appeared several pages of notes dealing with Jansenism with the comment that the "Truth of Jansenisme is efficacious Grace. They are great abasers of corrupt nature."[127] Sterry's interest in this shows clearly that he does not regard himself as moving away at all from the Calvinist commitment to efficacious grace, but welcomed, just as the high Calvinist Gale did, the discovery that Catholic Jansenism supported the Reformed view of grace.

Like other Puritan spiritual writers Sterry never tired of extolling grace: it is grace that causes saints and angels to cry out "Grace! Grace! Free-Grace!" in a "Rapture of Holy Joy and Wonder." Evelyn Underhill wrote that it was in "the joy of illumination" that are found "the most lyrical passages of mystical literature." And certainly an ecstatic tone and extravagant expressions of joy are frequent in Sterry's writings (though he could also warn that "false Raptures of Spirit are a sweet Poyson") as they are in many other Puritan spiritual writers; in an unpublished dissertation, Jean Dorothy Williams has described expressions of inexpressible joy in Puritan spiritual experience as their language for mystical ecstasy and rapture. And, contrary to the Calvinist stereotype, Sterry advised the Christian to "Bee Cheerful. Joy is oile to the wheele of all our Facultys; God and Men delight in a pleasant Countenance, and a glad heart."[128] Sterry exhorted the believer to "Make God thy Delight."[129] Ecstatic and rapturous language about delight in God joins Sterry to Joseph Alleine, as will be seen in a later chapter.

Parenthetically, it might be observed that Sterry's ecstatic and rapturous mystical language, like that of many other Puritan and dissenting authors and preachers, struck conformist opponents as "enthusiastic" and morally dangerous (the specter of Antinomianism), and a fitting object for ridicule. There were of course powerful political reasons for this, both before and after the Restoration, since the Cromwellian regime to which Sterry had close ties was attacked for its putative threats to social stability.[130] It is clearly the case that the most egregious instances of ecstatic and mystical piety in the second half of the seventeenth century in England were Puritan in provenance, not "Anglican," in spite of the supposedly more Catholic and mystical sensibility of the latter.

Sterry also speculated on the state of glorification, or final beatitude itself. In the fulfillment of the mystical quest in beatitude he thought that the redeemed "shall be capable of an immediate Sight, and Enjoyment of God, without any Vail, or Garment, without any Representation, or Distance; as he is in His own naked and simple essence, in his own proper and immutable

Form." This echoes an argument made by some of the medieval theologians.[131] But even in beatitude there would be growth: Sterry knew the writings of Gregory of Nyssa and hinted at something like that Greek church father's notion of a continuing spiritual growth beyond this life.[132]

But Sterry, in tune with most Christian mysticism, and certainly with the demands of his Calvinism, is careful, in spite of what might be inferred from much of his ecstatic language, to state that there is no such absorption of the human soul into the divine as would destroy the distinction of creature and creator. In *The Freedom of the Will*, Sterry argued that the soul is not one with God "formally," or "essentially," but "transcendentally," united to God by God's "infiniteness" and by God's transcending of God's own unity. Elsewhere in discussing this union he wrote that one must "Preserve carefully the distinction between God, and the Creature."[133] Sterry thought that the soul united to God and yet remaining partially what it was by its own nature was analogous to the humanity of Christ in relation to the divinity—real union but with real distinction, a union in which the humanity of Christ is never swallowed up by the divine nature.[134] Sterry condemned the Ranters for claiming the pantheist principle that "All is God."[135]

Sterry and Boehme

One matter that might call in question the description of Peter Sterry as a Calvinist is his interest in and use of the writings of Jacob Boehme. The writings of Boehme, an eccentric but enormously influential German Lutheran mystic whose orthodoxy was suspect and who died in 1624, had been translated into English between 1647 and 1661.[136] Sterry owned some of Boehme's books, including his *Aurora*,[137] spoke of having "much perused" them, and liked them so well that he asserted that the "Lord Jesus hath ministered, as much Heavenly Pleasure, & Profite to mee by reading of him, as of any Discourses, besides those of the Holy Scriptures." He found in Boehme "rich Depths" and "sweet Heights."[138] Sterry echoed Boehme in some of his language. He also used female imagery for God, as did Boehme, and even imagined Adam as originally androgynous, an important point in the thought of Boehme. The original Adam, Sterry says, was like the angels, sexless, although, insofar as "Every one is both Male and Female in himself," before God took Eve from his rib Adam was also both male and female, as Christ is "both Bridegroom and Bride." (Baxter criticized "Behmenism" for holding this notion of prelapsarian androgyny.) It has been claimed that Sterry's use of the image of the "Lily-seed" as a symbol for grace and perfection is derived from Boehme. Sterry also echoes

Boehme in his discussion of both wrath and love as being contrarieties within the Godhead, and his language about God's left hand and the law as a manifestation of it echoed Luther, upon whom Boehme drew for some of his ideas and imagery. Sterry also spoke of the "left hand" of Christ as his incarnation, humiliation, and suffering, also a "strange" work of God.[139]

Many fairly radical English religious writers showed interest in Boehme, including Sterry's friend Morgan Llwyd, who may well have introduced Sterry to the writings of the German mystic.[140] If one cannot speak exactly of a Behmenist sect in England, one can certainly catalogue his English disciples and some of what they borrowed from him.[141] A French scholar goes so far as to describe Sterry as one of these disciples; N. I. Matar gives a more nuanced analysis of their relationship.[142]

Nonetheless, in spite of these traces of significant influence, Sterry could be highly critical of Boehme (to whom he always refers as "Beaumont") and expressed differences with him precisely at those points where a Calvinist might be expected to do so. Writing to Morgan Llwyd in January 1652, Sterry balanced his praise of Boehme with some guarded and even dismissive comments: he thinks that there was "much Darkness mingled with his Light" and that any who read him should come to that reading already "well instructed in the Mystery of Christ, with a Heavenly Newness of Mind, by which they may bee able to try what the Good, Acceptable Word of God is." Those who do not come to the reading of Boehme with this kind of preparation "will be perverted by him." Indeed, Sterry disclosed that when he first read Boehme he "beleeved & saide, that which I have seen since prove true by manifold experience, that many by reading of him, have bin led aside from the Mystery of the Gospell, having lost themselves some in one maze of Darkenes, some in another. . . ." Furthermore, Sterry wondered whether it was indeed "our Lord Jesus" who appeared to "Beaumont" in his visions or rather "some Angell for the Ruler of the Darkenes of this Creation, cloathing himselfe with the Light," who did so, and "directed his Pen."[143] With such advice about comparing Boehme with the biblical message and trying the spirits where Boehme was concerned as well as with such advice about the danger of studying him, one can scarcely describe Sterry as a disciple of Boehme. These are rather the words of someone open enough to learn from the German mystic but with strong reservations about him.

When Sterry writes more specifically about these reservations they are of the sort one might expect from a Calvinist. Not only did Sterry think Boehme wrote confusedly of the Trinity, but he also thought that he exalted "free-Will after the manner of the Arminians." Sterry further remarked that Boehme involved himself too much with chemistry, that is, alchemy, a characteristic interest of occultist and spiritualist writers. More surprising is Sterry's remark that Boehme relied too much on "Heathenish Philosophy," insofar as Sterry's own considerable indebtedness to it has already been seen. It is also the case that Sterry occasionally uses images drawn from alchemy.[144]

Peter Sterry's willingness to draw on Boehme, then, does not compromise his Calvinism, though, like other Puritans who flourished in the 1640s and 1650s, he was attracted to various spiritualist, esoteric, and eschatological motifs and materials. Sterry seems to have had a remarkable capacity to synthesize disparate ideas that appealed to his own very idiosyncratic vision and yet ultimately render them compatible with the commitments of an anti-Arminian Calvinist. Nonetheless, Sterry's disciples persisted in these esoteric elements and borrowings in Sterry, and as W. R. Ward has pointed out, a generation of early evangelicals including some continental Reformed pietists were drawn to Boehme, Christian Cabala, and Platonic and vitalist philosophies, paralleling some of Sterry's preoccupations.[145]

Some of the same aspects of Sterry's thought that have been understood as excessive capitulation to the ideas of Boehme raise the suspicion that his ideas and language have Gnostic implications. But if so, it was a Christian Gnosticism like that of the great Alexandrian theologians Clement and Origen, for Sterry's dualism is always provisional, never ultimate, and while the created world is seen as a shadowy emblem of God, it is not in enmity with God. Most importantly in this respect, however, Sterry made clear that it is not body that is opposed to spirit, but "flesh," for the body is "an essential substantial Image, in which proper spirits dwell," and it is the "organ of the soul," upon which the soul plays "like a lute of many strings," while the flesh bears the implication, not of body but of that aspect of the human that is at war with the spiritual and divine, a mainstream Calvinist understanding of the matter.[146] Contrary to Gnostic dismissal of the body, Sterry emphasizes the embodiment and incarnation of the spiritual.

Sterry's Eschatology

The Peter Sterry who preached to the Parliament during the Interregnum spoke with eschatological fervor, declaring that God was shaking the nations and that the millennium was at hand.[147] How can this eschatological excitement of the earlier Sterry be reconciled with the near quietism of Sterry's later, somewhat withdrawn mysticism after the defeat of the Cromwellian regime on which he had pinned his hopes? For while many of the religious radicals of the Interregnum kept alive their revolutionary fervor and some of them engaged in revolutionary activity, as documented especially by Richard Greaves,[148] Sterry seems to have played no role of this kind. N. I. Matar has argued that Sterry was a classic case of how defeat transmutes eschatological fervor into an inward looking mysticism, a pattern that has been found repeatedly by historians, for example, in interpreting ancient Gnosticism or, in Renaissance Italy, with Savonarola. Matar argues, however, that in Sterry's case this was a strategy: one would confront the persecuting state not by the "language and zeal of the 1650s" but by turning inward to "the paradise within" in order to endure the new state of things. But, according to Matar, Sterry did not abandon his hopes for a millennium; but perhaps prayer, not agitation, would bring it about.[149] Elsewhere Matar goes a bit farther, suggesting that for Sterry after 1660 the millennium would not come as an external kingdom, but in the union of God with the souls of the redeemed: "Eschatology was subsumed by mysticism."[150] Clearly, Sterry has turned external hopes into a realized eschatology of inner spirituality and wrote about "The Kingdom of God in the Soul of Man" as inward growth and communion.[151]

Matar's point is helpful, but it might also be emphasized that there was much about Sterry's earlier ideas that persisted in his later thought. In a preface of 1653, written to recommend an eschatological work of another author, Sterry noted on the one hand the great "seasonableness" of the present time for discussion of the millennium while on the other hand he thought that there were many disagreements on the matter, and that it could be expected that not all would agree with the book he was introducing, since the interpretation of prophecy was a complicated matter.[152] Apparently, Sterry had some tentativeness about prophetic interpretation and was willing to encourage various perspectives but also retained great interest in such matters.

While Sterry had become more tentative about eschatology, the language and images by which he had expressed his eschatological views in the 1640s were strikingly similar to his later mystical language. In the earlier sermons, he spoke of the "mystical" and "allegorical" interpretation of scripture, referred to the Song of Solomon, and proclaimed the second coming of Christ as a wrapping up of all things in the unity of the cosmic Christ. There were even hints of universalism in these earlier sermons.[153] Thus his earlier eschatological fervor seemed to minister to his later full-blown mysticism.

At the beginning of this chapter, Baxter's negative assessment of Sterry was cited, with the implication that Baxter changed his mind, and later in the chapter Baxter's opinion of Sterry's style as opaque and confusing has been noted; at this point, since Baxter figured so largely as a spokesman and broker of dissenting concerns, it is appropriate to consider the later analysis of Sterry that Baxter provided. That revised assessment came in Baxter's book *Catholick Theologie: Plaine, Pure and Peaceable, for the Pacification of Dogmatical*

Word-Warriours, published in 1675, the same year as Sterry's *Discourse of the Freedom of the Will*, which Baxter read prior to finishing his *Catholick Theologie*, placing his comments about Sterry at the end of the second part of that work. It is difficult to date Baxter's earlier critical remark about Sterry, but the notes he made which became the basis for Edward Sylvester's publication of Baxter's autobiographical reminiscences date back at least to 1664,[154] and since the earlier comment was among Baxter's negative opinions about the excesses of Interregnum radicals, it was probably penned at the beginning of his jotting down of his narrative, and thus long before 1675. In any case, in *Catholick Theologie*, Baxter noted that Sterry was reputed a preacher "that few or none could understand," although admitting he never heard Sterry preach. Baxter added that having perused Sterry's book on the freedom of the will he found him to be of the same mind on many subjects as Sir Henry Vane (of whom Baxter disapproved as an extremist), but that Sterry handled these matters with much more ability than Vane. Moreover, Baxter declared himself favorably impressed by Sterry's "raptures of high devotion" and openness toward those of other opinions. Above all, by this time he concluded that Sterry was a person admirable in many respects:

> Doubtless his head was strong, his wit admirably pregnant, his
> searching studies hard and sublime, and I think his heart replen-
> ishcd with holy Love to God, and great charity, moderation, and
> peaceableness towards men: In so much that I heartily repent that
> I so far believed fame as to think somewhat hardlier or less charitably
> of him and his few adherents than I now hope they did deserve.
> Hasty judging, and believing fame is a cause of unspeakable hurt to
> the world, and injury to our brethren. But I found it no wonder that
> he was understood by few, For his sublime and philosophical
> notions, met not with many Auditors, so well studied in those things
> as to be capable of understanding them. It is a great inconvenience to
> men of extraordinary discoveries and sublimity, that they must speak
> to very few.

But this revised assessment was accompanied with some sharp strictures on Sterry's theology, which Baxter thought was far too deterministic, comparing it not only to several high Calvinist predestinarians, William Twisse and Samuel Rutherford, but also to Hobbes and Spinoza, two figures anathema not only to Puritans but also to the generality of late seventeenth-century Christians. But fault is found not only with Sterry's determinism but also with his seeming identification of philosophy and Christian revelation, his description of Christ as "an universal Intelligence or soul of the world" (read Sterry's cosmic

Christology), his treatment of "sin, death and hell" as but "Winter and Summer, Night and Day" to holiness and life, and his universalism. Baxter did not miss the parallel between Sterry and Origen on this last matter. Thus Baxter admired Sterry the tolerant and devout lover of God, but remained highly critical of his theological outlook.[155]

That seminal figure among the Cambridge Platonists, Benjamin Whichcote, however, approved of Sterry from first to last in his acquaintance with him. He was reported to have said after one of Sterry's academic performances when Sterry was his pupil at Cambridge that Sterry was "all pure intellect"; after Sterry's death, Whichcote was reported to remark that he would part with half his wealth to have a few hours conversation "with his enlightened friend."[156]

Granted the ambivalence of such a leading Dissenter as Baxter and the adulation of the leading Platonist Whichcote, and granted as well the circle of disciples gathered around him at West Sheen, Sterry was clearly not a standard-issue Calvinist Dissenter of the Restoration era. Rather, he was someone in whose thought there persisted central Calvinist emphases and doctrines which were reshaped and transformed by having their mystical implications pushed to the limit but not beyond it, as his recognition yet critique of Boehme makes clear. Although the trajectory of his thinking was rooted in the eschatological issues of the Interregnum, in its aftermath he worked out a mystical theology by pushing to the fore an inward focus already present even in his eschatological preachments, a focus which became a quietist mysticism after the Restoration. He at least passingly recognized the threats of atheism and Socinianism in a changed era, and found in the mystical cast of his mind the antidote: the reality of God was self-evident to his mystical experiences and ecstasies, and Trinity in unity clearly indicated by his mystical musings. As for the challenge of reason, Sterry, like other Platonists, met it by reaffirming an older intuitive, spiritual, and mystical understanding of that faculty, criticizing the Socinians for pushing a sterile and limiting concept of reason. The language he employed in discussing the soul's union with God, his mystical reflections on the primacy of Divine love and on the capacity for the divine in the human soul that led him to universalize election, and his interest in esoteric texts and motifs add up to a significant transforming of his Calvinist heritage and a distinct variety of Calvinistic and Puritan piety. In a mystical version of Calvinism it also represents a variety which much of the commentary on Calvinism is surprised to find there at all.

Calvinistic Puritanism was characterized by a particular kind of piety, and this piety had many aspects congenial to mysticism and a rich potential for it that increasingly came to be realized in the seventeenth century, not least in the life and writings of Peter Sterry. Of course Puritan and Protestant mysticism also had affinity and continuity with earlier forms of Christian mysticism, and Peter Sterry is illustrative of that as well. But Sterry was not a mystic in spite of his Puritan commitments and Calvinist theology, nor even someone mystical by inclination, who, coming of age in Puritan and Calvinist England, pushed his Puritanism and Calvinism in as mystical a direction as they could go, but was a mystic also because, like others before him, he drew out the mystical potential of Calvinist theology and Puritan spirituality. There was a strong mystical strain in the Cambridge Platonists generally, but Sterry's Calvinism brought a tone of ecstasy and a depth of awe and mystery that was rooted in that Calvinism's emphasis on the overwhelming surprise of divine grace and love towards sinful humanity. Yet in comparison with most other dissenting Calvinist spiritual writers there is enough distinctive about his mystical approach to it to set him apart as developing and presenting a distinct variation of Calvinist thought. For all his dependence on an earlier Calvinist tradition of mysticism his writings constituted a reformulation of Calvinism as a mystical theology. Thus Sterry in his idiosyncratic way of thinking and feeling added to and even transformed a variety of Calvinist thought in the later seventeenth century at the same time that he represented the persistence of older strands of Puritan piety and devotional expression.

3

Theophilus Gale

Calvinism and the Ancient Theology

In George Eliot's novel *Middlemarch,* the young and inexperienced Dorothea is astounded by the learning of Edward Casaubon, who explains to her that he is preparing a magnum opus that would show all the mythical systems and fragments "in the world were corruptions of a tradition originally revealed."[1] This nineteenth-century echo of seventeenth-century learning, intended to suggest erudite futility, fails to take the measure of the importance that the scholarly enterprise so described had for the savants of the seventeenth century, when Theophilus Gale set out to prove exactly that point and did so through his employment of a longstanding Christian apologetic strategy that conjured up a tradition of ancient texts and theologians, including the so-called Hermetic literature.

In the preceding chapter, it appeared that Peter Sterry found nourishment for his Calvinist mysticism in Platonism and some esoteric motifs drawn from a supposed "Ancient Theology"; that which helped nourish Sterry's outlook was the prime concern of the investigations of the massively learned Calvinist scholar Theophilus Gale. It is the intent of this chapter to place Gale in the context of the Renaissance tradition of a primal truth known to ancient theologians and show how he emphasized those aspects of this tradition that were compatible with his strict Calvinism to shape a Calvinist version of the ancient theology. This chapter is not an exposition of Gale's theological corpus in its entirety, nor primarily an effort to portray his exact role in the ongoing development of a Renaissance intellectual preoccupation, but an examination of his treatment of the ancient theology in relation to his Calvinist commitments. It is also, as with Sterry's mysticism, an examination of a tradition of Christian thought usually considered to be alien to the interests of Puritan Calvinists. And as with Sterry's Calvinist mysticism, this chapter finds that Gale's Calvinist version of the ancient theology not only represents a distinct variety of Calvinist expression but also entails a persistence of Calvinism and involves some transformation of it.

It has been typically assumed that Calvinism and Puritanism were inhospitable to the currents of Hermetism and ancient theology that were important elements in Renaissance thought. Especially after the Restoration of 1660, when many Puritans retreated to the confines of small and often clandestine congregations, dissenting Puritan Calvinists would seem unlikely to welcome such an expansive intellectual interest. In his classic study *The Ancient Theology*, D. P. Walker commented that Calvinists avoided this lore because of its magical implications and that it was "most unusual" for "an orthodox Calvinist" to accept it, although he noted the Huguenots Petrus Ramus and Phillipe de Mornay as exceptions. Similarly, Wayne Shumaker maintained that the influence of English Puritanism suppressed the impulse to find extra-biblical loci of truth so that "Hermetism" in England was restricted to "abnormally eccentric Englishmen like Robert Fludd and Thomas Vaughan." Frances Yates, on the other hand, spoke of John Milton as a Puritan "occultist" and referred to "Puritan Christian Cabalists," but her references are vague and relate to literary figures such as Edmund Spenser or Milton who had Puritan connections, not to leaders of the Puritan movement.[2]

The Ancient Theology

Greater precision in terminology for the description of these Renaissance currents is helpful. A useful distinction has been made between Hermeticism/Hermeticist on the one hand and Hermetism/Hermetic on the other, with the former pair of terms referring to Renaissance (and earlier and later) occultism generally while the latter pair have a more restricted reference to the texts, themes, and characteristics of the Hermetic literature of late antiquity. Both pairs, but especially the latter, are related to the so-called ancient theology or *prisca theologia*, described by D. P. Walker as a syncretistic Christian apologetic tradition going back to the church fathers which regarded Hermes Trismegistus, Orpheus, Pythagoras, and others as "ancient theologians" who possessed elements of true religion. These elements were particularly found in an extensive body of "Hermetic" texts, reputedly by Hermes Trismegistus, supposedly thought to be a near contemporary of Moses. This ancient theology was believed to be available to Plato, and to have been the basis of his philosophy and of the ongoing Platonic tradition. Moreover, these aspects of true religion, which foreshadowed such Christian truths as the Trinity, the immortality of the soul, and creation ex nihilo, were in turn usually described as deriving from Moses, or even much earlier biblical figures, including Noah, Enoch, or Adam.[3] Hermetism, referring specifically to the Hermetic texts, is thus a subtype and particularization of ancient theology. Ancient theology, insofar as it had been passed on as an at least semisecret tradition, might be considered part of the esoteric lore of Hermeticism; however, Hermeticism encompassed much else not necessarily related to ancient theology such as astrology, natural magic, and alchemy. Frances Yates has stressed yet other related intellectual impulses such as Christian Cabala (I have followed her spelling) and Rosicrucianism.[4] Christian Cabala bears on ancient theology because of its assumption that the truths of ancient theology were hidden in the secret meanings of the letters and words of the Hebrew Bible (this secrecy also makes it Hermeticist and occult), while Rosicrucianism was an early seventeenth-century movement that built on ancient theology but also included such Hermeticist elements as alchemy. Hermetism and Hermeticism both inclined toward mysticism, which was also present in Cabalism and Rosicrucianism, and aspects of this thinking have already been seen in Peter Sterry. Christian Euhemerism also belongs in this same context: it could be a secret Hermeticist lore about the true meaning of the pagan gods and heroes but also an apologetic strategy to retain the ancient gods for Christian purposes by treating them as human exemplars of ancient wisdom falsely exalted to divinity. Euhemerism was also important as a way to historicize ancient myth, and so reconcile myth and history.[5]

The notion of an ancient theology had a widespread and longstanding heritage. It went back to Hellenistic Jewish writers such as Josephus and Philo, who had claimed that the Greeks had taken their philosophical wisdom from the Jews, and to Patristic authors who put this idea to the uses of Christian apologetics, proving both that pagans were indebted to biblical traditions and that the pagan literature itself adumbrated Christian themes and even prophesied Christ's coming. St. Augustine thought Plato had learned from the Mosaic traditions and that Hermes, whom he considered later than Moses, had possibly gained his prophetic power through demons. Lactantius placed Hermes with the Sibyls as a prophet of the coming of Christ. Consonant with the tradition of ancient theology, medieval authors used allegory to justify the study of pagan mythology; the myths had meanings, hidden from the pagans, which spoke of Christian things. It was at Marsiglio Ficino's Platonic Academy in fifteenth-century Florence that the full *prisca theologia* flowered, with the Hermetic and

Orphic texts studied alongside those of Plato and the later Neoplatonists as a unified corpus in harmony with Christianity. Thus the mystical and magical elements of these texts became part of this synthesis of Christianity and Neoplatonism. Giovanni Pico della Mirandola added oriental lore including that of the "Chaldeans" and Zoroaster, the latter well known to the medieval world as a magician, to the ancient theology and also blended it with the mysticism and magic of Jewish Cabala.[6] The Italian Augustinian Agostino Steuco in his *De Perreni Philosophia* of 1540 seems to have been the first to designate this tradition as a "perennial philosophy."[7]

These motifs resonated in the northern Renaissance as well. The German humanist Johannes Reuchlin thought Adam had been the first cabalist and that Pythagoras had learned his wisdom from the Cabala. Jacques Lefevre, in a burst of French nationalism, added the Druids of Gaul to the ancient theologians; but he rejected the magical elements. These magical elements caused alarm in the case of Cornelius Agrippa, who was interested in Hermeticist magic; he was possibly the prototype for Marlowe's Dr. Faustus. The Swiss physician and alchemist Phillipus Paracelsus was a similar figure; he thought that Adam had invented the arts of astronomy, magic, Cabala, and alchemy, and that their secrets had been engraved in hieroglyphs; these secrets were rediscovered by Noah on Mt. Ararat, carried to Egypt by Abraham, and learned by Moses from the Egyptians.[8] A circle of Calvinist thinkers associated with the encyclopedist Johann Heinrich Alsted at the Herborn Academy in Rhineland Nassau in the early seventeenth century sought to harmonize Reformed theology with ancient theology, including cabalism, astrology, alchemy, natural magic and some of the ideas of Paracelsus in their mixture of full-fledged Hermeticism, although Alsted backed away from his earlier enthusiasm for such an amalgam after the Synod of Dort. But his interest in these matters later revived.[9]

The ancient theology apparently had considerable appeal for French Protestants. Phillipe de Mornay was a Huguenot statesman and lay theologian who developed a very detailed though nonmagical version of the ancient theology, integrating into it a great deal of Euhemerist interpretation of the ancient gods, and stressing the confirmation of Christian truths such as the Trinity from pagan sources, including the Hermetic literature. Joseph Scaliger, reputed one of the most learned persons of his time, is another indication of the appeal of this tradition to French Protestants. But another Huguenot scholar, Isaac Casaubon, who admired the Church of England and spent the last four years of his life in England as a prebendary of Canterbury Cathedral, in a work patronized by King James I and published just before Casaubon's death in 1614, disproved the antiquity of the Hermetic texts in a polemical work directed against the Roman Catholic church historian Cesare Baronius; Baronius had referred to Hermes Trismegistus as an ancient sage who predicted the coming of Christ. Casaubon, in an effort to establish the great distance between ancient paganism and Christian revelation, argued that the Hermetic literature was much later than supposed and interpolated with Christian elements. Casaubon was one of the greatest textual critics of his day; his view gradually came to be accepted and laid to rest the supposed antiquity of this literature.[10]

The synthesis of Hebrew and Gentile wisdom was not the only motive behind ancient theology; it was also an attempt to form a more universal and tolerant approach to religion. This was an aspect of Ficino's Platonic Christianity. Giordano Bruno went further in his effort to validate the wisdom of ancient Gentiles when he maintained that Hermes preceded Moses—the harmony of the biblical and the pagan represented a borrowing in the other direction, with Judaism and Christianity corrupting an original pure truth. Tommaso Campanella, another enthusiast for a universal religion of humankind, believed that the ancient Gentile theologians had received other revelations of truth in addition to the biblical.[11] Both Bruno and Campanella ran afoul of the inquisition in Italy. Alsted's circle was interested in Bruno and Campanella. It was apparently this universalistic implication of the ancient theology that both attracted and worried Alsted.

Frances Yates in her later work introduced Rosicrucianism as a seventeenth-century Protestant and mystical universalism built on Hermetic and magical elements with the addition of a mystical alchemy; she related it to the heterodox German Lutheran mystic Jacob Boehme in whom Sterry was interested, and the utopianism of another German Lutheran, Johann Andrae. She even connected, somewhat fancifully, Francis Bacon to these currents, though there are elements in his *New Atlantis* which suggest it.[12] Later, various esoteric and occult thinkers and movements, including freemasonry and the poets William Blake and William Butler Yeats, have drawn upon this variant of the ancient wisdom.[13]

The Restoration Dissenter Theophilus Gale, educated at Oxford by high Calvinists, and a card-carrying member of the Puritan brotherhood of spiritual writers, in his magnum opus *The Court of the Gentiles*, promoted a version of the ancient theology (including some Hermetism, but no occult Hermeticism or magic), which drew on the patristic, medieval, and Renaissance roots of this tradition and was consonant with the learning of his day, especially that of the historical-philological scholarship of international Protestantism but also of the wider republic of letters. Gale was a teacher who loved this ancient lore and also shared the late Renaissance urge for the schematization of all knowledge, which the ancient theology provided; on the other hand, he turned the ancient theology to a theological purpose of his own, a doctrine of revelation that was a Calvinist vindication of *sola gratia* which was of a piece with the anti-Arminian tenor of his theological career. In doing so, he brought attention to an important but underemphasized implication of the mainstream of ancient theology, its derivation of truth from Hebrew tradition. In accomplishing all of this, Gale illustrated the persistence of high Calvinism in Restoration England, the diversity of Calvinist expression in that age, and the continuing defense of Calvinism against the challenges of Arminianism, Socinianism, atheism, and scoffing irreligion. With his Platonism, like Sterry, he confronted the new meanings of reason with a more old-fashioned Neoplatonic meaning for it.

Gale's Career and Writings

Theophilus Gale was born in 1628 in Kingsteignton, Devon, where his father was vicar and a prebendary of Exeter Cathedral. In 1647 he entered Magdalen Hall, Oxford, and in 1648 he was by the parliamentary visitors appointed a demy (one receiving half the emolument of a fellow) and in 1650 a fellow at Magdalen College, Oxford. He received the B.A. in 1649 and the M.A. in 1652. In 1652 Gale also became Logic Lecturer. In Cromwellian Oxford he came under the influence of the high Calvinist Congregationalists or Independents Thomas Goodwin and John Owen: Goodwin had been president of Magdalen since 1650 and was closely associated with Owen, the vice-chancellor of the university. Gale preached frequently in the university. In late 1657 he accepted an invitation to serve as preacher at Winchester Cathedral, still retaining his Oxford fellowship.[14]

At the Restoration in 1660, Gale was ejected from his positions at both Winchester and Oxford, which reverted to their former incumbents. In 1662 he became a tutor for the family of a nobleman of Puritan sympathies, Philip, fourth baron Wharton. Few members of the nobility had been as committed to the parliamentary cause as Lord Wharton, though he had objected to the King's execution. He sat in the Westminster Assembly, and later led the Presbyterians in the Cavalier Parliament in opposing the Clarendon Code. He was an important patron and protector of dissenting clergy after the Restoration. In September 1662 Gale accompanied Lord Wharton's two sons to the Protestant academy in Caen, Normandy, and remained on the continent for two years, making the acquaintance of French Protestant scholars, especially Samuel Bochart. While there, he took a lively interest in the Jansenist controversy, about which he later wrote for an English Protestant audience. However, Gale's strictness as a tutor caused problems, and he was dismissed in 1664, with some suddenness if we are to credit his complaints. Before returning to England and Lord Wharton's estate in Buckinghamshire, he traveled for some months on the continent.[15]

Gale was back in England in 1666, just in time to see the flames of the fire of London, in which he feared many of the notes he had gathered for his magnum opus on antiquity ("the fruit of twenty years hard labour") were destroyed, since they had been left in a desk of a London friend. The friend's house had indeed burned, but the desk had been salvaged with other moveable goods. Edmund Calamy commented that had it not been for this stroke of good fortune *The Court of the Gentiles* would never have been published. Gale next settled near London at Newington Green and ran an academy for the education of the children of Dissenters. He also assisted his cousin John Rowe as pastor to an illegal Congregational meeting in the parish of St. Andrew's, Holborn; after Rowe's death in 1677, Gale succeeded him as pastor, assisted by Samuel Lee, another enormously learned Dissenter who wrote a major treatise on Solomon's Temple, and who later removed to New England.[16]

In 1669 Gale received permission from the vice-chancellor of Oxford, Dr. John Fell of nursery rhyme fame, to have the first part of *The Court of the Gentiles* printed at Oxford. This work was eventually completed in four parts in five volumes, but a lexicon of the Greek New Testament, reputedly on a scale greater than any other in publication, was left unfinished (he had gotten through iota) at his rather sudden death early in 1679. By his will Gale bequeathed his library, "except for the philosophical part of it," to Harvard College, including almost one thousand volumes of Hebraica—Bibles, Talmuds, and Rabbinic commentaries, which long constituted over half of the college library. The rest of his estate was left "for the Education and Benefit of poor Young Scholars, to be manag'd by his Nonconforming Brethren for their Use." Gale's former pupil Thomas Rowe, son of his cousin and former pastoral associate, was his successor at the Newington Green Academy and was one of the first in England to accept and teach the Cartesian philosophy. Gale was buried in Bunhill fields, the dissenting burying-ground in London.[17] His published writings came out in a flurry in the last decade of his life.

Gale's membership in the Puritan brotherhood of spiritual writers is attested by his authorship of typically Puritan works of "affectionate divinity." Included among these were two items celebrating the holy lives of members of the godly community: a brief biography, including letters, of Thomas Tregosse, a Cornwall minister, and a preface to a life of his uncle John Rowe, a Devonshire layman of exemplary piety and father of the John Rowe with whom he was associated in London. Gale also authored *A Discourse of Christ's Coming*, in which the earlier more communal Puritan eschatological expectations were given the individualistic and pietistic significance of a means to "awaken secure professors" and summon them to godliness as they look for the coming of the Lord, something of a parallel to the eschatology of the later Sterry.[18]

Two other works of affectionate divinity suggest some of the characteristics of Gale's *The Court of the Gentiles*. *The Anatomie of Infidelitie*, an analysis of unbelief, is interspersed with learned digressions on biblical words and passages and has many marginal references, often in Latin, to the Commentaries, translations, and other writings of Calvin, Franciscus Junius, Hugo Grotius, and Thomas Aquinas. *Theophilie*, another work of affectionate divinity, as the name suggested, stressed the necessity of friendship with God. In it, Gale quoted numerous classical authors as he exhorted to piety: for example, Pythagoras is quoted to the effect that virtue is nothing other than harmony. Plato is quoted more than twenty times, Aristotle ten, Seneca six, and there are one or two quotations each from Philo, Diogenes Laertes, Cicero, Juvenal, and Plutarch.[19] *Theophilie* also employed texts from the Song of Solomon in order to describe the friendship of Christ and the soul as a "conjugal affection," indicating that as sober a Dissenter as Gale could employ the same rhetoric that was so central to Peter Sterry.[20]

Gale's *The Court of the Gentiles*

But it was *The Court of the Gentiles* that gave Gale a reputation as a great savant. He began work on it at Oxford and continued with it while in France and later when heading an academy. It was published in four parts in five volumes between 1669 and 1678, with later revisions of some earlier parts.[21] Some revisions were undertaken as replies to objections, for after the first part had been published, Gale had seen "a Discourse of a learned man" which tended "to the subversion of my main Hypothesis," so that he felt himself obliged "to adde what I could for the confirmation of the same: Which I have endeavoured to do with all the Candor, Modestie, and Ingenuitie I could; without the least Reflexion on the Person, or so much as mention of his name," submitting "the Issue of it to the Judgement of the Learned Reader."[22]

The version of ancient theology that Gale presented was in its main outlines simple enough, although the particulars of the argument on its behalf were as complex as the detailed and seemingly endless etymologies and philological analyses scattered throughout *The Court of the Gentiles*. Gale accepted many of the usual ancient theologians as wise persons who knew at least significant fragments of divine truth: Plato and some of the later Platonists of course, but also Pythagoras; Orpheus; Zoroaster ("the first most illustrious Doctor of Magic in Persia"); the biblical Balaam, identified as a Chaldean magician and follower of Zoroaster's teachings; the ancient Thracian sage Zalmoxis; Atlas; Hercules; and the Druids are all on his list. He is familiar with the relevant sources of ancient theology, citing besides the ancient theologians themselves Philo (whom he thought had been a friend of the apostles), Josephus, and Augustine. He was also familiar with the later purveyors of the tradition, citing among others, Ficino, Pico ("that noble Earle of Mirandula"), Steuco, Vives, Reuchlin, Lefevre, and Mornay.[23]

Gale's Platonism

The philosophical outlook of Renaissance ancient theology was an eclectic Platonism; throughout his treatise Gale shows a preference for Platonism coupled with distaste for Aristotle. This is further evidence of the erroneousness of Ernst Cassirer's judgment that the revived Platonism of seventeenth-century England was incompatible with Puritan Calvinism. On the contrary, many Calvinists both in England and America synthesized Calvinism and Platonism in the later seventeenth century, locating the Platonic "ideas" in the divine mind.[24] Certainly Sterry was imbued with Platonism, and as will appear later, so were John Howe and John Edwards.

Gale is clearly such a Calvinist Platonist. The fourth part of *The Court of the Gentiles* bears the separate title *Of Reformed Philosophie. Wherein Plato's Moral, and Metaphysic or prime Philosophie is reduced to an useful Forme and Method* and begins with a critique of all the Greek philosophical schools before turning to a systematic presentation of his reworked Platonism. Gale lists precursors whom he considered had already tried to reform Platonism, including Pico, Savonarola, and John Wycliffe, as well as the Huguenot Ramus, who had sought to replace Aristotle's logic and, thought Gale, had been murdered at the St. Bartholomew's Massacre because of it. Norman Fiering has suggested that the implied Platonism in Ramist logic served as an entry into Puritan thought; Daniel Walker Howe refers to "the Ramist version of Platonism." Gale acknowledged that Platonism too had been a source of errors, especially in its late Alexandrian form, which had led to the errors of the Gnostics and Origen, whom Gale regarded as the heresiarch responsible for both Arianism and Pelagianism. As he saw it, the Neoplatonist Ammonius (d. 242) sympathized with the Christians, but his followers the "New Platonists" corrupted this by mixing it with magic and demon worship. Gale also mentioned contemporaries to reinforce the preference for Platonism: Cornelius Jansen (whose ideas Sterry also found interesting) "that great patron of Efficacious Grace, greatly prefers Platonic Philosophie before all other"; and so do "our New-philosophers," Pierre

Gassendi and Descartes, whom, Gale thought, merely imitated "the Contemplations laid down by Plato."[25] As a Platonist, Gale argued that God sees all things in himself (as the receptacle of the ideas), and that the world is a "universal Temple, wherein man may contemplate natural images . . . of Divine Wisdome and Goodnesse."[26] For God, as "the father of lights, has impressed upon the natures of things" a "reflex irradiation or shine of his eternal increated Wisdome" so that "all human Arts and Sciences, as gathered up into systems," or as innate in human minds, "are but the reflex ideas or images of that objective light, or internal law engraved upon the beings of things." Thus "all human arts and sciences are but beams and derivations" from God.[27] Much of the "reformed" Platonism of *The Court of the Gentiles* also appeared in a separate Latin text of 1676 under another title.[28]

Gale's Version of the Ancient Theology

Gale echoed earlier authors in making many figures of the biblical story progenitors of the arts and sciences as well as of true philosophy. Adam was the first philosopher and laid down the arts and sciences. Mathematics came from Seth. Seth and Enoch were skilled in astronomy but were also philosophers, Noah taught navigation, Abraham taught arithmetic to the Egyptians, Geometry came from the division of the land of Canaan by the children of Israel, and architecture from Solomon's Temple. Job knew natural philosophy and dialectics; Moses was skilled in all the arts and was a great philosopher.[29]

In developing this, Gale makes many conflations between ancient biblical figures and other ancient names. The ancient Greek Atlas, a philosopher-king of the Africans, was none other than Enoch (Gale was also aware that the Islamic world knew Enoch as "Edris," a knowledge that Gale thought had come to Mohammed from "Abdalla, the Talmudist." Hermes Trismegistus, or "Theuth" (Thoth) was a name of the Gentiles for both Joseph and Moses (Ficino had at the end of his life wondered if Hermes and Moses were not after all the same person). The Egyptian goddess Isis was based on the daughter of Pharaoh who rescued the infant Moses. The wise Chaldean Zabratus was really Ezekiel. Saturn may have come from Adam while Bacchus derived from Nimrod or Moses. Hercules was based on both Joshua and Samson. Apollo was derived either from Joshua or "Phut, son of Cham."[30] Most of these conclusions were based on philological arguments.

The last examples suggest Gale's reliance on the Euhemerist principle of treating pagan gods as deified ancient culture heroes. Such Euhemerist interpretation of the ancient pagan gods had been important to medieval and

Renaissance thinkers: through this method they could retain the study of ancient pagan lore. Thus Gale considered Neptune (whom he also identified with the biblical Japhet) to have been an ancient teacher of navigation. Hercules he thought was a Phoenician, contemporary with Moses, who sailed to Spain and Africa on the first great expedition of that people. Cadmus was a Phoenician from Sidon, and the story of his sowing serpents' teeth was a fanciful and mythologized way of saying that he raised a large army.[31]

But all these aspects of the argument of *The Court of the Gentiles* were ancillary to the main thrust of Gale's book, which was that all learning and truth had come from revealed traditions passed on by the Jews. This is the point of the title, for it was to "the court of the Gentiles" of the Jewish temple (metaphorically) that the Gentiles resorted "for their choicest Wisdome." This has already been seen in that Adam at the beginning had outlined the principles of language, philosophy, and all the arts. Plato, for example, merely built on "some broken traditions touching the Philosophie of Adam."[32] But since the fall, these arts and sciences cannot unaided be grasped from nature by fallen humankind but require the light of revelation to be known. This light was given to the Jews. And thus "the wisest of the Heathens were fain to light their candles at the fire of the Sanctuarie; to derive their knowledge from the Oracles of God, seated in the Jewish Church." Gale claimed, as had many before him, that this was acknowledged by the pagans and well known to the Jews and early Christians (although Gale also thought that the pagans often tried to hide this dependence because of their hatred of the Jews). From the pagans Gale cited Hermippus, the biographer of Pythagoras, who said that Pythagoras borrowed from the Jews; Plato and Plutarch, who acknowledge drawing on "old traditions" which must have been Jewish, thought Gale, though perhaps mediated through Egyptians or Phoenicians; and best of all Numenius, as quoted by Clement of Alexandria: "For what is Plato but Moses atticizing [i.e., speaking Greek]?" Among Jewish authors Gale called on Josephus's *Against Apion,* where the dependence of Pythagoras on the Jews is claimed, and Philo, who said that Plato drew from the Mosaic books and perhaps from Jeremiah for his philosophy. In addition, Plato had visited Egypt when the Jews were there. From the Christians various church fathers are cited, especially Clement of Alexandria and Justin Martyr.[33]

The first and second parts of *The Court of the Gentiles* outlined Gale's detailed evidence for the derivation of all knowledge from the Jews. Part I, "Of Philologie," is subdivided into three books, each of which examined a different aspect of that which had been derived by the pagans from Jewish sources. Book I shows that all languages and hence all literatures came from Hebrew. The Phoenicians learned from the Jews and took what they learned to Greece,

Spain, England and elsewhere, bequeathing alphabetic writing and language to all with whom they came in contact (although these other peoples did begin to write from left to right). In receiving the Hebrew language, these peoples all received that language which went back to Adam, and since Adam had originally named all things under God's direction, one could use these names to "pry into the very nature of things," since these names were essentially related to the things named, and contemplate the order and ideas behind them. There was such an exact correlation between names and things that just to know the language was eventually to have an understanding of things themselves. Emphasis on the importance of the Hebrew language as the primordial language enabling a more exact understanding of the things named was an idea that had appeared with various Renaissance promoters of Hebrew learning. This close relationship of names and things reflected the Platonic understanding of language, whereby words participate in the reality they represent; it draws, in medieval terms, on a "realist" rather than nominalist understanding of language. With Tommaso Campanella this view of language carried over to an almost magical sense of language having incantatory possibilities. Gale amassed philological evidence to show that Arabic, Persian, Gallic, and other languages were based upon Hebrew. It was at the Tower of Babel that the original language of Hebrew was first diversified and corrupted. Such a corruption of language, where words and things were originally closely connected, meant a loss of much of the primal truth.[34]

Book II of the first part of The Court of the Gentiles treated "Pagan Theologie, both Theogonie, Physic, and Politic; with its Derivation from sacred Names, Persons, and Stories." Here Gale showed that the names of ancient pagan gods were corruptions of Hebrew terms—as has appeared already in the case of Saturn and Bacchus. Serapis, for example, derived from Joseph, as did Osiris, of whom it was also said that he saved the Egyptians from a famine (though elsewhere Gale says he came from Moses). Physical theology, including worship of the sun and speculation concerning it, is likewise based on misunderstood Hebrew words. "Politic" theology, on the other hand, especially as practiced by the Romans (Gale seems to mean by it a combination of public ritual and civil religion), was borrowed from the temple at Jerusalem.[35]

The third book of part I treated "Of Pagan Poesie, Historie, Laws, and Oratory with their Traduction from Sacred Oracles." Here we learn that of all "artificial literature" poetry came first, and from the Hebrews. It originated in their astonishment at the miracles of God so that those who saw these miracles broke forth "in poetic Hymns and Raptures." Orpheus got his "poesie" from the Jews by way of the Phoenicians; Homer while in Egypt read the books of Moses, borrowing much from them. All oratory and rhetoric similarly came from the Jews, the oratory contained in scripture far surpassing all other, even that of Cicero. Furthermore, the sacred histories of the Old Testament are the earliest histories, which Egyptian, Phoenician, and Greek "annalists" copied and imitated, borrowing accounts of the creation and the flood, and garbling them with the passage of time. The Mosaic laws were the oldest laws, and Plato received the constitution for his ideal republic from them as did Aristotle the ideas for his *Politics*.[36]

The second part of Gale's magnum opus recounted the derivation of philosophy from the Hebrews, the books into which part II is divided being devoted to different philosophical schools. Adam has already appeared as the first philosopher, giving names to things. After the fall, this understanding began to grow dim, although "the learned also reckon Enoch amongst the first Divine Philosophers." Abraham was also a philosopher, teaching wisdom to the Chaldeans. Joseph taught Philosophy to the Egyptians, but after his death only a few rudiments remained. Moses's philosophy, found in the Pentateuch, was spread by the Phoenecians, Egyptians, and later the Greeks; from it Plato derived the creation story in the *Timaeus*. Solomon was second only to Adam as a philosopher and Aristotle's knowledge of animals as well as Theophrastus's knowledge of plants came from him—by way of the Phoenicians. Job was another of the great philosophers, skilled in dialectics. Gale goes painstakingly through the various schools of Greek philosophy, demonstrating that important aspects of the teaching of each came from the Jews. Pythagoras received his pattern of "collegiate life" from the Essenes; Socrates, whose mode of teaching was irony ("indeed his whole life was but a kind of Ironie") learned this from the "Jewish mode of disputation"; Stoic philosophy, with its contempt of earthly good was clearly based on Jewish ethics. Platonic philosophy is the most admirable, but insofar as it has come from the Jews, it is false to regard it as the "Product of Nature's Light."[37] But Jewish philosophy still lived on in the "Cabala," though corrupted by Greek Philosophy. However, Gale is doubtful about the antiquity of the Cabala, noting that Archbishop James Ussher considered it medieval, and certainly not as old as Moses. He did not include Christian cabalism as an element in his version of the ancient theology, although he does at one point refer to a "Divine Cabala," different from the "fabulous Cabala," which tells how the Old Testament points to Christ— presumably a reference to an ongoing Christian typological tradition of interpreting the Hebrew books.[38]

The wisdom of the East also came from the Jews according to Gale, including that of the Brahmins and the followers of the Buddha, who was himself the teacher of Manes, founder of the Manicheans. Much of this came by way of the Magi, whom Apollonius of Tyana knew to be philosophers; they in turn had learned from Zoroaster, who had learned from the Chaldeans, who of course had learned from the Jews. Having turned both east and west with Jewish influence, Gale adds the Ethiopian "Gymnosophists," who had learned from the Jews, and the ancient philosophers of Libya, who had learned from both Atlas and later Hercules, the latter of whom had gotten it from the Jews by way of the Phoenicians. But Gale's diffusionism was not finished: Thracian philosophy came from Pythagoras through their first philosopher Zalmoxis, and Spanish philosophy came from the Jews through the Phoenicians as did that of the Druids of Britain and Gaul.[39]

The importance to Gale of the Phoenician connection in diffusing this knowledge is apparent. They were the critical mediators of Hebrew wisdom to the world. The Phoenician philosopher Sanchuniathon, cited by Porphyry, Philo Byblius, and Eusebius as a Syrian native of Berytus (Beirut) who lived before the Trojan War and wrote a history, was for Gale one of the ancient theologians; Joseph Scaliger had given credence to his history as drawn from Phoenician temple records, but later in the seventeenth century Henry Dodwell proved the work a later forgery.[40] Sanchuniathon, according to Gale, had learned from the Jews. Gale claimed that many of the Greek philosophers had Phoenician ties: thus Orpheus learned from the Phoenicians; Pherecydes, Pythagoras's teacher, was a Phoenician; Pythagoras knew the Phoenician language and knew Jews who were in Phoenicia; Thales was of Phoenician descent, and derived his philosophy from them; even Zeno the Stoic got his ideas through Phoenicians. Gale was convinced that Plato too had been to Phoenicia: "Though we find no express mention of Plato's travelling to Phoenicia, yet that he visited that Country also, either in his Travels to, or from Egypt, seems very probable. For the Phoenicians being every way well furnished with Jewish Traditions, and Mysteries, we cannot conceive that Plato, who was so great an admirer thereof, would let pass such an opportunitie for satisfying his Curiositie therein." In addition, Gale cited Samuel Bochart as his authority for the conclusion that the Athenians as a whole were originally from Phoenicia.[41] The importance of the Phoenicians in this diffusion of Hebrew knowledge was a commonplace among seventeenth-century authors who treated these subjects, and Bochart was cited as an authority on the matter long after Gale had written.[42]

The knowledge of truth has had its vicissitudes, and in Gale's version this meant particularly that the baneful effects of sin had been at work. When Adam fell the purity of philosophy and of the arts and sciences fell with him: "Adam no sooner fell, but Philosophie fell with him, and became a common Strumpet for carnal Reason to commit folie with. And oh! how have the lascivious Wits of lapsed human nature ever since gone a Whoring after vain Philosophie?"[43]

But God did not leave humankind in darkness, vouchsafing the light of revelation through the Jews. However, those who had received so much light had trouble maintaining it because of the inevitable degradation that sin had brought into the world; thus the Greeks fell from what they had dimly known to an outright and reprehensible polytheism and idolatry; even the Jews, after a temporary restoration under Ezra, declined sadly from their original light. The new dispensation of Christianity took up the light of wisdom again, only to have it quickly dimmed, in spite of Tertullian's warnings, as vain philosophies, especially Aristotelianism and the corrupted Platonism of the Gnostics crept into the church, giving rise to Pelagian heresy. But Augustine was raised up by God "to give check and confusion to these proud sentiments." Gale also included Thomas Aquinas among the anti-Pelagian writers. Pelagians were yet later attacked by Thomas Bradwardine in "his never-enough to be admired Book *De Causa Dei*," and by John Wycliffe. Meanwhile Aristotelianism was made worse by the Arabian commentators. Gale quoted "pious Jansenius" against the medieval scholastics: they sought to be wiser than God and ended up by granting less to grace than did the wisest of the pagans! Then the Protestant Reformers arose, purging Christianity of the Pelagian and other errors into which it had fallen. Gale exhorted that it was the duty of sincere Christians to strive against such error, as the anti-Arminian Calvinists were doing in Holland and England and the anti-Jesuit Jansenists in France. Modern atheism, typified for Gale by Thomas Hobbes, was also the consequence of false philosophy with its assertion of human self-sufficiency.[44] It is apparent from this history that true Christianity needs a Reformed philosophy if future apostasies are to be avoided. This Reformed philosophy, as we have seen, will be based on Platonism, and accompanied with a reformed logic both Ramist and anti-Aristotelian.[45]

The Wide Currency of Ancient Theology

Thus Gale's *The Court of the Gentiles* was not out of step with the learning of his time. In William James's phrase, Gale's hypothesis was still live enough to tempt his contemporaries. He is praised by the Oxford antiquarian Anthony Wood, who generally scorned Puritans as vile rebels, but called Gale "a person of great reading, an exact philologist, and a philosopher."[46] The poet Thomas Traherne copied out large extracts from Gale for his notebooks, as well as from Ficino. In the next century, Jonathan Edwards also copied out many passages from Gale.[47] Many English authors in the century prior to Gale as well as contemporary with him expressed similar ideas, although without his systematic framework or exhaustive detail. There are echoes of Hermetic lore in the poetry of Edmund Spenser, for whose Neoplatonism it was congenial. Sir Philip Sidney accepted the ancient theology and helped translate into English Mornay's *De la Verite de la Religion Chrestienne.* Richard Hooker granted authority to the Hermetic texts. William Gilbert's treatise on magnets referred to Hermes, Zoroaster, and Orpheus as ancient teachers of great (and anti-Aristotelian) wisdom. Sir Walter Raleigh's *History of the World,* which Gale cited, alluded to Orpheus, Pythagoras, and Plato as ancient theologians.[48] Francis Bacon apparently believed that a better science would reproduce more of the perfect knowledge of nature that Adam had possessed and thought that Solomon had written a book on nature and its secrets. Robert Burton's *Anatomy of Melancholy* included many references to enthusiasts for the tradition such as Ficino, Pico, Paracelsus, and Campanella. Though he could be critical of the Hermetic tradition, he considered Pythagoras, Zoroaster, and Trismegistus to be ancient theologians. The treatise entitled *Mythomystes,* by Henry Reynolds, a friend of the poet Michael Drayton, probably published in 1632, showed dependence on Pico; according to it, all wisdom and learning is hidden in the Mosaic books, with the key to their meaning in the secret cabalistic wisdom God gave orally to Moses. The highest truth was also embedded in the ancient Egyptian hieroglyphs. Gale too thought that these hieroglyphs were ancient symbols and images that adumbrated "heavenly mysteries" but that they derived from the Jews and belonged only to the infancy of human wisdom, though eventually made known to the Gentiles by Zoroaster, Avenzoar the Babylonian, Orpheus, Trismegistus, Linus, Homer, Pythagoras, and Plato. *Mythomystes* also engaged in Euhemerist conflation, describing Noah and Bacchus as the same. Thomas Browne in *The Garden of Cyrus* commented of Ovid's description of creation that many thought it borrowed from Moses; Browne has been described by a recent author as both Calvinist and Hermeticist. Milton's allusion to "thrice-great Hermes" in "Il Penseroso" is well known. Thomas and Henry Vaughan have been treated as thinkers whose ideas were formed by Hermeticism. Thomas Vaughan even defended the magical and alchemical elements of this outlook as pious, seeking in particular to rehabilitate the reputation of Cornelius Agrippa; magic, he argued, was "nothing else but the Wisdom of the Creator revealed and planted in the Creature." Lord Herbert of Cherbury seems to have derived his first truths of natural religion from his understanding of an ancient universal wisdom but rejected the notion that all this wisdom had come from the Jews and that it had been impaired by sin; rather, it was a worthy ancient consensus.[49]

The Cambridge Platonists also generally accepted the ancient theology, since they too understood by Platonism a much wider lore than just the dialogues of Plato. Ralph Cudworth, writing as late as 1678, and well aware of Isaac Casaubon's disproof of the great antiquity of the Hermetic literature, argued that while the compilation of the whole may have been late, it nonetheless preserved ancient Egyptian wisdom. He also accepted Zoroaster and Orpheus as ancient theologians. Henry More believed that Pythagoras and Plato got their wisdom from Moses and was an enthusiast for the Cabala, considering it ancient. Nathaniel Culverwell, on the other hand, rejected the argument that all wisdom and knowledge came from the Jews, but the vehemence of his argument suggests that he felt opinion was against him: Plato, he insisted, had "many Spermatical Notions" not of Jewish sowing, and of the Greeks generally he asked, "Cannot they read Natures Alphabet unlesse a Jew come with his fescue and teach them?"[50] By the end of the seventeenth century, radicals such as the Deist John Toland were accused of Rosicrucianism and Freemasonry, the latter of which apparently drew on supposed traditions of ancient wisdom. Isaac Newton was quite interested in aspects of this material and accepted the same diffusionist and euhemerizing theories about the origins of the pagan gods that Gale did. He also thought that Moses had a full scientific understanding of the origin of the world and speculated about Hermetic lore in relation to alchemy.[51]

But perhaps the best evidence of the widespread acceptance of views similar to those of Gale is the recognition by opponents that in refuting such ideas they were fighting against the consensus of learned opinion. For example, when Samuel Parker wrote against Platonic philosophy, he acknowledged that in attacking Plato he would seem to be criticizing Moses, for that the former borrowed his system from the latter has "the unanimous consent of all the learned world." Against that consent, Parker insisted, refreshingly, that the Mosaic books and Platonism were quite different in outlook, while Hermes and Zoroaster are but "supposititious authors" and a "vocal cabala" going back to Moses "a late and silly Invention of the Jewish Rabbins."[52]

Gale's Sources

In developing his version of the ancient theology, Gale drew on learned contemporaries as well as earlier scholars of great repute, all of whom assumed some version of the truth of an ancient theology; he especially borrowed from an international Protestant historical-philological tradition that focused on biblical languages (particularly Hebrew as the original language of Adam; the flowering of Hebraic learning in the Reformation and its aftermath is an important context for Gale's work) and interpretation. Chronology was also an important concern of these scholars as evidenced in the work of Joseph Scaliger, and by it biblical and nonbiblical history were brought together, abetting the urge to engage in euhemerist interpretations of the origins of the pagan gods. This sort of learning was highly respected in its time for a breadth of coverage that ranged widely over classical, Hebraic, and Christian antiquity, and then put all this knowledge to the service of Christian theology. In its Protestant version, that service was especially the defense of the authority of scripture. Gale commented of his own labor in tracing all knowledge to the Jews that it was his main design to give greater glory to scripture.[53]

Gale himself claimed that the "concurrence of the Learned" supported his views, and listed some of them in a preface to *The Court of the Gentiles*. The list was long, and included major figures in the continuing development of the tradition of ancient theology as well as others who had given their consent to these ideas. Among fellow Calvinists he included John Preston and John Owen, Puritans who had been influential in Cambridge and Oxford respectively, as well as Irish Archbishop James Ussher; Church of England theologians who were not Calvinists included Thomas Jackson, Henry Hammond, and Edward Stillingfleet; among "learned Papists" he listed Agostino Steuco and Ludovico Vives; the Dutch scholars Hugo Grotius and Gerardus Vossius, both supporters of the Arminian cause in the Netherlands which Gale opposed; and the Huguenot scholars Joseph Scaliger and Samuel Bochart.[54] Some of these authorities listed by Gale and others too, not in his prefatory list, bear examination in order to discern the scope and nature of Gale's labors.

He particularly acknowledged the importance of Hugo Grotius in his preface as providing his inspiration for launching into the project of *The Court of the Gentiles* from his reading, during his Oxford years, of the *De Veritate Religionis* of the Dutch scholar, an important figure in international Protestant learning; Gale frequently cited Grotius as an authority on matters of biblical interpretation, calling him "a good Critic, well-skilled in Antiquitie," even though he was an opponent of Grotius's theology, maintaining that the great scholar's best work had been done before he "fell off" to Socinianism. Gale warned "young students" that "they imbibe not his erroneous Infusions, together with his Learned Annotations."[55] Gerardus Vossius, a friend of Grotius, was another Dutch scholar upon whom Gale relied and frequently cited. Amongst Vossius's historical studies was his voluminous *De Theologia Gentili* published in 1641. It was a treatment of the origin and progress of idolatry that argued that pagan religion was a degenerated derivative of the original revelation to the Jews and Christians, in which the figures of pagan religion are based on biblical characters. A huge work of Christian apologetics, it nonetheless granted some truth to natural religion and long served as a standard handbook of pagan mythology.

Vossius's work included the Hebrew text and Latin translation, with annotations of his own, on a treatise dealing with idolatry by Maimonides.[56] Gale
often cited Maimonides.[57]

Huguenot scholars, who had long given attention to the ancient theology,
loomed large on Gale's intellectual horizon: while ignoring Casaubon's disproof of the antiquity of the Hermetic literature (as did Gale's Jesuit contemporary Athanasius Kircher, another proponent of a version of the ancient
theology),[58] Gale drew frequently on Mornay, whose book was an important
early Protestant treatment of the ancient theology and its derivation from the
Jews (and whose euhemerizing Gale often followed). Mornay had also written
with a strong apologetic purpose, as did Gale, striving to prove the truth of
Christian revelation "against Atheists, Epicures, Paynims, Jewes, Mahumetists,
and other Infidels," as the English translation of his title declared. Gale also
relied on Joseph Scaliger (d. 1609), famous for his learning in chronology and
ancient languages, who also interpreted pagan mythology in Euhemerist
fashion, and on the Italian biblical translator and Genevan pastor Giovanni
Diodati, uncle of Milton's friend Charles Diodati, and author of a widely used
Bible commentary. More important to Gale than any of these was Samuel
Bochart, with whom he had conversed in France, whose name Gale usually
reverently coupled with some epithet, such as "acute and learned Bochart," and
whose book *Geographia Sacra* he described as "worth its weight in purest gold."
Bochart, whom Pierre Bayle was to call one of the most learned men in the
world, was a linguist who had added knowledge of Arabic, Persian, Coptic,
Ethiopic and Syriac to the usual humanist trilinguality of Latin, Greek, and
Hebrew, and wrote a definitive work on biblical animals in two large folios as
well as the biblical geography Gale used.[59] At one point Gale cited a less known
figure among the Huguenots, "eloquent Du Bosc," pastor of the Reformed
church at Caen, where Gale had lingered with his young pupils, on a matter of
the interpretation of ancient mythology.[60]

Among English scholars, Gale read the antiquarian John Selden, who had
written a work on the pagan gods that appear in the Bible, *De Dis Syris* (1617),
as well as a number of works on ancient Jewish law. Gale also depended on
John Owen, whom he knew from his Oxford days; Owen's *Theologomena
Pantodapa: sive De natura, Ortu, Progressu, et Studio, Verae Theologiae*, published
at Oxford in 1661, provided him "much light and confirmation." Owen too
discussed pagan philosophy as derivative from the Jews and treated Greek gods
as corruptions of Hebrew originals, though these points were not the main
focus of this work which was chiefly a kind of exercise in historical biblical
theology.[61] Owen specifically rejected the great antiquity of Hermes
Trismegistus, following Casaubon.[62]

Gale also drew on Church of England writers who were opponents of his Calvinism, including Thomas Jackson and Edward Stillingfleet. Thomas Jackson, Laudian ecclesiastic and president of Corpus Christi, Oxford, upheld Platonic philosophy there in the 1630s, including the view that Plato and Hermes Trismegistus received their light from Moses. His writings are filled with references to the ancient theologians Pythagoras and Orpheus. Jackson also thought that Greek myths and legends expressed mysteries of nature and were corruptions of biblical stories and that Plotinus had borrowed some of his ideas from Christian theologians. But he differed from Gale in thinking that Orpheus and Pythagoras had gotten some truths directly from their contemplation of nature. Edward Stillingfleet was a Church of England bishop and theologian whose *Origenes Sacrae* used similar lore for apologetic purposes, treating Greek gods and myths as corruptions of biblical persons and stories and arguing as Gale did that an earlier and purer philosophy had been corrupted into warring sects, but Stillingfleet followed Casaubon and rejected both the antiquity of the Hermetic literature and Hermes as an ancient person.[63]

Among earlier humanist writers Gale relied on the Spanish humanist Luis Vives, who came from a "new Christian" family (his mother was posthumously condemned by the inquisition for persisting in Judaic practices and her corpse exhumed for burning while his father was arrested for the same purpose) and emphasized the Hebraic elements in Christian truth. Vives left Spain and spent time in England; Protestants held him in high regard as a Christian apologist because of his apologetic work *De Veritate Fidei Christianae* (1543), from which Gale quoted, as he also did from Vives's commentary on St. Augustine's *The City of God*. Gale also shared Vives's Platonism, describing him as one who "made it his designe to detect the Vanitie and Abuses of the Aristotelian Philosophie, as depraved by Scholastic Theologues."[64]

Consideration of Gale's sources leads to reflection on his method as a scholar, the way in which he employed his sources, both ancient and modern. This could best be described as "bookish"—he ransacked relevant and not-so-relevant books related to his subject and then stitched it all together with little independent analysis of the validity of the many details, his contribution coming in the overall interpretation. It is the perpetuation of the medieval idea of the authority of "authors," whereby the written word of especially ancient books carried great weight virtually by having been written (of course ungodly books did not carry weight for the devout, but the extent to which skeptical writers sought authority from ancient skeptics suggests the power of the premise). "Authors" could mean authority, and writers sought precedent in earlier books for their opinions. Thus when Gale's authorities differed, his main recourse was to leave the matter undecided, citing several possibilities—for example, his sources differed as to whether Saturn was derived from Adam or Enoch, or Bacchus from Nimrod or Moses, and so in both cases he remained undecided. When it mattered to him for theological reasons, for example, as to whether the Cabala is really as old as Moses, he followed the authority he preferred for purposes of his own argument, but with little attempt to demonstrate why that was the correct choice. At such points he is obviously the victim of his bookish and old-fashioned method of citing "authors." Gale's fellow Dissenter John Howe, as will be seen later, wrote in the newer style that eschewed piling up authorities and instead sought to persuade by arguments appealing to the common sense of readers; that was the approach that came to be characteristic of the "moderns" who no longer thought that a case was established simply by reference to old books.

The Jewish Origin of All Truth

Gale's version of ancient theology was his own amalgam of ancient and modern sources, with its own peculiarities. But he made more of the Jewish derivation of all wisdom than did many of the later authorities he cited, for whom the point of ancient theology was to establish the universality of ancient truth and to enable them to enroll ancient Gentiles among the wise. In emphasizing the derivation of ancient theology from Jewish revelation, Gale did not promote the syncretism and universalism of Florentine Hermetism and its successors (though Ficino did think that all pagan wisdom was borrowed from the Jews, and used this argument apologetically against the rivals of Christianity),[65] but agreed with some of the principal Protestant proponents of ancient theology, including De Mornay, Vossius, Owen, and Stillingfleet, and with John Milton, whose Christ, rebuking Satan in *Paradise Regained,* declares that the Greeks received their "Arts" from the Hebrews, but "ill imitated" them. Gale was relatively uninterested in the Hermetic literature and did not acknowledge Hermes as an independent Gentile theologian since he thought Hermes or "Theuth" or as he sometimes has it, "Mercurie," were the appellations given by the Gentiles to Moses who had taught the Egyptians (and sometimes to Joseph),[66] perhaps not only because of the magical implications (he followed St. Augustine in considering even the learned magic of the Platonists dangerous trafficking with demons)[67] but also because of the uncertainty of its antiquity after Casaubon. The fact that the English translation of parts of the Hermetic literature (in particular the *Poimandres*) had been done by John Everard, one of the anti-Calvinist spiritualist radicals of the Interregnum era, cannot have whetted Gale's interest in that text as it was increasingly being associated with radical ideas.

Moreover, although for Gale there were vestiges of truth in the ancient texts and philosophies as his acknowledgment that foreshadowings of the Trinity appeared in pagan philosophy indicates, he nonetheless thought that the true understanding of that mystery was "altogether hid from them"; elsewhere he even speculates, in agreement with Jackson, that it may only have appeared among Neoplatonists because of their knowledge of Christian authors.[68] Clearly, his stress fell upon the corruption of original truth. Denunciation of pagan superstition was also prominent with Gale. He emphasized Hebrew lore and language, as did his most admired authorities. But Gale followed Archbishop Ussher in regarding the Cabala as late,[69] probably because he preferred not to admit all the mystical and magical elements that cabalism entailed into his version of ancient theology, which was, after all, derived from revealed truth.

The question remains as to Gale's motives for writing *The Court of the Gentiles*. He seems to have delighted in his learning and was pleased to find a system for its organization. Scholars contemporary with Gale were fascinated with schemes that would summarize or synthesize all knowledge. Gale's contemporary, the Oxford scholar John Wilkins, drew up tables to encompass all knowledge.[70] William J. Bouwsma has commented on the reappearance of the systematizing approach in the seventeenth century and regarded it as a reaction to some of the more daring approaches of the preceding century: as in the middle ages, many thinkers again in the seventeenth century sought to relate "all aspects of human experience to a central core of universal and therefore abstract truth." Bouwsma thought this was characteristic of Protestant scholasticism, Roman Catholic Counter-Reformation thought, and Cartesianism alike.[71] Encyclopedic scholarship arranged systematically certainly describes Gale's work, as it does that of such contemporaries of his as Vossius, Bochart, or Athanasius Kircher, and his labors at reforming Platonism suggest his metaphysical commitments.

As a teacher, Gale had a broad interest in all the arts and sciences. This may be why Lord Wharton considered him appropriate as a tutor for his sons, for that Puritan nobleman was a person of culture who collected the paintings of Van Dyck and Peter Lely[72] (his own portrait at age nineteen had been painted by Van Dyck). Gale corresponded frequently with Lord Wharton concerning his sons' education, noting on one occasion that they were making progress in their studies and that he was about to engage them in the study of "the more noble parts of human literature."[73] Furthermore, Gale simply loved this ancient lore, as no doubt did medieval apologists who worked out similarly intricate strategies for both condemning and studying it: condemned, for its corruptions; but studied for its glimmerings of borrowed truth.

Gale was quite explicit in the preface to *The Court of the Gentiles* that his purpose for writing down his scheme for encompassing knowledge was for the pupils he tutored and he was persuaded that it would be for the good of all young students. He also noted that "several Judicious, Learned, and Pious Friends" encouraged his writing, adding that there was in English nothing apart from the claims made in Preston and Jackson to support his main contention.[74] It was presumably prominent later in instruction in Gale's academy. The jumble of citations, authors, and information that characterize the pages of Gale's great work was part of its appeal to contemporaries—*The Court of the Gentiles* was a gold mine of information ready to be drawn upon by students, preachers, and theological authors. And Gale continued to exert influence in the Calvinist world through his magnum opus long after his death: Cotton Mather and Jonathan Edwards drew extensively upon his great work, as did others.[75]

Gale stated other purposes for the work too, purposes that came closer to the heart of his high Calvinist convictions. He declared that his "main and original design" was to confirm biblical authority "and so by consequence the Christian Religion" by demonstrating the perfection of scripture and showing that all knowledge had come from biblical revelation, an aim which he also says was the purpose of the ancient Jews and Christians who first asserted the claim as well as the intention of "many Moderne Divines," naming Preston, Jackson, Stillingfleet, and Bochart, the latter of whom he says explicitly told him that this was the purpose of his *Geographia Sacra*.[76]

This meant that his massive work was an exercise in Christian apologetics demonstrating that humankind really had no other access to a higher spiritual reality than that of biblical revelation. His argument in *The Court of the Gentiles* would show what "great Marks of Divine favor and rich Tokens of his Grace" Christ was pleased to grant to "his poor afflicted Church" that was despised by the Gentile world when it was realized that for wisdom they had originally turned to the fire of the Jews to light the candles of their wisdom. The temple of Jerusalem had a court for the Gentiles to which they were "fain" to resort. This would also "beat down that fond persuasion" that has lately crept among many of too great an admiration for pagan philosophy, falsely thinking that it was the "Product of Nature's Light" and serve to "disabuse the minds of many young Students" of false and blasphemous ideas about God which they had derived from too great an estimation of the "Ethnic Poets and Mythologists."[77]

Those who felt too much admiration for pagan philosophy and had too great an estimation of the worth of the ancient poets were in all likelihood those associated with Cambridge Platonism who had revived the more positive version of the ancient theology that went back to Ficino and the Florentine

Academy and whose love of the ancient classics and philosophers led them to shape a Christian apologetic that emphasized not that all this was a corruption of biblical revelation but that there was an ancient wisdom that showed that shadows of the truth known by Christian revelation had been recognized outside of the biblical tradition and independent of that revelation. For them, that recognition confirmed Christian truth; what the pagans had dimly known was confirmed in a Christian revelation that all humankind had been prepared for. Christianity was true because it completed truths already known by the light of reason, the "candle of the Lord." Even when these scholars acknowledged that much of this truth was derived from the Jews, their emphasis fell on the importance of the texts of the ancient theology as pointers to the truth, not on their inadequacy because they had corrupted the truth. No group in the Church of England contemporary with Gale had been more engaged with the ancient theology and interested in reason as a faculty for recognizing higher spiritual truths than those designated the Cambridge Platonists. Benjamin Whichcote was deeply interested in the ancient theology and its study, but unlike Gale he found it evidence of natural light among the Gentiles, regarding their knowledge of it through the Jews as only reinforcement of the light of nature. Henry More shared this attitude: the ancient theology evidenced in texts that included the Orphic, Platonic, Hermetic, and other ancient literatures established a widespread if fragmentary recognition of the truth known fully in the divine revelation found in scripture. Nathaniel Culverwell has already been seen complaining that some think there was no knowledge but what had been taught by Jews. It is especially in the massive *True Intellectual System of the Universe*, by Ralph Cudworth, that a more positive view of the ancient theology and some recognition of its independence of the Jews (although reinforced by contact with them) appeared, published at the same time as the last part of Gale's *Court of the Gentiles*. Something of the motivation for this line of thought can be detected in John Sherman's 1641 *A Greek in the Temple*, which employed the tradition of ancient theology to defend the study of the classics against radical religious thinkers who denied the importance of studying those ancient authors.[78] Perhaps the unnamed "discourse" that Gale had come across which disagreed with his argument in *The Court of the Gentiles* had come from the Cambridge group or one of their sympathizers.

Thus Gale turned the lore of the ancient theology to a purpose not primary among Renaissance thinkers: he used it to emphasize grace by showing that all knowledge had come from divine revelation. Everywhere in *The Court of the Gentiles* Gale found the pagan tendency to take credit for their borrowed philosophy reprehensible, describing it as "their proud affectation, or vain humor of ascribing unto themselves the original of those traditions, which they did really traduce from the Jewish Church." Equally reprehensible was their inability to remain steadfast in the light they had received, the consequence of the fall. The impact of sin on the clarity of human knowledge loomed large in Gale's version of the ancient theology. Gale admitted that this lack of clarity, however, was also because of the way God had clothed his revelation: "For God condescending to the childish capacity of the Infant Church [i.e., the Jewish], clothed the sublime Mysteries of Salvation with terrene habits, sensible formes, and Typick shadows," which "the carnal Jews themselves could not understand; much lesse could those blind Heathens . . . penetrate into their spiritual sense."[79] Ultimately, it would only be by means of the illumination of grace that one could truly understand the sacred oracles.

Gale's Calvinism and *The Court of the Gentiles*

This emphasis on grace was consistent with Gale's education under high Calvinists like Owen and Thomas Goodwin at Oxford and with the tenor of Gale's spiritual writings that constantly evidenced his anti-Arminian concerns. His preface to the biography of the older Thomas Rowe gave that life a very Calvinist theological point: Rowe's great holiness proved that grace can take a life to a degree of saintliness far beyond "the highest Attainments of the most Refined Morality."[80] A considerable portion of *The Court of the Gentiles* was devoted to ethics, especially in parts III and IV, and continued Gale's anti-Pelagianism, condemning much of medieval scholastic ethical reasoning as Pelagian, and rejecting the idea of natural virtue. True virtue comes from grace alone.[81] *Theophile* and *The Anatomie of Infidelitie* sounded similar anti-Pelagian chords.

Gale was also the first English author to write about the French controversy over Jansenism, a matter in which he was deeply interested while there, even conversing with some of the participants in the quarrel.[82] He sympathized with the Augustinianism of Cornelius Jansen, considering it analogous in relation to the Roman Catholic Church in France to himself and his fellow Calvinists in relation to the Church of England—true Augustinians lost in a sea of Pelagian compromise. The Jansenists, he announced, "seem good friends to Justification by Free Grace, and Faith in the blood of Christ, without any regard to human merits as abused in the Popish sense."[83] His discussion of the subject also showed his familiarity with postmedieval Catholic scholasticism. There are many references to Jansen and Jansenists in *The Court of the Gentiles*, where he says that it "ought to be the great wonder of pious Souls, that in this Age, wherein so many Professors of the Reformed Religion have turned their backs on the Doctrine of Free Grace, and imbibed so many

Pelagian Infusions" that God has raised up, "even in the bosome of Antichrist, Jansenius and his Sectators."[84] Parenthetically, the Jesuit opponents of the Jansenists accused them of having sold out to the Calvinists, a charge of which Gale was aware.[85] Gale's willingness to draw on near contemporary Roman Catholic authors if they were sound on the doctrine of grace also appeared in his laudatory reference to Paolo Sarpi, "that great Master of Wisdome, Padre Paul the Venetian." Protestants generally regarded Sarpi highly as the author of a critical history of the Council of Trent; but for Gale his strongly Augustinian theology probably counted as much.[86]

The Court of the Gentiles concluded with a book three of part IV (printed separately in 1678) dealing with "Divine Predetermination," which defended unconditional predestination, including an attack on John Howe, a moderate Calvinist allied with Baxter, as will appear in a later chapter. Part IV also contained vigorous polemic against Amyraldian modification of strict Calvinism, a development among French Calvinists that had repercussions in England and of which Baxter had been accused.[87] Thus whether as commentator on Jansenism, spiritual writer, or polemicist, it is clear that Gale was a staunch Calvinist, deeply imbued with the outlook in piety and theology of the great anti-Arminian theologians such as Owen (who wrote a preface to Gale's work on Jansenism) or Thomas Goodwin.

Much in The Court of the Gentiles reinforced Gale's Reformed or Calvinist outlook: by portraying all knowledge of God (and indeed all real knowledge) as coming from the Jews who received it by revelation, Gale undercut any basis for human pride and established absolutely the need of grace and revelation. Pelagianism meant to Gale the assertion of self against God; he quoted with approval the medieval scholastic Thomas Bradwardine's remark that Cain, Nimrod, and Nebuchadnezzar were all Pelagians. Thus it is not surprising that he regarded Pelagian free will as the principal doctrine of all corrupted pagan philosophy and "the most pestiferous Heresie that ever infected" the church. Gale further integrated his anti-Pelagian version of ancient theology with the covenants: human beings gravitate by nature to a covenant of works, for the aim of corrupt philosophy "was to put men under a covenant of workes." There can be no claim to any "Light of Nature, by virtue of the first Covenant"; not only is salvation by the grace of the second covenant, but also "some Divines of great note conceive, that those very common natural Notions, commonly called the Fragments or Remains of the Image of God lost by Adam, are vouchsafed to us by the Covenant of Grace in and by the Mediation of Christ," so that "not only supernatural light vouchsafed to the Elect, but even the natural notices or Light of Nature vouchsafed to the lapsed Sons of Adam is the effect of the second Covenant." Elsewhere Gale made clear that no one can be under both covenants: the redeemed are only under the covenant of grace so that whatever elements of law or natural light which benefit them are part of that covenant.[88]

So much of *The Court of the Gentiles* is directed to the refutation of heresies alarming to Reformed theologians that it is evident that this was another of Gale's motives in compiling it. It provided an etiology of heresy: just as there was a perennial truth going back to revelation so has there been a perennial tendency to heresy as the truth is corrupted by sinful humankind. For Gale the Arminian challenge of his own century, discussed by him as Pelagianism, was an archetypal heresy flowing from human pride. But that is not the only heresy: "Arian" denial of the Trinity, one of the key items of the original wisdom properly understood, is a recurrent heresy, connected by Gale to Origen and the Gnostics; it is also clear that Gale worried about the Socinianism of his time, accusing his sometime admired Grotius of having lapsed into it. True philosophy and theology, the uncorrupted stream coming down from the original revelation, rule out this heresy too, and thus his tracing of it served as a polemic against emergent Socinianism. As a Christian apologetic in a historical mode, it is interesting that Gale's work combined both evolution and devolution in its analyses: the truth is increasingly corrupted over time, an echo of the ancient notion of decline from a golden age, at the same time that the knowledge of God's grace increases over time, as Gale's Protestant belief that the passage of time brings out greater light from scripture counters the devolution of truth.

Gale's work can also be regarded as an attack upon "Gentilism," the religion of pagan peoples. So far as Gale is concerned, this Gentilism is true only insofar as it retains its reflection of original revelation, as it was never an independent revelation; in fact, it always existed in gravely corrupted form. That corrupted form can be summed up as idolatry, and there is an undertone of suggestion running through *The Court of the Gentiles* to the effect that heathen and "popish" idolatry were much the same. This can be construed as Gale's answer to the questions of natural religion, other religions, and a universal religion, as propounded not only by the Cambridge Platonists such as Cudworth but also by Lord Herbert and later Deists (it has been speculated that the tolerant version of ancient theology was in fact a root of Deism).[89] Gale's work was a defense of Christianity and its unique revelation in the face of the challenge of "extrabiblical" truths and a rejection of any universal natural theology.

In a publication of 1673, Gale complained that in recent years atheism had come into vogue and had "overspread the Christian world"; such atheists were "scoffers." Idolatry and corrupt philosophy, in spite of Plato's opposition to the atheists of his time, were thought by Gale to have led to atheism; he declared that there were too many "Mathematic Atheists" breathing "Christian air."[90] While it was the unbelief of nominal Christians who have not "closed" with

Christ that is the concern of his *Anatomie of Infidelitie,* he did describe such unbelief (as well as "popish" implicit faith) as at root "Antichristianisme," a form of blasphemy, if not "speculative atheisme." And as might be expected, Hobbes's putative atheism comes in for criticism in *The Court of the Gentiles:* "well indeed might that daring Atheist title his book of Politics *Leviathan*" since every atheist would be a leviathan, ready to devour his neighbors. Atheism, thought Gale, would undermine civil order. Thus Gale's magnum opus can be construed as an attack on anti-Christian atheism, by its confirmation of scriptural truth as the source of all knowledge. That attack on unbelief was continued in long sections of his work (particularly in parts II and IV) that develop Platonic-Christian arguments for the existence of God. The treatment of ancient theology by Grotius, which had helped inspire Gale's work, also had the refutation of atheism as one of its aims.[91]

Whether directed against Pelagian heresy, "Gentilism," a Deist-like primordial universal religion, or atheism, Gale's combating of these things through a historical approach is significant in its own right. He does not marshal arguments against these errors so much as show through his version of the unfolding of religious truth in history that these falsehoods are rooted in a process of falling away over time from an original revelation; that which he opposes is not only refuted by argument but also discredited by an unflattering version of its origin. This is in some ways a rather modern argument, akin to the dismissal of a viewpoint because one has explained the physiology, psychology, or sociology of its origins—what William James described as the "genetic fallacy." But it is significant that he is making his case through a historical approach, just as almost a century later Jonathan Edwards envisaged a new kind of theology through a history of redemption.

Gale's rather negative approach to the tradition of ancient theology can also be said to be a somewhat more "democratic" version of ancient theology than was usually the case. There is after all, something democratizing about the assertion of the human commonality of sin. As William Bouwsma pointed out, there was an elitist aspect of the ancient theology, insofar as it was a search for an esoteric and exclusive wisdom by "aristocrats of the spirit" who could rise above the vulgar masses. Its method was not a more public rhetorical or historical reading of texts but a ransacking of them for elusive clues of and insights into a perennial truth.[92] Gale on the other hand presented it as a Christian apologetic accessible to Calvinists lay and clerical, novice students and advanced scholars, which would serve to rebut all opponents.

Gale's conclusion that all real knowledge of God is revealed knowledge, which included his "reformed Platonism" which went back to Moses and even Adam, was his ultimate way of combating the rationalism of what would soon take shape as the dawning Enlightenment, and also the Arminian and Socinian trends of his day, with their claim that human works cooperated with grace in the process of justification. He made these points through a version of ancient theology that gave an ironic twist to that tradition, putting it to the service of a high Calvinist rejection of any knowledge of God apart from grace and revelation. This was certainly a different reading of the ancient theology from that which had put it to syncretistic and universalizing uses, but, as already seen, it was consonant with other Protestant versions of it and a shift of emphasis to a conclusion that had lain within the bosom of ancient theology all along. Many of the modern histories of the tradition of ancient theology so emphasize its harmonizing implications that they overlook how often it really boiled down to the claim that all truth came from the Hebrews and was thus a rejection of the independence of the Gentiles' knowledge of truth, although D. P. Walker does point out that G. F. Pico, the nephew of Giovanni Pico della Mirandola, having come under the influence of Savonarola, repudiated the more optimistic version of ancient theology in favor of the view that it was basically a corruption of the seeds of truth stolen from the Jews; however, Walker treats this as a repudiation of the tradition of ancient theology rather than simply another version of the tradition, like Gale's, that emphasized the corruption of an original truth. The passing on of an ancient theology is not denied; it is only evaluated more negatively.[93] It might also be noted that with Gale's version of the ancient theology its purpose had come full circle. The ancient theology had appeared among Hellenistic Jews and the church fathers as a way of denigrating any Gentile claim to independent access to wisdom or truth about God at the same time that the pagans were pulled into service to adumbrate divine truths, including even the truth of the coming of Christ and the doctrine of the Trinity. The late medieval and Renaissance uses were different. For them it was a way of claiming the lore of antiquity for Christian attention and scholarship (which Gale managed to do too), and so the emphasis often fell upon the truths known by virtuous pagans. A central Renaissance motif in the ancient theology was syncretism, emphasizing the oneness of the divine truth among all peoples. But Gale had brought it back to the patristic starting point: the denigration of independent truth apart from divine grace and the biblical record. His version of it revealed its inner tensions and contradictions. Perhaps such tensions had long been felt: Eugenio Garin has noted the fascination that Savonarola had for erstwhile Neoplatonists whom the fiery Dominican turned from syncretism to a renewed emphasis on grace. D. P. Walker commented on this too but noted that Savonarola was not opposed to the use of philosophy to defend Christian faith; in fact, Gale included Savonarola among his predecessors in reforming Platonic philosophy.[94] The question remains, however, why so many earlier proponents of the ancient theology did not worry that the derivation of all learning from an original revelation might compromise the independent truth of so much that they sought to include within their syntheses.

Clearly, Gale's emphasis on grace in *The Court of the Gentiles* represents a significant Calvinist persistence into the second half of the seventeenth century in England. But it also involved a transformation of Calvinism, a culmination of its apologetic fusion with the ancient theology which traced back to Mornay and others. His apologetic fusion of Calvinism and the ancient theology indicates something of the difference between Gale, as a later Calvinist, and Calvin and other thinkers of the earlier Reformed tradition. Calvin, who had been partly inspired to reform by the humanist Jacques Lefevre, a proponent of ancient theology, ignored it, not because he was worried about the implications of so much truth among the pagans but because he believed in the capacity of the pagans to know some religious truths, such as the existence of God, from the creation apart from special revelation; otherwise, they could not be held accountable for their sin and idolatry.[95] Calvin had an outlook expansive enough not to require the devices of ancient theology but believed that persons had an awareness of God's existence implanted in them by nature; furthermore, as William Bouwsma says, "Respect for the religious insights of the natural man, even after the Fall, is also implicit in Calvin's belief in the superiority of Greek religion to other expressions of ancient paganism." And while Calvin did not think that such general revelation was sufficient for a saving knowledge of God apart from special revelation, he did think that the fallen human mind retained sufficient light of reason for the development of the various arts and sciences and for the proper conduct of law and civil government.[96] But Calvin's approach did mean a rejection of the notion of the proponents of ancient theology that its adepts had knowledge of such matters knowable only by revelation as the doctrine of the Trinity—one of the principal points believed to be found in the Hermetic literature. It is also noteworthy that Calvin, who had some Platonism in his outlook and favored him over Aristotle, nonetheless rejected the kind of "realistic" understanding of language taught by Gale, commenting that "it is usage rather than etymology or intrinsic meaning [*proprieta*] . . . that distinguishes one word from another."[97] Different from Calvin, Gale and some of his fellow Calvinists such as Mornay and Owen defended Reformed theology by means of a historical scheme shaped to exalt divine grace. Such an exaltation of grace was, after all, the persistence of a prime desideratum of Calvin and Reformed theology; but it was also a transformative way of defending Calvinism that employed the idiom of the savants of the seventeenth-century republic of letters and a response to newer challenges that catalyzed the particular apologetic strategy of Gale against atheism, Socinian heresy, a redefined reason, and the suspicion of truths in other religions or in a primal religion independent of biblical revelation. There was also something transformative of Calvinism in the very fact that Gale's life was preoccupied with and devoted to studying and analyzing this lore, thereby encouraging its study within the Reformed heritage and opening up its pondering to a Calvinist clientele, with the possibility that others, fascinated by it as was Gale, might draw more expansive and even syncretic conclusions than he did. All those faded glimmers of truth and the literature in which they were found had their own attraction, and could open up new paths of reflection for those who entered upon them.

Not just the persistence and transformation of Calvinist expression but also its variety in the theological literature of the Restoration period is illustrated by the work of Gale. The conventional picture of the Calvinism of the Puritans or Dissenters after the Restoration portrays it as declining because of its subtle rejection by the Baxterians or through its rigid scholasticism and narrow pietism within the ingrown environment of the conventicle. The aspects of Restoration Calvinism that have drawn attention are the Baxterian Presbyterians, the rigid scholastics, and a bevy of spiritual writers, all of whom putatively "declined," respectively, into Unitarianism, hyper-Calvinist Antinomianism, and world-fleeing pietism. Thus the intellectual milieu of the Dissenters is seen as having little room for the traditions of Renaissance learning that were part of the education and mental equipment of pre–civil war Puritans; the transition from Milton to Bunyan would be seen in this view as typical. Gale indicates that the permutations of Calvinism among the Dissenters were more varied than often supposed. Pietism, Baxterian Latitudinarianism, and strict Calvinism tending to Antinomianism do not exhaust the English Calvinist possibilities of the Restoration era: Theophilus Gale's integrally Calvinist version of the ancient theology must rate as another variation of late seventeenth-century English Puritan thought, a variation with at least some kinship with that of Peter Sterry. Sterry synthesized an almost pantheistic mysticism with anti-Arminian Calvinism, creating a type of Reformed thought that shared some of Gale's interests but stressed quite different aspects of the ancient theology, such as Christian cabalist allegorism. If Gale illustrates Puritan Hermetism and ancient theology but never strays into Hermeticism, Sterry shows that even dabbling in the latter was possible for a Puritan. And perhaps strange to say, these esoteric and exotic elements in the intellectual life of the later seventeenth century also played into aspects of the Enlightenment, as would appear in their assimilation by Isaac Newton and early Freemasonry. Gale's version of Reformed theology, like that of Sterry, is a complex web of persistence and transformation, adding up to a distinct variety of Calvinist thought.

Perhaps parenthetically it should be noted that interest in the lore of the ancient theology to which Gale devoted so much of his life and integrated with his high Calvinism was to persist after his time and be used by others with sometimes different agendas. Gale's contemporary, the Jesuit Athanasius Kircher, wrote extensively on the ancient theology, convinced that the Egyptian hieroglyphics contained its secrets.[98] The Jesuit missionaries in China, disputing with the Dominicans over missionary strategy, found evidence of an ancient knowledge of the true God in the Confucian classics, derived, they thought, from Noah's son Shem. Shortly after 1700 the Protestant philosopher Leibnitz wrote to the Jesuit missionary Joachim Bouvet, noting that "what you tell me of the traces of the true revealed religion among the ancient Chinese, which are to be found in their characters and in their classical books, seems to be considerable." Bouvet was interested in the *I Ching*, supposed to be by a certain Fo Hi, whom Bouvet thought was perhaps none other than Hermes, whom he identified with the biblical Enoch.[99] The antiquarian clergyman William Stukeley asserted that the ancient Druids who built Stonehenge as a sacred place represented a continuation of the religion of Abraham which had come to Britain with their leader, the Tyrian Hercules, a pupil of Abraham. Gale had himself mentioned the Druids as part of the ancient "Hieroglyphic and Mystic way of philosophising."[100] The Anglican lay scholar John Hutchinson argued in a huge work entitled *Moses' Principia*, published in 1724, that all knowledge was locked away in the Hebrew Scriptures, and that he had found the key to the right interpretation of the Hebrew words and letters that would make indisputable what his predecessors had only dimly recognized. (Pico and Reuchlin had maintained not only that all knowledge went back to the Hebrews, but that it was encoded in the mystical meaning of Hebrew words and letters.) Hutchinson criticized Newton for looking for knowledge in nature rather than in the Hebrew letters. In 1757 the American Samuel Johnson, New England Puritan convert to Anglicanism and president of King's College in New York (later Columbia), announced a new direction for the curriculum of the college, based on his reading of Hutchinson. Not even the declaration of the archbishop of Canterbury, Thomas Secker, that he found the views of Hutchinson groundless, dissuaded Johnson. A Hutchinsonian influence was felt well into the nineteenth century by some American High Church Episcopalians.[101]

Finally, Gale's inquiry into the classical and Hebraic past, in which he explores the "uses" of a particular image of that past, represents a longstanding activity of western intellectuals. The past is always reconstructed selectively, and in particular, a perennial question in the West has been, what has Jerusalem to do with Athens? Because of their enormous intellectual and spiritual resonance for succeeding ages, what is thought about the classical and Hebraic pasts, their relative merits and their relationship, has often been the way that a later age had of arguing about its concerns—witness Matthew Arnold on the Greek and Hebrew elements in culture. Frank E. Manuel has shown how the age of Enlightenment pitted the classical against the Christian: "absorption with pagan artifacts was driving out the Christian word." Frank M. Turner in *The Greek Heritage in Victorian Britain* argues that many concerns of that time were cast into discussions and debates about the classical world.[102] Sigmund Freud used the interplay of Greek myth and biblical story to disclose the secrets of the human psyche. In the early twentieth century, Protestant neoorthodoxy tried to reclaim a biblical-Hebraic theology that was free of Hellenic intrusions. Do not discussions over harmony and conflict between the Hellenic and Hebraic still persist as an idiom through which pressing issues are discussed?

4

Joseph Alleine

Evangelical Calvinism

In George Eliot's novel *Felix Holt,* set at the time of the Reform Bill
of 1832, Lyddy, elderly housekeeper for the dissenting minister Rufus
Lyon, weeps when she prepares breakfast. "O Lyddy, Lyddy," says the
minister's stepdaughter, "The eggs are hard again. I wish you would
not read Alleine's *Alarm* before breakfast; it makes you cry and forget
the eggs." Lyddy replies, "They are hard, and that's the truth; but
there's hearts as are harder, Miss Esther."[1] At about the same time as
the setting for this story, the Victorian Baptist preacher Charles
Haddon Spurgeon as a boy listened to his mother read Alleine's
Alarm to the family on Sunday evenings.[2] Almost one hundred years
earlier David Brainerd in New England, whose story was to inspire
evangelical missions, noted in his diary that he was "refreshed and
invigorated" by reading Joseph Alleine, and then able "to pray with
some ardour of soul."[3]

It is the purpose of this chapter to show that Joseph Alleine's
brief life and few published writings both inspired and provided an
opportunity for a group of like-minded English Dissenters to launch
an effort to evangelize their nation with a program of spreading
conversion and holiness. Thus while this chapter is about Joseph
Alleine, it is also about the uses to which he was put by a circle of
those who treasured his memory and writings. These Dissenters
were no longer part of the established church, but they did not give
up on their ideal of deepening the Christian faith of their land, and in
the process they helped shape a distinct variety of Calvinism that

deserves the appellation "evangelical Calvinism" and was a significant step on the road to the later evangelical revivals. Their evangelical Calvinism was rooted in earlier English Puritan piety, aspects of which we have seen in the devotional works of Gale and the mysticism of Sterry (both of whom used the same image of awakening the mistakenly secure that appears in Alleine's title),[4] and represented the persistence of that tradition but also furthered its transformation. This evangelical Calvinism was a response to the challenges of the later seventeenth century that have been discussed already as ingredients of a dawning Enlightenment, but in this regard it was more of an end run around the proponents of a new rationality than a direct confrontation of it. And as in the later evangelical revivals this was less a conscious strategy than a vague and unspoken awareness that those deeply moved by an interior and personal religiosity would be inoculated against the dangerous viruses of a new intellectual world— though verbalized on at least one occasion by Richard Baxter.[5]

Publishing Alleine's *Alarm*

Perhaps no classic of Puritan and dissenting Calvinist piety other than *Pilgrim's Progress* has had more enduring popularity than Joseph Alleine's *An Alarme to Unconverted Sinners*, first published posthumously in 1671 and continuously in print ever since. Sometimes published under other titles, it was familiarly known as "Alleine's *Alarm*." It was reprinted under the original title in 1671, 1672, 1673, 1675, 1678, 1691, 1695, and 1696. It was printed under the title *A Sure Guide to Heaven* in 1688, 1689, 1691, 1696, 1700, and 1704. Edmund Calamy the younger, annalist of late seventeenth-century Dissent, claimed in 1702 that fifty thousand copies were sold under this title, thirty thousand "at one impression," adding that "no book in the English tongue (the Bible only excepted) can equal it for the number that hath been dispersed."[6] With the title *A True Way to Happiness*, it was reprinted in 1675 and 1678. Many of these printings, including the earliest ones, included as a second part *Divers Practical Cases of Conscience Satisfactorily Resolved;* this appeared with it as late as 1822. There were at least eighteen printings during the eighteenth century, including one printed in Philadelphia by Benjamin Franklin in 1741 and two in Boston, Massachusetts. At the end of the century, it came out with yet another title, *An Earnest Invitation* (1798).

The evangelical awakenings of the eighteenth century stimulated its reprinting. George Whitfield claimed to have been "much benefited" by it,[7] and John Wesley included a version of it in his Christian Library.[8] Methodist publishing houses reprinted Wesley's version several times, perhaps the last by the Southern Methodist Publishing House in 1920.

There were numerous nineteenth-century editions, some of them abridged and modernized, sponsored by such groups as the Religious Tract Society of London, the American Tract Society (as part of its "Evangelical Family Library)," the American Sunday School Union, and the Presbyterian Board of Publications. The geographical spread of its publication in the United States was wide: besides Philadelphia and New York, it was printed in Elizabeth, New Jersey; Charlestown, Massachusetts; Hanover, New Hampshire; and Newark, New Jersey. In the United States, it became common to print it in the same volume as Richard Baxter's *A Call to the Unconverted*. This was the case in printings of 1812, 1813, 1815, 1818, 1826, 1828, 1836, and 1855, which came out under the title *Solemn Warnings of the Dead or An Admonition to Unconverted Sinners*. Its pairing with Baxter's book was appropriate; it had been published in 1658, earlier than Alleine's *Alarm* and the latter probably drew inspiration from it. Baxter's *Call* was the only other title of this sort to match Alleine's *Alarm* in popularity.[9]

There have also been twentieth-century editions, the Banner of Truth Trust in London printing it in 1959 and then again in paperback in 1964 and 1967. Twentieth-century reprints in the United States have been in Grand Rapids, Michigan; Evansville, Illinois; Wilmington, Delaware; and Mobile, Alabama. In 2008 there were at least three versions of it in print. A cassette tape and Internet versions of it are also available.

Needless to say it has often been translated. Its first translation was in Welsh in 1693, reprinted in 1766, 1778, 1781, 1802, and 1812. It played a role in the Welsh revival sparked by Griffith Jones.[10] A translation of it into Scottish Gaelic was published in 1807 and again in 1822. There was a Dutch translation in 1717, a Greek translation in 1841, and a German translation in 1850. More recently it has appeared in a Korean translation, printed in 1974 and again in 1991.

The Life and Writings of Joseph Alleine

Joseph Alleine, however, had been relatively unknown before his untimely death in 1668 at the age of thirty-four. Joseph was born in 1634 in Devizes, Wiltshire (baptized April 8, 1634), where his father Tobie was a prosperous tradesman; his mother was Elizabeth Northie. He was the fourth child in a large family. His elder brother Edward had entered the clergy but died at twenty-seven years of age in 1645. His earliest education was in the Wiltshire village of Poulshot under William Spinage, who had been a fellow of Exeter College, Oxford, before his ejection as rector of Poulshot in 1662, an indication of his dissenting sympathies. Thus Joseph's education began with one of the "godly" and continued at Interregnum Oxford, where he entered Lincoln College in 1649. In November

1651 he switched to Corpus Christi and there received the B.A. in 1653. That same year he turned down a fellowship in order to take the post of chaplain to the college, a choice that surprised the ambitious but was in keeping with Joseph's reputation for strict devotion and long extemporaneous prayers.

In 1655 he moved to Taunton in Somerset, where he served as assistant to George Newton, vicar of the church of St. Mary Magdalene. He received Presbyterian ordination from the Somerset classis and on December 10, 1657, was named an assistant to the Somerset commissioners for the examination of the qualifications of the clergy and removing the unfit. In 1655 he married Theodosia Alleine, daughter of Richard Alleine, minister and author of many works of Puritan devotion. She was in all likelihood Joseph's cousin. In Taunton, he ministered harmoniously alongside of Newton with great success.

This period of peaceful ministry was threatened with the restoration of Charles II in 1660 and ended in 1662 when both Newton and Joseph Alleine were ejected for their refusal to submit to the Act of Uniformity. According to a letter to his wife, Joseph was offered preferment in the Church of England if he would conform but could not in conscience do so.[11] Alleine was unwilling to forgo unlicensed preaching in and around Taunton, even if illegal, and thus was indicted on July 14, 1663, for violation of the Act of Uniformity and sentenced to a fine of one hundred marks and imprisonment until he paid it. He was imprisoned in the jail at Ilchester, where he debated imprisoned Quakers, led other fellow prisoners in worship, and wrote endearing homiletic letters to his erstwhile flock. Released in May 1664, he was arrested again in 1665 and returned to imprisonment in Ilchester. In failing health, he was released and went first to the "waters" at Devizes, where he had been born, and then to Dorchester, where he stayed at the home of a Mrs. Bartlett, and consulted the "godly physician" Frederick Loss. Sent repeatedly to the waters at Bath, he languished through convulsions and bouts of paralysis until his death on November 17, 1668. While ill at Bath, he continued his evangelical witness. He was buried in the chancel of St. Mary Magdalene, Taunton, according to his wish.[12]

Joseph Alleine published little before his death and nothing that would have predicted his later popularity as an author. One fruit of his authorial labors was a Latin treatise on "natural theology," as Richard Baxter described it, of which the whole title was *Theologia Philosophica*. According to Baxter, who praised it highly, it consisted of sections on the knowledge, existence, attributes, perfections, decrees, providence, and worship of God. For every "Sheet or two of his doctrine on the Subject," Baxter said, there were eight or ten sheets by way of the testimony of ancient philosophers, so that the whole was "the fullest Attestation of Ethnicks consent that ever I have seen." Apparently, Joseph Alleine had collected numerous quotations in Greek and Latin from the ancients (including Plato, Aristotle, Iamblichus, Epictetus, Cicero, Seneca, and Plutarch) that demonstrated their consent to the principles of natural religion and found their completion in biblical revelation. However, Baxter added, only one part of it was in finished condition, that on divine providence, which, completed in 1661, had been licensed for publication but never printed because of the prohibitive cost and unlikelihood of sufficient sales. But the manuscript has not survived.[13] There are a few echoes of this interest in natural theology in his later works.[14]

Joseph Alleine did get into print with a very brief work in 1664, *A Call to Archippus: or An humble and earnest Motion to some Ejected Ministers, (by way of Letter) To take heed to their Ministry, That they Fulfill it.* Archippus, exhorted at the end of the New Testament letter to the *Colossians* (4:17) to "take heed to the ministry which thou hast received in the Lord, that thou fulfill it" (King James Version), served for Joseph Alleine as a warning to those who considered abandonment of their ministry because of persecution. Obviously addressing the ministers ejected between 1660 and 1662, Alleine reminds them of the "the sighs and groans" of their "helpless Flocks." Acknowledging his reverence for the "Gifts and Graces" of these "Fathers and Brothers" (Joseph was thirty years old, junior to most of those whom he was addressing), he nonetheless reminds them of their public promises to do the work of the ministry regardless of the cost: would Paul have deserted his post? Are not their flocks now defenseless before ravening wolves? Alleine further reminded these delinquent brethren that the Lord had appointed them to be prophets.[15] A profusion of other metaphors and tropes follows: protecting the ark of the Lord, having bowels of compassion, feeding others in time of famine, saving believers from Pharisees and seducers. His characterization of the conformist clergy was harsh—they are blind guides, "Spiteful Shepherds." If gospel ministers do not remain steadfast to their duty, they will be replaced by idle and ignorant ministers. Furthermore, how better can one silence slanderous tongues than by preaching in spite of the risk of punishment.[16]

Alleine's fiery tract takes a more dangerous turn when he addresses the question of the ejected ministers and the authority of the magistracy. He declared that the relation of pastor and congregation is not authorized by civil power but is a commission from Christ, and none but Christ can discharge a minister from that office. Thus the relationship is not based on a power "merely Political"; on the judgment day, if asked why one did not preach the gospel, it will not be adequate to respond, "Lord . . . the Magistrate did forbid us."[17] Alleine was also on dangerous ground when he suggested how the prohibitions of the magistracy might be evaded: write out a sermon and send it to those who will make copies and convey them "from hand to hand."[18]

In addition to this contentious tract, Joseph Alleine might also have been known to readers of pious works as the author of several insertions printed in the midst of a treatise by his father-in-law Richard Alleine. One of these insertions, "A Form of Words expressing mans Covenanting with God," appeared in his father-in-law's *Vindiciae Pietatis, or a Vindication of Godliness,* first published in 1660. By 1666, however, it had been moved to near the end of Richard Alleine's *Heaven Opened,* which came out as the third part of *Vindiciae Pietatis.* This five-page "Form of words" is presented as a model for declaring one's willingness to enter into the covenant of grace.[19]

Two further compositions by Joseph Alleine were inserted into Richard Alleine's *Heaven Opened,* where they are chapters 17 and 18, and identified as "by another hand," that of Joseph.[20] Chapter 17 is entitled "God speaking from Mount Gerizim. Or, the Gospel in a Map; being a short view of the exceeding great and precious promises"; chapter 18 bears the title "A Soliloquie, Representing the Believers Triumph in God's Covenant: and the various Conflicts and glorious Conquests of Faith over Unbelief." These two chapters of thirty-six and twenty-one pages respectively represent God speaking and then the soul soliloquizing in response to the divine speech. Both chapters consist of a pastiche of scriptural references and phrases (mostly identified in crammed margins) out of which tumble a profusion of biblical images, metaphors, and allusions, many strikingly vivid. Both God's speech (which chapter 17 can claim to be since it is made up almost wholly of biblical words of God spoken through prophets) and the human soliloquy (drawn extensively from biblical persons crying out to God) are rhetorical and hortatory rather than argumentative. The tone is emotional and sometimes ecstatic, as image is piled upon image to present God's amazing grace in the covenant and to plead for sinners to respond, and as the soliloquizing human voice stands in awe and astonishment at this grace, scarcely able to believe it. The soliloquy expresses surprise that God could forgive one so vile. Clearly, what Joseph added to his father-in-law's treatise, itself a rather logically organized discussion of the covenant, is a paean to the graciousness of God's forgiveness.[21] His interest in the covenant was not in the intricacies of covenantal distinctions, but in the covenant as a "promise" of forgiving and sanctifying grace for believers, as God says, "My design is to make you partakers of my Holiness."[22] But there is an echo of Joseph Alleine's prison experiences when he portrayed the voice of God assuring those who responded to the covenant that "no Prison shall hinder the presence of my grace from you. My presence shall perfume the noisomest Wards, and lighten the darkest Dungeon."[23] The themes and even some phrases in these chapters reappeared in Joseph's later writings.

Joseph Alleine had died in 1668, but between 1671 and 1674, a series of works by and about him were published and thereby made accessible to devout readers and religious seekers. The many printings of his *Alarm to the Unconverted*, which under various titles became such a popular work, began in 1671. The work itself is exactly what its title declares it to be, a book intended to awaken sinners to their need for conversion and an explanation of what is involved in such conversion. It is divided into seven parts, which consider "What Conversion is not," mistakes about it, "What Conversion is," its necessity, the marks and miseries of the unconverted, "Directions for Conversion," and "Motives to Conversion."

A treatise by Joseph Alleine entitled *Divers Practical Cases of Conscience Satisfactorily Resolved* appeared in 1672, and although sometimes printed separately thereafter, it was frequently printed as an addendum to *An Alarm*. An example of the literature of spiritual casuistry produced by those of Puritan and dissenting views, this work did not inquire into moral questions but into quandaries and puzzlements of the spiritual life, especially those related to gaining assurance of salvation and finding signs of God's grace. Alleine's "cases" were four in number: what must Christians do more than others in their obedience to God? What must a Christian be and do to please God? Whether one can match the example of Christ in pleasing God? And what slackness in religious duties may be compatible with having truly received God's grace?

In 1671, the same year as the *Alarm*, *The Life and Death of that Excellent Minister of Christ Mr. Joseph Alleine, Late Teacher of the Church of Taunton in Somersetshire; Assistant to Mr. Newton* was published. It was not uncommon for volumes commemorating beloved preachers to be published following their deaths; they typically included the funeral sermon and a sketch, more or less brief, of the life of the deceased, or at least a description of his ministry. This volume however had a number of sections: it began with an introduction by Richard Baxter, which in general praised the custom of memorializing worthy ministers and in particular the great virtues and labors of Joseph Alleine. Eight more chapters followed Baxter's introduction, which was designated the first chapter. The second was an account of Joseph Alleine's early life and university years, "written by an eye-witness thereof." The next is a description of his character and qualifications for ministry, written by his father-in-law, Richard Alleine. Chapter 4 was an account of his ministry and his godly life, from George Newton, whose ministry at Taunton Joseph had assisted. Two of the anonymous chapters (probably 5 and 8) are said to have been by "two Conformable Ministers of very great sincerity and abilities, who were long and intimately acquainted" with him—included to assure readers "that Faction and Partiality are not the Authors of this history," since these persons had accepted the

Act of Uniformity. These chapters attested to Joseph's holiness and the excellence of his ministry. Another chapter, the longest, is a narrative of his later life by his widow Theodosia Alleine "in her own words"—there is a note following the table of contents that informs the reader that she sent her text to a "worthy Divine" not imagining it would be published in her own words, but upon perusal by several persons, it was concluded that it should be printed as it was. Other chapters are "Some Notes by another, whose House he lodged in," and additional testimony to his character, "by his intimate Friend Mr. Richard Fairclough."[24]

In 1672 A Sermon Preached at the Funeral of Mr. Joseph Alleine, by George Newton, was published; this was added to three of the four reprintings in that year of The Life and Death of that Excellent Minister of Christ, Mr. Joseph Alleine. The funeral sermon was reprinted alone in 1673, 1677, and 1693.

Beginning with the first 1672 printing of The Life and Death of that Excellent Minister of Christ, Mr. Joseph Alleine, letters written by Joseph Alleine, mostly from prison to his former parishioners, appeared as an addition to the volume, with their own title page and pagination. The next year, 1673, an edition of the letters, under the same title by which they were appended to the memorial volume, Christian Letters Full of Spiritual Instructions, Tending to the Promoting of the Power of Godliness, both in Persons, and Families came out separately. These letters have echoes of the Pauline epistles in their salutations, their references to Alleine as an ambassador of Christ, and their frequent mention of his being a prisoner in bonds on behalf of his flock.[25]

Richard Baxter referred to a work published during Joseph Alleine's lifetime that was "an Exposition of the Assemblies Catechism," but if so, no copy printed that early has survived. So far as the Short-Title Catalogue of Books Printed 1641–1700 is concerned this was first printed in 1672, as part of the same explosion of the printing of books by and about Joseph Alleine enumerated here. The title encapsulates its contents: A Most Familiar Explanation of the Assemblies Shorter Catechism. Wherein their Larger Answers are broken into Lesser Parcels, thereby to let in the light, by degrees, into the minds of the Learners. To which is added, in the close, a most brief help for the necessary, but much neglected duty of self-examination, to be daily perused. And to this is subjoined, a Letter of Christian Counsel, to a destitute Flock. This was reprinted in 1674, 1682, 1690, and 1700, the last in Belfast, Ireland. The catechism explained was the Shorter Catechism of the Westminster Assembly. The explanation took the form of subquestions to the catechism's questions and runs for 160 pages. The questions and directions for self-examination take up a mere 4 pages and consist of questions to be asked in the evening before bed (e.g., "Wherein have I denied myself this day for God?") and directions for the morning (e.g., "Examine whether God were last in your thoughts when you went to sleep; and first, when you awoke?).[26] These pages on self-examination also appeared in *The Life and Death of Joseph Alleine*. The appended letter is another of his missives to his former flock in Taunton, presumably omitted from the earlier collection of letters. The prefatory "An Admonition to the Readers" bears all the marks of being by Joseph Alleine and is directed to his congregation so that they may continue catechizing while he is undergoing "tribulations for your sakes."[27] If not printed earlier, as Baxter thought, it must have been intended for publication by Joseph and might have failed to get the requisite permission, or simply was not considered by him to have been ready for publication. Nonetheless, the work might have been copied and used in manuscript form, not only by Joseph himself, but by others of his circle of associates, and only printed after his death along with his other works.

Last among these publications by or about Joseph Alleine was *Remaines of That Excellent Minister of Jesus Christ, Mr. Joseph Alleine. Being A Collection of Sundry Directions, Sermons, Sacrament-Speeches, and Letters, not heretofore Published. All Tending to promote Real Piety.* Printed in 1674, it went through no further printings. An introductory epistle by Richard Alleine declared that the Publisher collected these fragmentary remains, "it being pity they should be lost." He further added that all of them were assuredly the work of Joseph, some in his handwriting and others notes "taken from his mouth as he preached." Richard assured readers that they all reflected the same "divine and warm spirit" present in his other writings.[28] The contents are more miscellaneous than the other volumes, but among twenty distinct items, seven are "sacramental speeches" on biblical texts, several others are sermons, yet others are brief treatises on "The Art of dying well" and "self-examination," and in addition there are "A discourse made by Mr. Joseph Alleine, unto his people at Taunton, the night before his departure from them," "A Letter sent by him to an intimate friend," and "A serious call to Christians to win Souls to Christ."

Formation of a Circle Promoting Alleine's Piety

All these publications in two years suggests that a group of relatives, friends, and well-wishers had joined together to bring the life and writings of Joseph Alleine to wider attention. This was not uncommon after the deaths of major Puritan preachers, especially if they left materials in manuscript. In the seventeenth century, many manuscripts and their copies circulated among interested parties which were either not yet ready for printing or not thought significant enough for it, and there was often a good deal of manuscript material left behind by preachers. In Joseph Alleine's case, however, he had not published enough to have a wide following and he was still young enough that his reputation was mainly local. And yet he had been surrounded by a group of persons greatly impressed by his piety, preaching, and spiritual directions. Examination of the members of this circle and reflection on their purposes provide context for this publishing outburst.

Foremost among the circle was Richard Alleine, Joseph's father-in-law, in whose writings several products of Joseph's pen had been inserted, perhaps not only as a result of their merit but also as a way of introducing Joseph to the wider reading public of the godly. Richard had been born in Ditcheat, Somerset, where his father was rector, and according to Edmund Calamy, had been in trouble with his bishop, presumably for nonconformity. Richard was at St. Alban's Hall, Oxford, when he received the B.A. in 1631 and at New Inn Hall, Oxford, when he was granted the M.A. in 1634. That same year he was ordained and the year after licensed to preach. He probably assisted his father in Ditcheat for a period of time and also preached in nearby places. He briefly served as a chaplain to Sir Ralph Hopton, who, however, with the outbreak of civil war became an officer in the King's army. In 1642 Richard was installed as Rector in Batcombe, Somerset, after the death of longtime incumbent Richard Bernard. Bernard was a noted preacher of Puritan sympathies so that Richard presumably came to a parish ready for someone of his outlook. A notation of April 8, 1642, in the cathedral library at Wells named Richard Alleine along with two others as involved in breaking a window in the cathedral that they considered idolatrous. Anthony Wood reported him as several times harassed by royalist troops in the area. In 1648, at a time of alarm over sectarian extremism, he added his name to those of many other ministers on *The Attestation of the Ministers of the County of Somerset . . . Against the Errors, Heresies, and Blasphemies of the Present Times.* In 1654 he assisted the Somerset commissioners who worked at the task of removing unworthy (usually royalist) clergy. He was much beloved by his parishioners but refused to subscribe the Act of Uniformity at the Restoration so that he lost his position at Batcombe, though he remained there preaching for a while before settling elsewhere in Somerset. Several times threatened with imprisonment, he was once summoned to the sessions and "Soundly rated for Conventicling." In 1672 he was licensed to preach at Beckington as a Presbyterian under the terms of the Declaration of Indulgence. At the time of his death in 1681 he was living at the house of Robert Smith in Frome Selwood, Somerset, and reportedly had been keeping an illegal meeting there. His funeral sermon was by the conformist vicar of Frome Selwood, Richard Jenkins, according to the hostile Anthony Wood a "lukewarm conformist," who provided "pathetical encomiums." Jenkins had frequently visited

Richard during his last illness, an example of the permeability of the line between some conformists and moderate Dissenters noted in the first chapter.[29]

In a brief publication of 1661, Richard Alleine entered anonymously into the post-Restoration controversy over church government by defending Presbyterian ordination, and in it made many of the points later affirmed by Joseph Alleine in his *A Call to Archippus,* showing the extent to which the younger man was taking cues from his father-in-law. Entitled *Cheirothesia tou Presbuterou, or a Letter to a Friend,* this open letter began by declaring that until recently the "Reformed Churches" on the continent and the clergy of the Church of England agreed that Presbyterian ordination was valid. Therefore, he warned his brethren against re-ordination, since it implied that their previous ordination was "a meer nullity"—bishops and presbyters were not separate orders requiring the ordination of the latter by the former. Ordination was no more to be repeated than was baptism: corrupt as was the Church of Rome, English Protestants at the Reformation accepted even its ordination as valid. He noted that Archbishop of Canterbury Richard Bancroft had accepted the validity of ordination by presbyters in Scotland and Lancelot Andrewes had agreed. The ancient church fathers, Richard Alleine continued, also accepted ordination by presbyters as valid, Archbishop Thomas Cranmer agreeing with Jerome that presbyters and bishops had been one office in ancient times. He even cited Pope Damasus I in support of this view! Christ had appointed neither presbyters nor bishops, but apostles, who were "unfixed officers." This brief treatise cited contemporary scholarship, including that of John Lightfoot, John Selden, and Hugo Grotius, concluding that those who boasted of antiquity for their position knew little about the ancient church. Appended to it was a refutation of a recent treatise on re-ordination by a certain John Humfrey.[30]

Besides this work, everything else written by Richard Alleine exemplified that kind of spiritual writing and "affectionate divinity" for which so many Puritan preachers were known. His major work was the three part *Vindiciae Pietatis.* His intent to vindicate piety in an increasingly worldly age was a likely influence on the younger Joseph. In addition to this, Richard Alleine authored *The Best of Remedies for a plague-sick, Sinfull Soul* (1667), *Godly Fear* (1674), *A Rebuke to Backsliders, and a Spurr for Loyterers* (1677), *The World Conquered* (1676), *A Companion for Prayer* (1680), and *Instructions about heart-work* (1681). *Vindiciae Pietatis* as a whole of three parts and in its separate parts went through several printings. Many themes of these works of affectionate divinity appeared also in the writings of Joseph but were also commonplaces of Puritan affectionate divinity.

Richard Alleine was in all likelihood distantly related to Joseph, in which case their connection could have begun earlier than when Joseph married his daughter Theodosia; but in any case it was after that marriage that Richard and Joseph were connected to each other by a common publication and brought together in Somerset. Theodosia Alleine has to be regarded as another member of the circle that brought out Joseph's posthumous writings, especially since she was the author of a contribution to *The Life and Death of that Excellent Minister of Christ, Mr. Joseph Alleine*. But apart from what Theodosia Alleine tells us about her life with Joseph, we know little about her. As Richard Alleine's daughter, she would have grown up in the midst of fervent piety, helping to fit her for marriage with Joseph. They had no children, but she was busy with teaching a school that had fifty or sixty pupils, mostly from Taunton, and some from other places nearby. Many of these (twenty or thirty she claimed) were "tablers," who boarded at their house. She described herself as "having been always bred to work," and also supported her husband in his pastoral labors. As already noted, she was well-enough educated that her part for the memorial volume for her husband was printed exactly as she had written it. Anthony Wood, who slandered Joseph Alleine as "in actions busy, forward, (if not pragmatical) and meddling" also slandered Theodosia Alleine as having used "women's tricks" to entice Joseph and claimed that after his death, being of a "salacious humour," she married again. She did remarry, but to a godly widower who was a constable at Taunton. Wood also reported her as having died prior to Monmouth's rebellion in 1685.[31] The partisan Wood found the fact that a woman had written part of the story of Joseph Alleine a convenient handle for attacking the whole enterprise. Wood called *The Life and Death of Alleine* "a canting farce," and singled out Theodosia Alleine's part in it as especially "ridiculous."[32]

George Newton was also a member of this circle of friends and associates of Joseph Alleine. Newton had taken him under his wing as an assistant at St. Mary Magdalene, Taunton, and preached his funeral sermon. A Devonshire native, born in 1602 and educated at Exeter College, Oxford, Newton became vicar of St. Mary Magdalene, Taunton (Somerset) in 1631. When Joseph Alleine joined him in 1655, Newton was firmly ensconced there and had lived through the troubled years of Laudian ascendancy and civil war. It was reported of Newton that when in 1633 the clergy were once again ordered to read the "Book of Sports," which encouraged athletic endeavor on Sunday, Newton followed its reading with that of the Ten Commandments. Some from his congregation left for New England in 1636. In 1654 he was appointed by Parliament as one of the assistants to the commissioners for the removing of scandalous and ignorant clergy. Refusing subscription to the Act of Uniformity, he was ejected from his Taunton post in 1662. He occasionally preached illegally thereafter and was imprisoned for several years as a consequence. In 1672 he was licensed to preach as a Presbyterian in Taunton, under the terms of the Declaration of

Indulgence. After his death in 1681, he was buried in the chancel of St. Mary Magdalene.[33] Several of his sermons were published in 1660, as well as *An Exposition with Notes, Unfolded and Appllyed on John 17th*. This consisted of 564 pages of sermons he had preached on that one chapter to his Taunton congregation, exemplifying the expository form of affectionate divinity in which the "godly" delighted.

Richard Fairclough (1621–1682), like his father Samuel Fairclough, who had a notable career of preaching and pastoral work from as early as 1619, was another of the ejected ministers of 1662 who could not comply with the Act of Uniformity. Educated at Emmanuel College, Cambridge, long a Puritan stronghold, Richard Fairclough became rector of Mells, Somerset, in 1647, as a result of his impressive preaching. At Mells he was near Richard Alleine at Frome. In 1663, the year after his ejection, he published the summary of fourteen farewell sermons preached to his erstwhile parish at Mells, in which he told them that though he believed he had been designed by God from all eternity to be their pastor, to "keep a good conscience" he had to refuse conformity, fearing the wrath of God more than that of men. After ejection he spent some time in Essex and London, before removing to Bristol. He was probably located at Bristol when Joseph was at Bath, for in that last year of Joseph's life he often visited and conferred with him there. He was in London in 1672, when he was licensed to preach as a Presbyterian. He died in 1682, and his funeral sermon was preached by John Howe. Howe is mentioned by Theodosia Alleine as occasionally present with Fairclough and Joseph at Bath. Several other sermons of Fairclough were also published.[34]

John Norman (1622–1669), born in Devonshire, was educated at Exeter College, Oxford, while the godly disciplinarian John Conant headed that college, graduating with a B.A. in 1641. At Oxford he and Joseph Alleine were close friends, but they were also brothers-in-law, as Norman's first wife was Joseph's sister Elizabeth. In 1647 Norman became vicar of Bridgewater, only ten kilometers from Taunton, and it was from that parish that he was ejected in 1662. John Norman was imprisoned at Ilchester at the same time as Joseph, and in some of his prison letters Joseph sends greetings from "brother Norman." That they remained close friends is apparent from a surviving piece of correspondence between them, in which Joseph refers to himself as "Orestes" and Norman as "Pylades," who were close friends in Greek story, Pylades having married the sister of his friend. This letter, written a little more than a month before Joseph's death, is a protestation of his love for John Norman, and sorrow that they have not been able recently to see each other.[35]

Certain characteristics bound this group together. Obviously, they all were descended from the earlier Puritan and nonconformist movements and shared a Calvinistic theology with their predecessors. They were all sympathetic to the parliamentary cause in the civil wars and accepted or continued positions in the Cromwellian church. They had accordingly been ejected after the Restoration, although there were several unnamed conformists who sympathized with them, as attested by their contributions to *The Life and Death of that Excellent Minister of Christ, Mr. Joseph Alleine,* or by the conformist minister Richard Jenkins who ministered to Richard Alleine in his last days. All had engaged in illegal preaching after the Restoration, and Joseph Alleine, John Norman, and George Newton had all suffered periods of imprisonment because of it. Richard Alleine, George Newton, and Richard Fairclough had registered as Presbyterians in 1672, under the terms of the Declaration of Indulgence (Joseph and Norman died before 1672). Richard and Joseph Alleine had both written in defense of Presbyterian ordination. The group seemed to have misgivings about Independency or Congregationalism.[36] They also shared proximity, being distinctly a group connected to Somerset, with Taunton as their center.

These characteristics of the Somerset group, apart from proximity, were also shared with a wider circle including more prominent Dissenters than Joseph's immediate acquaintances. The wider group included Richard Baxter, John Howe, Nathaniel Vincent, and Samuel Annesley, with Baxter emerging as a prominent leader. Besides working in common in the publication of materials by and about Joseph Alleine, there had been and were later contacts among them. Howe had been friendly with Joseph Alleine at Bath and perhaps elsewhere in the southwest, as Howe spent most of the 1660s after his ejection in that region. After Richard Fairclough went up to London, he associated with this group: he preached in a lecture series associated with Nathaniel Vincent and Samuel Annesley,[37] and his funeral sermon was preached by John Howe, according to a request in Fairclough's will.[38] Baxter's extensive correspondence involved many of them, and he was in contact with Theodosia Alleine after Joseph's death.[39]

The central focus of both the Somerset circle and the wider group best typified by Richard Baxter was on the preaching of conversion and the cultivation of the spiritual life, as attested by the witness of their statements and the nature of their writings. In this respect they were the descendants of those earlier Puritans whom William Haller designated a brotherhood of preachers, such as Richard Greenham, Arthur Hildersham, John Dod, and Richard Sibbes.[40] Baxter's introductory epistle in the memorial volume continually returns to the theme of conversion; other contributors to the volume echoed this; and it was the subject of Baxter's own most frequently reprinted work, *A Call to Conversion.*[41] It was because of Joseph's focus on conversion and the spiritual life that they converged in bringing out publications by and about him.

Baxter is well known for seeking unity on a few fundamental doctrines related to piety, cultivating the pastoral task, and disavowing controversy (although continually embroiled it!).[42] A clear statement of the focus of this group is evident in the remark of Richard Alleine in his *A Letter to a Friend,* where, almost apologizing for being controversial, he declared that:

> For the author, thou art entreated to look upon him, as one who loves
> not to see his face in troubled waters, but would gladly spend his All
> upon those fundamental practical truths, in which all sincere
> Christians are agreed, having sadly observed all along this disgusting
> age, that the best of men in handling Controversies, have discovered
> more corruption in themselves, than mistakes in their adversaries.[43]

Elsewhere Richard Alleine commented that by stirring up religion he does not mean "hot and mistaken Zeal about the lower and more uncertain things of Religion," nor "headiness, and fierceness, and hot censoriousness" over religion.[44] Similar statements can be found in the writings of the other members of these circles: Howe in his funeral sermon for Richard Fairclough, for example, said that Fairclough "declined controversy."[45] This too is how they wanted to present Joseph Alleine.

This group is commonly designated as Presbyterian, but this does not mean that they were committed in a doctrinaire fashion to a strictly Presbyterian system of church government on the Scottish model, but, as already seen in chapter 1, that they were moderate English Puritans who did not object to an established church and a "reduced episcopacy" but would not deny the validity of ordination by presbyters. Joseph and Richard Alleine had defended ordination by presbyters and they and others participated in associations but did not demand the establishment of a full Presbyterian system. Baxter also participated in an association and made several attempts to bring moderate Dissenters and conformists together.[46] Such "Presbyterians" had friends and connections within the established church and worked cooperatively with them. They also had connections with the dissenting Independents, with whom they shared much—this was another porous boundary.

These "Presbyterians," both in Somerset and in the Baxter circle, were also moderate Calvinists who had misgivings about the high Calvinist doctrines favored by many earlier Puritans and later dissenting Independents. Differences on these matters kept Baxter and John Owen at arm's length from one another and caused the breakup of Presbyterian-Independent unity over their "common fund."[47] The issue of Antinomianism was prominent in that controversy, and the moderate Calvinist Presbyterians feared that it was something to which high Calvinism led. In his farewell sermons of 1663, Richard Fairclough warned his congregation against both Arminian and Antinomian teachings, staking out a middle ground where moderate Calvinists felt comfortable.[48] Baxter spent much of his career excoriating Antinomianism. These Presbyterians tried to keep theological as well as ecclesiological niceties from getting in the way of the primary task of laboring for the conversion and edification of souls.

The contributions of both the Somerset circle and the wider circle of Baxterians to the posthumously published writings of Joseph Alleine are clear. Richard Alleine wrote introductory epistles for *An Alarme* and the *Remaines,* and also "A brief Character of him" for *The Life and Death.* George Newton wrote an account of his ministry and "godly life" for the same volume, as well as the funeral sermon for Joseph. Richard Fairclough also added a chapter to *The Life and Death.* John Norman died shortly after Joseph so that while he may have helped shape the Somerset circle's thinking about Joseph, he had no direct hand in getting out the Joseph Alleine publications. And of course Theodosia Alleine wrote the longest of the sections in that same volume. Baxter was tapped for an introductory epistle to *The Life and Death* and also for a long introductory "Epistle to the Unconverted Reader" for *An Alarme.* Did the others seek out Baxter's support for their project of publishing Joseph Alleine, or had Baxter already heard of this promising young spiritual director who had died so untimely? Whatever the case, when a publisher was chosen for most of these texts by Joseph (except for the explanation of the catechism, published by Edward Brewster, and the *Remaines,* published by Peter Parker, who had brought out early publications of Richard Alleine), it was Nevil Simmons, who published a large number of Baxter's treatises and advertised Baxter's books in some of the Joseph Alleine volumes. In his introduction to *The Life and Death,* Baxter refers to Joseph's *Alarme* as "not yet printed," as though he knew that it was about to be, no doubt because he had written an introductory epistle for it.[49] Simmons was known as a publisher of pious works written by moderate Dissenters who had been ejected from the ministry of the Church of England.[50] Joseph himself several times mentioned Baxter in his writings, once recommending the books of Baxter and Richard Alleine and another time mentioning that Baxter had been scoffingly called a Puritan.[51]

The Portrayal of Joseph Alleine

These "Presbyterian" characteristics of ecumenicity, moderate Calvinism, and focus on piety are featured in the portrayal of Joseph in *The Life and Death of Joseph Alleine.* Richard Baxter claimed that by reading the story of lives like that of Joseph, "the factious Christian, may see that a man may be eminently Holy, that is not of his Opinion, Side, or Party" and "the proud domineering Pharisee may see, that eminent Piety is separated from his Traditions, Formalities, Ceremonies and Pomp." Further (and it is characteristic of Baxter to make an irenic point in an inflammatory manner) "the Opinionative Hypocrite" will see in Joseph's example that holiness is not a matter of "condemning of other mens outward Expressions, or Modes of Worship, or a boisterous Zeal against the Opinions and Ceremonies of others." Joseph on the other hand, Baxter continued, dwelt on "the great Essentials of Godliness and Christianity"; "Moderation and peaceableness" characterized "this holy Man," whose "Zeal was for Peace and Quietness, for Love and for good Works."[52] Baxter even defends Joseph against the insinuation that he was immoderate in wearing himself out in excessive pastoral labors.[53]

George Newton, whose pastoral assistant Joseph was, testified of him that he laid little weight on "Notions and Opinions in Religion," but would allow fellow Christians "Latitude" so long as they were sound in "the fundamentals of Religion," and "strict and holy in their lives." His moderation, Newton opines, was evident to all who knew him.[54] "Mr. G.," who contributed a chapter on Alleine's catechizing, also testified to Joseph's "peaceable Spirit," that "loathed all tumultuous carriages and preceedings," having no other design than the salvation of souls.[55] Richard Fairclough praised his "Charity and Meekness to Men of other Judgments and Perswasions."[56] Theodosia Alleine added that he was so moderate she thought he might have conformed at the Restoration, as he often said that "he would not leave his work for small and dubious Matters."[57] One of the anonymous contributors, perhaps a conformist, spoke of his moderate opinions on "Church-Communion," and the fact that he was not altogether opposed to the liturgy of the Church of England, feeling it important to maintain a general public worship. Further, it was at least three times mentioned in *The Life and Death of Joseph Alleine* that he showed great respect for magistrates and social order.[58] These claims of moderation regarding the liturgy of the Church of England and respect for magistrates are not easy to square with his fiery tract *A Call to Archippus;* however, his concern in that book was to vindicate the legitimacy of his ordination and ministry. Nonetheless one senses an effort on the part of those who were shaping the legacy of Joseph Alleine to play down some aspects of his story and emphasize other qualities more consonant with their purpose. Thus Joseph Alleine is repackaged in such a way as to minimize and neutralize the fierce dissenting spirit of that tract.

Joseph Alleine was also portrayed as a moderate Calvinist who agreed with Baxter regarding Arminianism. Baxter had been widely excoriated by high Calvinist defenders of strict orthodoxy for his compromises with Arminianism.

It was also claimed that Joseph agreed with the views of John Davenant on this matter. Davenant, a delegate to the Synod of Dort in 1618 and bishop of Salisbury, had defended predestination against Arminians but was thought by such a high Calvinist as John Owen to be unsound on the atonement, a charge also leveled against Baxter because of his Amyraldian view of that doctrine. The remark that Joseph was neither a "Solifidian" nor a legalist should be understood as testimony by his promoters to his freedom from the excesses of the Antinomians as well as of the Arminians. Neither enthusiast nor ritualist also would have been a statement designed to connect him with the Presbyterian middle ground between sectarians and Laudians.[59]

Apparently then, a group of godly Somerset clergy and their associates as well as a wider circle of "Presbyterian" Dissenters found in Joseph Alleine an ideal representative of their outlook, even if in their portrait they needed to smooth out a few rough patches: irenic though unable to conform to the Restoration Church of England, moderately Calvinist, and focused on the piety as were they, Joseph Alleine's legacy must have appeared to them as something to be presented to a larger public in the interest of promoting their ideals. Known before his death to a limited circle and having published little, Joseph Alleine had no wide following as a preacher of godliness. But he was a person greatly admired by those close to him for his excellence as a spiritual guide. They included a ministerial associate, a godly wife and father-in-law, and several bosom friends. No doubt something of his reputation had come to the attention of others whom they knew and whose views they shared, such as Richard Baxter. Joseph's life seemed worthy of memorializing and his manuscripts of publication. The same had been done for godly ministers before, with the same intention of furthering godliness. The same was to be done for others after Joseph Alleine as well, some of whom emanated from Baxter's network of association and claimed the influence of Joseph Alleine.[60] When Baxter wrote a preface for James Janeway's *Invisibles, Realities, Demonstrated in the Holy Life and Triumphant Death of Mr. John Janeway* in 1673, he noted that the story of Joseph Alleine's life had been so successful that he urged readers to examine the life of John Janeway also. Janeway, a paragon of piety, had died before even entering the ministry at all.[61]

Joseph Alleine's life story and writings must have seemed an opportunity for the furtherance of the cherished attitudes of this group about religion and the spiritual life. And thus took place the shaping of a hero of the faith in these volumes, a shaping that encapsulated and catalyzed a particular religious sensibility. It was also a point on a trajectory that was carrying an earlier evangelical Calvinist piety and thought toward later evangelical movements. It was a case of persistence yet transformation.

Defining Evangelical Calvinism

Clarification of the term "evangelical" is needed, though it is not easily defined. Evangelicalism in a broad sense can be identified with the Protestant Reformation, referring to a focus on the message of the gospel of Christ as a free offer of God's forgiving grace to those who accepted that gift in faith. This evangelicalism was shared by Lutheran and Reformed Protestants, was central in the English Reformation, and was developed in a variety of ways within the Protestant world over the several centuries following the revolt against Rome, including its development in continental European pietism.

English Calvinists, and especially those among them usually identified as Puritans, developed a particular style of piety that has given a further meaning to the word "evangelical" beyond that of the Protestant Reformation as a whole. This evangelical style became centered not just on the message of gospel forgiveness, but on its reception: the experience of conversion and growth in holiness of life, in response to the fervent proclamation of the gospel of Christ's atoning death for the salvation of sinners. Thus they spoke of the "new birth" and "holiness," and were intent on actively spreading the message. With reference particularly to the eighteenth century and after, such evangelicalism has been characterized as conversionist, Biblicist, activist, and crucicentric,[62] and although this definition is somewhat too restrictive for the more complex evangelical Calvinism of seventeenth-century England, it is suggestive of some of its core elements. Although this evangelical Calvinism was strongly laic, exalting the religious experience of the common Christian, it also emphasized the importance and authority of those spiritually minded ministers whose primary responsibility was the nurture of the community of believers.

This evangelicalism among Calvinists was rooted in the theology of Calvin and other early Reformed teachers, who had stressed faith and union with Christ, but much of it also exceeded Calvin in its introspection, subjectivity, focus on conversion and individualism.[63] The early Reformed theologians also stressed the doctrine of sanctification and the necessity of a holy life, arguing that this was the very aim of God's gracious election. By the late Elizabethan period and throughout that of the Jacobean, many sermons and devotional writings detailing the spiritual life were published in England, and persons who thought of themselves and others as the "godly" began to look upon those others as unconverted, even though formally or nominally Christian. To "close with Christ" was a very personal and individual thing that separated one from those who were ignorant and worldly. A distinct culture of preaching, spiritual direction, Sabbath-keeping, catechizing, and spiritual conference emerged during this period and was fed by an enormous output of homiletic and devotional writing. This concern with the spiritual life emerged as the central aspect of a wide swath of the Puritan movement, sometimes identified as "moderate Puritanism" or "mainstream Puritanism," if not with Puritanism as a whole.[64]

Dwight Bozeman has recently identified a "precisianist strain" in this Puritan piety which he argues gave it a distinct character that begot a backlash against its increasing legalism concerning the spiritual life; Bozeman's characterization of this development has considerable resonance and interpretive power for understanding the spiritual life as it was understood by Joseph Alleine and the circle that promoted his writings. As Bozeman sees it, the mainstream of Puritanism during the late Elizabethan and Jacobean periods, in spite of their solafidean language, "constructed Christianity as a disciplinary system both severe and punctilious" which rendered Puritan pietism "the most intensive and largest-scale ascetic project in early modern Protestantism."[65] In the background of this development, Bozeman argues, lay early English reformers who were "less categoric" than Luther about *sola fide,* informed by a Christian humanism with "a moralizing flavor," and indebted to Swiss reformers committed to the creation of a disciplined Christian society.[66] Contractual and covenantal themes and Deuteronomic urgency characterized the theological background of these "precisians" and gave impetus to their "second reformation" program of personal and social reconstruction.[67] The result was a piety and practical divinity focused on introspection, an experience of dramatic conversion considered normative, and the "disciplinary transfiguration of the self."[68] All this centered particularly on concerns about preparing for conversion and the search for assurance of conversion through recognition of its various signs and indications. For Bozeman, this preoccupation with assurance of salvation was the special and distinguishing feature of Puritan pietism,[69] and its pursuit through the analysis of "cases of conscience" its primary device. But such a hothouse of spiritual inquiry had the effect of creating greater doubt rather than bringing assurance and led to more anxiety.[70] Bozeman is also interested in the social meaning of all this: it was part of the turn to social discipline following the initial upheaval of the Reformation, it introduced a disciplined self into early modern European history, and it provided opportunity for a clerical elite skilled in spiritual direction.[71] It is no wonder that many either attacked these Puritans for an inhumane rigidity or rebelled against their reading of the gospel by appealing to a free grace that would preclude such burdensome preoccupations.

Many Puritan spiritual writers from the late Elizabethan period onward could be chosen to exemplify this concentration on the spiritual life in writing and preaching. Richard Greenham is widely acknowledged as a prime exemplar of this evangelical Calvinist piety, as also are Laurence Chaderton, George Gifford, Richard Rogers, Arthur Hildersham, John Dod, Richard Sibbes, and many others.[72] One could easily pick many of the dissenting and Calvinist preachers and spiritual writers of the generation after 1660 to represent the persistence of earlier Puritan piety and devotional writing at the same time that they crystallized its later seventeenth-century shape and prefigured the later directions into which this evangelical Calvinism was to move in the next century's awakenings. Others treated in this book such as Theophilus Gale, John Howe, Peter Sterry, and John Edwards produced works of Calvinist spirituality, but the center of their efforts was located elsewhere. On the other hand, Joseph Alleine, as he was promoted by the circle that had formed around him in Somerset and by the wider Baxterian circle, is an especially good example of evangelical Calvinism. Unlike someone such as Baxter, his story was not complicated by a number of other theological and ecclesiastical facets, and the drama and saintliness of his life made him an ideal representative of the piety he so winningly recommended to others. The popularity of his *Alarm* also helped, which together with his other writings presented so many of the themes and interests of what is here being called evangelical Calvinism.

Thus Restoration Dissent was a key moment in the flowering of evangelical Calvinism, and a stage in the transition from an earlier Puritanism to the evangelical Calvinism of the eighteenth century. The evangelical Calvinism of Joseph Alleine and the circle that promoted him can then be seen as transitional—a persistence but also a transformation—leading from key figures of an earlier Puritan age (Greenham, Sibbes) to some of the leading figures (Jonathan Edwards, Philip Doddridge, John Newton) and awakenings of the eighteenth century. Historians of later evangelicalism have noted in particular the importance of Alleine and Baxter as important in this transition, and Mark Noll has spotted one of the significant components of Puritanism that was sloughed off in the transition to eighteenth-century evangelicalism, namely the reform of church and nation through recourse to coercion.[73] This is apt in Alleine's case: his *A Call to Archippus* presupposes a national church gone awry; but increasingly for post-Restoration Dissent, piety was pursued and cultivated without recourse to a national church, and what the circle of Alleine's promoters offered was a Calvinist evangelicalism of individuals and freestanding congregations, a stage in that increasing privatization of religion which was such an important factor in the success of later evangelicalism. Alleine and the circle that promoted him thus represent persistence and gradual transformation, continuity but not identity. But running through all the stages of this evangelical Calvinism was the theme that souls were converted and sanctified by a supernatural grace, and that real religion was experiential.

The centrality of an evangelical Calvinist piety was characteristic of those loosely called "Presbyterians," who can be regarded as the continuation of the earlier more or less mainstream Puritans who tended to precisianism. They were relatively latitudinarian on matters of church government, moderate in their Calvinism, and focused on preaching and pastoral concerns related to the conversion of the ungodly—and also with the restoration of the monarchy in 1660 rather abruptly found themselves outside the Church of England. The cultivation of preaching and the spiritual life in "conventicles" outside the state church, some of which were, especially in London, fairly large congregations, and the writing and publication of a vast amount of spiritual literature (or "affectionate divinity") coupled with a lessened interest in reshaping the whole nation through a state church, with which an earlier Puritanism had been preoccupied, combined to provide a context for a concentration on the reshaping and nurturing of souls, one by one, within the fellowship of separate congregations. The individualism, separatism, and "turning inward" typical earlier of more extreme Puritans were now features of their situation and piety.

These Presbyterian Dissenters were somewhat detached from the radical politics and high Calvinism of other Dissenters such as many of the Independents and while the doctrines of predestination and limited atonement continued to loom in the background of their piety, making it distinctly a Calvinist evangelicalism (in sharp contrast with the Arminian evangelicalism of Wesleyanism in the next century), these doctrines were not foregrounded as prominently as in an earlier era. The doctrines of predestination and limited atonement had their uses in providing assurance and guaranteeing perseverance for those who believed, and had their ongoing legacy in rooting conversion and holiness in the gift of grace purchased for believers by Christ, but they were not the frequently proclaimed doctrines for these spiritual writers they had been for an earlier Puritan generation. But if these doctrines were muted, it was not just because they had become unfashionable but because they had to be prevented from complicating the evangelical labor of making saving appeals to sinners.

The particular elements of the evangelical Calvinism associated with Joseph Alleine and promoted by the circle that brought out the volumes by and about him can be divided into those that his life exemplified and those that were thematically central to his writings, although there is much overlap between them. The principal source for the first of these is of course the collaborative volume *The Life and Death of that Excellent Minister of Christ Mr. Joseph Alleine,* but there are additional comments scattered in some of the prefaces written by others for books authored by Joseph. The source for the second of these consists obviously of the writings of Joseph Alleine.

Constructing an Evangelical Calvinist Saint

In constructing an image of Joseph Alleine many of the hoary motifs of earlier Christian hagiographic lore resurfaced, as they often did in the lives of other Puritan "saints," as for example in the many accounts that appear in the volumes of Samuel Clarke and in the narratives of godly lives included in Puritan and Dissenter funeral sermons.[74] In the Protestant view as a whole, and certainly among Calvinists, the term "saint" had taken on a meaning different from that of the preceding centuries, as Protestants redefined it in keeping with their interpretation of the New Testament meaning of the term, in which Christian communities as a whole were dubbed "the saints." To Protestants a saint was any true believer in and follower of Christ. But in spite of that theological perspective, certain persons were singled out as exemplary for piety and holiness, and celebrated in funeral sermons and biographies in ways reminiscent of pre-Reformation saint's lives.[75] Baxter, in his introductory chapter to *The Life and Death of Alleine*, ruminated on this, commenting that in spite of the fact that "Popish Legends" of saints were filled with falsehoods, reading the lives of genuinely holy persons was edifying, inciting Christians to imitate "such excellent Persons." Those who produced these narratives of saintly living recognized the power of these exempla in encouraging holiness and the need for such reinforcement of the more abstract exhortations characteristic of sermons and devotional treatises.[76]

The longest account of the saintliness of Joseph Alleine comes from his widow Theodosia Alleine. This may well be a first in saint's lives, the story being told by the saint's wife! It adds an extra burden to the proof of sanctity that someone so close to the saint as that should serve as a witness to it. And there do seep through her account hints that living with a saint could involve strain, as Joseph sometimes had to neglect her for the sake of his saintly calling or rebuke her (but always she assures the reader, with that meekness and solicitude appropriate for the saintly). At one point in her narrative, she said that it worried her that he gave away so much of their money—evidence of sanctity perhaps but troubling to a spouse.[77]

Saintly attributes abound in the narratives and encomia about Joseph Alleine printed in *The Life and Death*. The ancient classical aretologies, lives that emphasized the many excellencies of their subjects, including their remarkable childhoods, influenced early Christian hagiography, and the same desire to praise the admired subject as excelling even prior to his or her maturation as saint appears in the description of Joseph Alleine. In his childhood he already showed "a singular sweetness of Disposition" and "a remarkable diligence" in all with which he was busied. By age eleven he was characterized by an "observable Zeal" for Religion, illustrated by time spent in private prayer and godly conversation; this eleven-year-old awakening was considered his conversion. After the death of his brother Edward, "a worthy minister," Joseph had a great desire to enter the ministry himself.[78] Arrived at manhood, he was tall, clear of complexion, and healthy (his early health was emphasized not least because it contrasted with his early death, which to his friends was the result of the necessity of furtive labors as a pastor after his ejection and his sufferings in prison).[79] His intellect was such that he could grasp difficult truths, and his learning while still young was prodigious. As a student at Oxford, it could be said that "Never had learning a truer Drudge since she kept House in Oxford." This learning included an interest in natural science, particularly anatomy, a knowledge that he improved with "frequent Dissections."[80] As a young minister, some at Taunton at first "despised" him for his youth, but were won over by his pastoral effectiveness.[81] He was grave and serene in manner, but at the same time affable and cheerful. In his manner of speech he was "Free, Eloquent, Sublime, and Weighty"; indeed, "It will be hard to tell what Man ever spake with more Holy Eloquence, Gravity, Authority, Meekness, Compassion and Efficacy to Souls." Like the great saints of the past, he gave an impression of power and authority, at the same time that he was charming and loving—a winsome personality, to whom even strangers were drawn. Theodosia related that when ill and taking the waters at Bath, strangers came to see and discourse with him, and even "The vilest of these Persons" declared that they had never in their lives spoken with such a person.[82]

Ascetic self-denial was also characteristic of Joseph Alleine, and suggestive of his assimilation of the precisianist model. As a student at Oxford he rose at four in the morning and often skipped one of his meals. Except that it would have been impious to think so, he almost felt regret that his soul had been tied to a body that required food, drink, and sleep. George Newton reported that Joseph was "much taken with Monsieur de Renty, (whose Life he read often) and imitated some of his Severities upon better grounds," suggesting the attraction of Roman Catholic asceticism for such as Joseph, although he was trying to practice it without the works-righteous implications of Catholic devotion which Calvinists found an abhorrent denial of the gospel.[83] Theodosia said Joseph was temperate in eating, "though he had a very sharp Appetite," adding that at every meal he denied himself, thinking that it conduced to his health,[84] a motive not conventionally attributed to the saintly. Also with regard to self-denial, "no thing was more conspicuous in this Blessed Saint," according to one of his anonymous admirers, than his "contempt of the World." He was truly "a stranger on the Earth."[85]

Rigorous observance of the Lord's Day was characteristic of English Calvinist self-denial. According to Theodosia, Joseph was "a very strict observer of the Sabbath," performing its duties with "such joy and alacrity of Spirit," that it was pleasant to join him in its observation.[86] This was a duty that he never tired of enjoining upon others.

Joseph also excelled at humility. His father-in-law described him as humble in spirit, and not "puffed up" in his own eyes, as he "despised the praise of men." He lived without ostentation, gladly condescending "to the Weakest or Meanest." Joseph complained to his father-in-law of being troubled by pride, but Richard Alleine observed that if he had a proud heart, no one ever saw any evidence of it, "so watchful was he," in checking it.[87] Theodosia testified that Joseph frequently kept solemn days of humiliation, especially in preparation for the sacrament of the Lord's Supper.[88]

It would be expected that he be ardent in devotion, prayer, and meditation. From early in his life he loved to go apart from others to pursue his devotions. He liked to perform them "in the view of Heaven, and the open Air," but at other times he would keep days alone by withdrawing to some unoccupied house, his friends gratifying him by providing him with such, and there he could use his voice "as his Affections led him," conversing with God without distraction. Even in prison he found private corners in which to offer his prayers, sometimes spending the whole night "in these Exercises." When ill at Bath, he retired for private prayer four times daily. But his prayers were not all private: he prayed with friends when they gathered, and maintained a time of prayer twice each day in his family, that is with Theodosia, their servants, and any children who were in the home for instruction at the time. But wherever he prayed, Richard Alleine said, his prayers were more taken up with thanksgiving than with requests.[89] Joseph delighted in meditation, meditating upon the "Divine Power and Wisdom in the Works of Creation," on the many providences of God (Theodosia said that when they had gone to bed he reckoned up the providences of God on their behalf that day), and, Theodosia notes, as the end approached, on death.[90]

The fruit of his holy life could be seen, according to this memorializing of Joseph, in his great charity. Thus his father-in-law said that he had compassion for those in distress and was "bountiful to those in want," giving them more than he could afford. Richard goes on to say that he gave alms daily, distributed much money to his relatives ("His Aged Father, and divers of his Brethren, with their large Families, being fallen into decay"), providing education for some of them, and gave liberally to a collection to relieve the needy after the great fire of London in 1666. George Newton added that Joseph considered the condition of the poor, devising "liberal things," and "holy Projects," for the advancement of their temporal as well as spiritual needs. Theodosia called his charity to the poor a "Charity that was ever beyond his Estate," but could not dissuade him from carrying it out. Another act of his charity was settling quarrels, a matter of great importance within the confines of small dissenting congregations as well as in traditional village life.[91]

This life of godliness, self-denial, humility, charity, prayer, and meditation was capped by a joyous and rapturous love of God in the accounts of those who knew him. One of the anonymous descriptions of Joseph declared that had not his zeal for an active life of saving souls so engaged him, he "could have even lived and dyed wholly in Divine Contemplation and Adoration." Richard Fairclough added that he looked upon Joseph "as one of the most elevated, refined, choice Saints that ever I knew, or expect . . . to know." So consecrated was he, Fairclough continued, that "he was carried with the highest and purest flame of Divine Love that ever I observed in any"; but it was a "Gospel Love" in which the gospel was for him a sight of such beauty and excellence that it "seemed perpetually to possess and ravish his Soul." He continued that he had "oft observed him in frequent and silent elevation of Heart, manifested by the most genuine and private lifting up of his eyes, and joined with the sweetest smile of his Countenance, when . . . he little thought of being seen by any." In such a state, he had the "dearest taste of divine Excellency and Goodness." The image of his great spiritual "taste," a metaphor well known from the later writings of Jonathan Edwards, appeared in another of the accounts.[92] His piety was also emphasized as a joyous one; he was not "morosely pious" said another.[93]

The piety of Alleine was also, in a term which had by that time become ubiquitous in Puritan and dissenting piety, heavenly-minded. Joseph's "conversation" was said to be in heaven; called exemplary for "Heavenliness of mind and life," he delighted in meditation on heaven, and especially liked to read Baxter's *The Saints' Everlasting Rest* as an aid to it. His untimely death was declared a reward for his heavenly mindedness, so that "he who made so great a haste to dispatch his Heavenly Work," should not have to wait "long without his desired Recompense."[94]

Joseph's saintly life reached a climax in the rapturous and ravishing sense of God's presence which he sometimes had, his piety at this point coming to resemble that of the more classically mystical Peter Sterry. Baxter's introduction to *The Life and Death of. . . . Joseph Alleine* prepared the readers of the memorial volume for this aspect of Joseph's piety by declaring that he lived and died in joyous praising of God, and at his death he revived out of "his long speechless Convulsion" in order to break out into "fervent Raptures, as if he had never been so impatient of being absent from the Lord, as when he was just passing into his Presence." But long before his end, Richard Alleine said, he "lived much in delightful Communion with God," and, according to Theodosia Alleine, "often in such ravishments of Spirit, from the Joys and Consolations that he received from the Spirit of God, that it was oftentimes more than he could express, or his bodily strength could bear." According to another witness, Joseph's will was entirely lost in God. Theodosia provided a moving account of his last day, alluded to by Baxter, in which, for sixteen hours he poured forth pious matter, only interrupted by the devil's last "surprising" of him as he was weak and dying, which he deflected triumphantly by crying out, "Away thou foul Fiend, thou Enemy of all Man-kind, thou subtile Sophister, I am the Lords, Christ is mine, and I am his: His by Covenant . . . therefore be gone."[95] In his funeral sermon, George Newton declared "Oh with what Exstasie, and Ravishments of Spirit did he flie away into the Bosom of his Saviour!"[96] From the viewpoint of evangelical Calvinist piety, this was a good death, faithful to the last and triumphing over Satan. Among the *Remaines* was published a brief treatise on "The Art of Dying Well," and Joseph according to his friends, followed his own advice.[97]

Joseph Alleine as Martyr

Over Joseph Alleine's grave in St. Mary Magdalene, Taunton, appears this epitaph: "Here Mr. Joseph Alleine lies, to you and God a sacrifice." Joseph Alleine's death was portrayed by his friends as the death of a confessor and martyr, for he had died as a consequence of persecution, connecting him with other martyrs. *The Life and Death of Joseph Alleine* made clear that he had been healthy and robust until his periods of imprisonment. He was ordered to stop preaching and refused to do so, suffering the consequences, paralleling the experience of early Christians who had been ordered not to testify to Christ. Theodosia's narrative is especially rich in bringing out this aspect of his story: when Joseph realized he could not conform he prayed that his way might be made plain to him, and determined that he would have to go on anyway with his work of saving souls, which he would do privately, preaching and visiting "from House to House, till he should be carried to Prison, or Banishment, which he counted upon." So they sold their goods, and awaited the result, he desiring that Theodosia would accompany him to prison and she willing to do so.

The last part of the story is assimilated to the biblical passion narrative, proceeding from Last Supper to arrest to trial to punishment eventuating in death. When summoned to appear at the house of a justice, he desired to finish his meal first, and ate cheerfully, and was then taken to prison. Released after a while, he was further troubled with warrants, but continued to preach in private houses.[98]

On the tenth of July 1665, two justices accompanied by attendants with swords came to arrest him at Taunton, and using "much deriding and menacing Language," brought him before the justices of the peace by whom he was confined in the prison at Ilchester.[99] From prison, he exhorted his followers not to revile their persecutors, but to bless them "and pray for them." In prison he found "a little church," and with these others spent much time in prayer and praise. After release from this imprisonment, his health seemed broken and he suffered greatly from convulsions, paralysis, and weakness, with a few periodic releases from these disorders, before further relapses.[100] But he "rejoyced that he was accounted worthy to suffer for the Work of Christ."[101] Theodosia provided a detailed account of Joseph's physical sufferings during periods of illness, emphasizing that his sufferings resulted from his mistreatment by persecutors. But through it all he remained patient in adversity.[102]

Joseph Alleine as Ideal Pastor

It was not inappropriate that such a picture of a saintly life as that of Joseph Alleine should have been shaped by a circle of evangelical Calvinists. The heart of Puritan and dissenting Calvinist evangelicalism was that the grace operating in the soul of those converted and sanctified would lift them to an extraordinary life of holiness, holiness that exceeded anything that could be attained by nature alone, a point that ran through the writings of Theophilus Gale. Credible examples of this were useful in furthering the cause of saving souls, and Joseph Alleine as he appeared in the collaborative volume about him was a winsome exemplar. But there is another motive lying behind this portrayal of a saintly life besides this general recommendation of a gracious holiness made possible by a supernatural work of God, and that was the portrayal of an ideal pastor, for the many aspects of Joseph Alleine's sanctity found their unity in a story of someone committed to the evangelical work of converting and nurturing souls.

There is something very Protestant about this. With the Reformation, religion had shifted from the presence of God in rite and sacrament to the presence of God as graciously indwelling the formerly sinful, transforming the sinner into saint. In the Puritan adaptation of Calvinism, this came to be focused with greater intensity on the individual believer than was generally the case in Protestant piety. Accordingly, the pastoral office changed greatly: the chief function was not the administration of collective rites, but the work of preaching, nurturing, and guiding souls in the inner life of grace. But the ministry had no less importance: the earlier Puritan Richard Greenham had maintained that ministers still had the power of the "keys" through their preaching of the word of the gospel, which opened the gates of heaven.[103]

This shift in the ministerial function had connections with what some scholars have been referring to as the disciplinary revolution in early modern Europe, a movement that influenced Catholics as well as Protestants, so that one finds pastor-saints in the Roman Church as well, such at Saint Charles Borromeo, who introduced disciplined pastoral oversight into his Milanese archdiocese. Eamon Duffy has called attention to the devising of new evangelistic methods as characteristic of both Protestantism and Counter-Reformation Catholicism.[104] The clergy were to be missionaries of the faith and trained guides of souls in this new model, and Joseph Alleine filled that niche admirably. The anonymous author of chapter 8 of *The Life and Death of Joseph Alleine*, identified as a close acquaintance of Joseph, described his chapter as "the Portraiture of a compleat Gospel-Minister."[105]

That Richard Baxter also recommended him in this way was especially appropriate, since he was deeply interested in the pastoral office, as his *The Reformed Pastor* indicates. Perhaps he found in Joseph the kind of saintly pastor he longed for and sought himself to exemplify in his Kidderminster ministry and described in that book, first published in 1656. Certainly the character and activities of Joseph Alleine, as portrayed in the memorial volume, echoed the pastoral ideal Baxter laid out in this book. In his introduction to that volume, Baxter said that Joseph was not one of those "weak well-meaning Ministers" who think their virtue alone is sufficient for the task, lacking ability, or worse, "one of those proud and empty Persons, who think that the Dignity of their Function is enough to oblige all to bow to them, and to be Ruled by them, without any personal Wisdom, Holiness, or Ministerial Abilities, suitable to their Sacred Office." No, Joseph was great in his "Ministerial Skillfulness in the public Explication, and Application of the Holy Scriptures," "Convincing and Powerful" in his "unaffected sacred Oratory," and so effective in his "private dealing with particular Families and Souls," that it is no wonder that God blessed him with success. In his pastoral work, Joseph "spake as one that spake from God." His joyous, rapturous piety, Baxter assured the reader, was a "wonderful help to the Converting of the World," and as for his martyr's death, "he died in Pulpit-Work." Thus for Baxter, who had already praised the importance of exemplary lives as models for Christians, the highest point of such holiness as Joseph's was its ministerial and pastoral worth.[106] In his introduction to *An Alarm*, Baxter again recommended Joseph as the ideal pastor and alluded to him as having sacrificed his life in fulfillment of his ministry.[107]

Baxter was not alone in striking this chord. If, as the epitaph for Joseph had it, he was a sacrifice for others, it was because of his ministerial labors on behalf of their souls. George Newton gave him a kind of intercessory role as pastor-saint, arguing that a "praying Minister" who bears the souls of his people on his shoulders before God in prayer, is a kind of "protection" for them, for God has a special "regard to the Intreaties of his faithful Ministers" for those under their care. He announced to mourners at Joseph's funeral that they were in great danger when a praying minister was removed from them, for "if any breach should happen between God and You," "you have lost your Covering, if a storm of Wrath should fall."[108] Thus there emerged a kind of Protestant version of the intercession of the saints, although only of living saints.

Continuing to speak to those who had once known Joseph's pastoral care, Newton urged that while the loss of such "painful" and zealous ministers as he should be much bewailed, they should much more bewail their own lot, that they no longer had him to nurture them. They should mourn that they will be no longer be "enlightened with his clear instructions," enlivened "with his zealous Exhortation," "quickened with his fervent Prayers," "warm'd with his heavenly Discourses," nor "guided by his holy Example." The Lord, he continued, took Joseph away from us because "we were not worthy of such a precious Gem as he was."[109] Joseph himself appeared in the narrative as aware of the importance of ministers as spiritual directors, declaiming against the sin of disrespecting ministers, dubbed "Korahism" in Puritan parlance. It was said of Joseph that he warned such sinners of "the Threatenings of God against them that despise his Ministers."[110] Perhaps his widow Theodosia best summed up the pastoral significance of his saintly life when she concluded that "his whole Life was a continual Sermon," evidencing the efficacy of the doctrines he proclaimed.[111]

If the center of his saintliness consisted of his pastoral labors, then his excellences at those labors provided further characteristics of his saintliness; many faithful pastors had excelled at these tasks, but Joseph Alleine was portrayed as an illustrious example of them. Those who sought to shape a legacy for Joseph Alleine and present him as a model to which pastors might aspire placed the many aspects of his pastoral excellence alongside of the other characteristics of his personal saintliness.

The first of the duties of faithful pastors at which Joseph Alleine excelled was fervent, impassioned, and effective preaching. Preaching had taken on a special importance in Protestantism, for the Word of the gospel had to be proclaimed for persons to accept the grace of God. The Puritan and dissenting heritage, if possible, further heightened the importance of preaching. The memorial volume often referred to Joseph as a diligent and effective preacher. It has already appeared how Baxter praised his "sacred Oratory," and Newton described him as always ready to preach and "spending himself" in that duty. Theodosia Alleine mentioned a week in which he preached fourteen times and portrayed him struggling with the issue of nonconformity primarily because of its implications for his preaching, and added that with his ejection he had to labor harder at preaching, traveling to distant places to speak to smaller groups in private houses. He tried to compensate for those ministers who had abandoned their flocks after ejection. He preached though ill, pushing himself to the limits of his strength. He preached in prison, made more appropriate by the presence there of many of his own flock, for their attendance at illegal meetings.[112] In an exhortation by Joseph inserted into Theodosia's account, he appears to have taken a special pride in the effect of "English practical Divinity" on foreign preachers who had spent time in England: upon return to their homelands their improved preaching was attributed to their having been in England.[113] Presumably Joseph and those who shaped his image took an understandable pride in their preeminence in preaching and practical divinity.

A ministry of preaching was a mission for Joseph, as he is portrayed by his circle. The task of preaching as the earlier English Puritans had conceived it also involved a concern for remote places where there was little or no preaching, the "dark corners" of the land. Eamon Duffy has singled out Samuel Fairclough (father of Richard), Baxter, and Joseph Alleine as examples of this concern.[114] Baxter expressed admiration for the missionary labors among Native Americans of John Eliot and prayed ardently for the conversion of "the heathen, Mahometan, and ignorant nations of the earth," and commented that he would be content with the silencing of so many good ministers by the Act of Uniformity if only these preachers "could go among Tartarians, Turks and heathens and speak their languages."[115] Both Richard and Theodosia Alleine claimed that Joseph considered going to Wales (one of the "dark corners") to preach the gospel, the latter mentioning an occasion after he had been to Bath in which he had agreed with two others to go there but was prevented by the recurrence of his illness. Baxter had been particularly interested in sending preachers to Wales.[116] More striking, and perhaps more Quixotic, Joseph told his wife right after the enforcement of the Act of Uniformity that he would leave England and go to China, "or some remote part of the World, and publish the Gospel there." That kind of missionary fervor and inclination was not common in late seventeenth-century England but adumbrates an expanding concern of later evangelicalism.[117]

Administering the sacrament of the Lord's Supper was another pastoral task undertaken by Joseph Alleine with earnestness and extensive preparation. According to Baxter, Joseph regarded it as an important part of covenanting with God. He is mentioned several times by Theodosia as administering (or failing to administer) the sacrament under trying circumstances, and in his preparation for it kept solemn days of humiliation. Among his remains there survived a number of sacramental sermons on various texts which demonstrate how seriously he took this preparation.[118] The importance of sacramental piety among Puritans and Dissenters should not be overlooked: one of the most popular works of affectionate divinity in the later seventeenth and early eighteenth centuries was Thomas Doolittle's *A Treatise Concerning the Lord's Supper*. Doolittle was a protégé of Baxter who had been converted by Baxter's preaching at Kidderminster and whose education Baxter had helped finance. Their correspondence documents Doolittle's closeness to Baxter and Baxter recommended Doolittle's writings.[119]

Besides preaching and administering the Lord's Supper, the ideal and saintly pastor engaged in family worship. Joseph Alleine is portrayed encouraging this, and his own practice of it, as described by his widow, was twice each day (which was Baxter's recommendation), consisting of reading a chapter of scripture, with comment, prayer, and singing, presumably of Psalms.[120] Such family worship had long been a Puritan desideratum and was to be a defining characteristic of later Victorian evangelicals, but it had a special role in Restoration England as a strategy for coping with the situation after ejection. Neighbors might be included so that it could become a sort of minimal gathered church although the presence of more than four outsiders in addition to the family was illegal.[121]

As noted already, Joseph Alleine sang Psalms twice daily in family worship. Such singing as an important part of worship and pastoral work is mentioned several times in the *Life and Death of Alleine*. In addition to singing in family worship, Joseph sang Psalms daily in his solitary morning hours of devotion. The author of chapter 8 of *The Life and Death of . . . Joseph Alleine,* identified as "one of his familiar acquaintance," said that Joseph "much delighted in Vocal Music, and especially in singing Psalms and Hymns." Theodosia speculated that "he is now shining in Heaven, singing Praises to God, and to the Lamb, which Work he much delighted in, whilst here on Earth."[122] Psalm singing had energized and popularized the Protestant cause from the early years of the Reformation, and proved effective in stirring up religious feeling and commitment among evangelical Calvinists, but had a controversial side to it: Psalms were approved, but what of hymns "of human composure"? Baxter approved of such hymns and Theodosia's remark that he sang hymns may have been intended to suggest that Joseph did too.[123]

Richard Baxter emphasized catechizing,[124] and the fifth chapter of the memorial volume, by a "Mr. G.," was entirely about Joseph Alleine's pastoral duty of catechizing.[125] Catechizing had become important with Protestantism from the beginning, Luther and Calvin having prepared catechisms, and it was also an aspect of early modern disciplined religious practice shared with Catholic reformers such as Borromeo or the Jesuit Peter Canisius. It had a special importance for Calvinist Protestants, for whom, according to Eamon Duffy, "a form of parochial discipline centered on rigorous catechizing became the principal instrument not merely of instruction but of awakening, conversion and Christian formation and reformation." A recent study of catechisms in Protestant England's first two centuries has made clear how important this was, not least by the staggering volume of catechisms published.[126]

Joseph Alleine, as seen already, wrote a commentary on the Shorter Catechism of the Westminster Assembly, and the memorial volume portrays his catechetical endeavors: he visited families in his parish at Taunton and catechized them, sometimes doing this for four or five afternoons in a week. After the Act of Uniformity, he seems to have expanded his labors at catechizing, the law having said nothing about ejected ministers catechizing in private houses. This made catechizing even more important than it had been as it now became a substitute for preaching. While ill and recovering at Bath, he spent much time catechizing, often in schools and alms-houses, during which occasions he also distributed copies of the catechism that he had himself purchased.[127] In his own writings, Joseph often mentioned catechizing; among his writings is a letter encouraging the distribution of catechisms and catechizing written jointly with Joseph Bernard that was directed to the ministers of Wiltshire and Somerset.[128] According to the memorial volume, Joseph also gave other books to young persons that were "suitable to their Capacities and Condition."[129]

Joseph Alleine is also portrayed as extremely active in household visitation, not only to catechize, but also to proffer spiritual advice. A practice earlier of Richard Greenham and a recommendation of Baxter, it is frequently mentioned in the memorial volume. It was said of Alleine that he sought to visit every family as often as he could, that he did it though weak with illness, and that it occupied him on many days from two o'clock in the afternoon until seven in the evening. Such visitation Baxter declared to be "a great promoter of his Successes." Joseph's conversation on these occasions was "always mingled with Heavenly and Holy Discourses."[130] In this way he pursued the task of spiritual direction which had long been a Puritan concern and continued to be an important aspect of evangelical Calvinism.

During imprisonment, Joseph Alleine wrote letters of spiritual counsel, many of which were little sermons. Letters of godly counsel had long been a device of Puritan spiritual guides, including Richard Greenham.[131] Such letters, like catechizing, increased in importance with the silencing of so many ministers during the Restoration. The circle of his promoters printed many of these letters in *Christian Letters* and in his *Remaines*.[132]

The intertwined networks of evangelical Calvinists connected with Joseph Alleine and Richard Baxter produced books of casuistry and presented Joseph as skilled in this matter, publishing sermons and letters of his that dealt with cases of conscience. These cases, pioneered by such earlier Puritans as William Perkins, William Ames, and Richard Greenham, focused less on moral questions than on dilemmas of the spiritual life, often related to the tortured question of assurance of salvation.[133] Baxter was well known for a major work of casuistry. A volume by Joseph Alleine's close friend John Norman, entitled *Cases of Conscience Practically Resolved*, was published after Norman's death by friends who praised his casuistical skill; only a certain William Cooper, author of the preface, is named among these friends, but they might have included some of those instrumental in bringing out Joseph's posthumous works.[134] The memorial volume says of Joseph that in his spiritual counsel to his flock he labored in "resolving their Cases."[135] As already noted a treatise dealing with such cases was appended to *An Alarm to the Unconverted* and also sometimes published independently, and a few "cases" also appeared in his *Remaines*.[136]

Finally, among Joseph's practices as an ideal minister admired by those who delineated him in the memorial volume must be mentioned the reproof and rebuke of sinners. Joseph is said to have practiced this with straightforward courage as well as sensitivity. This was not only the rebuke of degraded and lowly sinners but also of the high and mighty. While rebuke of sinners was long-standing Puritan policy, it functioned not only as a challenge to the rebuked but as a distinguishing mark of the godly. Such rebuke especially focused on scoffers who flouted the godly. As seen in the first chapter, after the Restoration Dissenters were deeply troubled by the scoffing directed at them by worldly persons who disrupted their meetings, informed on them, and harried them to prison. Sensitivity to scoffs and barbs directed at holiness of life lurks in the background of Baxter's introduction to the memorial volume and was a theme of Richard Alleine, who complained that to be a "Puritan" had become a worse reproach than to be a drunkard or fornicator.[137] But there was also need for reproof amongst the godly, as they admonished one another for their spiritual failures. As Richard Fairclough declared to the parishioners he was compelled to leave, "an upright heart delights in a serious reprover."[138]

Richard Alleine said of Joseph's rebukes that his "amicable and courteous converse" prepared the way for "his serious Counsels and severer Reproofs," making them more palatable. Although "he feared not the faces of Men, but where occasion was, he was bold in admonishing, and faithful in reproving," he managed this "ungrateful Duty" with "such prudence, and such expressions of Love, and compassion to Souls" as to make these reproofs successful. His colleague George Newton added that "none could live quietly in any visible and open sin, under his inspection," as he moved about the parish in visitation, "gently reproving them, where he found anything amiss among them." "Mr. G" mentioned Joseph's "faithfulness in reproving the miscarriages of Professors, sparing none, whether High or Low, whether Ministers or Private Christians." Theodosia Alleine also mentioned his reproofs, including reproofs directed at her, always done lovingly. She remembered that while taking the waters at Bath, where he mingled with worldly gentry, he reproved them for their "Oaths, and excess in Drinking," and "their lascivious Carriages, which he observed in the Bath." However, she added, "there was none of them but did most thankfully accept it from him, and shewed him more respect after, than they had done before," which encouraged Joseph to praise God's goodness to him. "His Reproofs were managed with so much respect to their Persons, and the honourable esteem he had of their Dignity, that they said, They could not but accept his Reproofs, though very close and plain." Finally, from "Mr. F.," with whom he lodged, came the testimony that he faithfully discharged "that great duty of giving seasonable reproofs."[139] Joseph's publicists included among his published letters one in which he reproved a former fellow student of whose backsliding he had heard.[140]

The ideal minister of the gospel had many duties and activities in the fulfillment of his calling. How were all these duties to be carried out with so many demands on the pastor? It could only be managed if there was a wise use of time, a recurring theme of Puritan and Dissenter spirituality, for pastors and people. Joseph Alleine rose "betimes," to begin his day of pious activity. His widow said he was ashamed when he heard tradesmen at work before he had begun "his Duties with God."[141] Among his pithy sayings recalled by his memorialists was "value precious time, while time doth last."[142] The valuing of time was a particularly Protestant and Puritan addition to the qualities of the saintly life.

Preaching, catechizing, singing, visitation, spiritual direction by letter or voice, distribution of pious books, administering reproof, and wise use of time were presented, in the materials by and about Joseph Alleine produced by the circle of his friends, as devices and strategies expressing a concern for souls. It would not be amiss to characterize this as "soul-winning," though that was not yet a widely used term in the late seventeenth century. This was above all the task of the minister, and this way of defining the office is clearly a central aspect of the crystallizing evangelical Calvinism that was a transitional phase between an earlier Puritanism and the later awakenings.

The circle that told Joseph Alleine's story and promoted his posthumous writings were themselves centered on this soul-winning. It was the burden of much that Baxter wrote and of his recommendations for the ministry in his *Reformed Pastor,* and there are frequent references to this concern in the writings of the others. They spoke often of awakening sinners, and the need to call sleepy souls to conversion, Richard Alleine asserting that "God hath sent forth his Ministers to Alarm this sinful world."[143] Naturally enough, they saw this as central in their portrait of Joseph Alleine. Richard Alleine spoke of Joseph's "ardent longing" for the souls of those under his pastoral care. George Newton and Richard Fairclough called him "greedy" for the salvation of souls. Baxter referred to the great numbers converted by him.[144] One of Joseph's sermons printed in his *Remaines* bore the title "A serious call to Christians, to win Souls to Christ with helps thereunto." In it he expounded the doctrine that "it is a chief part of a Believer's duty . . . to gain Souls unto God." After mustering many reasons, Joseph cries out, "O then labor to bring in Souls to Jesus Christ."[145]

Many of the contributors to the volume memorializing Joseph Alleine pointed specifically to his concern for the souls of the poor, those often overlooked by the religious elites of the time, and though this had been mentioned in the stories of many earlier Puritans who searched out "dark corners" to find the religiously needy, it received further impetus through the image of Joseph and was a theme in the eighteenth-century evangelical revivals. Baxter portrayed Joseph as showing great humility "in stooping to the meanest, and conversing with the poorest of the Flock"; Richard Alleine added that he "was of great condescension to the Weakest or Meanest," going among "the poor ignorant people that lived in dark Corners," and encouraging others to do so. His widow mentioned his visits to alms-houses, where he conversed with the inhabitants about their spiritual lives.[146]

The preceding consideration of all this saintliness and pastoral perfection in Joseph Alleine is not a primarily a search for the historical Joseph Alleine but a recapturing of the ideals of a circle of persons upon whom Joseph had made a great impact. Perhaps the real Joseph Alleine was not as flawless as portrayed, and some of his perfections, such as his ministry of reproof, seem for the modern reader to confirm the stereotype of Ben Jonson's "zeal of the land busy" meddling Puritan. Joseph may not have been an easy person to live with, and his widow who had lived with him showed a few faint signs of the strain of it. But his former associates and other promoters, impressed by his holiness and pastoral effectiveness, wanted to encourage the same thing in themselves and others, and hence their publications by and about Joseph. And besides the expected signs and evidences of sanctity in Joseph they found and promoted a set of qualities, devices, and strategies which collectively idealized the picture of the evangelical Calvinist pastor and the evangelical impetus which he typified. Preaching, catechizing children, visitation and letter-writing to promote spiritual direction, singing, literature distribution, evangelization of the poor and of foreign lands where they thought Christ was unknown, even cooperation with other promoters of the gospel that minimized possibly divisive ecclesiological commitments, above all "soul-winning" and the experience of conversion as the heart of the matter, prefigure the evangelicalism of a later time and represent one of the trajectories of English Calvinism at the end of the seventeenth century. None of these is a new element in Puritan-dissenting religiosity but a persistence of earlier things, yet collectively they expressed an emphatic and urgent tone as they distilled and crystallized earlier elements into a particular cluster of ideals and behaviors and as they nourished them within separated congregations and directed them especially at individuals, responsibility for nation and a national church having eluded them. To repeat, this evangelical Calvinism represents a blend of persistence and transformation within English Calvinism.

Joseph Alleine as Spiritual Writer and Theologian

The same evangelical Calvinism promoted by Joseph's life was also promoted by those of his writings that were brought out by this circle of his admirers, including the one that was to have the greatest impact, his *Alarm to the Unconverted*. Collectively, and not surprisingly, since those who promoted his life story selected what they published from his pen, the concerns and issues of this corpus conformed to the portrait of Joseph and illustrated the evangelical Calvinism presented through this striking exemplar.

As already noted, Joseph Alleine's writings published between 1671 and 1674 exemplified the genre of spiritual writing so characteristic of the output of the earlier Puritans and the later Dissenters. They are works of practical and "affectionate" divinity, sometimes systematizing the spiritual life, but not probing or even very often providing exposition of doctrinal matters. His circle and promoters apparently recognized in Joseph Alleine a mastery of this devotional genre and saw to it that these writings were published, whereas they did not put effort into the publication of his large manuscript on natural theology. For them piety was the meaning of Joseph's life and work that they wanted to feature. And apart from earlier years devoted to a more classical kind of theological learning, and a brief treatise which ventured into ecclesiological polemic, there was little doubt where Joseph's heart lay as well.

The style and tone of Joseph Alleine's spiritual writings echo those of the Puritan movement of which he was a late product, but they keep the emotional tone at a heightened pitch and sustain that pitch through page after page, especially through a profusion and repetition of images, metaphors, and phrases which often turn up in more than one of the letters, sermons, or treatises. The language of Peter Sterry was also characterized by heightened emotion and effusiveness, but it bore specialized meanings endemic to his personal mystical leanings and drew on a rich earlier mystical tradition in which Joseph Alleine had little interest. In contrast, Joseph's effusive language was homiletic and practical in its emotionality. This can be seen in his beseeching persons to be converted, in which he continually used the language and metaphor of "wooing" sinners to conversion and holiness. This appears at the beginning of *An Alarm* and is especially recurrent in his letters addressed to his former parishioners at Taunton. In the same vein, he referred elsewhere to the gospels as divine "love letters."[147] But sometimes Joseph warns more than he woos, reminding sinners that they are hell-bound.[148] Effusive emotionality is even more pronounced in his expressions of ecstatic and rapturous joy which he considered one of the benefits of salvation. And in the cases where the imagery used to express this became erotic, as in his references to embracing, kissing, and exchanging love tokens with Christ, or in his references to Christ as "husband," it paralleled the language of Sterry.[149]

The theological themes prominent in his books published by those promoting his spiritual life and writings were certainly in keeping with a long tradition of Puritan piety, but they also reflected the turn being taken by Joseph and the circle of his moderate Puritan-Dissenter admirers toward an evangelical Calvinism. The theme of Joseph Alleine's evangelical Calvinist message that he most celebrated with the language of rejoicing was that of God's unmerited grace. Astonished at God's free grace, "who but must needs cry Grace! Grace!" he writes in *An Alarm*.[150] This theme is pervasive in all his writings, as it is in so much of the rhetoric and theology of the Puritan and Dissenter tradition. This effusive language about free grace need not be taken as indicating a softening of the hard line against the more radical and Antinomian elements within the dissenting tradition, as it perhaps did with Sterry; Joseph's effusions about free grace are controlled and contextualized by his commitment to the disciplinary traditions of mainstream Puritan and Dissenter evangelicalism.[151]

Although predestination lurked in the background for Joseph Alleine and the circle of his admirers as it was to do in much later evangelicalism, there are few references to it in Joseph's writings. Near the beginning of *An Alarm*, Joseph explains that the subject for conversion is "the elect sinner" whom God has predestined to glory and effectually called to conversion. But then he warned the reader against being concerned whether or not he or she is among the predestined: "Prove thy conversion, and then never doubt of thine election." One should repent and believe, "cry to God for converting grace," and be assured, "Whatever the decrees of Heaven be," that "if I repent and believe I shall be saved."[152] This was the way the matter was addressed from the beginning of the English Reformation, and it was a commonplace of Calvinist spiritual thinking, but it was especially reiterated by moderate Calvinists such as Baxter and Howe, to which Alleine's immediate circle was connected. It was to be a frequent refrain of Calvinist evangelicals.[153] Thus the doctrine of predestination remained to fortify the pure gratuity of salvation at the same time that it was handled in such a manner as to prevent it from standing in the way of appealing to all to choose salvation. This avoided the pitfalls of that hyper Calvinism which began to develop about this time and flourished among some English Calvinists, especially some Independents and Particular Baptists.[154]

Joseph Alleine and his circle on the other hand spoke and wrote frequently of the atonement as a way of exalting God's grace, as had Reformed theology generally. God's unmerited grace toward sinners was possible and effective through the meritorious death of Christ in the place of sinners according to this theology, and the sufferings and death of Christ was appealed to as an encouragement to piety. In the "Sacramental Speeches" published in Joseph Alleine's *Remaines,* the theme of atonement was developed in a sustained fashion, appropriately since these sermons were meditations preparatory to receiving the sacrament commemorating Christ's sacrificial death. In one of these speeches in particular, Joseph described the atonement as expiation and satisfaction for sin, payment of the debt owed God by sinners, a substitution of Christ for the sinner, and a reception by Christ of the wrath of God the Father upon himself, all staples of English Calvinist teaching. Thereby, sinners were purified by the blood of Christ, cleansed from sin, and reconciled to the Father. But the affective language is foremost, as one would expect from Joseph: he urges his hearers to listen to Christ speaking from the cross: "Methinks I hear him calling upon you from the crosse"; "O see him, and hear him speaking from the crosse."[155]

Joseph Alleine's evangelical Calvinism also stressed, as had much of earlier English Calvinism, the theme of the covenant as an expression of God's grace. "Covenanting grace" is a repeated phrase in his writings.[156] Joseph's inclusions in the publications of his father-in-law dealt with the covenant, and he referred in one of his letters to the desirability of his former parishioners keeping at hand his directions for covenanting.[157] Presumably for Joseph, as for so much of the Puritan and Calvinist tradition, covenant was an appealing concept, sanctioned by the Bible, because while it presupposed predestinarian grace according to which only the elect would ever be covenanted savingly with God, it nonetheless used a language of reciprocity consonant with appeals to sinners to repent and believe. This language of reciprocity was in turn amenable to motifs of obedience to the obligations of the covenant. But as might be expected, Joseph's treatment of this subject is more homiletic than theologically precise, although he seems to have accepted the double covenant theology whereby a covenant of works, established with Adam, preceded a covenant of grace.[158] In *An Alarm* Joseph employs the covenant in order to urge sinners to conversion: they are exhorted to go to the covenant, to "lay hold on" the covenant, to covenant with God in Christ, to undergo "covenant closure with Jesus Christ," and are provided with the same form for covenanting which had been inserted earlier into a publication of Richard Alleine.[159] Elsewhere he dwells on the covenant of grace, sealed in the sacrament of the Lord's Supper, as a great comfort.[160]

Posited upon the basis of God's grace, the atonement, and the covenant, the center of gravity in Joseph Alleine's writings was conversion, and it was conversion that was at the heart of his evangelical Calvinism and of those in the circle that promoted his writings. This is the theme of *An Alarme to the Unconverted,* and much else that he wrote, including one of his letters that is a kind of miniature *Alarm.*[161] The emergence to centrality of the concept and phenomenon of conversion in the story of Puritanism has been extensively traced and studied.[162] Both the story and writings of Joseph Alleine illustrate this centrality for him and for the circle of his promoters, rendering apt their description as evangelical Calvinists.

But it was not doctrinal discussion of conversion[163] that preoccupied Joseph in *An Alarm* (and others, to varying degrees, within his circle of admirers) but the experience of conversion—his evangelical Calvinism was an experiential piety. This experience he referred to in a number of scriptural and homiletic phrases that had been long familiar in Puritan usage which come tumbling forth in his writings. Conversion is a new birth, second birth, or to be "born again";[164] it is to be a "new creature,"[165] to choose, receive, or accept Christ[166]; to "close with Christ"[167]; to be "saved";[168] and to give one's heart to Christ.[169] Many of the phrases of this richly metaphorical language continued to live on in the usage of evangelical Calvinists.

Of the utmost importance in Joseph Alleine's discussions of conversion published by those who promoted his piety was that it effected a real change in the believer. There was, to be sure, the change of justification, whereby the condition of converts was changed to a new relation to God, their sins covered by Christ's righteousness so that they were no longer condemned before the law.[170] But his ultimate interest was in the change that is suggested by the language of new creature and new heart. At this point, borrowing Dwight Bozeman's phrase, he has "in good Reformed fashion," equated the new birth "with personal transformation."[171] Theologically considered, this is sanctification, a real purifying and renewing of the sinner, and Joseph contrasted the red robe of justification (being covered by Christ's righteousness through his sacrificial blood) with the white robe of sanctification (being inwardly purified by the work of the Holy Spirit).[172] Theologically, Alleine also used the old formula that went back to the early years of the English Reformation and was a commonplace in Reformed theology, that election was an election to holiness.[173]

Joseph Alleine emphasized this great and real change that conversion entailed by calling it not a repair of the sinner but a rebuilding of a new creature.[174] The change is not just the forgiveness of sin, but a salvation from sinning; a change that regenerates the sinner, infusing new qualities and dispositions which bring about in the believer a hatred of sin and a desire for holiness for its own sake. Sin still dwells in the converted, but it no longer has dominion, so that the fruit of conversion is holiness of life. The language of "growing in grace" is used to describe this newness as a process. But Alleine is emphatic that no one can come to salvation apart from sanctification.[175]

The truly converted then, renewed by God's grace, must, as Theophilus Gale emphasized, go beyond any morality possible to human nature generally and "do more than others."[176] This holiness of the sanctified person is characterized by time spent in prayer, reading the Bible, meditating upon sermons, godly conversation, and the reproof of sinners.[177] But a holy life is also a life of self-denial. Believers should ask themselves, "Wherein have I denied my self today for God?" The converted must bear the yoke of the cross in this life and live as strangers and pilgrims in a sinful world.[178]

But the true Christian must complement piety and self-denial with a holiness of life in dealing with others. The truly converted person cannot be "a saint on his knees, and a cheat in his shop," for "Piety, without Charity, is but half of Christianity." Thus, according to Joseph, one must not "divide the Tables" but obey the whole law of the Ten Commandments, and this aspect of the holy life he described as "Second Table Duties," entailing the doing of good works, including showing mercy to the poor.[179]

The frequency with which Joseph Alleine spoke of fulfilling all the commandments and his repeated insistence on a truly sanctified Christian life suggest that although he never named it, he worried about Antinomianism, as did others among the moderate Calvinists such as Richard Baxter. But whether he named it or not, these passages in his writings supported his promoters' desire to stay clear of any hint of Antinomianism. This was not only a caution to their own following not to be so caught up in the joys of grace as to forget moral duties but also a rebuttal of the charge against the Dissenters that they were responsible for the sectarian disorders of the Interregnum. Baxter does name Antinomianism in connection with Joseph, assuring readers of the memorial volume that Joseph Alleine was not tainted with such errors.[180]

However, Joseph avoided that taint more circumspectly than had Baxter, who early in his career had been under suspicion for heterodoxy with regard to the doctrine of justification by faith because of his way of phrasing his insistence upon obedience to the covenant as necessary for salvation.[181] Alleine handled this matter without modifying the orthodox Calvinist and Protestant view of justification at all, but simply by including conversion, regeneration, and sanctification in his meaning of salvation in such a way as to make clear that one did not come to final salvation apart from a real holiness of life. The issue of Antinomianism was to dog the later evangelical revivals, but the path chosen by Joseph was characteristic of the mainstream of evangelicalism as it developed in the eighteenth and nineteenth centuries.

So demanding and different from common views was the expectation of Joseph Alleine and his evangelical Calvinist circle as to what a truly converted person was that they seemed to be searching for a new language to describe it. Earlier Puritan usage had distinguished the godly from the ordinary nominal Christian, and the simple term "believer" had also been widely used in the spiritual writing and "affectionate divinity" of Puritans and Dissenters. Especially as the term "conversion" came to be used in a way that distinguished those who had undergone an experience of grace setting them apart from all the nominal Christians of England, language needed to be found that would encompass this phenomenon and expectation. Several times Joseph Alleine spoke of those who had undergone or experienced a "sound conversion," presumably distinguishing them from many others who considered themselves converted but were not truly so. In one case, Joseph used this term to refer to the few among his former Taunton parishioners who had really been converted and not merely had the appearance of it.[182] Sometimes his usage simply fell back onto the term "Christian," using it in a somewhat invidious fashion to apply only to those who had a particular kind of religious experience and commitment rather than as a term that might apply to a whole population—a usage that became in time deeply embedded in the evangelical tradition. In a passage in one of his letters Joseph referred to those for whom "Christian" was only a name and who were at best "almost Christians." In the first chapter of his *Cases of Conscience*, Alleine used the term "Christian" to apply to those who, soundly converted, must be "singular" in their obedience to God's will.[183] The term "singular" is repeated in his writings in this connection: "singular" Christians are those who go beyond merely nominal profession to show the evidences of "new birth" or real change in their lives. In a passage in another letter, Joseph declared to those converted "that the Lord doth look for singular things from you."[184] There are also a number of references to sincerity and "sincere Christians," Christians whose sincerity is evident in their holiness."[185] Occurring most often however are references to being "strict" or to "strictness" in religion. And Joseph makes it clear that "if you are not holy, strict, and self-denying Christians . . . you cannot be saved."[186]

Several of these terms, especially "singular" and "strict," seem to be contextualized in adversarial settings and show Joseph's sensitivity to the scoffing world, in which the truly converted are ridiculed for their singularity and strictness, and in his *Alarm* he warned that one of the marks of being unconverted was "enmity against the strictness of religion," and that those who "make a scorn of precise walking, and mock at the messengers and diligent servants of the Lord" will have a "dreadful doom." On the other hand, it was an honor to "be vilified for Christ," or slandered with the name of "Puritan" for experiencing the "power of Christianity." The truly converted should not fret because of evildoers, for as God's enemies, "their foot shall slide in due time" (Deuteronomy 32:35, a text famous because of Jonathan Edwards's use of it in his sermon "Sinners in the Hands of an Angry God").[187] Scoffing adversaries were various: the profane and irreligious many, the haughty and high-born who deplored the fanaticism of irregular congregations, and the persecutors who gloated over the imprisonment of Dissenters. The sting of the scoffs of the unrighteous and of those with power to persecute was, as already seen, something that Joseph Alleine's circle and the promoters of his legacy found hard to bear and such scoffs and their rebuttals were, as seen in chapter 1, a way of establishing boundaries and distinguishing real Christians from the counterfeit. The distinction of the godly from scoffers sharpened by the years of persecution contributed to the invidiousness of the distinction between the truly and the merely nominal Christian, and served as a technique of self-definition for truly converted evangelical Calvinists—a major point for later evangelicals.

Assurance of Salvation

The earlier Puritan tradition had come to be greatly concerned with the question of assurance of salvation, as already seen in the consideration of Puritan and Dissenter casuistry. Whereas the early Protestant Reformation had connected assurance to faith so that those of strong faith thereby had assurance, the English Calvinist tradition, especially among those designated Puritans, increasingly connected it to sanctification. This led to a search for signs and evidences in the putative believer that he or she was truly among the elect. Thus there emerged anxious introspection, as more and more would-be saints wrestled with the problem of assurance, giving rise to discussions of the matter and to treatments of many aspects of it as cases of conscience.

The search for assurance perhaps created ever more doubt about assurance.[188] One consequence of this worry over assurance was that evangelical Calvinists found their efforts at evangelism stymied because some perceived their faith as "uncomfortable": Edmund Trench recounted the case of a "French papist" familiar with Trench's spiritual struggles who declared that Trench's religion lacked comfort.[189]

Richard Fairclough characterized Joseph Alleine as having "enjoyed the richest assurance of Divine Love to himself in particular, and his saving interest in Christ. I believe few Men were ever born that attained to so clear, satisfied and powerful evidence, that his sins were pardoned."[190] Joseph warned that merely having a strong persuasion of being converted was not sufficient, and urged his hearers and readers to strive mightily for certainty of assurance, doing so by looking for marks of salvation in themselves. In one of the items printed in the *Remaines,* he recommended that one learn what those marks were by reading some of the writings of Richard Alleine and Richard Baxter. Joseph advised that a person should strive to please God, and thereby find assurance and also pointed to the evidence of holiness and keeping God's commandments as a source of assurance, thus falling back on what has been called the "practical syllogism": if you show the evidence of good works, you should be assured of the soundness of your conversion.[191] Joseph also recommended self-examination as a means to assurance, a commonplace of the godly, and a brief formula for daily self-examination was placed both in the midst of the memorial volume and at the end of his *Explanation of the Assembly's Catechism.* He also devoted one of his *Christian Letters* to the subject.[192] He was himself said to have delighted in self-examination, and to have often recommended it in his preaching.[193]

However, Joseph does not seem to have pushed the extreme of self-analysis that has been found in some Elizabethan Calvinists and Stuart Puritans.[194] In his somewhat gentler version of the search for assurance, one could gain assurance by receiving the Lord's Supper, reflecting on the covenant of grace and the sureness of God's election, and by meditating on God's "promises," which he often discussed in the eschatological context of looking forward to heaven and glorification. Ultimately, Joseph wanted to encourage Christians with respect to assurance: "Come then Beloved Christian, be of good comfort, why shouldst thou doubt? Thou hast the mark of the sheep, and therefore thy portion shall be at the Right hand, and thy Sentence among the Blessed." Look over the "promises" and "count them thine."[195] In one of the chapters inserted into Richard Alleine's *Heaven Opened,* Joseph portrayed an assuring God speaking of the "promises."[196] Language about God's "promises" had long resonated in Puritan and Dissenter discourse; it was to persist in later manifestations of evangelical Calvinism.[197] This tendency to relax the stringency that had surrounded the problem of assurance was a significant component of later evangelicalism and it has been claimed that it wrought "a metamorphosis in the nature of popular Protestantism."[198]

Eschatology

Eschatology is not prominent in the writings by or about Joseph Alleine, but where discussion of the Second Coming of Christ appears in his writings, it has lost the social and political ramifications of the shaking of nations and vindication of God's rule that it bore earlier in the Puritan tradition, and has become focused on the reward and vindication of the individual believer, the final end and joyous expectation of the truly converted. Something of this appeared in Theophilus Gale's treatment of the Second Coming and was to be more and more characteristic of later Dissent and the evangelical tradition. In one of his letters to his former flock at Taunton, Joseph declared that the day of redemption when the Lord returns is drawing nigh, a source of joy to those who have experienced the second birth, and of awful warning to sinners. In a treatise in the *Remaines*, he asserted that in that Second Coming Christ will before the world declare as his very own "the very least, and lowest among poor believers," an encouraging thought for his audience. Believers should take comfort that at the second coming the elect will be gathered to God.[199] Earlier Puritan hopes for God's restoration of ecclesiastical purity and a godly state are in contrast with Joseph's interest in the future vindication of the converted individual.

Conclusions

In the generation after the Restoration, the published writings by and about Joseph Alleine that came from a group of moderate Dissenters presented an ideal of life, that of the saintly "born again" believer, the true "Christian," and the ideal evangelical minister. Most of the themes of this literature represented the persistence of an earlier Puritan and Calvinist piety, indeed distilled and concretized those themes into one exemplary life, but also represented transformations of that earlier piety into something different in nuance, language, emphasis, and sensibility. The circle that promoted the legacy of Joseph Alleine moved away from obsessions about church government, disputes about predestination, and an eschatology of the shaking of the nations toward a moderate Calvinism, a focus on practical piety, a central emphasis on the atonement and the experience of conversion, a strict Christian life separate from worldliness, a personalization of the second coming of Christ, and even a freer and more expansive hymnody. The ideal minister was preoccupied with practical activities of mission and encouragement of the spiritual life. Language about being "saved," born again, accepting Christ, "the promises," and winning souls came to the fore. Prominently, this body of literature proclaimed the message that the way to God was the way of conversion, a conversion that effected a real change in those who experienced it, and the warning that this is the only path to salvation. What was said about and by Joseph Alleine both shaped and illus-trated a particular trajectory of later seventeenth-century English Calvinism, as many earlier strands of Puritan, dissenting, and Calvinist thought and piety were drawn together into a particular constellation of themes, emphases, and concerns that can be designated evangelical Calvinism, and which persisted into the next century and beyond. It began to be, already at the end of the sev-enteenth century, a distinct variety of Calvinist expression, and one that was to grow exponentially in importance in succeeding generations.

This evangelical Calvinism was also a strategy, consciously or unconsciously, for coping with the early Enlightenment challenges of irreligion and critical rationalism that were subversive of the religious ways of the Dissenters. Calvinist experiential piety had long served alongside of theological systemati-zation and argument as a weapon in the arsenal of Reformed Protestantism in the warfare against Rome and what was taken to be the betrayal of the Protestant cause in Arminianism; after 1660 it was deployed against the challenge of Socinianism, Deism, and atheism, responding to these opponents not only by argument but also by a piety that insulated individuals and communities against their taint by the power of its self-authenticating intensity. Nourished within devout circles and congregational communities that reinforced its plau-sibility, such a piety was an inoculation against the bacteria of unbelief. The transformation of lives could also be a powerful argument in its own right. In sum, Joseph Alleine and the circle that promoted his story and writings sought to recast and present the gospel message as moderate and winsome at the same time that it had to alarm its audience.

5

Baxter, Bates, and Howe

Calvinist Natural Theology and "Evidences"

Natural theology, which seeks to demonstrate God's existence and determine what can be known of the deity from reason, has a long history in Christian thought. Rooted in the convergence of Christian faith and Greco-Roman philosophy that characterized Christianity in its first centuries, Christian natural theology flourished in the medieval era, as illustrated in the writings of Thomas Aquinas and other theologians of the time. Aspects of it carried over into the thinking of Reformation theologians, including John Calvin. But in the second half of the seventeenth century, as a way of opposing the challenge of atheism to religious belief that arose at that time, as outlined in the first chapter, it came into special prominence in Protestant thought, particularly in its use of the teleological argument, or the argument for the existence of God drawn from the wonderful design evident in the created world. It had considerable vogue in England during the Restoration era, as Church of England divines, especially those usually identified as Latitudinarians, considered it essential to answer objections to Christianity and to establish a case both for religion in general and for the necessity of Christian revelation in particular. The argument of these theologians branched out from proving the existence of God and the immortality of the soul to proving the validity and necessity of Christian revelation, specifically against Deists, a theological genre that came to be called the "evidences of Christianity." Among the most prominent of the Restoration Church of England works on natural theology and evidences were Edward Stillingfleet's *Origines Sacrae, or Rational Account of the Christian Faith,* more "evidences" than natural theology (1662), John Wilkins's *Of the Principles and Duties of Natural Religion* (1675), and Ralph Cudworth's *The True Intellectual System of the Universe* (1678). Stillingfleet became dean of St. Paul's, London, in 1678; Wilkins had promoted the new science as the head of Wadham College, Oxford, before becoming bishop of Chester; and Cudworth was associated with the Cambridge Platonists. Even earlier, in the decade before the Restoration, another Cambridge Platonist, Henry More, had published *An Antidote against Atheisme, or An Appeal to the Natural Faculties of the Minde of Men, whether there be not a God* (1653). This brief work, devoted to analyzing atheism, included a survey of arguments for the existence of God. A similar work by Seth Ward, Restoration bishop of Salisbury, also predated the Restoration, and particularly defended the soul's immortality against Thomas Hobbes. Similar volumes continued to come from English presses in the eighteenth century, such as those of Samuel Clarke.[1] Some of these Church of England efforts at natural theology drew not only on medieval and Reformation precedents but also on the Dutch Arminian Hugo Grotius, whose 1627 *De Veritate religionis Christianae* supplied an arsenal of arguments. Grotius maintained in this work that not only were there valid philosophical arguments to prove the existence of God and the immortality of the soul but also that there were solid reasons for accepting Christian revelation as the unique disclosure of divine truth. The continuing popularity of this book in England is clear from its frequent reprinting and its translation into English by the Church of England Latitudinarian Simon Patrick, whose translation was first published in 1680 and reprinted a number of times thereafter.[2] During the eighteenth century, this Church of England natural theology continued to flourish in order to meet the challenge of the continuing skepticism and Deism of that century, reaching major milestones in the works of Joseph Butler and William Paley.[3]

Dissenter Latitudinarianism and Natural Theology

But in the next century, when Samuel Johnson, Tory supporter of the established church, referred to this apologetic literature, he cited a work by the Dissenter Richard Baxter as "the best collection of the evidences of the Christian system."[4] Discussion of natural theology and evidences of Christianity in Restoration England has focused on its Church of England practitioners and overlooked the contribution of dissenting authors; it is the purpose of this chapter to examine the contribution to the natural theology and "evidences" that flourished during the Restoration of several Dissenters from the Church of England who have already been classified in earlier chapters as moderate Calvinist Presbyterians—Richard Baxter, William Bates, and John Howe. Restoration natural theology has not usually been treated in connection with Calvinist thought. Rather, the late seventeenth-century emphasis on natural theology has typically been seen as an outgrowth of the more liberal— Arminian and Latitudinarian—outlook of many within the Church of England, including the Cambridge Platonists, in the aftermath of the Puritan Interregnum. The Reformed or Calvinist consensus generally acknowledged to have prevailed in the Reformation Church of England up to the time of Charles I and Archbishop Laud had faded by the era of the Restoration, partly discredited by the putative disorder of Puritan rule, as Calvinism lost prestige and authority. While Church of England Calvinists by no means disappeared, as shall be seen in the next chapter, the Dissenters who found themselves outside the Established Church became the special proponents of Calvinist theology, but even among them, particularly the Presbyterian circle associated with Richard Baxter, Latitudinarian currents were flowing.

Baxter has been considered a central figure in the emergence of dissenting Latitudinarian Calvinism because of a number of theological opinions that he broached rather early in his career, such as his unorthodox views on justification.[5] Baxter struggled with his reputed heterodoxy, commenting early in his career that some cried out against him "Heresie, Poperie, Socinianism and what not," and later that he was considered some kind of "heresiarcha." He noted ruefully in 1691 that "above Sixty Books" had been written against him.[6] It was his fear of sectarian excess and especially of Antinomianism that led the young army chaplain to so stress the necessity of good works along with faith in his doctrine of justification that he fell under suspicion of Arminianism; that same fear of Antinomianism later in his career led him to say things about the imputation of Christ's righteousness that sounded Socinian to some, as appeared in chapter 1. He felt that he had carved out a middle ground between the Arminians and "the hot Anti-Arminians." Throughout his life Baxter decried, in Latitudinarian spirit, theological quibbling and argumentation and repeatedly advocated moderation (though never was any opponent of disputation so disputatious as he; a contemporary, playing with the title of one of Baxter's best-known books, dubbed him the author of "the saints' everlasting contention"). Thus on one occasion he criticized Francis Cheynell as an "overorthodox doctor" and on another John Owen as too eager in the multiplication of essential doctrinal articles. Baxter thought that there was too much disputing over small matters. He often—the point appears in his writings on natural theology—described his religion as that of a "meer Catholick" and advocated the Apostle's Creed, Lord's Prayer, and Decalogue as a sufficient basis for Christian union. Indeed, in reply to the argument of skeptics that Christians all disagreed with one another, Baxter replied that "Christianity is but One, and easily known," focusing on Christ as "Saviour of the world."[7] In this, Baxter reflected a growing tendency of the time to single out a few fundamentals of the faith in the search for a simpler and more rational Christianity, a tendency reflected among the Reformed on the continent as well as in England.[8]

However, Baxter's dissenting colleagues tended to treat him as a lax and confused Calvinist rather than no Calvinist at all. Thus the Scottish Presbyterian Robert Baillie advised that he be yoked with "some able divines to guard against his infection." On predestination and atonement, Baxter's views were akin to those of the Huguenot theologian Moise Amyraux, whose theology was, though a modification of strict Calvinism, still a Reformed option; eventually Baxter retracted some of what he had said about justification, admitting that in "the vigour of my youthful apprehensions" he had used "raw unmeet expressions" that had stirred up divines impatient of being contradicted.[9] And clearly, as already seen, Baxter was an exponent and promoter of the Reformed piety of conversion and holiness. Indeed, Baxter was primarily adept at practical divinity, and that he was not university trained perhaps accounted for some of his misadventures in heterodoxy.

Baxter's views, also already seen, were shared with a circle that included both William Bates and John Howe. While neither was as famous as Baxter as a spiritual writer, nor perhaps as important as a Presbyterian leader, both were university educated (after a few years at Christ's College, Cambridge, Howe removed to Magdalen College, Oxford, where he proceeded to the M.A., and was from 1652 to 1655 a fellow; Bates had been at both Emmanuel and King's, Cambridge, and had the Oxford D.D. conferred upon him by royal mandate in 1661) and more careful in the expression of their theological views, producing fewer and more considered works—Baxter admitted that his wife told him that he would have done better to have written fewer books more carefully.[10] Howe and Baxter conferred with one another prior to the Restoration in such a way as to suggest agreement on ecclesiastical and theological matters; Bates joined Baxter as a representative of the nonconformists before the bishops at the Savoy Conference in 1661, and in many other of Baxter's projects, and preached the sermon at his funeral, referring to Baxter as one who took the "middle way" in controversies, refusing to narrow God's grace and decrying the danger of Protestant division. Bates praised Baxter's "Pacifick Spirit." Howe preached the funeral sermon for Bates, acknowledging their close friendship ("his condescending affection to me" and Bates's own "reverential affection to him"), and praised Bates's moderation and commitment to the essentials of Christianity as a basis for wider Christian union. In this sermon Howe alluded to Bates's funeral sermon for "the admirable Mr. Baxter." Howe also preached the funeral sermon for Baxter's wife Margaret, noting his friendship and close acquaintance with her.[11] Howe's importance among the Dissenters is also evident from his meeting with the future King William III in Holland and his delivery of a welcoming address to the new monarch on January 2, 1689; he also spoke privately with the King on later occasions. Howe was present as leader of a deputation of dissenting ministers when William landed in England in 1688. Bates later made several speeches before the royal pair.[12]

These three moderate Calvinists, along with others such as Joseph Alleine (and later, Daniel Williams) while accepting the doctrine of predestination, stated it with moderation. Bates affirmed a single and sublapsarian predestination. Howe also had moderate views on predestination and was attacked by Theophilus Gale in 1677 for insufficient orthodoxy on the divine decrees.[13] Baxter seconded Howe on this matter as is apparent from a lengthy manuscript critique of Gale on "predetermination" and from an epistle to the reader with which he prefaced a book by another also directed against Gale—both of these date from 1679.[14]

Like Baxter and Richard Alleine, both Bates and Howe declared their dislike for controversy and their preference for the practical deeds of religion over theological niceties, although, also as with Baxter, this did not seem to preclude involvement in controversy—how indeed could one avoid that at such a time of theological volatility as the Restoration? Howe devoted two sermons to the point that contentiousness was a consequence of a worldly church, agreeing with Baxter that one should concentrate on essential and practical matters. Bates too was committed to "essentials."[15] Bates, when writing about natural theology, said he would avoid "nice and subtle Speculations" and concentrate on arguments that would help further the practical end of a good life.[16] But Howe and Bates were more careful theologians than Baxter and never shared Baxter's loose views on justification. These three together constituted a school of moderate Calvinists with somewhat "Latitudinarian" leanings who shared much with Church of England natural theologians (Howe had a long-standing friendship with the Cambridge Platonist Henry More) but also developed an approach to natural theology that reflected their Calvinist spiritual and theological provenance. It was with them that dissenting Calvinist writing on natural theology and the evidences of Christianity flourished. It might also have flourished with Joseph Alleine, had he lived longer; as seen in the preceding chapter, Baxter praised Joseph's eventually lost manuscript on what Baxter termed "natural theology."[17]

Natural Theology According to Baxter, Bates, and Howe

A publication from Baxter in 1655, *The Unreasonableness of Infidelity Manifested in Four Discourses*, was a foretaste of some of the themes he would address in his later works of natural theology and evidences, insofar as it addressed the need to strengthen the weak in faith who might be tempted to unbelief. In it Baxter stressed the argument that the best antidote to doubt was the witness of the Holy Spirit, both the inner witness present in the believer and the "extrinsic" witness as the Spirit called attention to such things as the miracles of Christ. This book also republished an earlier work of his that had relevance for Christian apologetics, *The Arrogancy of Reason*. But it was with *The Reasons of the Christian Religion*, published in 1667, that Baxter offered a mature work of natural theology. He was thereby the first of the Dissenters to write extensively on the general themes of natural religion and the evidences of Christianity and one of the first in England to employ the term "natural religion" as a contrast to revealed or supernatural theology.[18] Baxter wrote on these themes, he declared, because he wanted to eschew controversy over small matters and attend to the central issue of the defense of Christianity and the establishing of its "foundations."[19] A large portion of *Reasons* was devoted to answering the objections that might be put to Christian belief not only by learned skeptics but also by ordinary persons, indicating that his intended audience was not just the unbelieving, but "weak" believers, always a concern of the practical Baxter.

Baxter, who disclosed more of himself in his writings than his peers, put his natural theology in the context of his personal spiritual journey by adding that the considerations he was presenting were those which had helped him with his own "perplexities" about Christianity and which should help others "as weak as I" (a confession that to some must have seemed a dangerous concession). It was his own "temptations" (he even admits he had been tempted by the devil to doubt "the life to come") as well as his "inquisitive mind," that caused him to examine the "grounds" of the Christian religion. Therefore, his *Reasons* will disclose to his readers "what reasonings my own soul hath had about the way to everlasting life, and what inquiries it hath made into the truth of the Christian faith: I have gone to my own heart for those reasons . . . and not to my Books"— though Baxter proceeded to recommend books on the subject to his readers, including Grotius's *De Veritate* and Stillingfleet's *Origenes Sacrae*. Baxter intended his book to be useful for common Christians who are "surprised" by "melancholy" and so tempted to atheistic thoughts and ungodliness or who are "staggered" when they "hear subtle arguings against Christianity," and need help in defending it, thereby expanding what he had already proposed in his

Unreasonableness of Infidelity.[20] Something more of this personal approach to natural theology appears in his autobiographical musings, in which he says that as a young man he had come to question whether he was "a Christian or an infidel," and so he turned to the considerations of the foundation of his faith, and thus these temptations led to "great assistances to my faith." In a later reflection, Baxter says that his temptation when younger was not to doubt the truth of Christianity but to question his own "sincerity and interest in Christ," but that his later concern was over the truth of Christianity, perhaps reflecting a change in the mood of the later part of the century from the earlier.[21]

In 1672 Baxter followed his earlier work with two supplements in *More Reasons of the Christian Religion.* The first supplement answered the letter of an anonymous correspondent (which Baxter printed with his answer) who claimed that the contradictions in the Bible prevented him from being satisfied with Christian belief, particularly in the light of what Baxter had earlier said in his writings about the perfection and consistency of scripture. Baxter's reply had two prongs: first he argued that, theoretically speaking, not every "particle" of scripture need be "indefectible" for Christianity to be true since not every "particle" was "essential"; then he took up the various conundrums cited by the anonymous correspondent and showed that understood correctly (something that he acknowledged ultimately required the guidance of the Holy Spirit) the supposed inconsistencies vanish.[22] Yet later, in *Richard Baxter's Dying Thoughts,* published in 1683, almost a decade before he died, he enumerated the reasons he had found helpful for his belief; in this reflection on natural theology and the evidences he presented the arguments briefly in the context of comforting himself as he approached death.

The second part of *More Reasons* was Baxter's response to Lord Herbert of Cherbury's *De Veritate* which had been published in 1624. Baxter says that he wrote this supplement because no one had yet answered Lord Herbert and he feared that some might think that it remained unanswered because unanswerable. Baxter stated that Herbert acknowledged the general truths of natural religion (noting, for example, that atheism was "folly") but did not go beyond them to show the necessity of revelation and the particular truths of the Christian religion. Baxter thought that one should proceed methodically from "Natural Verities" to supernatural truths for which they were fundamental presuppositions. Thus his answer presented his version of the evidences of Christianity. To Baxter and the other natural theologians, it was particularly important to show that if one granted the truths of natural religion, logic would lead from those premises to affirm the truth of Christian revelation—therefore answering Lord Herbert was crucial. Baxter's *More Reasons* was dedicated to Henry Herbert, the brother of the deceased Edward Lord Herbert (and of George Herbert the poet, for whom Baxter professed great admiration). In the epistle dedicatory to Henry

Herbert, Baxter referred to his obligations to him, Henry Herbert having patronized the young Baxter. Henry Herbert also provided Baxter with the copy of Lord Herbert's book which he used in his refutation of it and apparently was not a follower of his brother Edward's religious ideas.[23]

Bates published his *Considerations on the Existence of God and the Immortality of the Soul* in 1676; the next year *The Divinity of the Christian Religion proved by the Evidence of Reason, and Divine Revelation* came out. The first of these was natural theology, the second evidences of the Christian religion. Later in 1677 the two works appeared in a single volume, since the latter built upon the former. In the preface to the first of these, Bates stated that he wrote in order to refute "an infidel age, wherein wickedness reigns with reputation," by showing from "the light of nature" and by reason that "a Sovereign Spirit made and governs" the world and that humans have a soul which may look forward to an immortality of either happiness or misery.[24] In the preface to the second work, Bates declared that it added a "Superstructure" upon the "the Foundations of Religion" that he had established in the previous book. Such a superstructure would show the necessity of honoring the God proved by reason in order for humankind to find happiness. Such an honoring of God must take the form of recognizing the true religion which God had revealed.[25]

John Howe wrote *The Living Temple* in two parts, published in 1675 and 1702 (he had, however, been at work on the second part long before its publication date). The first part was directed against "scoffing" and "Epicurean atheists," and the second, while returning to the fray against atheists, began with a long refutation of Spinoza's materialistic pantheism, which was at the time widely excoriated as atheism. But Howe also said that he wrote for those who already accepted religion but needed to examine its "fundamental grounds." They would, he thought, find "admiration and delight" in doing so.[26] Howe also left in manuscript a series of weekly lectures extensively devoted to natural theology delivered in London between 1691 and 1693 that bore the title of "The Principles of the Oracles of God."[27] Howe meant by "oracles" divine revelation, though the lectures described the "first principles" of religion as "partly of natural and partly of supernatural Revelation." Christian faith is founded on what is known by natural revelation, such as the existence of God, as its principles are "comprehended" in the specially revealed principles of Christian faith, such as that Jesus Christ is the Son of God.[28]

The Role of Reason in Natural Theology and Evidences

These nonconformist authors on natural religion and the evidences of Christianity paralleled the approach of conformist Anglican Latitudinarian apologetics in their insistence that Christian faith could be proved by reasoning. They claimed to be building a case for religion and Christianity that merely followed logic and examined evidence, a claim consonant with the growing vogue of the time for "reason."

Thus these dissenting natural theologians depicted themselves as defenders of reason against its detractors. Baxter noted that some objected that he appealed "too much to natural light" rather than relying simply on scriptural authority; of such objectors, he commented that he loved their zeal but would refrain from "opening their ignorance."[29] Howe warned against thinking "too meanly" of human reason, which separates humans from beasts; God gave us our "under-standings" so that we might use them.[30] Baxter agreed, and added that since God is eminently "intellection, reason, and wisdom," his revealed truth must be "the most rational in the world." According to Baxter, God made reason an essential part of human nature: reason is not our weakness but "our natural excellency" and God's Image in us; we must not therefore renounce it, for it is our natural way of knowing things by "their proper Evidence." Baxter also insisted that our "Natural faculties must be used in trying supernatural Truth." But Baxter cautioned that one should avoid the extremes of either claiming that we believe without reason or that we should not believe anything unless it could be entirely understood by reason. Bates thought that nothing in Christianity was "repugnant" to reason, though much Christian truth was "incomprehensible" to reason, for "'tis impossible that what is infinite should be comprehended by a finite Mind." That Christian truth could be above reason though not opposed to it was much repeated in Restoration natural theology.[31] In what must have been a nod in the direction of Roman Catholic fideist arguments, widely used in the Restoration era as already seen in chapter 1, Baxter defended the place of reason in religion by arguing that one must believe in religion on better grounds than custom or "the credit of the time and place" in which one lived.[32]

For the Dissenters the argument that one was only following reason and opposing irrationality played a special role in their controversy with Church of England conformists, by showing that their reliance on reason belied the Anglican charge that Dissenters were rude fanatics. Richard Ashcraft has argued that Restoration Church of England Latitudinarians deployed the "the hegemonic power" of reason, defining it in such a manner as to ensure that Dissenters were branded as irrational. Correspondingly, Ashcraft places a number of defenses of reason by Restoration Dissenters, including those of Baxter and Howe, in this context, as rejoinders and protests against a putative conformist monopoly on rationality. A brief book entitled *The Judgment of Nonconformists, of the Interests of Reason in Matters of Religion*, which bears the names of Baxter and Bates among fifteen subscribers to the opinions expressed, is an example of the dissenting rejoinder to conformist sneers. It predictably excluded Quakers and Antinomians from the ranks of rational Dissenters, and also alluded to "Papists" as irrational. (Baxter, in correspondence referring to someone who had converted to Rome, described such a conversion as a renunciation of reason.)[33] Baxter, who had so feared sectarians in the unsettled years of civil war and Interregnum, in his *Reasons of the Christian Religion* made clear that sound Christians avoided the evil of enthusiasm (frequently charged by conformists against the Dissenters, as already seen), which in that context he defined as "an unproved bare persuasion" that something was the case.[34]

Nonetheless, these nonconformist authors, like many of the Church of England Latitudinarians, employed as almost a commonplace the notion of the frailty of the human mind, and further insisted that reason in fallen human beings was defective and corruptible, and thus that wicked persons, as Baxter put it, would seem to have enslaved their reason to their lusts, turning themselves into "beasts."[35] Bates too declared that only fleshly lusts can lead one to reject the truth of Christianity, so evident is it to reason: "Those who are slaves to their eyes and appetites will raise Clouds to obscure the Truth that forbids their dear Lusts."[36] But this defect of reason can be overcome in faith, which Baxter described as "an act or species of knowledge," which is a "cleared" and "elevated" reason and not "an immediate intuition of God or Jesus Christ himself." This fits Baxter's affirmation that grace works through our natural capacities, as "it doth turn our natural powers to their right objects" rather than adding more powers to our natural capacity.[37]

William Bates, more than Baxter or Howe, thought it necessary to engage with the epistemological issue and describe the workings of the mind and reason in the course of his apologetic. Accordingly he restated a fairly standard Aristotelian and traditional Christian faculty psychology in arguing that persons were made up of both body and soul, and the soul of both the mind or understanding and the will. This rational soul was the image of God in humankind. The soul is the form of the body and animates it but also is superior to it since it can resist the senses. In fallen humankind the lusts of the senses can darken the mind and turn it away from its true divine end to which it otherwise tends like iron to a magnet. Evil works on human beings through the fancy and the senses; God works though illuminating the understanding and strengthening the will to overcome the attraction of the senses. The mind corrects sense impressions (such as the oar in water that appears bent) and reason or understanding should rule over the body and its senses. Within the soul the mind is nobler than the will. Reason then is preeminent in humans and God instructs and leads through this faculty: "the mind enlightened by sufficient Reasons that the Christian Religion is from God, represents it so to the Will, and the Will, if sincere and unbiased by carnal affections, commands the Mind not to disguise the Truth, to make it less credible, nor to palliate with specious colours the pretences of Infidelity." Thus belief in Christianity "results from conviction and love."[38]

These dissenting natural theologians were also in tune with their age and with the Church of England Latitudinarians in what they meant by reason. As Roland Stromberg has remarked, for that age "reason meant lucidity and common sense, not Scholastic obscurities."[39] Thus Baxter began his *Reasons* with a rather Cartesian musing that he was conscious of being a caused and dependent being and proceeded to describe his method in Cartesian terms: "Passing by all that is doubtful, and controverted among men truly Rational, and taking before me only that which is certain, undeniable, and clear, and wherein my own soul is past all doubt, I shall proceed . . ."[40] Howe added that his reasons for religion will be delivered, not by "way of brawling and captious disputation" but by "calm and sober discourse."[41] They scorned earlier scholasticism as trivial quibbling, Howe on one occasion referring to the "knots" and "snares" of argument "entertained by the school-men" (though Howe, described by Edmund Calamy the younger as well read in "the schoolmen," quoted Anselm, Aquinas, or Scotus when needed and Baxter on occasion praised the medieval scholastics).[42] They prided themselves on presenting a clear, straightforward case for the truth of religion and Christianity. Their stated preference for focusing on central and practical matters was also related to their understanding of reason and their scorn for scholastic quibbling. All three maintained that matters discussed should make a difference for human behavior and not be merely arcane mysteries.

But Bates also made a point important in the discussion of the function of reason in religious argumentation when he insisted that the rational proofs for religion and Christianity offered by theologians were persuasive in their cumulative effect, providing a moral rather than a mathematical certainty or the certainty of knowledge that derived from sense experience. In mathematics, said Bates, there are no infidels, since the "mind cannot suspend its assent." Arguments for belief in religion are of a "sufficient certainty" to convince the "considering dispassionate spirit," but do not "constrain the mind to give its assent," leaving "prudence and choice" in the matter. Baxter qualified certainty by maintaining that one could be certain without having a perfect knowledge of things and also without being able to answer all objections that might be raised. In his autobiographical reflections, Baxter made the personal comment that "among truths certain in themselves, all are not equally certain unto me," to which he added, in agreement with a remark of Richard Hooker in the *Ecclesiastical Polity* that "subjective certainty cannot go beyond the objective evidence." The same point was made in conformist apologetics, particularly by John Wilkins.[43]

Ancient and Modern Philosophers and Natural Religion

With respect to the citing of authorities, the style of argument characteristic of Baxter, Bates, and Howe in their writings on natural theology was in harmony with their emphasis on reason as it was increasingly understood by their more advanced contemporaries, including the Church of England Latitudinarians. Howe declared that he would not rely on authors but on clear and simply stated arguments—he thought the citing of authorities was needless to "unpreju-diced" minds as well as "useless" to the "prejudiced." Baxter stated that one could not cite Christian authorities because infidel opponents would not believe them; but classical authors were useful to show that the arguments for religion from reason alone were recognized by the wisest heathens—Baxter frequently cited Cicero and Seneca, Stoic moralists who were popular with Puritan authors and with others too, including Calvin, as part of the late Renaissance revival of Stoic philosophy. But there are also references to Plato and Aristotle in his natural theology, and occasionally he draws an argument from a patristic source.[44] Bates frequently cited classical authors in his *Considerations of the Existence of God,* but his citations and anecdotes from ancient Greek and Roman authors served to illustrate points he was making and often seem little more than decorative, except for those occasions when he is refuting the materialism or skepticism of some ancient thinker. The approach of these three contrasts with the mode of argument of such a contemporary Calvinist scholastic as Theophilus Gale. Gale buried opponents under mountains of citations (admit-tedly more appropriate for his task of proving points about antiquity), but when his authorities differed, he either sought to reconcile their statements or out-weigh the assertions of one side with those of the other. He never professed to take a fresh look at a subject independent of "authors." This gives to Gale's work a kind of baroque flavor, whereas Baxter, Bates, and Howe argue in a manner more typical of the early Enlightenment. But there is in these natural theologians an affinity for Platonic thought akin to Gale and reflective of the influence of the Cambridge Platonists: there is much Platonism in Howe's *Living Temple;* Bates called Plato the greatest of the philosophers; and Baxter agreed with Gale's view that Plato received his knowledge from Moses and remarked that he had read such authors as Ficino, Vives, and Mornay.[45]

But when these natural theologians did significantly cite ancient authors it was to oppose materialism and skepticism, and they sometimes framed their arguments in an ancient rather than modern context, with citation of Greek and Roman thinkers, such as Epicurus, Democritus, and other ancient skeptics refuted by classical authors regarded as closer to the truth, such as Plato, Cicero, and

Seneca. But Baxter, Bates, and Howe added their own arguments, too. One reason for framing the argument in this way was the seventeenth-century revival of interest in the ancient skeptics who had become precedents for radical ideas: Isabel Rivers has commented that "freethinkers gave scriptural status to classical authors," and so their opponents found it necessary to argue against those authors. Bates described his work on natural theology as in opposition to "Epicurus with his Herd" and engaged in a substantial critique of the materialistic atomism of Epicurus and Democritus. Howe also began *The Living Temple* with the assertion that the work was directed against Epicureans. He further used the Augustinian notion of a continuous creation against Epicureanism, arguing that the created world required for its maintenance God's continual communication of his power and influence. Baxter made frequent references to Epicurus and Epicureans, particularly in his defense of the soul's immortality, where he connects them with "somatists," perhaps a reference to Hobbes.[46] These dissenting natural theologians were in agreement with the Cambridge Platonists who in their concern to uphold the causality of spirit also directed their arguments against Epicureans. This was notably true of Ralph Cudworth in his *True Intellectual System of the Universe*.[47]

Of course, ultimately this was not argument with ancient authors but with contemporary skeptics in England and on the continent who had revived the materialistic skepticism of these ancient authors and employed them in attacks upon conventional Christian belief. Bates defended animal souls against Descartes, distinguishing them in the conventional manner from human souls as not being rational souls but merely souls that as a principle of causation animated bodies. Howe similarly objected to Cartesian mechanism, particularly the idea that animals were mere machines, and argued for the real causality of spirit with respect to matter, and the necessity of a self-acting soul.[48] However, the dissenting natural theologians approved of much that they found in the philosophy of Descartes, as Baxter revealed by his own approach to defending Christianity. Howe called Descartes "that famed restorer, and improver of some principles of the ancient Philosophy." Elsewhere Howe approved of Descartes' discussion of divine excellence. Howe's ambivalence about Descartes was typical of the era: many were pleased by his defense of God's existence but disturbed by his denial of souls to animals, an aspect of materialistic mechanism. As seen in chapter 1, some of the dissenting academies had added the philosophy of Descartes, usually through handbook summaries, to their curriculum. The Church of England natural theologians also drew on Descartes: Henry More asserted that the truest philosophy "did consist of what we now call Platonism and Cartesianism"; Simon Patrick agreed; and Edward Stillingfleet argued in Cartesian manner that the idea of God is so clear and distinct that God must exist.[49] Henry More, however, was later to have serious misgivings about Descartes' philosophy.[50]

If the natural theologians were ambivalent about Descartes, they were certain that Hobbes and Spinoza were enemies of religion, natural and revealed. Howe considered Hobbes to have restated the atomistic materialism of Epicurus[51] and attacked Spinoza as a pantheistic materialist. The second volume of Howe's *The Living Temple* begins with a lengthy refutation of Spinoza in which Howe accuses Spinoza of so confusing his deity with all substantial being that any scheme of religion at all is overthrown, since religion is worship, and there is no distinct God to worship for Spinoza. The claim of followers of Spinoza that they had religion Howe thought entirely fraudulent. Spinoza he asserted had overthrown any doctrine of creation. Such views Howe considered against reason.[52]

Contra Deism, Antitrinitarianism, Atheism, and Scoffing

There were other opponents that these three dissenting natural theologians and practitioners of the evidences of Christianity had in mind besides prominent skeptics ancient and modern. It has been argued that Howe was aiming at the Deist phenomenon in the first part of *The Living Temple*, and this is clearly the case where Howe attacks those who acknowledged that a God exists, "provided he be not meddlesome."[53] Howe's argument that the work of creation was continuous and therefore unfinished might also be understood as anti-Deist. As N. H. Keeble notes, for Howe a God not immanent and present in the world, not "conversable" (Howe's term) with men, was no God at all.[54] Although not using the term "Deism" to describe the views of Lord Herbert, in responding to him so extensively about the necessity for a divine revelation that would disclose truths unknown to reason and carry persons beyond the "common notions" of natural religion celebrated by Herbert, Baxter was in effect attacking the kind of religion of nature alone without revelation that came to be known as Deism.[55] Bates rebutted the argument, a Deist commonplace, that religion was a "politic" invention, noting in the process however, that religion was indeed necessary for civil order.[56] Baxter added that the Dissenters could hardly have anything worldly to gain from their religious convictions, since they were subject to persecution.[57] And whenever the dissenting natural theologians moved to "evidences" of Christian revelation, as all three did, they were in effect refuting Deism. Also anti-Deist was the critique of Epicureanism when it declared that while the Epicureans did not deny the existence of a divine realm they thought that it had no relation to the lives of human beings—Howe noted that Epicurus did not disbelieve in gods though he was "irreligious."[58] Baxter, who was more disarmingly frank than the others, commented autobiographically that "mere Deism" was Christianity's "most plausible competitor" although refuted by the recognition that without a mediator one cannot come to God.[59] Evidence of Baxter's continuing concern with Deism is reflected in the fact that he owned a copy of Stillingfleet's 1677 *Letter to a Deist,* a work in which the author, like Baxter, credits Deism as a serious alternative that might be held by persons of civility, who nonetheless need to be shown the rationality and credibility of Christian belief.[60]

The subject of the Trinity was obviously not something taken up in natural theology or necessarily even in discussion of the evidences of Christianity. But Baxter, Bates, and Howe were certainly aware of the rising tide of criticism of this doctrine especially associated with Socinianism, and it is not surprising that the topic occasionally intruded into their writings. Baxter in his *Reasons of the Christian Religion* takes up the Trinity as a "mysterious" doctrine that "hath always been a difficulty to Faith," observing that while "nothing is so certainly known as God," yet God is known "imperfectly"; he argued that power, intellect, and will, present in humans made in God's image, make the Trinity analogically credible. In any case, Baxter continued, the doctrine is "the very summe and kernel of the Christian Religon."[61] Bates in discussing Christian truth and reason observed that while beyond reason, the doctrine of the Trinity was in no way opposed to reason. And at the end of his *Divinity of the Christian Religion,* he brought into his apologetic argument the "three that bear witness" from I John 5:7–8 as a Trinitarian proof of Christian truth.[62] The second part of Howe's *The Living Temple* contains extensive discussion of the persons and interrelations of the Trinity, the latter a favorite theme of Sterry. Howe also thought, in an echo of ancient theology reminiscent of Gale, that the wise among the heathen had some dim notion of the Trinity.[63] In "The Oracles of God," Howe acknowledged that it was commonly objected that the doctrine of the Trinity is against reason; in response Howe says the doctrine is above the weak rationality of fallen creatures, the arguments against it are "unreasonable," and it is reasonable that the same thing can be both three and one "in different respects."[64] In 1694, between the publication of the two parts of *The Living Temple,* Howe published a defense of the doctrine of the Trinity bearing the title *A Calm and Sober Inquiry Concerning the Possibility of Trinity in the Godhead.*

However, it was atheism in all of its ramifications and various meanings that Baxter, Bates, and Howe avowed to be the main focus of their natural theology and evidences. Baxter, after opening his *Reasons of the Christian Religion* with an introductory letter to Christian readers who were encouraged to read it in order to find arguments against unbelievers, proceeded to another letter to "Doubting and Unbelieving Readers," in which he says that his book's purpose was to overthrow the "Atheism, Infidelity, and ungodliness" of the "brainsick sceptick." A third epistle, directed to "Hypocrite Readers," described them as Christians in name but who had the hearts and lives of "Atheists."[65] Bates more gently opened his *Considerations of the Existence of God* with the intent to refute the atheism and infidelity that prevailed among so many of his contemporaries.[66] Howe began the first volume of *The Living Temple* with the assertion that "the Epicurean Atheist is chiefly designed against in this discourse, that being the Atheism most in fashion." The second volume opened, as already seen, with reference to Spinozan atheism.[67]

All three authors were convinced that atheism was irrational and should be attacked on that ground. Atheists and infidels, Baxter averred, had debased their reason. Bates thought atheists only pretended to be following reason, and have "sunk below the rational nature." Howe echoed the thought that unbelievers only pretended to reason, and declared that atheists had "dethron'd and abjur'd Reason," thereby banishing "all manly rational joy." Atheism was for Howe accordingly a kind of "dementia."[68] What then could account for atheism? All three agreed that it arose from a sinful mind and disposition that sought to be freed from moral constraints. For Baxter atheists hated holiness and preferred their sensual desires to pleasing God; Bates described them as seeking to satisfy their carnal appetites, having abandoned reason and invented weak and specious arguments against God's existence; Howe thought them victims of "a vile appetite" that stifled "all the relishes of intellectual pleasure" in seeking to satisfy their senses. Howe declared that none who have the use of their understandings "can ever be innocently ignorant of God."[69] The argument that atheism was irrational and rooted in sinful rebellion against God echoed what conformists said about atheism, and no doubt the dissenting natural theologians emphasized it in order to establish their credentials as "rational" in the face of conformist charges to the contrary.

The perception that atheism was rooted in sin and was essentially irreligion and godlessness resulted in Baxter, Bates, and Howe still sometimes treating it as what the age called "practical" atheism—the principal meaning of atheism throughout most of their century, as seen in chapter 1. Baxter's introductory epistles to *Reasons of the Christian Religion* expressed fears that doubting Christians might lapse into such practical atheism, connected atheists with infidelity and ungodliness, and described merely nominal Christians as living like atheists. Baxter introduces the category of "latent atheism" to describe this phenomenon. Bates's preface to *Considerations of the Existence of God* described his era as an "infidel age" and wrote his book as a "cure" for such godlessness. He makes reference to those who, whatever they say they believe, live as atheists. Elsewhere Bates described "incogitant practical Atheism" as every bit as destructive as "Absolute and Speculative" atheism.[70] This focus on atheism as godlessness is appropriate for authors who in the largest proportion of their writings concerned themselves with practical and devotional themes: natural theology and practical divinity overlapped for them.

But for all that Bates considered practical atheism as bad as the speculative kind, and even thought that atheists who altogether denied the existence of God were rare,[71] he recognized the phenomenon as real. This recognition forced him to deal with that fact in the portion of his natural theology where he asserted that the existence of God was proved by the universal consent of humanity that the divine was real; but Bates denied that the very existence of atheism weakened the argument against a divine being since the atheist's disbelief violated his own reason. Bates thought that no atheist could long live without doubting his own position, for "no violence can entirely choke this natural notion and belief of a Deity," since it has "such deep and strong root in the Human Spirit."[72] Baxter too acknowledged the existence of atheists who altogether rejected the existence of God and regarded this question as the essence of the matter in the pursuit of natural theology.[73] John Howe seems generally to have meant by atheism a real mental disbelief in the existence of God (which he thought was also the real meaning of Spinoza's conception of God) and, revealing how tinged his mind was with Platonism, suggested that the increase of atheism might be the result of the world's growing older and sinking into "a deeper oblivion of its original." Nonetheless, for Howe atheism was a fact, and he declared an atheist to be "a Prodigy, a Monster amongst mankind. A dreadful spectacle, forsaken of the common aids afforded to other men, hung up in chains, to warn others" and to show them "what an horrid creature man may make of himself by voluntary aversion from God." Bates too called the atheist monstrous, and in New England Samuel Willard also referred to atheists as prodigies, in what apparently had become something of a commonplace among the godly.[74] Granted such a view of the atheist, it is not surprising that Baxter observed that "the vilest Atheist" did not want to be thought of as evil, but claimed to be good.[75]

Atheists of either kind—practical or theoretical—were typically presented as scoffers at religion, and these natural theologians concerned themselves with the evils of such scoffing more than one might have supposed appropriate to natural theology. It has already been seen that conformist Christian apologists also addressed the problem of scoffing, and that Dissenters, so often the butt of scoffing, had a special sensitivity to it. Howe declared that atheists regarded "jeers and sarcasms" as "the most weighty arguments."[76] Baxter also rebutted scoffers and also thought that scoffing at religion, rooted in the unbelief and sensuality of those "capricious brains who deride our ordinary preaching," presented a serious temptation to the weak. Baxter warned them, however, that "God will not be mocked."[77] The objections to godly religion that Baxter was at pains to refute often seem to be the sort of scoffing thoughts expressed by the common folk, or at least by those who might get the ear of the common folk. A sermon by Bates published in 1699 evinces his concern with scoffers and provides a critique of scoffing consonant with the tone of his natural theology: nothing could be more "unreasonable" than scorn directed at holy persons who seek to serve God: the scorn of the ungodly he says should be worn by the godly as a "diadem" aligning them with the apostles who suffered shame for the gospel.[78]

Arguments for the Existence of God

Foremost among the reasons for belief in the existence of God according to the dissenting natural theologians Baxter, Bates, and Howe was the fact that human beings had commonly and universally recognized the reality of a divine order transcending the world. For them, such common consent was a powerful evidence of God's existence. This universality of religion as the recognition that there was a higher power to whom worship was due became an occasion for them to cite such ancient authors as Cicero, Seneca, and Plutarch, and thus to commend even the wisdom of "Gentilism." For Bates, "no societies of men are without the belief of a first being superior to all things in the world." "To the still voice of Reason, the loud voice of all Nations accords in confirming this truth." Bates thought such an idea was innate, "indelibly stamped on the minds of men," God having "so framed it, that by the free use of its faculties" the human soul "necessarily" comes to a belief in God. It was "as natural to the human understanding . . . to believe there is a God, as 'tis the property of the Eye to see the light." And while the nature of God may have been misconstrued, no ignorance can entirely destroy the notion.[79] Howe too thought that it came from a universal search for a higher power, which was an "instinct" implanted by God, citing Cicero, Plutarch, and even Epicurus to that effect.[80] For Baxter God left testimonies of his reality in the "Natural Conscience of mankind," which account for the continuation of "Natural Religion in the world."[81]

The dissenting natural theologians drew on many of the traditional arguments for the existence of God which had appeared in the scholastic tradition. Thus Baxter, Bates, and Howe all developed the argument from a first cause, the recognition that the world was an effect of a supreme God. Bates thought it evident from the "visible frame of the world" that there must be a first cause, as the world cannot have come from mere chance.[82] Baxter discussed God as the first cause of all being and remarked, quoting Francis Bacon, "God never wrought a miracle to convince atheism, because his ordinary works convince us."[83] Howe agreed that there must be an uncaused cause, and that this was God.[84] Baxter and Howe also gave a version of the argument from possibility and necessity, that there must exist a necessary being, put tersely by Howe, "if anything is, something hath always been." And one can find in Howe the argument from motion: all motion comes from God who is alone "self-active."[85]

But these dissenting natural theologians showed a clear preference for the teleological argument from design, an argument whose force was greatly enhanced during the Restoration because of the advances of natural science and the perception of the purposeful intricacy of the workings of nature. Baxter included this argument in his *Dying Thoughts,* finding comfort in the consideration that all things in creation had been designed for an appropriate end or goal, showing the purpose and design of a beneficent God.[86] Bates provided long descriptions of the natural world and the purposeful design of everything in it: "Now if we survey the universe, and all the Beings it contains, their Proportion, Dependence and harmony, it will fully appear that antecedently to its Existence, there was a Perfect Mind that designed it, and disposed the various parts in that exact order, that one beautiful World is composed of them." Bates's first example was the sun, ideal in its placement and motion, providing colors, directing human work, and guiding those who take journeys; its cycles provide the darkness which enables us to admire the beauty and order of the stars and induces sleep, providing "a fit succession of Labour and Rest." He dilates on the thought of how much better a twenty-four hour cycle is for human beings than would be six months of light and six months of darkness. This is followed by discussion of the benefits of air, wind, plants, and animals; even the bees and swallows are guided by "an excellent mind." How wonderful it is, he declares, that the earth is divided into mountains and valleys, which delight us, but also provide minerals and plants for our benefit. From this he turns to the intricate and ideal design of the eye and the hand, perfectly fitted to their tasks, and the wonder of faces that can "make known our inward motions to others." This artful universe points to an "artificer" who designed it. Bates also adds that there are many other mysteries of nature still to be discovered that will even more highly proclaim the existence and designs of God.[87] This kind of discourse certainly qualifies Bates for the company of those who have been described as physico-theologians, although in the fullest sense of the word, the term probably best describes those such as William Derham and John Ray who wrote about the natural world at greater length than Bates, calling attention to its details and intricacies as evidence of a designing God.[88]

Howe described God as an "intellectual designing cause," and like Bates called attention to the "orderly frame of things" in the human eye and the motions of the heavenly bodies. He was impressed that the argument from design was clearer than in former times because of the advances made in searching out such matters. He also presented the watchmaker argument, observing that if we "pitched upon" a clock or watch we would immediately acknowledge "a designing cause." He added that there is incomparably greater evidence of wisdom and design in the "contrivance" of the bodies of animals "than in that of a watch or a clock." (Howe was not the only or first Puritan author to mention this argument; it also appeared in the writings of Baxter's protégé Thomas Doolittle). Howe also conjectured that a miniature universe would so impress us as to demand a designer, while the macrocosm does not because of its very familiarity, and also asked his readers to consider that if their skins were transparent so that all the body's inner workings with their intricacy were visible, they would indubitably believe in a designer, especially when it is added that these intricate bodies have the power of generating new ones: "who can by his own contrivance find out a way of making any thing that can produce another like itself?" For Howe the world and its inhabitants "carry about" the "prints and foot-steps of a Deity," with everything accommodated to its use.[89] Howe and Bates clearly reveled and delighted in this argument from design and accordingly showed interest in the developing natural science of the time. Howe was aware that the "vastness of the Universe" was much greater than earlier ages had supposed and felt that this revealed even more strongly the glory and inventiveness of the creator.[90] Their arguments are better known from the writings of such later Christian apologists as William Paley but were already becoming commonplaces by the end of the seventeenth century. Bates and Howe evinced an enthusiasm for the advances of scientific understanding because they had become so useful in strengthening the Christian argument. They also illustrate something of that rhapsodizing over the "elegance and beauty of creation" which Barbara Shapiro describes as characteristic of the Anglican Latitudinarians during the Restoration. Basil Willey described William Derham's *Physico-Theology* (1713) as consisting of "a long catalogue of relevant characteristics of the terraqueous globe and its living inhabitants, punctuated frequently by pious exclamations."[91]

From the acknowledgement of the existence of God arose discussion of the divine attributes, the definition of which they thought followed logically from the assumption of a first cause and creator. First among them was the oneness of God, Bates declaring that even idolatry and polytheism promote "a strong presumption that there is a true God," and attention to the light of Nature" will make clear that, as rational persons always knew, God is One.[92] That the existence of anything more than one God was irrational was a shared conviction of these natural theologians. Baxter and Bates both asserted that God's attributes of power, wisdom, and goodness could be known from his works in creation and from the necessary perfection of a first being and creator.[93] Bates stated that the attribution of qualities to God could be done on the basis of the analogy of creatures and their creator, by "removing all imperfections" from creatures. Howe too discussed the principle of analogy and stated that "we attribute to God the greatest thing that can be said or thought." Since God is by definition a perfect being, "all the excellencies that are requisite to make up the most absolute perfection" can be attributed to God. He also introduced the idea of divine attributes that only declare what God is not, such as God's invisibility, asserting that such negative attributes always imply something positive about God. Howe devoted the most attention to the divine attributes, not surprising since his *Living Temple* was more than natural theology and evidences, being rather a whole system of theology. He insisted on God's incomprehensibility, a traditional attribute to be sure, but one that was perhaps not always featured when presenting a rational apologetic. God, Howe maintained, is self-active and vital, characterized by life and power (God is "Life, Originall Selfe-springinge in the highest perfection of it"); he is also a good and an intelligent power, as the design of the world shows. The particular emphasis of Howe on life as a divine attribute is related to the design of his book, entitled, after all, *The Living Temple,* in which the life of God is that which ultimately leads to the connections between God and persons.[94]

Spirits and Immortal Souls

The vindication of the reality and immortality of the soul was as central to these dissenting natural theologians as were the reasons for believing in God. Bates devoted much more space in his *Considerations of the Existence of God and of the Immortality of the Soul* to the latter than the former topic. Howe was especially interested in countering the ideas of Descartes about the soul and continually returned to the point in *The Living Temple*. Baxter included an argument for the immortality of the soul among his *Dying Thoughts*[95] and on the title page of *The Reasons of the Christian Religion* declared that his book sought to prove "a future Life of Retribution." This book also contained an appendix defending "the Soul's Immortality against the Somatists or Epicureans, and other Pseudo-Philosophers." Baxter published an additional defense of the soul's immortality in 1682.[96] Bates was the most systematic in approaching the topic and began by noting that God alone was immortal in the absolute sense of the word. His arguments for the soul's immortality included the spiritual and rational nature of the soul and the soul's restless desire for an eternal felicity not attainable in earthly life, with holy souls the most so inclined, but his principal argument was that without immortality and retribution the virtuous would not be properly rewarded and the wicked appropriately punished, and this would violate the justice of a good and powerful God. He added that there has been a common consent on this matter among humankind. Baxter concurred with these points.[97] Much of their argument on behalf of immortality flowed out of their previous proofs for God's existence and attributes, and its use was practical: to warn atheistic, ungodly, and heedless persons of their fate unless they turned to God.

Upholding the existence of human souls, the causality of the spiritual, and God as spirit, led to a line of argumentation important to late seventeenth-century Christian apologists because of what seemed its empirical base, namely, the defense of the existence of supernatural and spiritual phenomena such as ghosts, witchcraft, demon possession, and satanic voices. This proved the reality of the spiritual, even if mainly its dark and negative aspects. Among the Calvinist natural theologians examined in this chapter, it was Baxter who showed greatest interest in the occult lore that was the basis for this argument. In doing so, he depended on two conformist natural theologians, Henry More and Joseph Glanvill, who had especially developed this line of thought. In his *Antidote against Atheisme,* More called attention to supernatural phenomena including snake charming, vomiting of nails and glass, ghosts and apparitions, elves, fairies, werewolves, "field fights and sea-fights seen in the Aire," and even the story of the pied piper. To deny such things, declared More, was a prelude to atheism; in metaphysics, he concluded, "No Spirit, no God."[98] Defending the reality of witchcraft and other supernatural prodigies had thus become a way to defend the truth of the Christian religion with its spiritual view of ultimate reality. In 1681 Baxter was grieved to hear of the death of Joseph Glanvill, a leading figure in the Royal Society and a publicist for the society's scientific endeavors, for he was aware that Glanvill had been at work on a "Collection of Histories of Apparitions" that would be of great use "against our Sadducees," and to firm up doubters, but had been relieved to hear that Henry More had preserved it. This was presumably a reference to Glanvill's *Sadducismus Triumphatus,* published later that year (Glanvill had published an earlier version in 1668 as *A Blow at Modern Sadducism*). Glanvill's book attacked the denial of the reality of a world of spirits as "Saduceeism" and catalogued examples of ghosts and other supernatural occurrences in order to refute atheistic materialism. Earlier, in a letter from Glanvill to Baxter in 1662, Glanvill reported that he had just heard the details of supernatural events associated with a certain "Drummer of Tedworth" that will be "as palpable & convictive a Testimony against Atheism as this age hath afforded."[99]

In his *Reasons of the Christian Religion* Baxter gave examples of witchcraft and satanic possession which he thought proved that some souls were punished after death and commented that while atheists may not believe in an afterlife, Satan certainly does, as he seeks to pact with witches in order to bring them to his hellish domain. He recounted several stories of apparitions and satanic possessions, citing the chemist Robert Boyle among others as a source.[100] In his 1682 *Dying Thoughts*, Baxter returned to this theme, asserting that the persistence of separate souls in an afterlife was proved by apparitions and witches.[101] In 1690 Baxter wrote a commendatory preface for Cotton Mather's *Late Memorable Providences Relating to Witchcraft and Possession*, describing that work as providing material for the refutation of Sadducees.[102] So important was all this to Baxter that one of his last writings dealt at length with occult matters, *The Certainty of the World of Spirits* (1691), also directed against "Sadducees," so called because the biblical Sadducees had denied an afterlife. Baxter thought that supernatural phenomena not only proved empirically the reality of spirits and souls but also proved Christianity to be true. Both witches and those possessed by the devil usually blasphemed Christ and Christianity, which, if so hated by the powers of evil, must be from God who is good. Even the temptations of Satan felt by so many faithful Christians "are so palpable, malicious and importunate, that they do much to confirm me of the truth" of Christianity, Baxter announced. He found comfort in the thought that should the devil appear to him in person, it would free him from temptations to unbelief. Atheists and infidels would be converted if they would only recognize the truth of the narrations of apparitions and "operations of Spirits."[103] Acknowledgement of such spiritual phenomena aided in the movement from natural to revealed religion.

The Transition to Revealed Theology

For Baxter, Bates, and Howe natural theology led up to supernatural or revealed theology, rendering the latter plausible and necessary. Bates spoke of proceeding from the "foundations" of religion to the "superstructure." Howe called natural theology the "vestibulum" to the temple of God and remarked that it was important in building a case for Christianity to begin "lower" than "written Divine Revelation," with the unwritten revelation of nature, as "preparatory" and "fundamental," in the sense of foundational, before moving on to scripture. According to Baxter, natural theology was a "preparative to faith," and the "alphabet of nature"; it developed points which "supernatural revelations presuppose." Thus Christianity is comprised of both "theological verities which are of Natural Revelation" and "much more which is supernaturally revealed;" as Baxter went on, "where Natural light endeth, Supernatural beginneth," grace being "medicinal to nature." This point of view had become common among the Cambridge Platonists. For example, Nathaniel Culverwell, who, like Sterry, was more Calvinist than was usually the case with the Cambridge group, had written that "Nature and Grace may meet together, Reason and Faith have kissed each other."[104] Howe's thought was permeated with Platonism, and while this is less evident in Bates's case, Bates did refer to Plato and his followers as a group with whom "Natural Reason ascended as high as in any of the Gentiles," glimpsing the "true blessedness of Man."[105] Richard Muller has noted that Reformed scholasticism did not typically treat natural theology as a foundation for a superstructural revelation as these Reformed writers did, suggesting another way in which they were innovative and transformative within their Reformed heritage.[106]

Baxter added that revelation gave greater certainty and made it possible for those who lacked time, philosophical ability, and perhaps even the requisite rationality—the great majority of humankind—to come to these truths, a point that John Locke was later to emphasize in *The Reasonableness of Christianity*.[107] This was a point about which Bates and Howe were more cautious than Baxter, since this might imply that the content of revelation and reason were the same, or nearly so. Howe related revelation more organically to natural theology, rooting it not in human need for knowledge but in the divine nature: the God who has so many excellent attributes certainly has that of "conversableness" with human beings, and, granted the capacity, because of his goodness, would converse with them, that is, bring them into a relationship with divinity.[108] Bates was perhaps closer to the opening of Shorter Catechism of the Westminster Assembly when he argued that religion was necessary for properly honoring a creating God and coming to eternal happiness in God.[109]

But there was another way of relating revelation to human need and the human situation than understanding it as almost an informational knowledge, and all three of these Calvinist natural theologians agreed that there was a yearning within human beings that made them reach out for fulfillment in the divine; for the more Platonically inclined Bates and Howe, this seems to have been something implanted by God, Bates saying that the creator of our souls framed it so that the human soul necessarily comes to believe in God, the idea of God being "indelibly stamped on the minds of Men." Thus Bates thought there was a "general inclination" to worship God and that it was a duty to acknowledge and admire this God, giving our obedience. Howe argued that, granted the existence of a blessed self-existing being, human beings will move toward that being to find blessedness for their souls. Religion is necessarily the path for "viatores," wayfarers, a term taken from medieval scholastic theology, suggesting a tending toward God. In this world such wayfarers are "coming to God" and yet always short of the divine perfection. Furthermore, this yearning involved the recognition that something more was needed than just natural knowledge; there was a need for a mediator, as Baxter had put it in arguing with Lord Herbert's book, so that sinful beings could come to their divine goal.[110] Thus, in the words of Howe, "by common consent of mankind some Divine Revelation or other is necessary to the Ends of Religion besides Natural Light."[111]

But which was the true revelation? Restoration dissenting natural theology was modern in its discussion of Christianity as a religion whose claims to validity must be judged alongside those of other religions, though it turned out that there was not much to be said for those other religions. As seen in chapter 1, "religion" in the sense of the relativizing possibilities of the awareness of many religions had become a challenge by the later seventeenth century.[112] This approach also suggests that religion was beginning to be understood as a general phenomenon, of which Christianity was one example. Nonetheless, Baxter, Bates, and Howe, once they had arrived at that point in their arguments where it had been shown that revelation was necessary, took up the question of which revelation was the true one by engaging in a bit of comparative religion (Bates spoke explicitly of comparing Christianity with other religions). Howe dealt with it in the manuscript left behind at his death on "The Principles of the Oracles of God." There, having noted that all agreed some revelation was needed, Howe added that the only plausible competitor with Christianity was the claim of revelation to Mohammed in the Quran. However, this work he says is "so manifestly contrary to the common light of reason," with its affirmation of the corporeal nature of God and of bodily pleasures in heaven, as well as its many contradictions, that it can easily be discounted as God's ultimate revelation.[113]

Baxter claimed that he took it as his duty to examine other religions to see if they had discovered greater truth than he had but agreed with Howe's assertion that Christianity really had no competitor.[114] Baxter and Bates both drew on a fourfold classification of religion that went back to the earlier part of the century, as described in chapter 1: there was "Gentilism," or mere pagan idolatry (usually thought of in classical Greco-Roman terms, but applicable to contemporary idolators), Judaism, Islam, and Christianity. The first of these, Gentilism, was irrational, absurd, and contradictory, with its trivial superstitions and obscene stories and so without claim to serious attention as an option (although Baxter conceded that the wisest among them had religious notions far closer to the truth than the vulgar, and all three certainly admired Plato, Cicero, and other pagan authors). Baxter made much of the many differences of opinion among the ancient philosophers and the squabbles of their sects—an argument, granted the divisions of Christians at his time, that seems imperceptive. Islam was discredited by its founders' resort to imposture and its use of the sword and promise of a sensual heaven (and besides, even Mohammad acknowledged Christ as a true prophet); while the other two represented genuine revelation. But that which was true in Judaism was also professed by both Christians and Muslims; its revelation was provisional and had been fulfilled in Christianity. Since that time it had degenerated into a tissue of "fopperies" (Baxter) and "the carcass of a dead religion" (Bates). Judaism had become a "carnal" religion of ceremonies, replaced by Christianity as a spiritual religion.[115]

Christianity was the clear winner in their reckoning, but it is significant that the argument had to be made at all—a new world of relativism was dawning. It is also to be noted that these authors granted, as has been seen, that the religious sense of all peoples, however corrupted by entanglement in idolatry, represented some real searching for God and an outgrowth of a universal recognition of a God. Baxter treated the other religious alternatives with somewhat more respect and gentleness than did Bates, drawing on the logos theology of such early church fathers as Justin Martyr and Clement of Alexandria (without naming them) to observe that such truth as the virtuous heathens Socrates, Plato, Cicero, Seneca, and others received no doubt came from the work of that "eternal logos that had undertaken man's Redemption" even if those worthies did not recognize this true source of their wisdom. He spoke of Islam as a religion of "much good," though he also noted that it pointed to Christianity, since Mohammad recognized Christ as a prophet. He conceded that there was truth in other religions and even raised the possibility of the salvation of the virtuous and God-fearing heathen: "I find not my self called or enabled to judge all these people as to their final state, but only to say, that if any of them have a holy heart and life, in the true love of God, they shall be saved."[116] Howe also thought about the matter, asserting that one need not worry about the virtuous heathen for that was in God's hands; it was enough for persons to know the terms upon which God dealt with them.[117] Nathaniel Culverwell and John Wilkins both thought salvation was possible for the virtuous heathen,[118] but neither they nor the dissenting natural theologians approached the position of Lord Herbert of Cherbury, made most forcefully in his posthumously published *De Religione Gentilium* (1663), that the agreement of the various claims to revelation on a number of points (more or less identical with the common notions of religion that he had outlined in his earlier work that Baxter had refuted) suggested the common truth of these revelations.

Evidences of Christianity

The Christian revelation was not proved true, however, by the fact that other religions did not qualify as that revelation which humanity needs and seeks.

This then was the stage in the argument where the "evidences of Christianity" entered. Bates was perhaps the most systematic at this point, dividing his evidences into the "intrinsick excellencies" of Christianity that proved it divine in origin and external proofs that verified this origin. Among the intrinsic excellencies are that Christianity "illustrates and establishes" all the natural principles of truth and goodness known to reason, reveals just those supernatural things needed to glorify God and bring about the happiness of humankind, explains both the human condition of sin and misery and the way of redemption from that condition (simultaneously disclosing God's justice and mercy) that is suitable to human need and worthy of the highest supreme being, and sets forth a perfect ideal of life commending all virtue, providing rewards fitting for those who receive them. Bates added that this is set forth in revelation in a manner suited to human capacities.[119] Baxter went further, asserting that without such a revelation suited to the capacities of the weak the "vulgar" would have no religion at all, as they were unable to reason out the truths of natural religion.[120] In summarizing, Bates proclaimed that the Christian religion was so wonderful that it could not possibly be a human invention.[121] Howe also used another argument for the truth of Christian revelation that calls to mind Karl Barth's essay "The Strange New World Within the Bible" and was not exactly calculated to appeal to an incipient age of reason: biblical revelation must come from God, having contents "so repugnant to common inclination."[122]

The excellence and consistency of scripture also belonged to the intrinsic arguments for the truth of Christianity and became a standard part of treatises on the evidence for the truth of Christianity. Baxter's concern about the consistency and perfection of the Bible has already been noted; Bates thought it necessary to insist that the New Testament had been preserved in its original state without any falsification or "material alteration."[123] Bates argued that if Jesus Christ was not what he claimed to be, Son of God and Savior, then he was an imposter; such a thought, granted his evident goodness, was preposterous, even heathen thinkers acknowledging his excellence.[124] Baxter thought the biblical revelation was proved true by the credibility of its apostolic witnesses, who gave their lives for their testimony and by its perfection and consistency. He also devoted considerable attention to answering objections that had been raised about scriptural truth, including the charge that its account of creation contradicted the "physics" of natural philosophers, which Baxter denied. Baxter anticipated the later argument of Joseph Butler's *Analogy of Religion Natural and Revealed* (1736) in his remark that "the State of this present world is exceeding suitable to the Scripture-character of it."[125] Howe agreed, noting that the written revelation so comported with the natural that we have thereby a "rational Inducement" to receive the former from what we know of the latter.[126]

John Howe was deeply concerned with the issue of scriptural accuracy and authenticity, perhaps more aware of an incipient skeptical biblical scholarship that had appeared with Spinoza and others than Bates and Baxter had been— Howe being particularly engaged with the refutation of Spinoza. Thus Howe raised, but dismissed as inessential and diversionary, the status of the Hebrew vowel points (a more conservative Calvinist such as John Owen had defended the antiquity of the Hebrew vowel points against the argument of the biblical scholar Brian Walton that they were medieval additions to the text).[127] Howe also dismissed, as not essential, an understanding of the exact epistemology of biblical revelation, a matter that began to concern Christian apologists at the end of the seventeenth century, as evidenced by Daniel Whitby's discussion of it in his influential biblical commentary. Whitby felt it important to state just how various biblical authors received their revelation, by audible voice or inner inspiration, for example. Howe considered it unnecessary to know whether God communicated with biblical authors by voices or visions, or simply "by an immediate Irradiation of the Intellect."[128] Stating as his premise that there is a book claiming to be the word of God, it must either be that or one of the "boldest Cheats." Howe echoed Bates in arguing that the Bible has come down to the present intact and uncorrupted (had the Jews tampered with the text of the Old Testament they would not have left in it the passages condemning themselves), but he featured the comprehensiveness ("nothing can be pretended to be wanting") of the scriptural text. It was also proved true by the majesty of its style, the "sublimity" of its content, its "correspondency" whereby it was fitted to the needs of humanity, and by "the wonderful efficacy this Word hath had upon the Souls of Men from Age to Age."[129] So convincing did Howe think these arguments that he commented that although there is "no effectual believing of the things contained in the Scriptures unto Salvation, without the special Operation of the Divine Spirit," this was not necessary to bring persons under a divine obligation to believe it.[130] Baxter, Bates, and Howe were not alone in presenting such arguments: a major compendium defending scripture was that of Charles Wolseley, Parliamentarian during the Cromwellian years, who defended the truth of biblical revelation in a large work directed against Deists and atheists.[131]

When he had completed his discussion of the intrinsic evidences of Christianity and of the Bible as revelation, Bates turned to external proofs. Here Bates argued that Christianity was proved true by the witness of its martyrs, the success of the apostles in converting others without any recourse to compulsion ("an unanswerable proof that the Christian Religion came from heaven"), and its good effects in the world, including the comforts it brought to humankind, ridding people of their fears and superstitions.[132] Baxter found further proof in the many providences of God, especially in answers to prayer.[133]

But an important argument serving as an external proof was the timeworn one, utilized by Baxter, Bates, and Howe, as it also was by the Church of England natural theologians, that Christian revelation was proved true by the prophecies which foretold it and the miracles which accompanied it. But Baxter also took up miracles as a problem for the Christian apologist, raising the objection that "there are things so incredible in the Scripture-Miracles, that it is hard to believe them to be true." His argument from miracles then had to make evident that they should be believed: miracles were to be believed because some were plainly seen by multitudes, others reported by multiple testimonies, and all handed down from the accounts of reliable witnesses "who were not crafty deceivers." Their credibility established, the miracles of the apostles "sealed" their verbal witness, and the miracles of Christ along with his miraculous resurrection and ascension authenticated his claim to be the Son of God. But while miracles were necessary to establish Christian truth at the beginning, they were not needed to provide for its continuation, a Protestant argument against the Roman Catholic claim of continuing miracles.[134] Bates agreed that there was no need for new miracles, as there were already sufficient reasons for believing Christian truth.[135]

Bates crafted a more focused and carefully stated argument for miracles as evidence of Christianity than had Baxter. He began by defining a miracle as "a supernatural work that requires an extraordinary Divine Power to effect it." Thus only the God who created the world could so suspend "the Universal Laws of Nature"; while the works of darkness wrought by Satan astonish and deceive us (such as in the putative miracles claimed by the heathen, which Baxter acknowledged had been raised as an argument by those seeking to discredit the miracles of Christ), "a true Miracle is a work reserved to God." Thus God accompanied the "mysteries of the Gospel" which transcended human reason with miraculous testimonies, in order to confirm them. In condescension, God recognized that since gospel truth was necessary for the salvation of humanity it would have to be attended with "such signs as may convince all."[136] Having laid the groundwork of these premises, Bates turned to the miracles of Christ, who while veiling his divinity in his humanity nonetheless on occasion disclosed his true nature through works proper only to God, which Bates then analyzed in their number, variety, manner of performance, and certainty. Thus he healed the sick, cast out demons, stilled the winds, and was transfigured before his disciples. Their manner of performance was by his word, so that just as at creation God said "let there be light," Christ said to the blind, "Receive thy Sight." He did not perform miracles by "commission from an extrinsick superiour principle," but by a power "inherent in his Person, the natural proper Attribute of his Deity," thus proving himself God become human. The witness of his followers and of bystanders confirmed their certainty as does the consideration that God would not have allowed a deceiver to perform such works. Even the opponents of Christ such as the Jews "in Their Talmud" confessed that he did miracles, though attempting to explain them away. Christ's miracles drove from the field the pretended miracles of the heathen.[137] Next Bates turns to the resurrection of Christ, "the great principle upon which all Christian hopes depend," and seeks to show what "rational assurance" there is for it: here he stresses the number and "quality" of the witnesses as evidence of the truth of their testimony. These witnesses did not depend on hearsay but on what they had seen, and even when the disciples who reported it were "tried by the sharpest Sufferings," they yet persevered in their testimony, thereby ruling out the charge that they conspired to invent a falsehood.[138]

The fulfillment of prophecy as an evidence of the truth of Christianity also received full treatment in these dissenting works on the evidences of Christianity. As in other cases, Baxter considered prophecy in the context of objections: for example, he says, the obscurity of many prophecies, and the unlikelihood that they could all be fulfilled constitute "one of the difficulties of our Faith." Moreover, expositors differ about the meaning of the prophecies in the Book of Revelation. Baxter responded with several considerations: prophecies may be obscure in their particularities and understood fully by few, but they are not meant as a rule of life, which must be clearly set forth, but as "encouragement to hope"; since no one can say that any prophecy has failed yet, why should one think that hereafter they will; many prophecies have been misunderstood, as with the Jewish expectation of a carnal rather than a spiritual kingdom, when they should have been understood in a more spiritual way, which is admittedly a matter most clear to "but a few of the extraordinary wise."[139] Elsewhere Baxter recounted the biblical passages that foretold the coming of Christ, calling attention in the process to the various "types" of Christ to be found in the Old Testament, such as Abel and Isaac.[140] Howe made an interesting move when he argued that once one believed that the New Testament carried the weight of divine authority, it carries the Old Testament with it, as that which it fulfilled.[141]

Once again, Bates is the one who treated the subject with the most clarity and focus. Again, he stated general premises: only God can know the future and no one can be a prophet by the light of reason alone. Then he turned to the prophecies fulfilled in Christ, which together provided a narrative of his life: born of a virgin, of the house of David, born in Bethlehem, worker of miracles, betrayed by Judas, ignominiously scorned by his enemies, his death and resurrection.[142] Next Bates called attention to the consequences of Christ's coming as the fulfillment of prophecy: the curse upon the Jews for killing Christ and the destruction of their kingdom followed by their continual misery for the sixteen hundred years since that time; and the conversion of the Gentiles with the abandonment of the heathen gods and the triumph over the eloquence of the Greeks and the power of the Romans.[143] His conclusion to the discussion of prophecy puts it succinctly: "The success justifies the truth of the Prophecy, and the truth of the Prophecy justifies the Divinity of the Christian Religion."[144] This motif of the persistence yet suffering of the Jews as a proof for Christianity was fairly common in Christian apologetics and in the seventeenth century is most famously connected to Blaise Pascal's *Pensées*.

With Christian revelation having been proved true, it was only Baxter who then went a step further and asked which form of Christianity was the true one, answering the question with his own notion of a "mere Christianity" based on the Apostle's Creed, Lord's Prayer, and the Decalogue, and thus consisting of a few central truths of the faith and realized in an invisible church of true believers everywhere—an indubitably Latitudinarian point, and one which Baxter had made as early as 1655 and continued to repeat at the end of his career.[145]

It is clear then, that Restoration Dissenters, as well as conformists, were active as natural theologians and authors on the evidences of Christianity, and were significant contributors to the development of this literature. Of course, there were reasons why Church of England Latitudinarians and dissenting liberals should both write on these themes: both sought a wider and more comprehensive Church of England (Baxter, Bates, and Howe all favored comprehension within a more flexible establishment rather than toleration outside of it, and Wilkins, Simon Patrick, John Tillotson, and Stillingfleet at various times hoped to include the moderate Dissenters within the established Church), and both opposed the more rigid members of their own party, finding reasons in the common pursuit of a broad Christianity for rejecting the viewpoints of Tory High Churchmen and strict Calvinist Dissenters. Howe, for example, stated that it was past time for disputing over "modes of religion"; the issue had come to be whether there should be any religion at all. Thus Latitudinarianism of either the churchly or dissenting kind had a clear social context.[146] For the dissenting natural theologians this was another indication of the widening gap between them and the more strictly Calvinist Dissenters among the Independents and Particular Baptists. There were also close connections between these dissenting natural theologians and the conformists: Baxter often attended the prayer book worship of the Church of England on Sunday mornings before preaching in the afternoon in his house to family and friends; Howe was an occasional conformist, sometimes taking communion in the established church.[147] Baxter corresponded with Glanvill and Stillingfleet, and recommended their books as well as those of Henry More. Howe had been acquainted with More and Cudworth at Cambridge, cited them both in his writings, and, according to Edmund Calamy the younger, Howe received his "Platonick Tincture" from them and had "a particular intimacy" with Archbishop Tillotson.[148] Bates had been sought out by the Earl of Clarendon and Bishop Morley in 1660 for discussions about the comprehension of the Presbyterians in the established church and had even been offered the deanery of Coventry and Lichfield if he would conform; he also had conversed with Wilkins and Tillotson.[149] Not that the relations of these two groups with each other were always smooth: Baxter in particular felt betrayed by Glanvill and Simon Patrick who both seemed friendly to the Dissenters but then circled the Church of England's wagons against them at critical moments.[150] And like the conformist natural theologians, the dissenting ones drew on the work of Hugo Grotius. Baxter admired the ecumenical spirit of Grotius but worried that he went too far in his irenicism toward Rome.[151]

Distinctive Aspects of Dissenting Natural Theology and Evidences

However Bates, Baxter, and Howe were more than just an echo of Latitudinarian Anglican authors on natural theology and the evidences of Christianity during this period: there were distinctive notes in their treatment of the these topics that connected them to their Calvinist heritage and dissenting milieu.

One distinctive note separating the dissenting and conformist versions of natural theology and the evidences of Christianity from each other was a matter frequent in conformist apologetics and muted in dissenting ones—the advantageousness of religion and Christian faith. Barbara Shapiro has noted that some of conformist writers in defending Christianity did so by reference to its earthly benefits, leading to riches and honor in this world as well as beatitude in the next. John Wilkins in particular stressed earthly happiness, stating that "Religion is the cause of Riches," promotes pleasure, and conduces to reputation, observing that this was an important matter in Christian apologetics because "the generality of men are chiefly swayed" by such things. John Tillotson, Isaac Barrow, and John Ray all echoed this theme, sometimes referring back to Wilkins.[152] Simon Patrick advised that one should present Christian faith with a face "fair and beautiful."[153] Seth Ward defined religion as resignation to God "with an expectation of reward," and that reward as he discussed it has a ring of earthly happiness.[154] That persecuted Dissenters would not warm up to such an argument is not surprising: Baxter warned of the deceit of riches and power, and called attention to the sincerity of the ejected and dissenting clergy who had nothing to gain and much to lose from their convictions.[155]

Bates did refer to temporal blessings as part of God's promise to believers but noted that they were "in the lowest rank of good things," to be desired only "subordinately to our chief good." Bates spoke of them as things that would give "support and refreshment under the troubles of the present life," noted that for those who had no hope of a future state of blessedness they loomed larger than for believers, and that contentment with one's earthly lot was only really possible for those who had such hope. Bates called the view that the coming of the Messiah would bring earthly happiness an error of the Jews.[156]

Perhaps the most pervasive distinction between conformist and dissenting works on natural theology was the extent to which these works by Baxter, Bates, and Howe were much more than apologetic and intellectual exercises, being also treatises of practical and affectionate divinity intended for the edification of their readers. All three authors were in their whole careers producers of such homiletic and devotional material, and there are many indications of this interest in these apologetic works, especially in those of Baxter. Baxter's title page to *The Reasons of the Christian Religion* described the book as about "godliness"; and after developing many of his arguments, Baxter remarked that better than all his reasoning was a fervent desire for God and "a penitent tear"—and then he broke into a long prayer reminiscent of Augustine's *Confessions*, asking God to transcribe his "sacred precepts on my heart." Howe concluded the second part of *The Living Temple* with the exhortation to look to Christ, "That God may have his Temple in your Breast."[157] Bates concluded his *Divinity of the Christian Religion* by noting that the "Mysteries of Godliness are not confined to the speculative mind" but are moral, to regulate our lives and mortify our sins, and that there are no greater enemies of God than Christians who wear "the Livery of his Servants" but defame this holy profession—"unholy Christians are the most guilty Sinners in the World."[158]

However, it is possible to be more theologically precise about this difference between conformist and dissenting authors on natural theology and the evidences of Christianity. The Church of England Latitudinarian discussions of the necessity of revelation tend to stress revelation as propositional and faith as assent to those propositions,[159] whereas when the Dissenters arrived at the transition from natural theology to revealed theology, engineered by the argument for the necessity of revelation, they either built their arguments around or adverted to the necessity of the atonement to reestablish a fellowship between God and humanity which had been broken by the depravity entailed by original sin. And the renewed fellowship with God so brought about was not primarily a matter of assent to revealed teachings and then a following of them, but a union of the soul with Christ effected through a supernatural regeneration by the Holy Spirit. At this point, the dissenting natural theologians would have seemed unduly enthusiastic to their Establishment counterparts. Barbara Shapiro notes that Anglican natural theologians avoided references to grace, original sin, and God's justice, and comments that "Latitudinarians made little if any distinction between moral righteousness and evangelical righteousness."[160] Richard Westfall goes farther in saying that the Anglican natural theologians gave "scant notice" to the spiritual life.[161] Perhaps more measured in summing up the difference is the comment of John Spurr that while Anglicans conceived of the edification of the spiritual life as a kind of instruction, for Dissenters it was part of experiential religion.[162] In any case, the fall, atonement, and the holiness resulting from regeneration by supernatural grace were significant elements in the works of the dissenting natural theologians and were less prominent in the works of natural theology by conformist authors, although Stillingfleet did discuss the atonement in his *Origines Sacrae,* asserting that God sent his Son into the world to die in order to show his love and beget repentance. Stillingfleet had earlier authored an entire treatise on the atonement.[163]

Baxter, Bates, and Howe all stressed that the loss of fellowship between God and humankind brought about by the fall made revelation necessary, thereby giving original sin a place in their apologetics. The fall also accounted for human blindness so that God's truth was more hated than disbelieved, as Howe put it; Howe elsewhere stated that because of sin men became so "loathesome" that God could no longer dwell with them. Baxter agreed: we come into the world, he said, with a "natural pravity" which is worsened by "vicious education." He also echoed Hobbes: humankind is so anarchic that government is necessary; humans require God's government "that they may not live as in a continual war, in danger and fear of one another, . . . as so many fighting cocks or Dogs, every one would fight or flie for himself; for fighting, or flying, injuring and being injured would be all their lives."[164] Among the intrinsic proofs of the truth of Christianity for Bates was his argument that Christian faith explains the cause and nature of human sinfulness and misery.[165]

All three also made the atonement crucial as a necessary satisfaction of God's justice and the restoration of fellowship with God. Bates spoke in *The Divinity of the Christian Religion* of the incarnate Son of God being offered on the cross as a full payment for human sin and of Christianity being true because it outlined a way of redemption in which "justice and mercy triumph with equal Glory," the gospel displaying the excellencies of God in the redemption of sinners. Had Christ come in his glory, "the design of his coming had been frustrated." His lowly death was thus not "unbecoming" for God, but the appearance of his infinite mercy. "Where might such a contrivance of Wisdom be framed but in the Divine mind?" Thus the atonement of Christ becomes an indication of the divinity of the Christian religion for Bates. But this manner of redemption was also a means to draw humankind to Christ, for the reasonable creature cannot "resist the sweet Violence" and the powerful attractions of such love.[166]

Baxter and Howe equaled Bates in their attention to the atonement within their defenses of Christianity. Baxter emphasized the atonement in his argument against Lord Herbert: where Herbert had maintained that repentance alone was sufficient to gain God's favor, Baxter argued the necessity of atonement and, granted the need of revelation going beyond a mere religion of nature, connected the revealing Christ with that act of atonement. He also maintained that the act of sacrificing in religion generally represented humanity's inchoate recognition that God's justice demanded atonement.[167] Howe developed the doctrine of atonement at great length, starting with the premise that Christ, as the incarnate God, was himself "a most perfect Temple" from whom "Life and Influence" could be spread to fallen humanity, but not without a sacrifice of himself, necessary to atone for sin, and to reestablish God's moral government, making the abandoned temple of God on earth fit again for human habitation. Only the mediator, the God-Man, could do this. But the death of Christ was not unjust or vindictive on the Father's part, rather it was necessary for the vindication of the Father's majesty and honor "without wrong to himself" or to the dignity of his moral government.[168] Baxter introduced into his treatment of the atonement some of the elements of Grotius's view that the rectifying of God's moral government was necessary before fellowship with God could be restored.[169] Thus the answer to the question of why God became man was part of the argument of these three dissenting practitioners of the evidences of Christianity. It would show to doubters and unbelievers the necessity of Christian revelation as not only further knowledge about God but as a means to restore human fellowship with God, granted the observable brokenness and idolatry of human efforts to find God.

But the ultimate aim of God's plan according to these dissenting writers was to restore persons to holiness of life. Thus not only original sin and the atonement played important roles in the dissenting version of Restoration Christian apologetics but also the evangelical Calvinist conviction that the end of Christianity is a faith and holiness in the believer which is the effect of supernatural renovating grace. Baxter argued that the human desire for holiness was itself a proof of religion, and declared that the holiness of a regenerate soul was "the just continuation and use of a reasonable soul." The suitableness of the gospel to the good loved by holy souls was one of the reasons for believing Christianity to be true, according to Baxter, and the fact that persons were made holy by the gospel further evidenced its truth. This holiness of a regenerate soul as evidence of Christian truth was overlooked by the ungodly but persuasive in self-authenticating fashion to the godly: love of God and holiness steadied the believer in the hour of temptation, when reasoning was too weak to withstand temptation: "O what a blessed advantage have the sanctified against all temptations to unbelief: And how lamentably are ungodly sensualists disadvantaged, who have deprived themselves of this inherent testimony." To seal his argument Baxter provides an analogy: "If two men were born blind, and one of them had been cured, and had been shewed the candle-light and twilight, how easie is it for him to believe his Physician, if he promises also to shew him the Sun in comparison of what it is to the other who never saw the light?" Baxter added that it was a work of the Holy Spirit to effectuate this and that the Holy Spirit is "the great evidence of the Christian Verity." Baxter also maintained that for believers the internal testimony of the sanctifying Holy Spirit was an infallible indication of truth.[170]

Howe agreed that personal holiness was an evidence of the reality of Christianity. But he was more interested in the "conversableness" of God with humanity as a fundamental principle of religion and an aspect of his temple metaphor, insofar as that temple was to be a place on earth for God's presence. Howe too connected this holiness to the coming of the Holy Spirit, for if one benefit of Christ's sacrifice was the remission of sin, another was the "emission" of the Holy Spirit to sanctify believers. By the work of the Spirit there is a "Personal indwelling Presence" of God within believers, and this is what brings to a conclusion God's restoration of God's temple on earth, the regenerate becoming God's "living temple."[171] Holiness of life brought about by the Holy Spirit who renewed the image of God within believers was also affirmed by Bates in his development of the evidences of Christian truth.[172] Such reliance on the inner work of the Holy Spirit would have been scorned by many Restoration Anglicans as enthusiastic; though they agreed that an upright life was the goal of Christian faith, they conceived it in more moralistic terms.[173]

Summing Up

For all their similarities, these three dissenting natural theologians went about their tasks rather differently. Baxter's treatment of the subject is a listing of arguments, sometimes randomly and digressively, with practical concerns to the fore, and with the personal asides so characteristic of his writing. Bates's work is compact, clear, logical, sober, and measured in its argumentation, with the greatest similarity of the three to the Church of England versions of natural theology. Howe's *The Living Temple*, on the other hand, with its central image of the temple of God among humankind providing unity, from the original founding of that temple, to its decay, to its restoration, is architectonic in a way untrue of Bates and Baxter. It can be compared to a medieval summa in the way it proceeds from things coming from God as creator and then returning to God as redeemer (Christ descended, in order to "make way for a glorious ascent" of redeemed humanity, Howe says)[174] first through the earthly divine footprints of natural theology and then through a necessary revelation which picks up where the footprints of nature and reason end.

Such a coherent plan and structure was available to Howe because of his Platonic (or more precisely, Neoplatonic) formation and gives his work a depth lacking in that of Bates and Baxter. Barbara Shapiro has made a distinction between the more empirically inclined of the Church of England Latitudinarians (Wilkins, Tillotson, and obviously Locke) and those, centered on Cambridge, who represented a Platonic orientation. The first of these relied on common sense and everyday observation while the second sometimes defended innate ideas, stressed the necessity of spirit as a cause in nature, and inclined to a more mystical spirituality.[175] This distinction is helpful in understanding the differences between the works of these dissenting Latitudinarians, with Baxter offering some severe strictures against "platonizing" while Howe, who had connections to the Cambridge group or their ideas (as did those very different Dissenters, Peter Sterry and Theophilus Gale), developed a Christian apology suffused with Platonism.[176] Bates was somewhere in between the other two on this issue.

In developing natural theology and the evidences for Christianity in the way they did, Baxter, Bates, and Howe were true to salient elements of their heritage of Reformed theology and Puritan piety, with their stress on sin, grace, atonement, supernatural regeneration by the Holy Spirit, and holiness of life. They also followed some of the themes related to natural theology found in Calvin (although none mentioned his name in their writings on natural theology), as they pointed to a common human recognition of deity drawn (especially by Bates) from such classical sources as Cicero and Seneca, recognized the creation as a mirror of divine activity, stressed the corruptions of idolatry which obscured the original knowledge of God, maintained the absolute necessity of revelation if there were to be restored fellowship with God, and treated atheism as irrational heedlessness of God.[177] Richard Muller has observed that while Reformed theologians employed the causal, cosmological, and teleological arguments for the existence of God typically associated with Thomas Aquinas, they also "tended to follow patterns of Renaissance logic, and to develop discursive rhetorical arguments for the existence of God—as much for the purpose of persuading so-called practical atheists as for the sake of rational demonstration of the existence of God." This clearly fits much of the argumentation found in the natural theologies of Baxter, Bates, and Howe, and further evidences their Reformed provenance.[178]

But their version of natural theology was different from earlier Reformed thinkers in several ways. It has already been seen that both their considering Christianity alongside other religions and their constructing evidential arguments upon a previously developed base of natural knowledge of God were departures from an earlier Reformed approach. If their approach remained fairly spiritual and rhetorical, they nonetheless developed in considerable detail the teleological argument from design, drawing on many appropriate analogies like that of the watchmaker deity and pondering the human usefulness of many of the cosmological arrangements and bodily functions in a manner characteristic of the physico-theological apologetics that was to flourish in the hundred years after their writings were published, and which seemed such an effective response to the discoveries of a new natural science. Because the challenges they faced and the "proto-Enlightenment" tenor of their times differed from that of earlier Reformed theologians, they struck out in some of the same new directions of argument as did the much less Calvinistic conformist authors who were their contemporaries in writing on these subjects, and in all of this they were in company with Reformed thinkers elsewhere who were widening the scope of natural theology and honing evidential arguments for the truth of Christianity in order to defend Christian truth in their time and place.[179] Clearly then, a natural theology and argument for Christianity from the evidences attuned to new philosophical challenges and to the new scientific interests flourished in the Restoration era among Dissenters, particularly in a circle associated with Richard Baxter, as well as among Church of England conformists; but this dissenting version differed significantly from most conformist versions in being integrally related to a Calvinist and Reformed sensibility. This "Baxterian" or moderate Calvinist natural theology was not only a step toward a new religious world but also one late seventeenth-century variant of the Calvinist theological heritage.

6

John Edwards

Church of England Calvinist

John Edwards was a staunch Calvinist and a Church of England conformist at the turn of the eighteenth century, when such a combination was not as common as it had once been. Although the only conformist among the Calvinists examined in this book, he was the most self-consciously Calvinist, repeatedly and proudly using the label as a designation for his viewpoint, and he was also the only one who showed interest in Calvin himself.

It is the purpose of this exposition and analysis of John Edwards's thought and writings to show that he wrestled with the same challenges of scoffing, atheism, Deism, anti-Trinitarianism, and the new meaning of reason as did the other Calvinist and Reformed thinkers considered in this book, and added to that a strong defense of Calvinist anti-Arminian theology as the proper and historic viewpoint of the Church of England. He furthered scholastic Reformed theology as did Gale; evangelical Calvinist grace-centered piety as did Joseph Alleine and the circle that promoted Joseph Alleine; natural theology and the evidences of Christianity as did Howe, Bates, and Baxter; and a Platonically tinged philosophy in the company of Sterry, Gale, and Howe. He represented a Calvinist variety not only by his own peculiar polemical approach to the faith but also by his embattled insistence that as a conformist he was defending the Calvinist faith of the Church of England against those who had departed from it. In that defense he stressed his conformist credentials and joined others in the Church of England who increasingly defended their church by appealing to the ancient church fathers.

With respect to his background, Edwards's Calvinism is less surprising than his conformity. Born in 1637, he was the second son of Thomas Edwards, militant Presbyterian nonconformist opponent of Archbishop Laud and eminent heresiographer of the 1640s, who died when John was only ten years of age. The younger Edwards was educated in Interregnum Cambridge at St. John's College from 1653 to 1661, at that time presided over by the Puritan-inclined and staunchly Calvinistic Anthony Tuckney, who played a significant role in drawing up the Westminster Confession and catechisms (at the Restoration Tuckney was soon pushed out as Master of the College). Awarded the B.A. in 1658, Edwards became a fellow of St. John's in 1659 and received the M.A. in 1661. He was ordained both deacon and priest in 1662. In 1664 Edwards began preaching at Trinity Church, Cambridge, while remaining a fellow. His preaching was popular and he gained favor during an outbreak of the plague in 1665 when he ministered to the stricken. In 1668 he received the B.D. degree and was appointed lecturer in Bury St. Edmunds. After about one year there, he returned to his college at Cambridge.

Edwards's Calvinism and Puritan sympathies caused conflict with Tuckney's successors at St. John's, leading him to resign his fellowship, after which he took up the study of civil law. But before long he was once again a parish incumbent, at St. Sepulchre's, Cambridge. In 1683 he was given the vicarage of St. Peter's, Colchester, where he then resided. But ill health and marriage to a widow of some means led to his retirement from that post in 1686 and his settlement first in a Cambridgeshire village and then in Cambridge itself in 1697, where he devoted the rest of his life to study and publication—a torrent of books came from his pen beginning in the late 1680s. In 1699 he was made Doctor of Divinity by Cambridge University. He died in 1716.[1]

Polemicist, Affectionate Divine, Scholastic

Like his father, the younger Edwards became notorious as a theological writer on the lookout for heresy. Perhaps his conformity was related to a commitment like that of his father to the need of a national church to combat heresy, and like his father he cultivated "a populist literary strategy"[2] in his invective against opponents. Perhaps the younger Edwards felt a mission to complete his father's labors against heresy that were so untimely ended in 1647 by a fatal ague when the elder Edwards was only forty-eight years of age. In any case, the younger Edwards became a harsh harrier of heretics with a style so polemical and with such a reputation for controversy that he was rather isolated within the Church of England. He is perhaps now most well known for his attack upon John Locke, but he also crossed swords with an array of opponents, including numerous Church of England divines and some proponents of the new natural science.[3] The title page of a book of 1713 summed up his opponents neatly, declaring that it was written against Papists, Arians, Socinians, Pelagians, Remonstrants, Anabaptists, Antinomians, Deists, atheists, Skeptics, enthusiasts, and libertines. The same work ended with a separate "Index to Writers Censured."[4] He could be apt with an insult, excoriating one opponent for "an Amphibious and Trimming conscience."[5] Nor did he suffer attacks on his views gladly: he declared his motto was that of a "neighbouring nation," that "no one shall insult me, and go Scot-free."[6] One exasperated opponent made reference to Edwards's "insolent way of expressing himself," as "his peculiar Talent."[7]

Aware of his reputation, Edwards offered in one of his writings "A Defence of Sharp Reflections and Censures on writers and their Opinions, when there is Occasion." Acknowledging that some had faulted him for being too harsh and "a stranger to civility" in controversy, he seemed to prove their point by countering that his accusers were ignorant of all the precedents for "smartly" reflecting on errors, as the biblical prophets, John the Baptist, Jesus, and innumerable authors did so. He amassed a list of precedents that consisted of pagans as well as Christians, including Dionysios of Halicarnassus, Lactantius, Minucius Felix, Photius, Luther, and Calvin. Should it be objected that he was only citing "foreigners," he provided a list of English polemicists, from John of Salisbury to his near contemporary John Bramhall.[8]

But Edwards also turned the tables on his critics and assailed others for being too disputatious in theological argument, condemning those "whose Trade and Work it is to raise Controversies"; such captious love of quarreling he considered a significant source of error—one should not be too quick to accuse another of heresy but "be content to speak Probably, not certainly," taking a middle way.[9] After all, good Christians might err, and again seeking examples, he took the case of the Lutheran doctrine of consubstantiation, which served as a warning that not every doctrine taught by godly persons should be received as truth.[10] That Edwards was not as inconsistent as might first appear is evident from his remark that he favored liberty and avoided "dogmatizing" except where the "Necessary and Fundamental Points" of Christianity were concerned.[11] Of course, there were major differences of opinion in the England of his time as to exactly what those fundamental points were. He also insisted that he sought to follow scripture, insisting that he did not consider whether or not he would displease other persons when he had scripture on his side.[12]

But there is much more than polemic in the writings of John Edwards. There is a certain baroque excess in the long rambling passages of his books which displayed recondite and miscellaneous learning, not unlike Cotton Mather in New England, who, by the way, recommended that students for the ministry read John Edwards's books. At other times, he is a witty and engaging if occasionally hectoring author—certainly he paraded his learning with less heavy-handedness than did Theophilus Gale. Sometimes his books, especially some of the later ones, are rather random, intermixing crotchety opinions with impressive biblical exegesis and astute theological argumentation—such as his judgment that poetry was something "unnatural, strain'd, and out of order; it is as if Men and Women should affect to Dance and Caper, instead of plain-walking."[13]

The first published work of Edwards was neither polemical nor pedantic but standard "godly" affectionate divinity not unlike that of Joseph Alleine, a forty-eight- page treatise based on sermons he had preached to his congregation in Trinity Church, Cambridge, which pastorally addressed the outbreak of plague in that city. Entitled *The Plague of the Heart,* it developed an extended "metaphor" (his word) of spiritual plague, a plague far worse, he declared, than the physical kind. While bodies are sickening "in your streets," souls suffer from the plague of sin, which is then analyzed as to its symptoms (such as "swelling tumours of pride"), its spread ("epidemicall and catching"), its prevention (shun those infected with it), and its cure, for which a true spiritual physician will prescribe the needed "strong and bitter" medicine, unlike a "quack" who would palliate the disease with "wine and merry company." The true cure is the blood of Jesus.[14] *A Treatise of Repentance,* published posthumously, but based on sermons he had preached during his "regular ministry," which could have been any time between 1664 and 1686, reveals his commitment to the preaching characteristic of Calvinist spirituality.[15] But Edwards, especially when compared to others examined in this book, published relatively little that could be described as affectionate divinity, though he seems to have practiced it in his pastoral charges, and he certainly recommended the Reformed piety of renovation by grace to his fellow pastors in the Church of England, exhorting them to stress "Supernatural power in conversion" and not just "nibble on some Moral Topicks."[16] Like others examined here, in what was perhaps becoming a commonplace of the time, he stated his preference for practical religion over disputation—even if the latter seemed his main preoccupation.[17]

His three volumes entitled *The Preacher; A Discourse Shewing, what are the Particular Offices and Employments of those of that Character in the Church,* published between 1705 and 1709, evidence his commitment to affectionate divinity as a pastoral strategy. He recommended that "an evangelical preacher" should preach in a plain style, informed by learning, with neither anything "rude or boorish" nor "too much care and art," preaching "with all tenderness of affection," and exuding "Warmth and Vigour in the Pulpit." Prefiguring a motif of the later evangelical awakenings, he declared that a preacher "who is himself altogether cold and frozen" cannot "kindle in others an ardent desire ... after the things of eternity." Edwards added that "Personal Holiness makes our preaching effectual," for a good life is a "convincing Sermon." Preaching he declared excelled all other pastoral activities, even that of the prayers of the church service, since in preaching God addresses us, while in prayer we address God. In making this point Edwards was refuting those in the Church of England who claimed that too much emphasis on preaching was "done to vilifie the Prayers of the Church" in the liturgy. Perhaps in a compensatory effort to mollify his critics in the established church, he criticized those preachers who spoke in "a strange and uncouth tone," a charge that had often been leveled against the radical preachers of the Cromwellian years and was still being repeated against the Dissenters. On the contrary Edwards said, echoing many Church of England authors, the language of sermons should have "comeliness and beauty."[18]

But Edwards also contended that preaching should include a large dose of refutation of error and heresy.[19] Indeed most of what Edwards wrote belonged to the genre of controversial divinity, nor was controversy absent in his systematic theological treatises and his sermons. In his attacks against opponents, Edwards responded to many of the same social and intellectual challenges as did the other English Calvinists that have been examined in this book, but for Edwards, living and writing well into the eighteenth century, some of these challenges were more clearly delineated than they had been for Gale, Sterry, Joseph Alleine, or even the Calvinist natural theologians (though Howe too lived into the new century). In addition to his many works of controversial divinity, Edwards also produced a systematic "body of divinity" that came out between 1707 and 1713 in three parts and four large volumes—it too was filled with theological polemic.[20]

In these works of controversial and systematic theology, Edwards employed the tools of Protestant scholasticism, in spite of his occasional severe strictures against scholastic theology—these strictures echoed the earlier views of Renaissance Christian humanists such as Erasmus and paralleled contemporaries who wanted to cut through the thicket of university jargon. Edwards scorned the medieval "schoolmen" for obscuring the truth with "Barbarous terms," decried the "Dry and Sapless niceties of the Schools," and upbraided an opponent as too "scholastical and metaphysical," but this was the abuse and misuse of scholastic method, for Edwards defended "Metaphysical and Scholastick Learning" as "serviceable" in its terminology and "useful distinctions," particularly since in controversies those skilled in this learning have "the advantage of their Adversaries." Logic, Edwards said, citing Clement of Alexandria, is a "Hedge and Fence to the Truth, to keep it from being trodden under foot by Sophisticall Heretics." Metaphysics, he added, echoing Cartesian terminology, helps us to "a clear and distinct apprehension of things."[21] Edwards thus joined the persisting scholastic theologians of the era in his use of logic, philosophy, and concern for precise terminology and also in his view that there were certain matters of theological prolegomena that must be attended to in developing Christian doctrine, including epistemological and methodological concerns. He stated this latter point in the preface to his *Sermons on Special Occasions and Subjects* (1698) where he noted that he was writing a book that would survey all religion from the beginning of time (it came out the next year as *A Complete History or Survey of all the Dispensations and Methods of Religion*) and preparing another that would constitute an inquiry into truth and method in religion (presumably his *Free Discourse Concerning Truth and Error,* published in 1701); both of these books would be, he asserted, preliminary to treatises against Arminianism and Roman Catholicism and to a proposed body of divinity. In his *Free Discourse* he noted that not only it but also his books on scripture and God's existence were preliminary to doctrinal treatises that he planned to write. His doctrinal treatises came out as a body of divinity under various titles between 1707 and 1713. Richard Muller identifies John Edwards as a significant practitioner of the systematic theology of Reformed orthodoxy, and accordingly Edwards should be accounted one of the later representatives of scholastic Calvinist orthodoxy among English theologians.[22]

Scoffing and Atheism

Edwards's controversial treatises worried about scoffing at religion, but like other conformists he perhaps felt it less sharply than did Dissenters, for whom scoffing was part of the general opprobrium directed against them by cultured despisers. But when Edwards portrayed scoffers as those who "laugh at conversion and Regeneration as mere Canting Terms," and mock the way of salvation by Christ's satisfaction for sin, he echoed the Dissenters, as it was the Reformed theology of supernatural grace that was the object of ridicule, unlike his fellows in the established church, many of whom themselves scoffed at such piety as dangerous enthusiasm. Edwards sounded the more general denunciation of scoffing that both conforming and dissenting clergy shared when he declared that it was not strange that those who resolved to be wicked "hate reproof."[23] Scoffers "come upon the stage like Buffoons," and especially target those clergy who are "strict and religious"; such "laughing Philosophers" consider themselves "witty" when they "scoff at virtue and Piety," and "mock God himself" in their atheism. It was their very scoffing that led them and others to atheism—they would "laugh God out of his being."[24]

Conflict with atheism loomed large in the writings of Edwards. His books mention atheists and atheism with frequency, but in one, *Some Thoughts Concerning the Several Causes and Occasions of Atheism, Especially in the Present Age,* he gave the subject sustained attention (appended to this work was also his first attack on John Locke's *The Reasonableness of Christianity* as Socinian). While Edwards used the familiar language about atheists as libertine and immoral,[25] and employed the slippery slope argument that much of what he opposed tended to atheism (Socinianism, for example, he declared, had an "Atheistic tang"),[26] it is clear that what he generally meant by atheism was a complete denial of the existence of God and other spiritual realities, not just practical atheism—though the latter led to the former.[27] Atheists, with whom "this present age" is "pestered," think that to believe in God is a "Melancholick conceit," the result of ignorance and credulity, and claim that there is no God, "no Supreme Over-ruling Being of Infinite Perfection," but that "an everlasting Juncto [sic] of Atoms did without Counsel and Knowledge club together to make the World" and that "Religion is a mere Invention of Politick Heads to awe the Multitude, and to keep the world in good order."[28] Edwards included among the causes of atheism the quarrels among Christians (to which he had contributed his part);[29] he also counted as a source of atheism the hypocrisy and corruption of church and clergy, citing Roman Catholic examples.[30] Edwards shared the conviction of many of his contemporaries that atheism was becoming more widespread, and that it was fashionable to talk like an atheist.[31] He seems to connect it also with belles lettres, as in his observation that the "Amorous Sallies" and "Lascivious Flights" of poetry led to atheism.[32] And like Baxter, Edwards thought the denial of the reality of demons and witches, who evidenced spiritual realities, was a road to atheism.[33]

Edwards loved to cite authors, so his discussion of atheism named some of those considered atheists but began with the case of Socrates, famously accused of atheism, and exonerated him of the charge: Socrates, he said, echoing a hoary patristic theme, criticized inadequate ideas about God and died "a martyr for a Deity."[34] Other philosophers accused of atheism do not fare so well: the mechanical philosophy associated with Descartes, whom Edwards knew was no atheist, explained natural phenomena better than the "Aristotelian way," but when taken to an extreme by reducing all causality to natural and material causes it denied the spiritual and turned men into "Senseless Puppets," encouraging atheism. Descartes was also at fault for abandoning final causes, which undercut the argument from design. Edwards especially rejected, as Bates and

Howe had, the Cartesian description of animals as mere machines, and asserted that many philosophers recognized spiritual and "incorporeal" causality, including "Learned Dr. More," Robert Boyle, and John Ray. But Edwards acknowledged that as clarified by Nicolas Malebranche, the ideas of Descartes were not inimical to religion.[35]

Nothing positive, however, is said about either Spinoza or Hobbes, both widely accused of atheism at that time. Spinoza is faulted for his destructive views about the Bible such as the denial of the Mosaic authorship of the Pentateuch and his opinion that the Bible was filled with contradictions; God and religion will fall with the Bible, if such views gained ground, according to Edwards.[36] Hobbes is a special target of Edwards, as he was of so many others at this time: not only was he associated with dangerous ideas about the Bible like those of Spinoza, but also his denial of spiritual reality constituted atheism, and his notion of a "corporeal God" was no God at all—the ideas of Hobbes were destructive of "all Religious Principles." Elsewhere Hobbes's skepticism, mortalism, and annihilationist denial of hell's eternity are decried. Characteristically, Edwards was particularly incensed with Hobbes's claim that preaching fails to improve morals and is dangerous to the state (an opinion of Hobbes obviously related to that philosopher's distaste for the rabble-rousing preaching that played into rebellion in the 1640s).[37]

Natural Theology and the New Science

Edwards not only railed against atheism but also developed arguments against it, engaging in the same kind of natural theology characteristic of Baxter, Bates, and Howe, further illustrating its vogue. At the end of his treatment of atheism, Edwards exhorted his readers to labor to develop "a profound sense of that Great God with whom we have to do." This he thought could be cultivated by examining the works of creation by which God "is made visible" as the footsteps of God in the world are seen.[38] In 1696, the year after the publication of his book on atheism, Edwards followed it up with A Demonstration of the Existence and Providence of God. This work refuted atheism by means of the argument from design, showing it in the first part of the work in the macrocosm, revealing "the Excellent Contrivance of the Heavens, Earth, Sea" and in animal life, and in the second part in the microcosm, "the Wonderful Formation of the Body of Man." In doing this, Edwards avers, he has amassed sufficient evidence of the harmony of all things in the cosmos to show that the "pulchritude and consent of things cannot be without an Eternal Mind," a "Supreme Director," and to rule out the possibility that this could have been a mere matter of chance.[39] He repeated what he had said in his refutation of atheism, that it was "vain" to think that all this could be accounted for by the "Mechanick Philosophy" of Descartes, and again noted that both Henry More and Robert Boyle had shown this.[40] Edwards also took gravity and magnets to be examples of spiritual rather than mechanical causation.[41] The natural theology of design of Edwards, however, was not like the terse argumentation of Bates, content with a few illustrations of design in nature, or the comments of Howe, or even the lengthier arguments of Baxter, but went beyond the earlier natural theology into a full panoply of detailed physico-theology of the sort that was becoming common in writers such as John Ray (whom Edwards occasionally cited) and others. Such physico-theology had grown out of the earlier natural theology but differed from it in that instead of focusing on the design of creation as a whole, it celebrated the way in which the details of nature worked for the practical convenience of human life and society, resorting to an expanded body of recent scientific observation in making this case.[42] Accordingly, in the first part Edwards discussed the sun's motion and warmth, winds, clouds, rain, storms, meteors, and the whole "frame" of the earth. In the process he defended mountains (which he said are not just a result of Noah's flood, a point that had been asserted by Thomas Burnet) against those who argued that the earth's jagged surface is not ideally suited for human habitation; on the contrary, mountains provided boundaries between nations, supplied minerals, sheltered the plains from winds, and, in a foretaste of the later Romanticist view of mountains, enabled the contemplation of "greatness." In the same vein of nature as sublime, he thought the seas "a great ornament to the world."[43] Echoing the themes of what was eventually referred to as "vegetable sermons," Edwards pointed out the alimentary and medicinal uses of plants, uses sometimes borne as a "signature" on the plant itself (as with walnuts, which resemble the human brain and are nutritious for it).[44] Animals also "set forth God's Power and Wisdom," providing food and medicine (citing Galen, he instanced ground-up earthworms as good for the ears and teeth), and are used by God's providence to call us to repentance (as lice created to plague the Egyptians). The elephant is a "monument of the Divine Power." But he rejected the opinion of Pliny the elder that the purpose of poisonous snakes was to enable suicide without bloodshed.[45]

The second part of Edwards's *Demonstration* focused on the intricate design of human beings. As the most perfect of animals and the "Prince of Creation," humans only, appropriately, stand and walk upright, have chins, laugh and weep, and are able to blush out of modesty. A large body of data about design in human anatomy and physiology followed, all directed at revealing intricacy of design: the teeth, the eye, the heart ("Mr. Harvey" is mentioned), the hand and the intestines, among much else, are discussed; he even mentions a muscle, "whereby untimely Excretion is prevented and hindered; the Benefit of which cannot sufficiently be expressed."[46]

As befits an author engaged in physico-theology, Edwards apparently read about the natural science of his day which was gaining so much attention. And more than the other Calvinists treated in this book, he worried about some of the implications of recent discoveries in natural science. His first foray into these matters came in 1684 and dealt with comets at a time when he thought there was much alarm over them. His title sets forth the book's purpose: *Cometomania. A Discourse of Comets: Shewing their Original, Substance, Place, time, magnitude, motion, Number . . . and, more especially, their Prognosticks, Significations and Presages. Being a brief Resolution of a seasonable Query, viz. Whether the Appearance of Comets be the Sign of approaching Evil?* Although the book treated the science of comets, canvassing learned opinion on the matter at length, it is apparent that what was really at stake was God's providential intervention in the world through "prodigies" to warn of calamities to come and to call persons to repentance; he wrote to refute those who denied the "ominous" and "portentous" nature of comets. The loss of belief in this would weaken the sense of God's activity in the world. Thus Edwards was pleased that so many classical authors (Seneca, Virgil, Cicero) as well as many persons important in making recent discoveries in natural philosophy (Tycho Brahe, Kepler, Galileo, and Descartes) agreed that comets had a providential dimension. For Edwards was certain that comets were "signs of future Evils," portending great changes in earthly affairs, such as the deaths of princes. He listed many examples of comets that warned of disasters but acknowledged that often the evil presaged by a comet was deferred and that many evils occurred in the world without any such warning.[47] In his treatment of providential design in his natural theology, Edwards argued that earthquakes were providential acts of God's just judgments on the world. But he also observed that both earthquakes and comets had natural causes as well—comets could be treated by both natural philosophers and theologians as things may be both "Natural Causes and Effects, and yet Divine Tokens." Such he thought was even the case with certain biblical events, such as the burning of Sodom and Gomorrah.[48]

Edwards's second foray into the burgeoning world of natural science came in 1697 with a rejection of Copernican astronomy (at a rather late date for this) in his *Brief Remarks Upon Mr. Whiston's New Theory of the Earth.* William Whiston, clergyman and mathematician, was attacked for replacing the Mosaic account of creation with one based on "the strict laws of the Mechanick or Corpuscular Philosophy," which Edwards thought played into the hands of Deists, undermining belief in biblical revelation. We have no reason, he said, "to quit Moses for Copernicus." The Mosaic account he added, was literal and historical, not allegorical. Edwards also opined that the Copernican hypothesis would soon be "exploded."[49] In another book of four years later, he referred to himself as no friend of the Copernican hypothesis but seems to have softened in his opposition to it. Considerably later, in a publication of 1714, Edwards only stated that Copernican astronomy was "uncertain" and while criticizing Henry More's animistic view that gravity was the love of bodies for one another, accepted More's view that gravity was an immaterial agent and form of spiritual causation dependent on the existence of a God.[50] In that same work, Edwards, with Isaac Newton in his sights, asserted the uncertainty of the first principles of natural philosophy; however, in another publication of that year he praised Newton as one "who hath justly merited the Applause of the learned World, for his admirable Efforts in Natural Philosophy and Mathematics."[51]

Deism and the Evidences of Christianity

Deism loomed on the intellectual horizon of Edwards, as he lived well into the eighteenth century when it seemed flourishing. He thought the admirers of Locke's religious views were Deists, claimed that without revealed religion and with the Deists' rejection of mystery in Religion, Deist natural religion without revelation would soon be abandoned, and wondered if Deists were not really just "sly" atheists, disguising skeptical ideas more radical than even Deism under a false name, an impression that many anti-Deist writers had and that may not be altogether false.[52] But generally, even though he consistently maintained that Deism led to atheism, he treated Deism as a distinct form of error, to be refuted by the evidences of the truth of the Christian religion.

In 1693 Edwards published a book on the authority and perfection of scripture, thereby making his contribution to the literature of "evidences." In it, he cleared up certain seeming scriptural inconsistencies, defended the integrity of the text (including the Hebrew vowel points as original to it), and argued that the perfection, consistency, and sublimity of scripture proved its truth. He also maintained, as had Theophilus Gale (whom he dubbed "a Person well versed in Critical Learning"), that much in non-Jewish ancient writings was derived from the original revelation to the Jews even if garbled in the transmission, and that some of this borrowing antedated Moses and went back to the aftermath of the Tower of Babel. He thought the Old Testament was the most ancient literature, and that Hesiod, Plato, and Sanchuniathon received their accounts of the world's creation and other matters unknowable to reason alone from it.[53] But ancient theology did not play the central role in Edwards's thought that it did in Gale's.

Defense of scriptural integrity and perfection was not the only weapon against the Deists in Edwards's arsenal; he deployed others in a treatise that followed up his books attacking atheism and providing its antidote in natural theology. This treatise was *A Compleat History or Survey of all the Dispensations and Methods of Religion, From the beginning of the World to the Consummation of all Things . . . In which also . . . the Certainty of the Christian Religion [is] demonstrated, against the Cavils of the Deists,* a work of two volumes which is somewhat reminiscent in its historical approach of Augustine's *City of God* as well as prefigurative of Jonathan Edwards's *History of Redemption.* In it he described the various economies of God in dealing with the world to refute the claim that Deism was the original religion. These volumes addressed certain conundrums that opponents might raise, for example, the reason for the ceremonial laws among the Jews or the reason why the Christian dispensation came so late. They also employed the well-worn arguments from biblical miracles and prophecy as well as the miraculous character of "the wonderful prevailing and spreading of Christianity." There is in addition an argument from the "transcendent worth of the Christian Religion," and another from the great improvements in the world already brought about by Christianity and yet to come from it: the world "is much amended, and is like to be improved yet further in future times."[54]

Epistemology

Having wrestled with some of the implications of the new science and refuted atheism with natural theology in 1696 and Deism with evidences of Christianity in 1699, in 1701 Edwards published a book on the question of whether and how one could know truth. This clarified the epistemological base upon which he had developed earlier arguments and was entitled *A Free Discourse Concerning Truth and Error, Especially in Matters of Religion.* It expanded an earlier sermon on truth which Edwards had delivered in the presence of King Charles II at Newmarket (there is no indication of the date of this sermon which was published after the King's death). Edwards reported that he wrote the discourse after being asked by others to enlarge upon what he had said in the sermon.[55]

In the sermon Edwards noted that some claimed a monopoly on true religion while others said that all religion was a "cheat"; in opposition to such extremes Edwards says that the truth can be known by the "light of nature and of scripture," or by reason and revelation. Reason he defined as "the free and impartial use of our Understandings and Judgments which God hath naturally endued us with," and which we "improve" by the aid of our bodily senses, the testimony of others, and "by serious and steady Observation of well-grounded experience." If we seek truth we will find it, for human reason is "the Candle of the Lord" (a frequent phrase with the Cambridge Platonists that had Augustinian illuminationist implications) given us by God that we might discover the truth. However, more is needed for gaining the full truth of God, and that was provided by supernatural revelation, which is necessary for the eternal happiness of salvation. Much of what scripture reveals consists of "mysteries" beyond reason.[56]

The larger *Discourse* referred to those atheists, Deists, libertines, and skeptics, including ancient ones like Pyrrho, who doubted revelation and that ultimate truth could be known. We can be assured, Edwards stated, that ultimate truth is available to us because it is the innate nature of the soul to eagerly pursue it as "the genuine food and repast of Humane Minds," because God would not plant false notions in the human mind (ignorance and error are a "blemish" on the mind), and because of that moral goodness which resulted from conscience perceiving truth. Edwards further thought that the many claims to truth meant that truth exists, just as no one would counterfeit coins unless there were real ones. From the actuality of truth, his argument took a Neoplatonic turn as he proceeded to the nature of truth: it is the correspondence between "things themselves" and the words we use in our discourse about these things, which are based on the presence in God of the "Essential and Eternal Ideas of all things which were afterwards to be created." This argument suggests his kinship with the Cambridge Platonists (Cudworth and Benjamin Whichcote as well as Plato are cited) and depended on the prior existence of ideas in the divine mind which are implanted in human minds as the image of God in which humans were created; these ideas are in humans "derivatively and secondarily." Such ideas in the divine mind convey truth to us: knowing the archetypes innately, humans assent to their truth without deduction or ratiocination. Reason means then not only discourse and argumentation but also recognition of truth through innate ideas. Descartes, now dubbed "the Incomparable French Philosopher" and else-where "that man of France who was as great a Reformer in Philosophy as Calvin, his Country-man, was in Divinity" (perhaps the highest compliment Edwards could offer), is drawn into the argument as one who proved that the ideas of God and the Soul are innate to us, for even though with Descartes the mind is methodologically stripped of all ideas to start over with what cannot be doubted, those ideas that are part of God's image in human hearts cannot be expunged. For Edwards there is a valid natural law as well as recognition of moral and other truths by means of common consent; moreover, religion "is inlaid in the very Nature of the Soul." Edwards associated the denial of innate ideas with Socinianism.[57]

As in the brief sermon, so in the larger treatise discussion of what is known by reason is followed up by discussion of the perfection of religious knowledge through divine revelation, as found in scripture, which conveys mysteries unknowable to reason and confirms what was known by the natural light of reason, revealed truth not erasing the "Reasonable Nature of Man" but improving and exalting it.[58]

But Edwards in his epistemological musings also stressed the ease and likelihood of error and the limits of human knowledge. In *A Free Discourse*, he explained why human error was so widespread, citing that "Great Wit of this Nation," Francis Bacon, who "admirably shew'd how many mistakes may be committed in our conceiving and judging of things." One explanation was the weakness of human understanding, another was the "transcendency" of some of the truths of religion which "dazzle" us like the rays of the sun dazzle our eyes.[59] As for the first of these reasons for ignorance, Edwards lists many causes and examples of human error, and devoted one of his last books to the subject, *Some New Discoveries of the Uncertainty, Deficiency, and Corruptions of Human Knowledge and Learning*. The book is an astonishingly miscellaneous catalogue of errors in all fields of learning, including history, chronology, mathematics, philosophy, and medicine.

Among the errors Edwards considered were those of other religions, but while some non-Christian religions are listed as examples of error in *A Free Discourse*, nowhere does he give very sustained attention to non-Christian religions (apart from Judaism), though he did reveal an awareness of their existence as a problem, noting in a sermon that for some Christianity is to be weighed in the same scales as Judaism and "Turcism" (Islam).[60] And in *A Free Discourse* Edwards followed Gale and other proponents of ancient theology in finding a garbled version of primeval truths in the ancient pagan beliefs he sometimes referred to as "Gentilism," although "Christ's Gospel broke in pieces Gentilism." He also thought that ancient pagans, along with the Brahmins of India, the Japanese, and Muslims sometimes lived upright lives, as did even some Papists and heretics such as Quakers; but while admirable, none of this was that true inward holiness wrought by the grace of God.[61] On the other hand, a universal moral sense is not undermined by what is said about the utter immorality of the "Brasilians or Caribes" and the Hottentots, "with the noise of whom our Ears are mightily grated of late."[62] Edwards also used Islam to prove the necessity of revelation: all peoples, he says, best illustrated by "Mahomet" and his "Alcoran," but also by many examples from the ancient Greeks and Romans, claim a revelation, showing that it is universally thought that more is needed for true spiritual fulfillment than what can be provided by reason alone.[63] But in the vagaries of Edwards's catalogue of errors his main point must not be lost, that the weakness and corruption of reason in post-fall humanity means that revelation is necessary for the knowledge of God in this life, and that even as persons "passionately" seek after truth it will only be perfectly known in heavenly beatitude.[64]

That is when the full truth, including revealed truth, will be clearly known to the redeemed who will no longer be hopelessly dazzled by its light. Edwards may have tried to meet his opponents with reasoned argument, but ultimately he maintained that the fullness of Christian revelation involved mystery, the ways of God being so far beyond human ken, in their mystery transcending human calculation and reasoning. To Edwards, heretics, Deists and atheists rejected mystery in their oversimplified presentation of truth as entirely accessible to human reason and blasphemously railed at the mysteries of Christianity. But the Bible and the Christian gospel contain the mysteries of salvation and the nature of God that surpass reason altogether, and indeed sometimes still surpass comprehension when known by revelation—there are "Profound Abysses in the Christian Religion" which utterly surpass our conceptions; some of the teachings of Christianity are "Incomprehensible and Inconceivable, and will not submit to the nicer Scrutinies of Humane Reason." "The Sublime truths of the Christian Religion still retain, and ever shall the nature of a Mystery." God is the greatest of all mysteries, whose good pleasure it is sometimes "to render Divine Truths more venerable by their Obscurity." Only an inward illumination of the mind by the Holy Spirit, "the Great and heavenly Mystagogue," can enable believers to apprehend these mysteries, and of course that illumination is not available to wicked scoffers. Such mysteries, however, are not contrary to reason but above it, Edwards assured his readers. Many of these points were made in a sermon on "Christianity Mysterious" that Edwards preached in St. Mary's Church in Cambridge in 1697, and then greatly enlarged before publishing.[65] It is noteworthy that both John Locke's *The Reasonableness of Christianity* and John Toland's *Christianity Not Mysterious* had been published the year before. An earlier age would not have questioned that Christianity involved mysteries, but this became an issue after the Restoration when natural religion was emphasized and the rationality of Christianity challenged. Even defenders of Christianity were reluctant to speak of Christian mysteries, although the Deist controversy sometimes forced it upon them.[66] But some insisted upon the mysterious aspects of Christian teaching, notably Blaise Pascal in France, and the physician Thomas Browne in England, in spite of the vogue for rationality and clear and distinct ideas; and later opponents of Deism such as William Law also did so.[67] Certainly Edwards would have to be included among those defenders of Christianity such as Baxter and Howe who had a real sense of Christian mysteries, as seen especially in their discussions of the Trinity.

Edwards tended to leave no stone unturned, and so he proceeded to take up the question of false mysteries, as found in enthusiasm, mysticism, and the Church of Rome ("the mystery of Iniquity"). In spite of his inclination to Platonism, and his favorable references to Henry More, Edwards was deeply suspicious of pantheism and "allegoric theology," warning his readers about them. In *A Free Discourse of Truth and Error,* he listed among causes of error "A Fond Affectation of Obscurities and Mysteries" lacking in plain intelligibility. Such misguided thinking led to the Gibberish of the Gnostics, the "barbarous terms" of the medieval schoolmen, "Sooty Cheymists" such as Paracelsus and Van Helmont who "speak as Darkly and Obscurely as if their Brains were infected with the Smoak of their Furnaces and Laboratories," "the whole Enthusiastick Tribe" of Cabalists, Behmenists, Familists, and Quakers, and, "the Allegorizers" (Philo, Dionysios the Areopagite, and Averroës are mentioned) who are "the most Shameful Corrupters of the Sacred Scriptures and all Theology by their Obscuring and Darkening them." He makes an exception with respect to allegorizing, however, acknowledging a "mystical divinity" for those parts of scripture that have a double meaning, for example, the book of Canticles, which would otherwise be "useless."[68] In a sermon Edwards damned pagan mysteries for their "dark recesses" and lewd ceremonies, and condemned Druids, "Gymnosophists," and Egyptian hieroglyphics for sowing false mysteries (the Deist John Toland thought that the pagan mysteries had corrupted Christianity with their mystifications).[69] Astrology too came in for his opprobrium, and he claimed that the great astronomers Galileo, Brahe, Kepler, and Newton all rejected it (Thomas Browne, "that learned Knight," however, is faulted for accepting it).[70] Although he seems to have made no reference to Peter Sterry, it is likely that Edwards would have been suspicious about some of his writings.

Dissenters such as Baxter and others inveighed against enthusiasts not least because they themselves suffered from the accusation of it by many within the Church of England and wanted to clear themselves of the charge. Although Edwards was no Dissenter, the charge of enthusiasm was often enough directed against Calvinism itself, giving him motivation to firm up his conformist credentials by denouncing it. And he gave this condemnation a nice twist when he declared that some "Popish saints" who claimed immediate revelations were just like Quakers and Ranters in their "delusions and impostures."[71]

Defense of the Trinity

In discussing those aspects of Christian faith that are true mysteries in both his sermon on mysteries and his treatise *A Free Discourse,* Edwards mentioned the doctrine of the Trinity.[72] This was, as already seen, extensively debated at the time, precisely because it seemed a test case for the rationality or irrationality of Christianity. Edwards's most specific defense of the Trinity came in arguments against his fellow Cantabrigian, Samuel Clarke, and secondarily against Isaac Newton and William Whiston. Clarke was a highly reputed philosopher and Whiston had succeeded Newton as Lucasian Professor of Mathematics at Cambridge in 1703. His first salvo against Clarke came in 1712, the year Clarke published his *Scripture Doctrine of the Trinity*, a book widely thought to teach an Arian subordination of Son and Spirit to the Father. Edwards declared that by that time the controversy was about twenty years old[73] (the 1690s had been a particularly vexed decade for the discussion of Trinitarian theology, and in that decade Edwards had accused John Locke of denying the Trinity.)[74] The next year Edwards published a supplement to his first work against Clarke and a year later a third refutation which also contained a postscript refuting Isaac Newton for Spinoza-like ideas mixing God with matter and misusing biblical terminology. In these treatises Edwards depended extensively on patristic argument, maintained that even Plato, "by the light of nature," had asserted a trinity of divine persons, and accused Clarke of idolatry for worshipping a Christ who was a mere creature of God.[75] Edwards also maintained that in their views of the Trinity Clarke and Whiston had "drunk deep" of Socinianism, and it was a commonplace in Edwards's writings (and those of others) that the Socinians made reason the sole judge in matters of faith and rejected mysteries— derision of mysteries and orthodoxy, he said, were "infallible marks" of Socinianism.[76]

Calvinist and Conformist

Socinianism seemed to sum up many heresies as well as lead to Deism and atheism and mockery of orthodox faith; and as Edwards saw it "a Man must be a Calvinist, unless he be a Socinian."[77] Calvinism was the term he used to sum up the true version of Christian faith which he proffered as the antidote to Socinianism and all to which Socinianism was but a slippery slope. Thus one comes to Calvinism as the center of Edwards's commitments, and the way in which he self-consciously and with a bit of lonely desperation represented the persistence of Calvinism within the Church of England.

After the Restoration Calvinism lost ground in the established church, as Arminian and Latitudinarian outlooks became increasingly acceptable and even fashionable. Bishops who had held fast to Calvinist theology were disappearing from the scene: Robert Sanderson died in 1663, and in any case his Calvinism had become somewhat attenuated after the Restoration, though Edwards denied this; Edward Reynolds, bishop of Norwich, who had had strong ties to Puritanism as well as Calvinism before the Restoration, died in 1676; George Morley, bishop of Winchester, who had been an opponent of Arminianism, died in 1684; and Bishop Thomas Barlow of Lincoln, who had once taught John Owen and had continued to produce Calvinistic polemics against Rome, died in 1691. Thomas Tully, longtime principal of St. Edmund Hall, Oxford, defended the Calvinist position from within the Church of England, dying in the same year as Reynolds.[78] John Conant was a moderate Calvinist conformist who eschewed preferment and stayed out of theological controversy while doing his pastoral best;[79] Ralph Josselin was another.[80] Nonetheless, significant strands of Calvinist and Reformed thinking did persist in the established church and have been identified as an "Anglican Reformed Tradition" in a book published in 2008.[81] But Edwards left little sign that he considered himself part of a group.

While Edwards's self-avowed Calvinism perhaps marginalized him within the established church and he had few if any ties to its leadership, he sought to give the impression that he was a loyal son of the church, addressing one bishop (Thomas Tenison) as "Your Grace's Most Dutiful Son," in spite of polemics which belied such a relationship. He was proud of having preached before Charles II,[82] and dedicated a number of his writings to bishops, including Seth Ward, Edward Stillingfleet, John Tillotson, Thomas Tenison, and Simon Patrick, all bishops with whom he had significant theological differences, and several of whom, especially Tillotson, were objects of his attacks. Upbraided for attacking Tillotson, Edwards replied indignantly that Tillotson was not "an exempt person" whom none should call to account. However, Edwards often strove in his dedicatory letters to these dignitaries to find some common point of interest or commitment with the bishop he was addressing: thus a dedication to Stillingfleet compliments the bishop for his opposition to Socinianism, and one to Thomas Tenison praises him for having attacked atheists.[83] In one of his controversial treatises, he tells his readers that he is pleased to have been placed in the company of three "learned prelates" by a "Nameless Socinian."[84] Edwards called the by then deceased bishop of Chester, John Pearson, who shared Edwards's commitment to Reformed theology, "the Incomparable Bishop Pearson" for his defense of the divinity of Christ.[85] In a list of books recommended to those who would be preachers and theologians, Edwards included the works of such Church of England stalwarts as Stillingfleet, Pearson, Henry Hammond, and Jeremy Taylor, even though elsewhere he depicted Taylor as inclined to Socinianism.[86] The pattern is fairly clear: whenever he could praise a Church of England bishop or leading theologian for upholding doctrines dear to him such as the Trinity, atonement, or divinity of Christ, he did so, whether or not they maintained a Calvinist perspective on soteriological matters.

In spite of parading his Church of England credentials, he nonetheless on occasion alluded to his marginality—in one case referring to himself as "not all alone like Athanasius was" (suggesting that it might be heroic and orthodox to be all alone), noting that "several" of his "learned brethren" in the ministry of the established church agreed with him.[87] In another case he acknowledged that the "Calvinian doctrines" have been rejected by the "Generality of our Brethren the Clergy" but that this was no argument against their validity.[88] Occasionally, he expressed hope that this might change, declaring in a publication of 1705 his expectation that with Queen Anne and her bishops there might be a turning back to Calvinism. Later he voiced the expectation that the union of England and Scotland augured a return to a purer faith, as England would be leavened by Scottish Calvinists.[89]

There are many other touches in the writings of John Edwards which suggest conformist commitments and sensibilities. In one treatise he attacked an opponent for showing disdain for "the Clergy of the Church of England"; in another he defended the Book of Common Prayer against any implication that it was Arian, and in yet another he assaulted the Socinians for treating the Eucharist as nothing more than a means of stirring up thankfulness to God.[90] More generally, he declared that the Church of England "as to the main," excelled all other churches, as it was "the most apostolical in the world," a point made at the time by other Church of England clergy.[91]

The Church Fathers

Edwards also showed his kinship to the Church of England by his patristic learning and his habit of making reference to the church fathers in theological debate. "Luther and Calvin are great names," he declared in a sermon "Preached before the Clergy at the Archdeacon of Ely's Visitation," but their study should not lead to neglect of the fathers.[92] He also recommended study of the fathers as preparation for preaching.[93] Emphasis on the literature and authority of the church fathers was a distinctive characteristic of the Church of England in the seventeenth century and grew stronger as the century wore on. However, when Elizabethan bishop John Jewel defended the English church against Roman Catholics by claiming the authority and precedent of the church fathers for changes made in the English Reformation, he was not taking a step that was particularly different from other Protestant reformers. Luther and Calvin asserted that the church fathers of the early centuries were more on their side than that of Rome; study of the church fathers was a factor in Ulrich Zwingli's turn to Reformation; and his Zurich successor Heinrich Bullinger gave weight to the fathers in interpreting scripture. The continental Reformed theologians Martin Bucer and Peter Martyr Vermigli, who came to England to help with its reformation, had a deep knowledge of the fathers and used them extensively in anti-Roman polemics. Jewel was a protégé of Vermigli, and Bucer labored on a collection of patristic quotations which was finished by the first Elizabethan archbishop of Canterbury, Matthew Parker. But while the reformers followed the fathers in matters of Christology and Trinitarian theology, valued their interpretations of scripture, and found in them an arsenal of historical data for argument with Rome, they always subordinated them to scripture;[94] the seventeenth-century Church of England theologians would not have thought otherwise.[95] And, related to that father's theology of sin and grace, Protestant theologians especially used and cited St. Augustine. Beyond polemic uses, the study of the church fathers helped shape Protestant theological writing and discourse, particularly in the development of Protestant orthodoxy throughout the seventeenth century.[96]

One of the problems involved in patristic citation, however, was that the available texts of the fathers were so flawed, and so many spurious medieval writings were included among them, that much of the Catholic-Protestant argument concerning the church fathers dealt with questions of textual authenticity. Furthermore, citations were often drawn from collections of the sayings of the fathers and lacked context.[97] These problems gave rise to the flowering of a more historical and philological study of patristic literature, and during the seventeenth century, advances were made in the editing of the fathers and the gaining of a more accurate and critical reading of them.[98] The Protestant appeal to the church fathers differed from the Roman Catholic insofar as it restricted the authoritative fathers to an early period, variously defined as the first four to six centuries of the Christian era, whereas Catholics usually included medieval authors among them. Exactly where the era of authoritative fathers came to an end was contested in the Church of England.[99]

Thus Protestant patristic scholarship flourished in the established churches of the British Isles. A cadre of such scholars emerged that included the staunchly Calvinist archbishop of Armagh in Ireland, James Ussher, Henry Savile, John Fell, Henry Hammond, William Cave, William Beveridge, Henry Dodwell, and Daniel Whitby. Archbishop Laud gave early encouragement to this development. On the continent England gained a reputation for patristic learning and for being an established church that gave weight to the fathers and the kind of Christianity they represented. This drew some continental Protestants to

England in search of a faith different from both militant Protestantism and Tridentine Catholicism, one that offered a particular style of theological discourse that gave "a much greater consideration for the Fathers than that which was commonly associated with continental Protestantism." Such a theology and piety seemed to offer the possibility of a more irenic Christendom and brought the Huguenot Isaac Casaubon and the Lutheran John Ernest Grabe to England.[100] Church of England patristic scholars were particularly determined to rebut the arguments of the French Reformed theologian Jean Daillé, who had maintained in 1632 that since all Protestants acknowledged that scripture was the primary authority, the fathers could be ignored as unnecessary; his views were taken up by some among both Dissenters and the Church of England. After the Restoration, when it became especially important to establish the point against both Dissenters and Roman Catholics that the Church of England best continued the Christianity of antiquity, the English patristic scholars William Beveridge and William Cave penned refutations of Daillé.[101] Ralph Cudworth and others among the Cambridge Platonists also studied the church fathers for a somewhat different reason, their attraction to the Neoplatonic philosophy and spirituality of the Alexandrian fathers Clement and Origen.[102]

Richard Hooker used the authority of the fathers in an intra-Protestant dispute when he found evidence in them against Presbyterian and other nonconformist notions among the Puritans in his debate with Thomas Cartwright.[103] This explains much of the emphasis upon the fathers by Church of England conformists: patristic literature was ransacked to provide a theological base for the liturgy and government of the national church other than that of the Reformation theology which had provided the impetus for the original separation from Rome. As conflict over Puritanism developed within the English church, an element in the established church sought an outlook which would better support conformity to those aspects of traditional church fabric which had been retained in the course of the English Reformation than did the Reformed theologians of the continent. Lutheranism, with its more pliant Erastianism and its relative indifference to matters of government and ceremony was helpful; but a broad appeal to the church fathers became characteristic of the Laudian divines of mid-century, as they exploited a rift in the use of the fathers within the Church of England that had begun with some within it who became increasingly anti-Calvinist in their theology, such as Lancelot Andrewes and John Overall. They went beyond the standard arguments that Protestant orthodoxy could be vindicated by Protestant consonance with the theology of the early fathers and the Protestant cause defended against Rome by patristic citation to a willingness to use the fathers on behalf of an emerging "new ceremonialism."[104] This pattern of patristic deployment persisted among many conformist divines of the Restoration era and beyond.

A patristic focus also appeared in Edwards and became for him a personal apologetic strategy: like other sons of the Church of England, he would demonstrate his learning in the church fathers and his skill in arguing from their writings, though his use of them would be like that which had prevailed before the Laudian turn. Edwards was especially pleased when he could cite the church fathers against Church of England authors with whom he disagreed, upstaging them as being himself more faithful to patristic antiquity than they. Thus Edwards declared that many in the Church of England who extolled the fathers were in fact undermining "the Ancient Primitive Faith," mentioning Dodwell, Whiston, and Whitby.[105] Edwards corresponded concerning matters of patristic scholarship with Dodwell, who was a representative of the High Church faction bent on emphasizing patristic authority and downgrading Calvinism. But in spite of their mutual interest in the fathers, Edwards accused him of promoting the "High Flyers Divinity" and of trying to "explode" Calvinism by claiming it derived from the Pharisees. Dodwell he considered one of those in the Church of England who misused the fathers in order to revive "Popish tenets and Practices." The basis for attacking Whiston and Clarke for rejecting patristic authority was more clear cut, Edwards observing that they had no "Regard for the Fathers" since they dismissed the conclusions of the "whole Assembly of them at the Council of Nice," though he was aware that they appealed to some of the pre-Nicene ecclesiastical authors to support their Arianism.[106]

This highlights a vexing problem with patristic authority, namely, who is to be included among the authoritative fathers, for Whiston and Clarke found support for their heterodoxy in the absence in the pre-Nicene fathers of a full Trinitarian theology, an argument frequently raised by the English Arians of the time.[107] In some cases it may even have been pre-Nicene patristic texts, which were, after all, chronologically closer to earliest Christianity than Nicea, which led to Arian views. Controversy over Arianism and Socinianism was likely another factor generating deeper study of the church fathers.[108]

Edwards as a conformist thus had an intra–Church of England reason for stressing his commitment to the fathers which was not typical of dissenting Calvinists. But he also frequently cited the fathers in pursuit of his primary aim of defending Reformed theology. This required a more exact definition of the role of patristic authority in the Reformed theology, since Edwards was also quite aware that the fathers could be cited in defense of many teachings and matters of ecclesiastical practice inimical to Reformed belief and usage. Such definition was important, since Edwards both appealed frequently to the authority of the fathers while otherwise cautioning against the errors into which some of them had fallen. Edwards would have been aware of Daillé's view that in the light of the primacy of scriptural authority, the church fathers were superfluous and could be ignored, but apparently did not agree with it since he so frequently used the church fathers to bolster an argument. Edwards had also read William Reeve's preface "On the Right Use of the Fathers" in that scholar's 1709 edition of patristic apologies in which Daillé's position was attacked. But his interest in Reeve focused on the latter's slurs on Calvinism and denial that the fathers taught predestination, which he refuted.[109]

Edwards provided two full discussions of the authority and use of patristic literature. The first of these was in *A Free Discourse of Truth and Error* (1701), where he took up epistemological issues, devoting a lengthy chapter to extolling the usefulness of the church fathers in seeking truth as well as cautioning against blindly relying on them. Here he maintained that one should strive to follow the ancient councils and fathers, insofar as "the Universal Consent of the Church of Christ is allowed as a Good Argument by all Sober Persons," and that "Catholick Suffrage in some cases is an Evidence of Truth"—indeed, "the Joint Testimony of the whole Church of Christ is one source and means of conveying Truth to us." However, many individual fathers erred, and some of their errors opened the door to the worse errors of later "popery"—therefore, the final arbiter of truth must always be scripture. Antiquity alone is no guarantee of knowledge of the truth: the divines of the last two centuries have been better interpreters of scripture than were the fathers, not least because most of the fathers knew so little Hebrew. This same work contains a long chapter to illustrate the errors into which some of the church fathers fell. Moreover, the fathers often criticized one another, and St. Augustine freely acknowledged his errors and those of other esteemed authors. Anselm, Luther, and even some of his Roman Catholic contemporaries have admitted that the fathers sometimes erred.[110]

Edwards's most sustained discussion of this matter came in a posthumous publication entitled *Patrologia: Or A Discourse Concerning the Primitive Fathers and Antient Writers of the Christian Church Designed to undeceive Those who have entertained wrong Apprehensions concerning Them and their Writings.* In this work the points made in *A Free Discourse* were repeated in greater detail, but in a more guarded fashion and with less confidence in the wisdom of the fathers, whom, he said, were excellent persons meriting our esteem, particularly "serviceable to confirm and establish the Catholick Doctrines" such as the Trinity and the Incarnation; yet they "abound with sundry Dangerous opinions and Superstitious Practices." The fathers are especially vulnerable as biblical interpreters, "diluting" the divine word "with their own weak Reasonings," for example, placing the Garden of Eden in heaven.

Their etymologies were often absurd and they have been much excelled by modern commentators in understanding the literal sense of scripture.[111] Whitby was another English patristic scholar who found considerable fault with patristic exegesis and even seemed to agree with Daillé that too much veneration was accorded to patristic literature.[112] Elsewhere Edwards noted that scripture was much better understood since the Reformation and that divines of the last two centuries have more clearly stated scriptural doctrines than all the fathers and medieval theologians and that overvaluing of antiquity is a source of error.[113] That the fathers were important guides in defending dogmas such as the Trinity but less useful in exegesis had long been asserted by Church of England Calvinists, having been remarked upon much earlier by William Perkins.[114]

Edwards excused the errors of the fathers (showing in the process that he was no mere follower of the ancients against the moderns—an argument that had become lively by the end of Edwards's life, and in which High Church clergy had generally taken the side of the ancients[115]) by noting that often, as in the arts and sciences, "it cannot be denied" that in the present "All Arts and Sciences are improved." Edwards, sounding like Francis Bacon, added that in the sciences "the first essays are seldom perfect," and advance (which he especially found in biblical exegesis) is to be expected. Besides, if antiquity is alone the criterion, what about the ancient heretics? Moreover, there are many problems with early noncanonical Christian literature: some of it was spurious and much of it full of "fabulous narratives." Many of the fathers were fond of "Needless Rites and Ceremonies."[116] He was even uncertain of the usefulness of the fathers in anti-Roman polemic: while many Church of England divines had used them for this purpose (William Whitaker, Andrew Willet, Jewel, and Stillingfleet are mentioned—Edwards's encyclopedic mentality seldom let up), in fact, the fathers could be cited on both sides of many issues, and in any case "Romanist authors" rejected the authority of the fathers whenever it suited them.[117] But he elsewhere acknowledged that "opposing Antiquity to Antiquity" could occasionally be useful in argument.[118] But the "best and most Valuable Antiquity" was to be found in scripture.[119]

There is one final point of great importance about the fathers which Edwards made in his *Patrologia*, that the fathers, with reference to the doctrines of faith, predestination, and grace, upheld views consonant with Reformed theology, as when Augustine upheld the doctrines "we now call Calvinian." Elsewhere he commented that the articles of the English church were "according to Augustine's Mind: Which is as much as to say, they were Writ according to Calvin's Mind." Former archbishop of Canterbury Whitgift, among others, is cited for making this equivalence of patristic and Calvinist opinion. The point was further made by Edwards when he asserted that "what is call'd Calvinism was the True Primitive Doctrine of the Christian Church" and not a novelty.[120] And why not, since Calvin was himself "no stranger to Antiquity and the Primitive Fathers."[121]

But even though Edwards's use of the church fathers fits a pattern and growing emphasis in the theological writings of Church of England authors, there is no major point in it that does not echo the views of most earlier Calvinist theologians and of Calvin himself: recent investigations of Calvin's approach to the church fathers describes views much the same as those of Edwards, and no doubt Edwards was aware of this and influenced by it. Calvin considered the church fathers subsidiary authorities to scripture, drew on Augustine more than any others, and used them primarily in polemical contexts, especially in defense of the Reformation against Roman Catholic arguments and against opponents of the doctrine of the Trinity. Calvin also thought the fathers through the fifth century represented a better and purer age of the church.[122]

An Uneasy Conformist?

In spite of sharing an albeit qualified commitment to the patristic learning favored in the Restoration Church of England, Edwards sometimes voiced complaints about the Church reminiscent of earlier Puritan worries, such as Sabbath-breaking, pluralism, and nonresidence among the clergy, and its reluctance to bar even "Scandalous Offenders" from communion.[123]

A more striking difference that set Edwards apart from the Church of England than even his Calvinist theology and denunciation of abuses was revealed in print after his death, and that was his view of episcopacy. Calvinistic bishops such as Thomas Barlow and George Morley were staunch Episcopalians and critical of Dissent, but Edwards in a posthumous *Discourse of Episcopacy* upheld a straightforward Presbyterianism, arguing that while the primitive church had a distinction of clergy and laity, it had no distinction of clergy—all were presbyters or bishops, that being a single office. But eventually "some Presbyters affected to be above the Rest," making others "trucke to them," clearing the way for the development of prelacy, which eventually "made Way for Popery." Even here Edwards claimed patristic support and argued that sources used to defend Episcopacy, such as the Ignatian epistles, were interpolated with later additions. According to this posthumous treatise, early English reformation bishops, including Cranmer and Jewel, as well as later Church of England theologians, such as Whitaker and William Fulke, did not think of episcopacy as of divine right; and entering into a lively Church of England debate about the authenticity of the later books of *The Laws of Ecclesiastical*

Polity that spanned the Restoration era and later, Edwards opined that even "the Judicious Mr. Hooker holds, that Episcopacy may be abrogated, and consequently is not of Divine and Apostolical Right, but is the Political Institution of the Church." Archbishop Ussher's reduced episcopacy he thought recognized the same thing, and all moderate churchmen in England have held that those foreign Reformed churches which do not have bishops are nonetheless true churches. "Presbytery was the Government left in the Church by the Apostles."[124] Here he echoed his father.

As for monarchy, Edwards was clearly on the side of the Whigs in his rejection of the divine right of kings and his support for those changes of regime that had maintained the Protestant succession. In a sermon entitled "The Extreme Danger of Intestine Divisions in a Kingdom" preached before the Lord Mayor and Aldermen (presumably of London) he referred to the "late change of affairs" and the "Happy Revolution" of 1688 which he thought a providential deliverance just when national divisions had made the land vulnerable to popery.[125] He struck the same note in a sermon on November 5, 1709, in which he celebrated deliverance from the gunpowder plot and also gave thanks "for the happy Arrival of King William, and the Great blessings that accompanied it." That arrival had also been on the fifth of November, so on that date loyal English preachers could celebrate a double deliverance from Roman treachery and continued to do so long after 1688. Edwards also on this occasion praised Queen Anne as a ruler of exemplary religious devotion.[126] In 1714 Edwards welcomed the Hanoverian dynasty with a sermon "Occasioned By the late Happy Accesion of King George to the British Throne," in which he condemned those who overvalued the past and nourished "a willful spirit of opposition." King George, he proclaimed, had been given the nation by God in order to defend its faith, laws, and liberties as well as "to unite all his Protestant subjects in one Body." Sounding almost millennial, Edwards added that the best state of religion is yet to come, an age during which Christians will pursue brotherly love and holiness of life.[127]

It is not surprising that Edwards sounded Whiggish on the duty of obedience to rulers. In a sermon published in 1698, he had argued that persons were obliged to obey their rulers in all their "lawful demands," a telling exception, and even a perilous one if the sermon had been preached earlier than 1688, which cannot be determined from its content.[128] He was even more explicit in a posthumously published work in which he gave sustained attention to the question of obedience and maintained that if rulers act against true religion or subvert the constitution of the state, they may lawfully be resisted.[129] That Edwards could sometimes take a jaundiced view of state power is apparent in his observation that "the chiefest Art of State hath been generally to

Dissemble,"[130] a remark that echoed not only Puritan distrust of the hegemonic state's suppression of the godly but also St. Augustine's *The City of God.*

With such views as these, it is no surprise that Edwards believed in leniency toward those Dissenters from the Church of England who were doctrinally orthodox; they were not, he thought, guilty of the sin of schism, a point he had made in an earlier work in which he noted the irony that it was the schismatic Non-Jurors who were particularly insistent that Dissenters were schismatics.[131] Edwards thought it an embarrassment to the Church of England that many of its clergy were less orthodox on the doctrinal portions of the Thirty-Nine Articles than were Dissenters. The real Dissenters and separatists from the Church of England were those who denied central articles of its faith, like the Arminians and the Arian Samuel Clarke. The Arminian clergy in the Church of England "cannot fairly and honestly fasten the Name of Dissenters upon the Non-Conformists (as they do) unless at the same time they suffer these to call them by the same Title. For they both Dissent from the Church of England."[132] Moreover, Edwards considered it folly that the Church of England should "hold fast our Rites and Ceremonies" given by the Reformers of the Church of England, some of which "perhaps they would in a short time have laid . . . aside" while abandoning "the Doctrines they transmitted to us."[133]

The question arises as to why Edwards was a conformist at all: for at least the last two decades of his life he had sufficient wealth to be in no need of preferment in the state church. But his marginality in the Church of England did not mean that he had close ties with the Dissenters; there were various Calvinist-inclined clergy in the state church such as John Conant who had closer ties to the Dissenters than Edwards seems to have had.[134] There was something of the loner about Edwards. And, as earlier noted, he felt the need of a state church in order to protect the orthodox faith in the nation, even though he was embattled in doing just that.

The Church of England Should Be Calvinist in Its Theology

Edwards was thus at best an uneasy conformist to the Church of England, but his principal point both in defining the identity of the Church of England and in arguing against apostasy within it had to do with the question of the Calvinism of the established church. Edwards insistently reminded his readers that from its reformation the Church of England had been one of the Reformed or Calvinist churches and claimed that that identity was currently under attack from a bevy of corrupters within it. Thus a principal burden of Edwards's career as a writer was to defend Calvinism as the valid and historic theology of the Reformation Church of England and to refute those alternative theological systems which threatened or perverted it. He marshaled extensive evidence to prove the Calvinist character of the established church, and in addition to his refutations of Anti-Trinitarianism, Deism, and atheism, he attacked Arminianism as a threat to the established orthodoxy of the Church of England.

The argument from precedent that the Church of England was Calvinist since its reformation appears throughout Edwards's writings. Unlike those Dissenters who assailed the established church for departing from Reformed orthodoxy, as an insider he could say that "of all humane Testimonies and Authorities, that of our own church ought to have the greatest sway with us."[135] Examining the question historically, Edwards maintained that the English church was originally independent of the Papacy, regained that independence at the Reformation,[136] and was reformed with considerable help from foreign Reformed divines such as Martin Bucer and Peter Martyr.[137] In asserting this, Edwards was countering an emergent tendency in the Church of England to exaggerate the indigenous character of the English Reformation: such an emphasis helped support the argument that the English church should go its own way and not stress its connection to foreign Reformed churches.[138] Edwards insisted that the early English Reformers such as Cranmer, Ridley, and Latimer agreed with Calvin—"our Church was founded by such as were Friends to Mr. Calvin's Doctrines," and "all the Archbishops in Queen Elizabeth's Reign professed themselves Calvinists."[139] The Thirty-Nine Articles were Calvinist in tenor—anyone who denied a point so obvious was engaged in Jesuitical reasoning.[140] He particularly found specious the arguments of Bishop Gilbert Burnet about flexibility in interpreting the articles: Burnet he pronounced had made the articles a nose of wax with his "equivocating" and obscuring exposition of them and had thereby opened the door to skepticism and infidelity.[141] Edwards also pointed out that the leaders of the Church of England held Calvinist doctrines in common with their Puritan opponents, differing from the latter mainly on matters of discipline,[142] and that the Church of England agreed with the Synod of Dort,[143] Calvinist doctrines prevailing with the bishops, clergy, and universities of England until the end of the reign of James I.[144] Edwards tellingly included Richard Hooker among those who accepted Calvinist doctrines.[145] The villain who undid this harmony was Archbishop Laud, who was "well affected to Rome," and did much that was destructive of Protestantism.[146] Edwards was not alone among conformists in blaming Laud for the civil wars: Gilbert Burnet and other Latitudinarians thought Laud deserved some blame in the matter.[147] And not surprisingly a Dissenter such as Baxter also blamed Laud for the disruption of the English

Church.[148] According to Edwards, it was only after the Restoration that non-Calvinist views come to be adopted by many of the clergy of the Church of England.[149]

Foremost among those who rejected Calvinism had been the Arminians, and Edwards appeared on the scene as a defender of Calvinism against Arminianism at a time when it was more often the Dissenters who were battling it and calling attention to the triumph of Arminianism in the Church of England. Attacking Arminianism was also a shift from his assaults on such looming threats of a new era as those on Socinians, Deists, and atheists, to an old nemesis of Puritans and Calvinists. Edwards had frequently condemned Arminianism in his writings, but in a work published in 1711 he offered a systematic rebuttal of it. *The Arminian Doctrines Condemn'd by the Holy Scriptures, By Many Ancient Fathers, By the Church of England, and even by the Suffrage of Right Reason* was his response to Daniel Whitby, a Church of England cleric known for his biblical commentaries, anti-Roman polemic, treatises on behalf of comprehension for Dissenters, and, in his last years, Arianism, as already seen. In 1710 Whitby had published a critique of the five articles of the Synod of Dort in which he attacked Edwards's *Veritas Redux* and portrayed Calvinism as outmoded and rare among Church of England divines (William Twisse, a rigid Calvinist who played a leading role in the Westminster Assembly, was his exemplar of it). The Church of England, thought Whitby, generally agreed with the Remonstrants condemned by the Synod of Dort. Whitby referred to Edwards as a "warm but weak" defender of "Calvinistical Doctrines" who, in doing so, "cordially embraces the Doctrine of Mr. Hobbs, and the Turks," a frequent charge of anti-Calvinists that identified Calvinism with fatalism, and must have especially galled Edwards. Whitby charged that predestination had not been taught in the church before St. Augustine and that its intricacies had been borrowed from the medieval scholastics. Whitby had also challenged Edwards's claim that the church fathers were predestinarians, a sally certain to inflame Edwards. But Edwards responded that he had never claimed that all the church fathers taught predestination, only that predestination could be properly designated a patristic doctrine.[150]

Another work of Edwards against Arminianism was *A Letter to the Reverend Lawrence Fogg,* published in 1715, which assailed that author, the dean of Chester, for the Arminian error that predestination was based on God's foresight of those who would repent.[151] Besides the usual Reformed arguments against Arminian teaching, and a determination to find patristic authority for the doctrine of predestination (citing Origen, Cyprian, and Ambrose as well as Augustine) in spite of acknowledging that the majority of the fathers may have thought otherwise, what is noteworthy about Edwards's refutation of Arminianism is its constant reference to Calvin and Calvinism.[152] Thus he declared that Whitby wished to overthrow the "Calvinian Scheme" whereas he was defending "the Calvinian Verities" that were the doctrines of the Church of England at its Reformation.[153]

Edwards Against Rome and the Socinians

It was a long-standing refrain of Calvinists writing against Arminians that the latter opened the door to Rome, undermining Protestantism by their reintroduction of merit into the process of salvation, and Edwards shared this contention.[154] Edwards thought Roman Catholic views about salvation were dangerous and perverted the essence of Christianity and therefore assailed Laud and his post-Restoration theological progeny for denying that the pope was Antichrist. He even turned on Richard Baxter (long suspect for Arminian sympathies) for making too little of the differences between Protestants and Roman Catholics.[155] Edwards maintained that insofar as the Church of Rome was a false church and the church of Antichrist (which, he asserted, was the teaching of the Church of England), salvation cannot be attained in it; otherwise separation from it would not be justified. The erosion of this conviction he thought was a reason for the decay of Protestantism. In making the case, he cited persons with good Church of England connections: John Jewel, William Whitaker, and Thomas Barlow. He is especially indignant about any in the Church of England who have so succumbed to "popish" error as to consider the clergy "real and proper" priests who offer "a proper sacrifice" in the Lord's Supper, on this occasion pointing to Laud, George Bull, and "our nonjuring Brethren."[156] Such ideas were dangerous, because, as he noted elsewhere, even a little "popery" was a Trojan horse.[157] In 1724 there appeared posthumously a lengthy treatise written by Edwards, *The Doctrines controverted Between papists and Protestants . . . With an Introduction, Giving an Account of the Rise and Gradual Progress of Popery, and of the Decay of it at the Reformation,* which debated the full range of doctrinal and historical issues setting the two groups apart. His sermon of November 1710, which applauded the discovery of the gunpowder plot, also celebrated Britain's triumph over papal idolatry, reminded his auditors of the victory over the Spanish Armada and the recent rescue of the nation from "a bigoted Popish Prince, in league with France," through the instrumentality of King William.[158] Clearly Edwards, like other defenders of Calvinism in his time, found it appropriate to confute Roman Catholic claims. Although, somewhat surprisingly, Edwards elsewhere noted that there were some Calvinists among the Papists ("there are Roman Catholicks of all Perswasions, Socinian, Arminian,

Calvinistic"), presumably for the last of these with the Jansenists in mind as well as some medieval theologians. Edwards, like Theophilus Gale, approved the books of Cornelius Jansen.[159]

In refuting Whitby's Arminianism, Edwards had focused on Whitby's denial that grace was an external moving power giving rise to Christian virtues that went beyond Arminianism to "moralist" error, by rendering salvation nothing more than a human moral achievement.[160] For Edwards, this amounted to a rejection of that justification and regeneration by supernatural grace that was the heart of experiential Calvinism. Among his criticisms of Archbishop Tillotson was that the primate of the English Church had taught justification by works. That such criticism of the then deceased but revered archbishop was resented is evident in the rebuttals it brought forth.[161] Edwards also included Lawrence Fogg (whom he handled roughly for Arminianism, as already seen), Henry Hammond, William Sherlock, and Edward Fowler with Tillotson for teaching this same error.[162] For Edwards this moralist error entailed a rejection of those soteriological themes of justification by the imputation of Christ's righteousness to the believer and sanctification by supernatural renovating grace that were the heart of his Calvinist theology. His three-volume magnum opus on practical theology, *The Preacher,* prescribed a warm and affectionate manner in pressing home the truths of a gracious piety, and promoted a morality that was not a mere morality of nature, but one of grace that far exceeded the capacity of nature,[163] which has already been seen as an insistence of Theophilus Gale.

Edwards identified such moralism with his constant adversary, Socinianism.[164] Socinianism, with its denial of the Trinity and the atonement as well as its grace-denying moralism, was a more complete challenge to Calvinist orthodoxy than Arminianism had been, as Edwards recognized. For him, Socinianism was not only the denial of the divinity of Christ and the Holy Spirit but a combination of errors "about Christ's Incarnation and his Design of Coming into the World, and his Satisfaction, and the Doctrine of Justification, and several Other Great Mysteries and Sacred Verities of the Gospel."[165] Conversely, as already seen, Calvinism was its antidote and a "preservative" against it: to repeat, "a Man must be a Calvinist, unless he be a Socinian."[166]

Much else of the theological output of Edwards was directed against the Socinians: his notorious attack on Locke, for example, whom he accused of being "all over socinianized,"[167] of concealing the sufferings of Christ like the Jesuits in China,[168] of denying the Trinity,[169] and of deriving his religion from Hobbes.[170] Edwards's treatise *The Socinian Creed: Or, a Brief Account of the Professed Tenents and Doctrines of the Foreign and English Socinians,* published in 1697, continued the assault upon Locke but broadened its scope to a more general treatment of Socinianism, charging that "mocking" at salvation through the grace of the atonement opened the way for Deists, atheists, and scoffers at religion.[171] Edwards's *Thoughts concerning Atheism* joined Jeremy Taylor and Arthur Bury, author of the anti-Trinitarian tract *The Naked Gospel,* with Locke as fellow Socinians.[172] Practically the same thing was said about Whitby, whose rejection of the received doctrines of the Church of England, Edwards averred, had encouraged Deists and atheists.[173] Edwards's critique of Socinianism was thus central to his defense of Calvinism; Socinianism was for him the thin end of a wedge that led to Deism, skepticism, and atheism. Interestingly enough, a recent historian sympathetic to Socinianism has drawn the same conclusion.[174]

Edwards finally arrived at the production of a systematic "body of divinity" in the last decade of his life, publishing it between 1707 and 1713 in three parts and four volumes. These volumes concentrated on the issues dear to Calvinist theologians which he had been pressing throughout his theological writings. The first volume, *Veritas Redux: Evangelical Truths Restored,* dealt with God's eternal decrees, the nature of human willing, Grace and conversion, the atonement, and perseverance. The second volume, *The Doctrine of Faith and Justification Set in a True Light,* covered the doctrine of the imputation of Christ's righteousness to the believer and the relationship of faith and good works. The third part, in two volumes under the title *Theologia Reformata,* followed the articles of the Apostles' Creed, and in its preface alerted readers that the author espoused the "Calvinian" doctrines which prevailed at the Reformation of the Church of England.[175]

Edwards's Defense of Calvin and Moderate Calvinism

In making the case for the Calvinist character of the Church of England, in refuting Arminian, Roman Catholic, Socinian, Deist, and atheist views, and in developing a system of theology, Edwards revealed himself as a very self-conscious Calvinist who had much to say about Calvin and Calvinism, unlike all the other Calvinists this book has examined, who referred to Calvin sparingly— for example, I have found only one reference in Joseph Alleine, although that is to "holy Calvin," and the author of a recent book on John Howe found only one reference to Calvin in the marginalia of Howe's books. One section of Theophilus Gale's *Court of the Gentiles* is titled "Vindication of Calvinists," and in a preface to a book written by Thomas Hotchkis, Baxter explained that while he believed "that no one party on earth is so sound in Doctrine, and way of Worship, as those called Calvinists," nonetheless he did not think that any one group was infallible or in no need of learning from others.[176] The same reticence appeared among earlier English exponents of the theological emphases associated with Calvin such as Thomas Cartwright, John Prideaux, and Robert Abbot, who all rejected "Calvinist" as a description of their views, preferring to describe their outlook as Reformed.[177] This reticence about Calvin continued with those in the Restoration era and later whom Stephen Hampton has connected with the "Anglican Reformed Tradition," a tradition including figures such as Pearson, Barlow, and William Beveridge. They found Calvin too tainted with Presbyterianism, Rebellion, and Dissent to suit their tastes as Episcopalians, Royalists, and defenders of the English liturgy.[178] Edwards, on the other hand, continually identified his views as Calvinist, using the term (most commonly "Calvinian") to describe the scheme of theology which he was defending ("the Calvinian Verities")—such references are scattered throughout his writings, from his earlier to his later ones. Furthermore, Edwards cited Calvin and discussed Calvin's views with some frequency, showing familiarity with Calvin's opinions on obscure points. He was also interested in Calvin as a historical figure, "that worthy man," "that eminent Servant of God," "the Famous Calvin, who with indefatigable Pains promoted the Protestant Religion and Interest." Calvin is especially praised as one who "revived, refreshed and renewed" doctrines on grace, predestination, and perseverance, which, though taught in earlier periods by the fathers and especially St. Augustine, and never completely forgotten (Edwards mentions the Carolingian-era monk Gottschalk, the Dominicans, and Bradwardine as keeping these doctrines alive), had been greatly obscured. These doctrines, he thought, had been accepted at the English Reformation, partly because of the influence of Calvin upon those who prepared the Articles and Homilies.[179]

Edwards was aware that these doctrines were out of fashion, not only in England, but even in Geneva itself, and asserted that his opponents were "wounded . . . under the fifth Rib" by his attempt to restore them in the English church.[180] He was further aware that this disfavor was partly a matter of what later would be called "image"—his opponents were "frighted out of their Wits with Calvin's Ghost," and "wonderfully disordered and enraged, because they see some of his Doctrines revived and restored."[181] In spite of this, and indeed because of this, he sought to defend "Calvin's Reputation."[182] Asserting that Calvin's teaching had been misrepresented and abused, Edwards vindicated Calvin from some of the common charges made against him, revealed himself an astute interpreter of Calvin, and separated Calvin from the extremes of some later Calvinists. Thus Edwards appears to be a moderate rather than high Calvinist. According to Edwards, not only do Calvin's enemies slander him for teaching things he never taught, but some supposed supporters of Calvin pervert his teachings and "fasten that on him which he never said or meant."[183]

Foremost of the slanders against Calvin taken up by Edwards was that the Genevan reformer made God the author of sin through his doctrine of reprobation. As a good Augustinian as well as Calvinist, Edwards pointed out that God never compels the will of a sinner, but that in all sin there was the "cooperative Agency" of the will of the sinner. God "induces no Coactive Necessity in the Agent." In sinning, persons are "free agents." The sins of sinners come from themselves, who "sin voluntarily and freely," so that their sin "becomes their own proper Act." God is thus not the author of sin. Edwards also affirmed that it was entirely erroneous to claim that Calvin held that innocent and guiltless persons were damned.[184] Moreover, Edwards argued that although teaching a decree of the reprobation of sinners, Calvin was not a supralapsarian since he maintained that the decree of reprobation was directed toward persons not as they were created but as fallen sinners. This view, Edwards said, taught by Augustine and the Synod of Dort as well as Calvin, was the correct one, in spite of the fact that some putative followers of Calvin, including the Dutch theologian Gomarus and "our Perkins and Twisse," thought they followed Calvin in their supralapsarianism.[185]

There was one other rather peculiar theological point that appeared in Edwards which suggests his moderate Calvinist unease with a too emphatic teaching about the reprobation of sinners. In *Veritas Redux* he speculated that in addition to those whom God has elected to salvation and reprobated to damnation, there may be a third sort of persons who do not fall under either decree but are in a "state of probation," neither predestined to salvation nor damnation, so that a door is "kept open for Hope and Relief." For these, God is "at liberty to give Grace to them, or to deny it." However, he stated this as a matter of probability rather than certainty ("it would be great Arrogancy to be positive here"). One reason for this suggestion was that he thought it might be the explanation for certain ambiguous biblical passages. If true, Edwards went on, it would be "most congruous" with God's mercy and pastorally helpful in dealing with those who despond and despair.[186]

Edwards's moderate Calvinism also surfaced in his attack upon the revived Crispian Antinomianism of the 1690s, launched by a reprinting of Tobias Crisp's notorious sermons which had first appeared almost a half-century earlier. This set off a vigorous controversy which became a defining moment for the Dissenters, further dividing them between moderate and high Calvinists; it also led John Locke, as Locke himself obliquely confessed, to write *The Reasonableness of Christianity* in order to define the nature of justifying faith, his definition being precisely what Edwards judged Socinian.[187] In this controversy, moderate Calvinists rushed to attack Antinomianism and make clear that they had no truck with this error, which had so frequently been seized upon by conformists as a weapon against Calvinism and Dissent. The Church of England conformist Edwards joined the fray with his *Crispianism Unmask'd,* published in 1693, declaring that Crisp's "Zeal for Christ's imputed Righteousness, makes him vilifie, and almost exclude, an internal righteousness of our own." Antinomians, he thought, were not only in error because they excluded the inherent righteousness of sanctification but also because they taught that God's predestination did not work through the human means of actual faith and good works (i.e., that justification was from eternity), and because they held such "wild" opinions as denying that God is pleased with the good works of believers. Such opinions, Edwards declared, were fit for Ranters, not sober Christians.[188]

There were other charges against Calvinism that Edwards refuted, for example, that according to Calvinists one may commit sins with impunity so long as one is in a state of grace (claimed by enemies to be an aspect of Calvinist Antinomianism), that Calvinism excused criminals from responsibility for their crimes, and that Calvinism drove persons to "melancholy." He does acknowledge, however, that by comparison Arminianism is "a pleasant and Jolly doctrine."Judging by Samuel Taylor Coleridge's much more insightful comment a century later that Calvinism was a far more comforting doctrine than Arminianism, Edwards may have missed an apologetic opportunity here. As for the slander that Calvinism bred rebellion, Edwards answered that while some Calvinists may have been rebels, it was not because of their Calvinism. Such a charge was "mere raillery."[189] Earlier Calvinists and Dissenters had been driven to defend themselves against this charge which had become a very effective piece of anti-Calvinist rhetoric in the aftermath of the Restoration. And granted that it was a Puritan inclined Parliament that brought about the execution of Charles I, it was difficult to counter; the argument found its classic statement in Peter Heylyn, who dubbed "Presbyterians" a "dangerous sect" descended from those rebels against Moses, namely Korah, Dathan, and Abiram (Korahism again), who imitated Calvin and his disciples in insulting monarchs and fomenting revolution.[190]

Edwards's defense of Calvin did not mean that he never differed from him. As Edwards put it, Calvin did not think himself an "unerring Oracle," and neither should Calvinists; Calvin had no monopoly on truth, and put some matters more harshly than necessary.[191] On various points Edwards disagreed with Calvin, for example, on his interpretation of the meaning of Christ's descent into hell. Calvin had thought the descent a psychological event, in which Christ on the cross suffered in soul the agony of abandonment, whereas Edwards followed the more common Reformed view that the descent referred to Christ's humiliation of remaining under the power of death until the Resurrection—although many

Reformed theologians continued to teach that Christ on the cross had suffered abandonment, they did not connect it to the descent into hell of the creed. By Edwards's time, Reformed theologians had generally abandoned Calvin's inter- pretation of the creedal descent, particularly because of the pressure of a growing consensus in biblical scholarship that the word "hades" referred to the grave. Edwards's view was that of most learned opinion in England at the time and was shared by Theophilus Gale.[192]

Edwards also disagreed with Calvin as to whether Christ's mediation referred only to his divine nature, and not to both: medieval theologians had especially related Christ's mediatorial work to his human nature, whereas Reformed theologians established a consensus that this aspect of Christ's work required the involvement of both the human and divine natures. Edwards asserted that both Calvin and Melanchthon, in overreacting to papist error, thought that it was only the divine nature that fulfilled this role. Ultimately for Edwards, as for all Reformed theologians, Calvin's authority was based on his fidelity to scripture, as scripture alone could establish a point of doctrine, not Calvin or the Synod of Dort.[193]

Summing Up John Edwards

John Edwards represented the persistence, transformation, and variety of English Calvinism. Clearly, he stood for its persistence in the Church of England at a time when the most influential conformists had abandoned it, even if he regarded himself as a lonely voice throughout much of his career— there is little evidence that he was connected to other Church of England Calvinists or to the Calvinistic Dissenters whom he sometimes defended and whose polity he seemed to share. But he stands out as the most self-consciously Calvinist of the Calvinist theologians considered in this book, proud of the des- ignation and defiantly using a name for his theological outlook that even the Dissenters for the most part avoided. For Edwards, Calvinism was true Christianity, the faith of the New Testament, of the fathers of the Church, of the English Reformation and of the great theologians of the Church of England. In this regard he reminds one of William Prynne, who so stoutly defended Calvinist theology in another era, and like Edwards argued from precedent. But the Calvinism Edwards defended was a somewhat transformed moderate version, not a copy of John Owen or Theophilus Gale, and thus he oscillated between the attempt to make Calvinism more winsome and a querulous defen- siveness about it. In the process, he did something few English Calvinists did, whether conformist or Dissenter; that is, he showed an interest in Calvin himself and recognized that not all that passed as Calvinism in later times was to be found in Calvin. His interest in Calvin certainly served the strategic purpose for him of presenting a more moderate Calvinism, enabling him to disavow certain later Calvinist excesses. But in polemics, a more hard-edged Calvinism often reappeared.

Edwards was both old-fashioned and an adumbration of new directions. He was old-fashioned in his overuse of the argument from authors, in his persistence as a Church of England Calvinist, in his ties to the ideals of an earlier Puritanism, and in his insistence that true religion involved elements of mystery not reducible to rational terms (persistence), but also modern (transforming) in his recognition of, if not in all his responses to, the late seventeenth-century challenges of natural science, full-fledged atheism, Deism, Socinianism, and the growing discontent with central Christian doctrines such as the Trinity.

So far as variety is concerned, Edwards is distinguished from the other Calvinists treated in this book by his conformity at a time when conformist Calvinism was becoming much rarer than it had been earlier in the seventeenth century. Emphasizing his conformist credentials (even though elsewhere revealing some uneasiness about conformity) and presenting a version of Calvinism more endued with patristic learning and references than that of the dissenting Calvinists, he represented both by ambience and emphasis a distinct version of Calvinism.

Edwards is also notable for the range of his productivity as a theologian. He wrote long, rambling, occasionally cranky books which sometimes dissolved into a barely connected series of topics by which he could vent his exasperations. He was impassioned, contentious, sometimes inconsistent, but he could also be witty (though he would not have liked the word applied to himself), surprisingly open-minded, and moderate in judgment. A modern reader might be at first put off by the strident polemics and crotchety asides that pepper his books, as well as entertained by some of their baroque eccentricities, but Edwards as a theological author grows on one. When all is said and done, his books are often interesting, and when the scope of his whole project as an author is grasped, the range of his writings and the consistency of its central themes are impressive. At a critical time when it seemed necessary to concentrate on defense, Edwards undertook nothing less that a grand restatement and defense of the Christian faith in its Calvinist or Reformed version, beginning with an expression of its heartfelt piety and then moving on to epistemological and apologetic labors to establish a preface and groundwork for major works of biblical exegesis, doctrinal controversy, systematic theology, and practical/pastoral theology. His work has a kind of unity, given it partly by the opponents whom he undertook to refute. The seriousness, erudition, and even judiciousness of what he wrote is impressive, and he stands as a representative and transitional figure of English Calvinism between the older Church of England and Puritan Calvinism on the one hand and the newer evangelical Calvinism of the British awakenings on the other. He kept alive in the established church that emphasis on supernatural renovating grace that revived in the work of the Anglican evangelicals of the later eighteenth century such as George Whitefield, Augustus Toplady, and John Newton, and continued in the established church in the nineteenth century with Charles Simeon. It is no surprise, then, that some of those later Calvinists, including another Edwards in colonial America, looked back to this Edwards.[194]

Conclusion

The preceding chapters have explored the ways in which some English theologians and spiritual writers shaped and reshaped their Calvinism in the period from the beginning of the Restoration through the reign of Queen Anne. They did so in the context and idiom of five different but overlapping patterns of discourse: mysticism, "ancient theology," evangelical pietism, natural theology and the evidences of Christianity, and Church of England conformism. Each case, with the possible exception of Joseph Alleine's evangelicalism, also reveals Calvinist comfort with an aspect of religious life and thought typically considered inimical to Calvinism. This applies to the mystical and Platonic Calvinism of Sterry, Gale's deployment of the ancient theology, the natural theology of Baxter, Bates and Howe, and the belated Church of England Calvinism of Edwards. Joined with the experiential spirituality of the Alleine circle this constitutes five exfoliations of English Calvinism and accentuates the variety of Calvinist expression at the time.

Each of the five varieties was firmly rooted in Puritan religiosity and Calvinist theology and spirituality. Sterry's roots were in the flowering of Platonism in Emmanuel College, Cambridge, during the 1630s; the millennialism of radical Puritan preaching in the 1640s; and the Cromwellian Independency of the 1650s. Gale imbibed Puritan spirituality and scholastic Calvinist theology in the Oxford of John Owen and spent time in the 1660s in the company of Huguenot scholars in France; he had long planned a great work that would unify knowledge in what was beginning to be an outdated scheme. Joseph Alleine, younger than all but John Edwards, was also educated at Oxford during the years of Puritan hegemony, was saturated with the traditions of Puritan spirituality, and, bespeaking a nonconformist outlook, authored a fiery tract against conforming to the established church of the Restoration. Of Richard Baxter, William Bates, and John Howe, the latter two were educated at the universities and committed to the Puritan and Parliamentary cause, while Baxter, as a town minister and chaplain in the Parliamentary army, came to fear religious radicals, especially the Antinomians. All three belonged to the Puritan brotherhood of preachers of the spiritual life, and none conformed at the Restoration of the monarchy in 1660. John Edwards, in spite of his father's Calvinist Presbyterianism, did conform in 1660, but he also carried on the fight against anti-Calvinist Arminians that had roiled the Church of England in the early decades of the seventeenth century.

All of these Calvinist thinkers and writers lived into the Restoration period, and the two who died in its first two decades, Sterry and Joseph Alleine, were followed by disciples and sponsors respectively, who published posthumously most of what Sterry and Alleine had written, and kept their names and influence alive. Baxter had been active as a theological author before 1660, but Gale, Bates, Howe, and Edwards produced either most or all of their theological output after 1660. Howe and Edwards both published major works in the early eighteenth century.

It was during the second half of the seventeenth century that developments in western cultural and intellectual life emerged that can be regarded as an early phase of the Enlightenment. It is a cliché to refer to a century as an age of transition, but much can happen in one hundred years, as the gap between the mental and cultural worlds of 1600 and 1700 illustrates. As a recent book has put it, "Suddenly by the last quarter of the seventeenth century, what the pious labeled nonbelief threatened to become a religious alternative."[1] When, late in the seventeenth century, as has already appeared in this book, John Howe could comment that with atheism become fashionable contention is no longer about the true mode of religion but whether there ought to be any religion, and Richard Baxter could muse that when young his doubts had to do with whether or not he had genuine faith whereas in later life his doubts were about the truth of Christianity itself, it is clear that a new sensibility and mental universe had arrived. Religious discourse had undergone a transition from preoccupation with internal Christian debate where Reformed or Calvinist thinkers refuted Rome, Anabaptism, Arminianism, and Lutheranism, to a point where Christianity was challenged by the rejection of ancient orthodoxy by Socinians, of Christian revelation by Deists, and even of the existence of God by atheists, accompanied by scoffing at Religion not only by the rabble but by fashionable elites. At the same time, increasing awareness of other Religions and changing understandings of what counted as rational played a role in the exchange of ideas in a republic of letters.

While the three individuals and two groups analyzed in the preceding chapters are of interest in their own right, each was engaged in finding a way through the thicket of early Enlightenment modernity. The five varieties of Calvinism they represented became five responses to new challenges in a changing mental climate. Sterry was perhaps least self-conscious about the new challenges but also most expansive in pointing to new directions through his tolerant esoteric mysticism of "a paradise within" and his universalizing scheme of redemption. Gale shaped the body of systematic learning he purveyed into a defense of biblical revelation against the burgeoning irreligion and misbelief of atheism and Socinianism. To that mix he added an updated Platonism as a basis for true religion. From Joseph Alleine and his admiring circle came a reshaped evangelical Calvinism that aimed to spread conversion and holiness, and, by self-authenticating experiential religion, counter the challenge of irreligion by inoculating persons against it. Baxter, Bates, and Howe shaped their moderate Calvinism into an intellectual defense of Christianity that confronted atheism, Deism, and other religions by the arguments of natural theology and the "evidences of Christianity." John Edwards in an array of publications attacked head-on the challenges of Socinianism, Deism, and atheism. Most regarded Hobbes and Spinoza as their quintessential opponents, and were at least tinctured by the traditional Christian use of Neoplatonic philosophy, but with some misgivings came to see Descartes, who for many epitomized new ways of thinking, as updating philosophical truth, several even succumbing to the appeal of Cartesian "clear and distinct" ideas. In their variety they may have represented continuations of older ways of thinking and acting, but they also reshaped their older Calvinism into responses to new challenges. Each had one foot in an old battlefield while with the other stepping into a new one.

Peter Berger has remarked that "the history of Protestant theology is a paradigm for the confrontation of a religious tradition with modernity,"[2] and the five ramifications of Calvinism considered in this book had resonances for future theological paths, although reversion into the Whiggery of reading these authors through later outcomes must be guarded against. Nonetheless, it may be posited that they represent five overlapping trajectories to modern religious thought. A trajectory to the modern applies most readily to the ways in which the moderate Presbyterian triumvirate of Baxter, Bates, and Howe reshaped their inherited Calvinism into a Latitudinarian version compatible with the times by a focus on the rationality, in the newer sense of the word, of the

Christian religion. Theirs was becoming a "rational Christianity" in something of the later meaning of the term, and a prototype of much modern Protestant thought. Sterry seems a point on a different trajectory, the esoteric reappearing in such as William Blake, the mystical in Schleiermacher, and the universalism in the modern understanding of divine benevolence and in openness to other religions. The trajectory of evangelical pietism that appears with Alleine and his sponsors has been enormously influential as a modern religious response, eventually reformist, willing to break with state supported religion, and centered on religious experience, not dogma. Gale is perhaps a more ambiguous case, but his historicizing of religion in his magnum opus and his insistence that all knowledge of God is ultimately revealed knowledge foreshadows the thinking of Karl Barth in the twentieth century. Edwards would appear to represent many of these trajectories, as moderate Calvinist, natural theologian, and evangelical pietist. Calvinist Anglicanism is also surely partly his legacy.

However, when all has been said about varieties, persistences, transformations, trajectories to the modern, and reshaping theology and practice to meet the challenges of the early Enlightenment, there remains with all these thinkers a Calvinist, or Reformed core, that of divine grace. It pervades all of them: for Sterry God's grace is of such overwhelming force that it would appear to include all—an affirmation of the triumph of grace. For Gale not only the knowledge of God but also in some sense all knowledge ultimately derives from revealed scriptural truth, a revelation of God's grace. For Joseph Alleine and those associated with him the piety and personal holiness promoted and claimed to be the very heart of Christian faith, in spite of their emphasis on a religion of discipline, is finally one of grace alone as well. For Baxter, Bates, and Howe, the Christian faith for which natural theology provided a base and "evidences of Christianity" a springboard is ultimately an atonement-centered religion of divine grace. And for Edwards, running through all his polemics against Arminian, Socinian, scoffing, Deist, and atheist enemies, is the same centrality of divine grace. Finally, for all that they saw the clear light of a dawning age or reason and responded to it with various theological and spiritual adjustments and transformations, these Calvinists remained faithful to the celebration of the mystery of grace.

Abbreviations for Notes and Bibliography

Ath. Oxon.	Anthony Wood, *Athenae Oxoniensis,* edited by Philip Bliss, 4 vols. 1813–1820. Reprint, Hildesheim, Germany. Georg Olms, 1969).
Backus, *Reception*	Irena Backus, ed., *The Reception of the Church Fathers in the West: From the Carolingians to the Maurists,* 2 vols. (Leiden, the Netherlands: Brill, 1997).
BDBR	*Biographical Dictionary of Seventeenth-Century British Radicals,* edited by Richard L. Greaves and Robert Zaller, 3 vols. (Brighton, U.K.: Harvester 1982–1984).
Calamy, *Account*	Edmund Calamy, *An Abridgement of Mr. Baxter's History of His Life and Times, With an Account of the Ministers, etc., who were Ejected after the Restoration of King Charles II,* 2 vols. (London, 1713).
Calamy, *Continuation*	Edmund Calamy, *A Continuation of the Account of the Ministers, Lecturers, Masters and Fellows of Colleges, and Schoolmasters, who were Ejected and Silenced after the Restoration in 1660,* 2 vols. (London, 1727).
CH	*Church History*
CR	A. G. Matthews, *Calamy Revised* (Oxford, 1934).

CSPD   *Calendar of State Papers Domestic*
JEH   *Journal of Ecclesiastical History*
JHI   *Journal of the History of Ideas*
JURCHS   *Journal of the United Reformed Church History Society*
ODNB   *Oxford Dictionary of National Biography*, 60 vols.
RB   Richard Baxter, *Reliquiae Baxterianae. Or Mr. Richard Baxter's Narrative of the Most Memorable Passages of His Life and Times*, edited by Matthew Sylvester (London, 1696).
SCJ   *Sixteenth Century Journal*

Notes

INTRODUCTION

1. Gerald R. Cragg, *From Puritanism to the Age of Reason: A Study of Changes in Religious Thought Within the Church of England, 1660–1700* (Cambridge: Cambridge University Press, 1950), pp. 13–36. See also Daniel Walker Howe, "The Decline of Calvinism: An Approach to Its Study," in *Studies in Society and History* 14 (June 1942): 306–27.

2. Christopher Hill, *A Tinker and Poor Man: John Bunyan and His Church, 1628–1688* (New York: Norton, 1988), p. 344.

3. *Puritans and Predestination: Grace in English Protestant Theology, 1525–1695* (Chapel Hill: University of North Carolina Press, 1982), pp. 149–57.

4. Carl R. Trueman, *The Claims of Truth: John Owen's Trinitarian Theology* (Falmouth, UK): Paternoster Press, 1998); Sebastian Rehnman, *Divine Discourse: The Theological Methodology of John Owen* (Grand Rapids, Mich.: Baker Academic, 2002).

5. John Owen, for example, wrote a commendatory preface for a book that some Calvinists considered heretically Antinomian, William Eyre's *Justification Without Conditions* (London, 1653).

6. Peter Toon, *The Emergence of Hyper-Calvinism in English Nonconformity, 1689–1765* (London: Olive Tree, 1967).

7. Jacques Le Goff, *The Birth of Purgatory*, translated by Arthur Goldhammer (Chicago: University of Chicago Press, 1984), p. 96.

8. Hans Frei, *The Eclipse of Biblical Narrative: A Study in Eighteenth and Nineteenth Century Hermeneutics* (New Haven, Conn.: Yale University Press, 1974), p. 51.

CHAPTER I

1. Donald Davie, *A Gathered Church: The Literature of the English Dissenting Interest, 1700–1930* (New York: Oxford University Press, 1978), p. 74.

2. Alister McGrath, *A Life of John Calvin* (Oxford: Basil Blackwell, 1990), p. 203, considers Calvinism influential through its "moral and social deposit," as well as doctrine; Philip Benedict, *Christ's Churches Purely Reformed: A Social History of Calvinism* (New Haven, Conn.: Yale University Press, 2002), p. xvi, says that it inspired a vision of moral and social transformation.

3. Patrick Collinson, "England and International Calvinism 1558–1640," in *International Calvinism 1541-1715*, edited by Menna Prestwick (Oxford: Oxford University Press, 1985), pp. 197–224.

4. Benedict, *Christ's Churches Purely Reformed*, p. xxiii, uses "Calvinism" in his subtitle but says "Reformed" is a better term; Diarmaid MacCulloch, *The Later Reformation in England, 1547–1603*, 2nd ed. (New York: Palgrave, 2001), p. 60, calls "Calvinism" a limiting term; see Dwight Bozeman, "Forum: Neglected Resources in Scholarship," *Religion and American Life: A Journal of Interpretation* 7 (Winter 1997): 14–20.

5. Cited by Peter Iver Kaufman, *Prayer, Despair, and Drama: Elizabethan Introspection* (Urbana: University of Illinois Press, 1996), p. 5, from Walter Travers's *An Answer to a Supplicatorie Epistle of G. T.* (London, 1583), p. 352.

6. John Bunyan, *The Miscellaneous Works of John Bunyan*, vol. 4, *A Defence of the Doctrine of Justification, by Faith; A Confession of My Faith, etc.*, edited by T. L. Underwood (Oxford: Clarendon Press, 1989), pp. 38, 122.

7. John Milton, *The Works of John Milton*, vol. 6, *English Political Tracts*, edited by William Haller and Frank Patterson (New York: Columbia University Press, 1932), p.169.

8. *RB*, bk. I, part II, p.143; Geoffrey Nuttall, *Richard Baxter* (London: Thomas Nelson and Sons, 1965), p. 128; J. Alleine, *Remaines of that Excellent Minister of Jesus Christ, Mr. Joseph Alleine* (London, 1674), sig. A3v; William Ames, *The Marrow of Theology*, edited by John Dykstra Eusden (Durham, N.C.: Labyrinth Press, 1968), p. 288; Samuel Lee, *Orbis Miraculum, or The Temple of Solomon* (London, 1659) p. 214; Jollie, quoted in William Lamont, *Puritanism and Historical Controversy* (London: UCL Press, 1996), p.89, from Jollie MS folio 8, Dr. Williams's Library.

9. B. A. Gerrish, *Grace and Gratitude: The Eucharistic Theology of John Calvin* (Minneapolis, Minn: Fortress Press, 1993), p. 2; McGrath,*Life of Calvin*, pp. 202–3; Benedict, *Christ's Churches Purely Reformed*, pp. xxii–xxiii.

10. Basil Hall, "Calvin Against the Calvinists," in *John Calvin: A Collection of Distinguished Essays*, edited by Gervase E. Duffield (Grand Rapids, Mich.: Eerdmans, 1966), pp. 19–37, emphasizes the distinction between Calvin and later Calvinists; William J. Bouwsma, *John Calvin: A Sixteenth-Century Portrait* (Oxford: Oxford University Press, 1988), stressing the humanist roots of Calvin's thought also distinguishes him from later Calvinists; Richard A. Muller in *The Unaccommodated Calvin: Studies in the Foundation of a Theological Tradition* (Oxford: Oxford University

Press, 2000) and *After Calvin: Studies in the Development of a Theological Tradition* (Oxford: Oxford University Press, 2003) emphasizes the continuity of later Calvinists with Calvin.

11. For what amounts to a "Calvinist International," see Alastair Duke, Gilian Lewis, and Andrew Pettegree, eds., *Calvinism in Europe, 1540–1620* (Cambridge: Cambridge University Press, 1994), Prestwich, ed., *International Calvinism,* and Anthony Milton, *Catholic and Reformed: The Roman and Protestant Churches in English Protestant Thought 1600–1640* (Cambridge: Cambridge University Press, 1995), esp. pp. 377–447.

12. For the first English Protestants, see William Clebsch, *England Earliest Protestants* (New Haven, Conn.: Yale University Press, 1964). Dewey D. Wallace, Jr., *Puritans and Predestination: Grace in English Protestant Theology, 1625–1695* (Chapel Hill: University of North Carolina Press, 1982), pp. 3–28, and Carl R. Trueman, *Luther's Legacy: Salvation and English Reformers, 1525–1556* (Oxford: Clarendon Press, 1994), modify Clebsch's conclusions. For Cranmer, see Ashley Null, *Thomas Cranmer's Doctrine of Repentance* (Oxford: Oxford University Press, 2000) and Diarmaid MacCulloch, *Thomas Cranmer: A Life* (New Haven, Conn.: Yale University Press, 1996).

13. Wallace, *Puritans and Predestination,* pp. 29–111; MacCulloch, *Later Reformation in England*; Patrick Collinson, *The Religion of Protestants: The Church in English Society, 1559–1625* (Oxford: Oxford University Press, 1982); Nicholas Tyacke, *Anti-Calvinists: The Rise of English Arminianism* (Oxford: Oxford University Press, 1987); Lorrie Anne Ferrell, *Government by Polemic: James I, the King's Preachers, and the Rhetoric of Conformity, 1603–1625* (Stanford, Calif.: Stanford University Press, 1998).

14. David P. Field, *"Rigide Calvinisme in a Softer Dresse:" The Moderate Presbyterianism of John Howe (1630–1705)* (Edinburgh: Rutherford House, 2004), p. 4.

15. *RB,* bk. I, part I, p. 6.

16. Muller, *After Calvin,* pp. 26, 29, 72–75, 81–82; Muller, *Unaccommodated Calvin,* pp. 43–44.

17. Muller, *After Calvin,* pp. 9–11, 33, 46, 49–51.

18. *RB,* bk. I, part I, p. 6.

19. Martin Luther, *Three Treatises,* 2nd rev. ed. (Philadelphia: Fortress Press, 1970), p. 93.

20. John Patrick Donnelly, *Calvinism and Scholasticism in Vermigli's Doctrine of Man and Grace* (Leiden, the Netherlands: E. J. Brill, 1976), pp. 19, 100; McGrath, *A Life of John Calvin,* p. 213.

21. *RB,* bk. I, part I, p. 6.

22. Norman Jones, *The English Reformation: Religion and Cultural Adaptation* (Oxford: Blackwell, 2002), p. 179.

23. Bouwsma, *Calvin,* pp. 227–28 stresses Calvin's theology as pedagogical.

24. Donald K. McKim, *Ramism in William Perkins* (New York: Peter Lang, 1987), Keith L. Sprunger, "Ames, Ramus, and the Method of Puritan Theology," *Harvard Theological Review* 59 (April 1966): 33–151; Ames, *The Marrow of Theology,* pp. 37–47 (Eusden's introduction); Muller, *After Calvin,* pp. 32–33, 74–75.

25. Michael McGiffert, "Grace and Works: The Rise and Division of Covenant Divinity in Elizabethan Puritanism," *Harvard Theological Review* 75:4 (1982): 463–502; McGiffert, "From Moses to Adam: The Making of the Covenant of Works," *Sixteenth Century Journal* 19 (Summer 1988):131–56; McGiffert, "The Perkinsian Moment of Federal Theology," *Calvin Theological Journal* 29 (1994):117–48; see also J. W. Baker, *Heinrich Bullinger and the Covenant: The Other Reformed Tradition* (Athens, Ohio: Ohio University Press, 1980), John von Rohr, *The Covenant of Grace in Puritan Thought* (Atlanta, Ga.: Scholars Press, 1986), and David A. Weir, *The Origins of the Federal Theology in Sixteenth-Century Reformation Thought* (Oxford: Clarendon Press, 1990).

26. Theodore Dwight Bozeman, *The Precisianist Strain: Disciplinary Religion & Antinomian Backlash in Puritanism to 1638* (Chapel Hill: University of North Carolina Press, 2004), p. 23.

27. *RB*, bk. I, part I, p. 126.

28. Richard A. Muller, *Post-Reformation Reformed Dogmatics: The Rise and Development of Reformed Orthodoxy, ca. 1520–ca. 1725*, 4 vols., 2nd ed. (Grand Rapids, Mich.: Baker Academic, 2003), vol. 1, pp. 340–43; Ames, *Marrow of Theology*, p. 77.

29. R. Po-Chia Hsia, *Social Discipline in the Reformation: Central Europe 1550–1750* (London and New York: Routledge, 1989), pp. 1–3; Bozeman, *Precisianist Strain*, pp. 40–43.

30. Philip Benedict, *The Faith and Fortunes of France's Huguenots, 1600–1685* (Aldershot, UK: Ashgate, 2001), pp. 220–27; Benedict, *Christ's Churches Purely Reformed*, pp. 317–19, 491.

31. William J. Bouwsma, *The Waning of the Renaissance, 1550–1640* (New Haven, Conn.: Yale University Press, 2000), pp. 143–64; Jonathan Sheehan, *The Enlightenment Bible* (Princeton, N.J.: Princeton University Press, 2005), pp. 20–24.

32. Muller, *After Calvin*, p. 47.

33. Dwight Brautigan, "Prelates and Politics: Uses of "Puritan," 1625–40," in *Puritanism and Its Discontents*, edited by Laura Lunger Knoppers (Newark, Del.: University of Delaware Press, 2003), pp. 49–66, shows how the Laudians used the word to taint Puritans with political extremism.

34. David R. Como, *Blown by the Spirit: Puritanism and the Emergence of an Antinomian Underground in Pre-Civil-War England* (Stanford, Calif.: Stanford University Press, 2004), p. 10; For the return of the term "Puritanism" see Peter Lake, "Defining Puritanism—Again?" in *Puritanism: Transatlantic Perspectives on a Seventeenth-Century Anglo-American Faith*, edited by Francis J. Bremer (Boston: Massachusetts Historical Society, 1993), pp. 3–29; see also Margo Todd, *Christian Humanism and the Puritan Social Order*, (Cambridge: Cambridge University Press, 1987), p. 9: "The people who called themselves the 'godly,' 'professors,' and even 'saints,' and were called 'puritans' by their foes, were a sufficiently self-conscious and popularly identifiable group in their own day to deserve a name, and the traditional 'puritan' seems as good as any."

35. Cited in John Spurr, "From Puritanism to Dissent, 1660–1700," in *The Culture of English Puritanism, 1560–1700*, edited by Christopher Durston and Jacqueline Eales (New York: St. Martin's Press, 1996), p. 234.

36. Tim Harris, "Introduction: Revising the Restoration," in *The Politics of Religion in Restoration England,* edited by Tim Harris, Paul Seaward, and Mark Goldie (Oxford: Basil Blackwell, 1990), p. 2; Mark Goldie, "Danby, The Bishops and the Whigs," in Ibid., p. 79; Burke W. Griggs, "Remembering the Puritan Past: John Walker and Anglican Memories of the English Civil War," in *Protestant Identities: Religion, Society and Self-Fashioning in Post-Reformation England,* edited by Muriel C. McClendon, Joseph P. Ward, and Michael MacDonald (Stanford, Calif.: Stanford University Press, 1999), pp. 158–91.

37. Diarmaid MacCulloch, "Richard Hooker's Reputation," *English Historical Review* 117 (September 2002): 799.

38. Griggs, "Remembering the Puritan Past," pp. 160–62; Mark Goldie, "The Theory of Religious Intolerance in Restoration England," in *From Persecution to Toleration: The Glorious Revolution in England,* edited by Ole Peter Grell, Jonathan I. Israel, and Nicholas Tyacke (Oxford: Clarendon Press, 1991), p. 331.

39. James C. Spalding and Maynard F. Brass, "Reduced Episcopacy as a Means to Unify the Church of England, 1640–1662," *Church History* 30 (December 1961): 414–32; John Spurr, *The Restoration Church of England, 1646–1689* (New Haven, Conn.: Yale University Press, 1991), pp. 26, 34–36, 143–45; Gary S. DeKrey, "Reformation in the Restoration Crisis, 1679–1682," in *Religion, Literature, and Politics in Post-Reformation England, 1540–1688,* edited by Donna B. Hamilton and Richard Strier (Cambridge: Cambridge University Press, 1996), pp. 241–43, 247, argues that Baxter and his associates in the midst of the crisis over the "popish plot" launched a more radical attack on diocesan episcopacy than his professions of moderation bears out.

40. *RB,* bk. I, part II, pp. 140, 278.

41. Roger Thomas, *Daniel Williams, "Presbyterian Bishop,"* Friends of Dr. Williams's Library Sixteenth Lecture (London: Dr. Williams's Trust, 1964) shows Williams's importance; Gerald R. Cragg, *Puritanism in the Period of the Great Persecution, 1660–1688* (Cambridge: Cambridge University Press, 1957), pp. 15–16, 191, 246, 250–51; Michael R. Watts, *The Dissenters: From the Reformation to the French Revolution* (Oxford: Clarendon Press, 1978), pp. 217–19, 260; Field, *"Rigide Calvinisme in a Softer Dresse,"* pp. 18–32, 166–79, describes the moderate Presbyterians, listing in an appendix those he thinks belonged to that party.

42. John D. Ramsbottom, "Presbyterians and 'Partial Conformity' in the Restoration Church of England," *JEH* 43 (April 1992): 249–70; John Spurr, *England in the 1670s: "This Masquerading Age"* (Oxford: Blackwell, 2000), pp. 227–28.

43. Edmund Trench, *Some Remarkable Passages in the Holy Life and Death of the late Reverend Mr. Edmund Trench; Most of them drawn out of his own Diary* (London: 1693), pp. 59–60, 77.

44. E.g., George Trosse, *The Life of the Reverend Mr. George Trosse, Written by Himself, and Published Posthumously According to his Order in 1714,* edited by A. W. Brink (Montreal and London: McGill-Queen's University Press, 1974), p. 119.

45. *RB,* bk. I, part II, p. 387.

46. Francis Bremer, *Congregational Communion: Clerical Friendship in the Anglo-American Puritan Community, 1610–1692* (Boston: Northeastern University

Press, 1994), pp. 249–52; Roger Thomas, "Partners in Nonconformity," in *The English Presbyterians: From Elizabethan Puritanism to Modern Unitarianism,* edited by C. G. Bolam, Jeremy Goring, H. L. Short, and Roger Thomas (Boston: Beacon Press, 1968), pp. 99ff.; R. W. Dale, *History of English Congregationalism* (London: Hodder and Stoughton, 1907), pp. 474–84; Watts, *The Dissenters,* pp. 289–97.

47. B. R. White, *The English Baptists of the Seventeenth Century* (London: Baptist Historical Society, 1983), pp. 93–138; T. L. Underwood, *Primitivism, Radicalism, and the Lamb's War* (Oxford: Oxford University Press, 1997).

48. Nicholas Tyacke, "The 'Rise of Puritanism' and the Legalizing of Dissent, 1571–1719," in *From Persecution to Toleration: The Glorious Revolution and Religion in England,* edited by Ole Peter Grell, Jonathan I. Israel, and Nicholas Tyacke (Oxford: Clarendon Press, 1991), p. 32, underlines the dissatisfaction of many Dissenters: "Under Cromwell the main body of Puritans had tasted power. It was hardly to be expected that for the future such people would enthusiastically embrace the status of a tolerated sect."

49. Nicholas Tyacke, "The 'Rise of Puritanism'," pp. 39–40; B. R. White, "The Twilight of Puritanism in the Years Before and After 1688," in *From Persecution to Toleration: The Glorious Revolution and Religion in England,* edited by Ole Peter Grell, Jonathan I. Israel, and Nicholas Tyacke (Oxford: Clarendon Press, 1991), pp. 306–30; Hugh Trevor-Roper, *From Counter-Reformation to Glorious Revolution* (Chicago: University of Chicago Press, 1992), p. 268, describes the Toleration Act as the best that could be obtained at the time; Geoffrey Holmes, *Politics, Religion and Society in England, 1672–1742* (London: the Hambledon Press, 1986), pp. 191–92, 224–26, regards it as grudging and precarious; but William Gibson, *The Church of England, 1688–1832* (London and New York: Routledge, 2001), pp. 183, 191–203, minimizes the division between Church of England and Dissent in the eighteenth century.

50. Craig Rose, *England in the 1690s: Revolution, Religion and War* (Oxford: Blackwell, 1999), p. 169; Judith Maltby, *Prayer Book and People in Elizabethan and Early Stuart England* (Cambridge: Cambridge University Press, 1998), p. 235.

51. Rose, *England in the 1690s,* pp. 204–205. Howe had been a chaplain to William and Mary.

52. Ramsbottom, "Presbyterians and Partial Conformity," p. 270, avers that "the passage of the Toleration Act of 1689, coupled with the failure of comprehension, removed the middle ground on which 'occasional' or 'partial' conformists had stood."

53. Spurr, *Restoration Church,* p. xiv; For Latitudinarianism see W. M. Spellman, *The Latitudinarians and the Church of England, 1660–1700* (Athens, Ga.: University of Georgia Press, 1993) and Martin I. J. Griffin, Jr., *Latitudinarianism in the Seventeenth-Century Church of England* (Leiden, the Netherlands: Brill, 1992).

54. C. John Sommerville, *The Secularization of Early Modern England: From Religious Culture to Religious Faith* (Oxford: Oxford University Press, 1992), p. 15; J. G. A. Pococke, "Post-Puritan England and the Problem of the Enlightenment," in *Culture and Politics From Puritanism to the Enlightenment,* edited by Perez Zagorin (Berkeley: University of California Press, 1980), p. 100, says that "the church of the Restoration

was to be Arminian rather than Calvinist, but Erastian to a degree that dispelled many of the suspicions formerly attached to the Laudians. That is, it laid much less emphasis on jure divino episcopacy than on jure divino monarchy."

55. For congregational fellowship see Geoffrey Nuttall, *Visible Saints: The Congregational Way, 1640–1660* (Oxford: Basil Blackwell, 1957), pp. 70–100; for the spiritual "network" of the godly see Diane Willen, "Communion of the Saints: Spiritual Reciprocity and the Godly Community in Early Modern England," *Albion* 27 (1995): 20, 25, 40; for a group portrait of the Dissenters see Cragg, *Puritanism in the Great Persecution*, pp. 156–93; for decline of the Puritan gentry, see Spurr, "From Puritanism to Dissent," p. 254.

56. Sharon Achinstein, *Literature and Dissent in Milton's England* (Cambridge: Cambridge University Press), pp. 3, 11, 21, 34.

57. N. H. Keeble, *The Literary Culture of Nonconformity in Later Seventeenth-Century England* (n.p.: Leicester University Press, 1987), p. 184.

58. S. L. Bethell, *The Cultural Revolution of the Seventeenth Century* (London: Dennis Dobson , 1951), p. 12.

59. Paul Hazard, *The European Mind: 1680–1715*, translated by J. Lewis May (1952; reprint, Cleveland: World Publishing,1963), pp. xv, xviii; Jonathan I. Israel, *Radical Enlightenment: Philosophy and the Making of Modernity, 1650–1750* (Oxford: Oxford University Press,2001) pp. 4–5, 11, 13, 15.

60. Barbara J. Shapiro, *Probability and Certainty in Seventeenth-Century England: A Study of the Relationships Between Natural Science, Religion, History, Law, and Literature* (Princeton, N.J.: Princeton University Press, 1983), p. 270.

61. Spellman, *Latitudinarians*, pp. 1, 4–6; Spurr, *Restoration Church*, p. 385. Roy Porter, "The Enlightenment in England," in *The Enlightenment in National Context*, edited by Roy Porter and Mikulas Teich (Cambridge: Cambridge University Press, 1981), p. 6, "Enlightenment goals . . . throve in England within piety;" cf. also Gerard Reedy, S. J., *The Bible and Reason: Anglicans and Scripture in Late Seventeenth-Century England* (Philadelphia: University of Pennsylvania Press, 1985), pp. 3, 11–12; Gibson, *Church of England, 1688–1832*, plays down the skepticism even of the later eighteenth century, and surveys recent literature that emphasizes the conservatism of England's version of the enlightenment, pp. 4–24.

62. John Gascoigne, *Cambridge in the Age of the Enlightenment:Science, Religion and Politics from the Restoration to the French Revolution* (Cambridge: Cambridge University Press, 1989), p. 21.

63. J. C. D. Clark, *The Language of Liberty 1660–1832* (Cambridge: Cambridge University Press,1994), pp. 15, 22, 141.

64. Pococke, "Post-Puritan England," pp. 93, 106, 108. But J. A. I. Champion, *The Pillars of Priestcraft Shaken: The Church of England and Its Enemies, 1660–1730* (Cambridge: Cambridge University Press, 1992), pp. 8–9, 14–15, 23–24, notes the attack of radicals on the privileged position of the Church of England.

65. Michael P. Winship, *Seers of God: Puritan Providentialism in the Restoration and Early Enlightenment* (Baltimore, Md.: Johns Hopkins Press, 1996), pp. 7, 50–51.

66. Henry F. May, *The Enlightenment in America* (New York: Oxford University Press, 1976), pp. 3, 65.

67. The term came from Pierre Bayle's journal "Nouvelles de la Republique des Lettres," Anne Colgar, *Impolite Learning: Conduct and Community in the Republic of Letters, 1680–1750* (New Haven, Conn.: Yale University Press, 1995), p. 13; John Locke, *An Essay Concerning Human Understanding*, 2 vols., edited by Alexander Campbell Fraser (New York: Dover Publications, 1959) vol. 2, pp. 428–29; John E. Wills, Jr., *1688: A Global History* (New York: W. W. Norton, 2001, pp. 219–20; W. R.Ward, *Christianity Under the Ancient Regime 1648–1789* (Cambridge: Cambridge University Press, 1999), p. 155; Gerard Cerny, *Theology, Politics and Letters at the Crossroads of European Civilization: Jacques Basnage and the Baylean Huguenot Refugees in the Dutch Republic* (Dordrecht, the Netherlands: Martin Nijhoff Publishers, 1987), p. 163. The republic of letters has been traced back to Erasmus and also connected to the learned of the early seventeenth century, Constance Furey, *Erasmus, Contarini, and the Religious Republic of Letters* (Cambridge: Cambridge University press, 2006); J. P. Heering, *Hugo Grotius as Apologist for the Christian Religion: A Study of His Work De Veritate Religionis Christianae* (Leiden, the Netherlands: Brill, 2004) p. 186.

68. David Ogg, *England in the Reign of Charles II*, 2 vols., 2nd ed. (Cambridge: Cambridge University Press, 1956), II, 514–16; S. H. Steinberg, *Five Hundred Years of Printing*, 2nd ed. (Baltimore, Md.: Penguin Books, 1961), pp. 266–68; Warren Chappell, *A Short History of the Printed Word* (New York: Dorset Press, 1970), p. 113.

69. Tyacke, "The 'Rise of Puritanism,' " p 44.

70. Elizabeth Eisenstein, *The Printing Press as an Agent of Change*, 2 vols. in one (Cambridge: Cambridge University Press, 1979), pp. 409, 645–47, 655.

71. Carl L. Becker, *The Heavenly City of the Eighteenth-Century Philosophers* (New Haven, Conn.: Yale University Press, 1932), pp. 29–31.

72. Richard Ashcraft, "Latitudinarianism and Toleration: Historical Myth Versus Political History," in *Philosophy, Science, and Religion in England, 1640–1700*, edited by Richard Kroll, Richard Ashcraft, and Perez Zagorin (Cambridge: Cambridge University Press, 1992), pp. 156–57.

73. John Vincent Cane, *Fiat Lux, A General Conduct to a right understanding in the great Combustions and Broils about Religion here in England*, 2nd ed. (London, 1662), pp. 49, 53, 56, 66, 79, 82, 198, 213–14.

74. John Owen, *Animadversions on a Treatise Entitled Fiat Lux*, in *The Works of John Owen*, edited by W. H Goold, 16 vols. (London and Edinburgh, 1853), vol. 14, p. 73.

75. John Owen, *Vindication of the Animadversions on Fiat Lux* in Ibid., vol. 14, pp. 356–57; for the English debates over Cane's book, see Louis I. Bredvold, *The Intellectual Milieu of John Dryden* (Ann Arbor: University of Michigan Press, 1934), pp. 73–98; for fideism see Richard Popkin, *The History of Scepticism from Savonarola to Bayle*, rev. ed. (Oxford: Oxford University Press, 2003), pp. 64–79.

76. Griffin, *Latitudinarianism*, pp. 99–100; Robert Crocker, *Henry More, 1614–1687: A Biography of the Cambridge Platonist* (Boston: Kluwer Academic, 2003),

pp.52–53, 71–72; For the Cambridge Platonists generally, see Gerald R. Cragg, *The Cambridge Platonists* (Oxford: Oxford University Press, 1968).

77. Gascoigne, *Cambridge in the Age of the Enlightenment*, p. 52; Joseph M. Levine, "Latitudinarians, Neoplatonists, and the Ancient Wisdom," in *Philosophy, Science, and Religion in England 1640–1700*, edited by Richard Kroll, Richard Ashcraft, and Perez Zagorin (Cambridge: Cambridge University Press, 1992), pp. 91, 96–97.

78. Gascoigne, *Cambridge in the Age of the Enlightenment*, pp. 7, 52, 54–55; Jonathan Israel, *Enlightenment Contested: Philosophy, Modernity and the Emancipation of Man, 1670–1752* (Oxford: Oxford University Press, 2006), p. 64; Jonathan Israel, *The Dutch Republic: Its Rise, Greatness, and Fall 1477–1806* (Oxford: Clarendon Press, 1995), pp. 889–90; Norman Fiering, *Moral Philosophy at Seventeenth-Century Harvard* (Chapel Hill: University of North Carolina Press, 1981), p. 241; Anthony Grafton, *Defenders of the Text: The Tradition of Scholarship in an Age of Science, 1450–1800* (Cambridge: Harvard University Press, 1991), p. 2.

79. J. W. Ashley Smith, *The Birth of Modern Education: The Contribution of the Dissenting Academies 1660–1800* (London: Independent Press, 1954), pp. 87–88, 90.

80. Martin I. Klauber, *Between Reformed Scholasticism and Pan-Protestantism: Jean Alphonse Turretin (1671–1737) and Enlightened Orthodoxy at the Academy of Geneva* (Selinsgrove, Pa.: Susquehanna University Press, 1994), pp. 37–38, 42; Israel, *Radical Enlightenment*, p. 14.

81. Roland N. Stromberg, *Religious Liberalism in Eighteenth-Century England* (Oxford: Oxford University Press, 1954), p. 17.

82. Peter Gay, *The Enlightenment: An Interpretation*, 2 vols. (New York: Alfred Knopf, 1967, 1969), vol. 1, *The Rise of Modern Paganism*, pp. 127, 133, 427.

83. Nicholas Atkin and Frank Tallett, *Priests, Prelates and People: A History of European Catholicism Since 1750* (Oxford: Oxford University Press, 2003), pp. 35–37; Samuel Parker, *A Free and Impartial Censure of the Platonick Philosophie* (London, 1667).

84. Israel, *Radical Enlightenment*, pp. 3, 14.

85. Charles G. Nauert, Jr., *Humanism and the Culture of Renaissance Europe* (Cambridge: Cambridge University Press, 1995), p. 193.

86. Richard S. Westfall, *Science and Religion in Seventeenth-Century England* (1958; rpt, Ann Arbor: University of Michigan Press, 1973); Rogers Miles, *Science, Religion, and Belief: The Clerical Virtuosi of the Royal Society of London, 1663–1687* (New York: Peter Lang, 1992), p. 1.

87. Barbara Shapiro, *John Wilkins, 1614–1672: An Intellectual Biography* (Berkeley: University of California Press, 1969).

88. Margaret Jacob, *The Newtonians and the English Revolution, 1689–1720* (Ithaca, N.Y.: Cornell University Press,1976), esp. chapter 4; Jan W. Wojcik, *Robert Boyle and the Limits of Reason* (Cambridge: Cambridge University Press, 1997), pp. 40, 46, 55, 97, 122, 217, 219.

89. I. Bernard Cohen, ed., *Puritanism and the Rise of Modern Science: The Merton Thesis* (New Brunswick, N.J.: Rutgers University Press, 1990).

90. Smith, *The Birth of Modern Education*, pp. 56–59; Fiering, *Moral Philosophy*, pp. 207–8; F. A. Turk, "Charles Morton: His Place in the Historical Development of

British Science in the Seventeenth Century," *Journal of the Royal Institution of Cornwall*, n.s. 4 (1961–1964): 353–63.

91. Charles Coulton Gillespie, *Genesis and Geology: The Impact of Scientific Discoveries Upon Religious Beliefs in the Decades Before Darwin* (1951; reprint, New York: Harper and Row, 1959), pp. 3–6; Michael J. Buckley, S. J., *At the Origins of Modern Atheism* (New Haven, Conn.: Yale University Press, 1987), p. 347; James R. Jacob, *Henry Stubbe, Radical Protestantism and the Early Enlightenment* (Cambridge: Cambridge University Press, 1983), p. 213; Miles, *Science, Religion, and Belief*, pp. 109–10; Shapiro, *Probability and Certainty*, pp. 15–16, 27–29, 117–18; Israel, *Enlightenment Contested*, p. 64.

92. Peter Harrison, *"'Religion' and the Religions in the English Enlightenment* (Cambridge: Cambridge University Press, 1990), p. 39; Henry Smith, Gods *Arrow Against Atheists*(London, 1604), table of contents, pp. 7–8, 42, 48; various books from the seventeenth century took as their subject "Gentile" religion, including Lord Herbert of Cherbury, *De Religione Gentilium* (1663) and Gerard Vossius, *Libri Quatuor de Theologia Gentili* (1642).

93. Sommerville, *Secularization of Early Modern England*, pp. 3–7.

94. Harrison, *"Religion" and the Religions*, pp. 1–2, 5, 15.

95. Edward, Lord Herbert, *De Veritate*, translated by Meyrick H. Carre (Bristol, UK: J. W. Arrowsmith, 1937), pp. 289–307; Champion, *The Pillars of Priestcraft Shaken*, pp. 140–47.

96. Nathaniel Culverwell, *An Elegant and Learned Discourse of the Light of Nature*, edited by Robert A. Greene and Hugh MacCallum (Toronto: University of Toronto Press, 1971), pp. 165–66; Peter Harrison, " '*Religion' and the Religions*, pp. 49–51.

97. John Bunyan, *Grace Abounding to the Chief of Sinners*, edited by W. R. Owens (London: Penguin Books, 1987), paragraph 97.

98. *RB*, bk. I, part I, p. 131.

99. Isabel Rivers, *Reason, Grace, and Sentiment: A Study of the Language of Religion and Ethics in England 1660–1780*, vol. 2, *From Shaftesbury to Hume* (Cambridge: Cambridge University Press, 2000), p. 51.

100. James R. Jacob, *Henry Stubbe*, p. 64–75; Stubbe died in 1676.

101. Peter Harrison, *Religion and the Religions*, pp. 61–74.

102. John Calvin, *Institutes of the Christian Religion*,2 vols., edited by John T. McNeill and Translated by Ford Lewis Battles (Philadelphia: Westminster Press, 1960), vol.1, bk. I, chapter 3, section 2; Robert Burton, *The Anatomy of Melancholy*, edited by Floyd Dell and Paul Jordan-Smith (New York: Tudor Publishing, 1955), pp. 928–29.

103. [William Stephens], *An Account of the Growth of Deism in England* (1696; facsimile reprint, William Andrews Clark Memorial Library Publication Number 261, Los Angeles: University of California, 1990), pp. 5–7.

104. [Robert Howard], *History of Religion Written by a Person of Quality* (London, 1694), pp. iii–xx.

105. John Toland, *Christianity Not Mysterious: Or a Treatise Shewing, That there is nothing in the Gospel Contrary to Reason, Nor Above it: and that no Christian Doctrine can be properly call'd a Mystery* (London, 1696), pp. xxiii–xxiv, 7, 20, 27–28, 171.

106. *RB*, bk. I, part I, p. 23.

107. Dryden, "Religio Laici," lines 66–69; [Edward Stillingfleet], *A Letter to a Deist, in Answer to several objections Against the Truth and Authority of the Scriptures* (London, 1677), sig. A3.

108. [Stephens], *Account of the Growth of Deism*, pp. 4–7, 13.

109. C. John Sommerville, *Popular Religion in Restoration England*, (Gainesville: University of Florida Press, 1977), p. 116; John Redwood, *Reason, Ridicule and Religion: The Age of the Enlightenment in England, 1660–1750* (Cambridge, Mass.: Harvard University Press, 1976), p. 14.

110. Francis Bacon, "Of Atheism," *Essays, Advancement of Learning, New Atlantis, and Other Pieces*, edited by Richard Foster Jones (New York: Odyssey Press, 1937), pp. 46–49.

111. Bozeman, *Precisianist Strain*, p. 55.

112. Ibid., p. 87.

113. Samuel Gardiner, *History of the Commonwealth and Protectorate, 1649–1656* (London: Longmans, Green and Co., 1903), vol. 2, p. 336.

114. Samuel Butler, *Hudibras in Three Parts* (London, 1684), pp. 29–31.

115. J. G. A. Pococke, "Post-Puritan England," p. 101.

116. Henry More, *Enthusiasmus Triumphatus* (1662; facsimile reprint, Los Angeles: William Andrews Clark Memorial Library Publication Number 118), pp. 2–11, 15–19, 45–46.

117. Ibid., pp. 2, 39.

118. Sharon Achinstein, *Literature and Dissent*, discusses enthusiasm in relation to dissenting literary culture, see pp. 154–81.

119. Zachary Taylor, *Popery, Superstition, Ignorance, and Knavery . . . very fully proved upon the Dissenters* (London, 1698), pp. 5, 8, 19–20, 23–24.

120. T.[homas] J.[Jollie], *A Vindication of the Surey Demoniack* (London, 1698); Zachary Taylor, *Popery, Superstition, Ignorance, and Knavery Confess'd, and fully proved upon the Surey Dissenters* (London, 1699).

121. For this case, see Jonathan Westaway and Richard D. Harrison, "The 'Surey Demoniack:' Defining Protestantism in 1690s Lancashire," in *Unity and Diversity in the Church: Papers Read at the 1994 Summer Meeting and the 1995 Winter Meeting of the Ecclesiastical History Society*, edited by R. N. Swanson (Cambridge, Mass.:Blackwell, 1996), 263–82, and Michael P. Winship, *Seers of God*, pp. 117–18.

122. Trosse, *Life of Trosse*, pp. 48, 50, 71, 79, 104.

123. John Milton, *Paradise Lost*, edited by Merritt Y. Hughes (New York: Odyssey, 1935), bk. VI, line 630; Benjamin Keach, *A Trumpet Blown in Zion, or An Alarm in God's Holy Mountain* (London, 1694), pp. 5–6.

124. Benjamin Keach, *The Travels of True Godliness, From the beginning of the World to this present Day; in an apt and Pleasant Allegory* (London, 1684), pp. 59, 60, 63.

125. John Bunyan, *Some Gospel Truths Opened, A Vindication of Some Gospel-Truths Opened, A Few Sighs From Hell*, in *The Miscellaneous Works of John Bunyan*, vol. 1, edited by T. L. Underwood (Oxford: Clarendon Press, 1980), pp. 254–55, 277.

126. *RB*, part III, p. 84.

127. *ODNB*, "Ellis, Clement"

128. [Clement Ellis], *The Vanity of Scoffing* (London, 1674), pp. 1–5, 8–9, 11, 14–18–19, 28, 30, 33–35.

129. Joseph Glanvill, *Some Discourses, Sermons, and Remains of the Reverend Mr. Jos.Glanvill* (London, 1681), pp. 192–93.

130. Quoted in Gascoigne, *Cambridge in the Age of the Enlightenment*, p. 18.

131. Quoted in Spurr, *Restoration Church*, p. 219.

132. Stephens, *An Account of the Growth of Deism*, p. 5; perhaps the first appearance of the word "Deist" in English print was in 1596, in Josias Nichols, *Order of Household Instruction*, where it appears to be a synonym for atheist, Michael Hunter, "The Problem of Atheism in Early Modern England," *Transactions of the Royal Historical Society*, 5th ser., 35 (London, 1985): 156 n. 99.

133. John Bunyan, *The Pilgrim's Progress*, edited by W. R. Owens (Oxford: Oxford University Press, 2003), pp. 129–30; Ellis, *Vanity of Scoffing*, pp. 1–2, 10.

134. Hunter, "Problem of Atheism," p. 143.

135. Ibid., p. 136.

136. Trosse, *Life of Trosse*, pp. 48, 50, 54, 56, 60, 62, 66, 73, 132.

137. Lucien Febvre, *The Problem of Unbelief in the Sixteenth Century: The Religion of Rabelais*, translated by Beatrice Gottlieb (Cambridge, Mass.: Harvard University Press, 1982), pp. 131–33, 275, 314–15, 329, 352–53, 377, 442, 456, 460; Popkin, *History of Scepticism*, pp. 87, 95–96, 143–44; Elizabeth Labrousse, *Bayle*, translated by Denys Potts (Oxford: Oxford University Press, 1983), pp.1, 11, 18, 52–63; Karl C. Sandberg, *At the Crossroads of Faith and Reason: An Essay on Pierre Bayle* (Tucson: University of Arizona Press, 1966), pp. 37–39, 43–44, 108–109; Willis B. Glover, "God and Thomas Hobbes," *CH* 29 (September 1960): 275–97; J. G. A. Pocock, "Thomas Hobbes: Atheist or Enthusiast? His Place in a Restoration Debate," *History of Political Thought* 11 (Winter 1990): 737–49; C. A. J. Coady, "The Socinian Connection—Further Thoughts on the Religion of Hobbes," *Religious Studies* 22 (June 1986): 277–80; Richard Tuck, "The Christian Atheism of Thomas Hobbes," in *Atheism from the Reformation to the Enlightenment*, edited by Michael Hunter and David Wootton (Oxford: Clarendon Press, 1992), pp. 111–30; Leopold Damrosch, Jr., "Hobbes as Reformation Theologian: Implications of the Free-Will Controversy," *JHI* 40 (July–September, 1979): 339–52; David Wootton, "New Histories of Atheism," in *Atheism from the Reformation to the Enlightenment*, edited by Michael Hunter and David Wootton (Oxford: Clarendon Press, 1992), pp.13–54. G. E. Aylmer, "Unbelief in Seventeenth-Century England," in *Puritans and Revolutionaries: Essays in Seventeenth-Century History presented to Christopher Hill*, edited by Donald Pennington and Keith Thomas (Oxford: at the Clarendon Press, 1978), pp. 22–46, focuses on atheism as outright denial of God's existence, but notes that while there were many scoffers and blasphemers there were almost no real atheists; John Redwood, *Reason, Ridicule, and Religion* devotes three chapters to atheism.

138. Apparently among the ancients Plato made such a distinction and considered most people to be practical atheists, Walter Burkert, *Greek Religion* (Cambridge, Mass.: Harvard University Press, 1985), p. 315.

139. Wootton, "New Histories of Atheism," p. 27, suggests that denial of God's "relevance to human concerns," was what "contemporaries felt did most to undermine belief in the Christian God."

140. Dewey D. Wallace, Jr., "George Gifford, Puritan Propaganda, and Popular Religion in Elizabethan England," *Sixteenth Century Journal* 9 (April 1978): 27–49.

141. Hunter, "Problem of Atheism," pp. 146–47.

142. Henry Smith, *Gods Arrow Against Atheists*, p. 1.

143. Lord Herbert of Cherbury, *De Veritate*, p. 295.

144. Burton, *Anatomy of Melancholy*, p.925.

145. Michael P. Winship, *Making Heretics: Militant Protestantism and Free Grace in Massachusetts, 1636–1641* (Princeton, N.J.: Princeton University Press), p. 39.

146. *Paradise Lost*, bk. VI, line 370; XI, line 625.

147. Roger Ascham, *The Schoolmaster (1570)*, ed. Lawrence V. Ryan (Charlottesville: Published for the Folger Shakespeare Library by the University Press of Virginia, 1967), pp. 71–72; Hunter, "Problem of Atheism," p. 144; Cyril Tourneur, *The Atheist's Tragedie: or the honest Man's Revenge* (London, 1611), sigs. C2r, I[sic]v.

148. Burton, *Anatomy of Melancholy*, p. 933.

149. Burton, *Anatomy of Melancholy*, pp. 925, 935.

150. Henry More, *An Antidote against Atheisme, or An Appeal to the Natural Faculties of the Minde of Man, whether there be not a God* (London, 1653), sigs A1-2.

151. Ralph Cudworth, *The True Intellectual System of the Universe* (London, 1678), p. 134.

152. Buckley, *At the Origins of Modern Atheism*, pp. 33, 222; David Berman, *A History of Atheism in Britain: From Hobbes to Russell* (London: Croom and Helm, 1988), p. 61; Jonathan Israel, *Enlightenment Contested*, pp. 45–46.

153. Thomas Wise, *A Confutation of the Reason and philosophy of Atheism* (London, 1706), as quoted in Berman, *A History of Atheism*, p. 11.

154. Wootton, "New Histories of Atheism," pp. 46. 50.

155. Bunyan, *Grace Abounding*, paragraph 44; Christopher Hill, *A Tinker and a Poor Man: John Bunyan and his Church, 1628–1688.* (New York: Norton, 1988), p. 75.

156. Wootton, "New Histories of Atheism," p. 49.

157. Calvin, *Institutes of the Christian Religion*, bk. I, chapter 3, section 2; Martin Fotherby, *Atheomastix: clearing foure Truthes, Against Atheists and Infidels* (London, 1622), sig. B3v.

158. Bacon, "Of Atheism," pp. 46–49.

159. Heering, *Hugo Grotius as Apologist*, p. 99.

160. Harrison, *Religion and the Religions*, p. 123.

161. Cudworth, *True Intellectual System*, pp. 123–34.

162. Osmund Airy, ed., *Burnet's History of My Own Time*, part I, *The Reign of Charles II*, 2 vols. (Oxford: Clarendon Press, 1897), vol. 1, p. 335.

163. *RB*, bk. I, part I, p. 22.

164. Bunyan, *Grace Abounding*, paragraph 44.

165. Anne Bradstreet, *The Complete Works of Anne Bradstreet*, edited by Joseph R. Elrath, Jr., and Allan P. Robb (Boston: Twayne Publishers, 1981), p. 217.

166. Gascoigne, *Cambridge in the Age of the Enlightenment*, p. 81.

167. Jonathan Israel, *Enlightenment Contested*, pp. 122; J. C. D. Clark, *English Society, 1688–1832* (Cambridge: Cambridge University Press, 1985), p. 277.

168. Stromberg, *Religious Liberalism*, pp. 34–51.

169. Richard F. Lovelace, *The American Pietism of Cotton Mather: Origins of American Evangelicalism* (Grand Rapids, Mich.: Christian University Press, 1979), p. 42.

CHAPTER 2

1. *RB*, bk. I, part I, p. 75. Vivian de Sola Pinto, *Peter Sterry, Platonist and Puritan, 1613–1672: A Biographical and Critical Study with Passages Selected from His Writings* (1934; reprint, New York: Greenwood Press, 1968), pp. 221–22; David Parnham, *Sir Henry Vane, Theologian: A Study in Seventeenth Century Religious and Political Discourse* (Madison, N.J.: Fairleigh Dickinson University Press, 1997), p. 14.

2. Anthony Wood, quoted in Pinto, *Peter Sterry*, p. 28; Robert Baillie, *Letters and Journals*, ed. David Laing (Edinburgh, 1841), vol. 3, p. 443; for his relationship to Milton, see Pinto, *Sterry*, pp. 20–21, 32, 48. N. I. Matar, "Aristotelian Tragedy in the Theology of Peter Sterry," *Journal of Literature and Theology* 6 (December 1992): 310, claims that Sterry and Milton kept in contact after the Restoration.

3. Pinto, *Sterry*, p. vi; Eliot cited in Gordon Rupp, "A Devotion of Rapture in English Puritanism," in *Reformation, Conformity, and Dissent: Essays in Honour of Geoffrey Nuttall*, edited by R. Buick Knox (London: Epworth Press, 1977), p. 127.

4. For example, "Puritanism and mysticism were antithetical." R. M. Jones, *Mysticism and Democracy in the English Commonwealth* (Cambridge, Mass.: Harvard University Press, 1932), p. 113.

5. Richard F. Lovelace, "The Anatomy of Puritan Piety: English Puritan Devotional Literature, 1600–1640," pp. 294–323, in *Christian Spirituality: Post-Reformation and Modern*, edited by Louis Dupre and Don E. Saliers (New York: Crossroads, 1991), pp. 318–19; Joel Beeke, in his *Assurance of Faith: Calvin, English Puritanism, and the Dutch Second Reformation* (New York: Peter Lang, 1991), p. 248, comments that Owen "safeguards this experience [assurance] from becoming unbiblically mystical"; he also refers to Richard Sibbes as having "curtailed his mysticism," p. 256.

6. Though Max Weber granted a mystical union in Lutheran piety, he thought Reformed piety centered on proving a state of grace by activity in the world, thus ruling out mysticism, Max Weber, *The Protestant Ethic and the Spirit of Capitalism* (New York: Charles Scribner's, 1958), pp. 112–14. For Ritschl on mysticism see his "Prolegomena to *The History of Pietism*," reprinted in Albrecht Ritschl, *Three Essays*, translated by Philip Hefner (Philadelphia: Fortress Press, 1972), pp. 51–148; Adolf Harnack, *History of Dogma*, translated by Neil Buchanan, 7 vols. (1896–99; reprint, New York: Dover Publications, 1961), vol. 4, p. 271 n. 3; Ernst Troeltsch, *The Social Teachings of the Christian Churches*, translated by Olive Wyon, 2 vols. (1931; reprint, New York: Harper & Brothers, 1960), vol. 2, pp. 740–41, 795.

7. For dismissal of Puritan mysticism, see Louis Bouyer, *Orthodox, Protestant, and Anglican Spirituality* (London: Burns and Oates, 1969), p. 143; E. I. Watkin, *Poets and Mystics* (London: Sheed and Ward, 1953), pp. 56–59 claimed that Puritan devotional and mystical writings returned to "the Catholic type of spirituality rejected by the Reformers," but that, "lacking the fullness of Christian truth contained in the teachings of the Catholic Church, and dispossessed of a public religious authority divinely instituted," they "went to individualist excesses and vagaries of individual interpretation." He cited Sterry as an example. Louis L. Martz, in *The Poetry of Meditation: A Study in English Religious Literature of the Seventeenth Century* (New Haven, Conn.: Yale University Press, 1954), pp. 156, 158–61, 168, 174, argued that Calvinist predestinarian theology left no room for meditative devotion, and that Puritans borrowed from medieval and Catholic materials in order to remedy this. That the Puritan Edmund Bunny modified a Catholic devotional work by Robert Parsons has been used as evidence of this point. All this overlooks the fact that the sermon form so much Puritan devotional writing took was different in presentation from the mystical literature, largely monastic in provenance, which came from medieval Catholic authors. For Bunny and Parsons, see Gordon Wakefield, "Mysticism and its Puritan Types," *London Quarterly and Holborn Review*, 6th series, 35 (January 1966): 39 and Elizabeth Hudson, "The Catholic Challenge to Puritan Piety, 1580–1620," *Catholic Historical Review* 77 (January 1991): 1–20, where it is argued, however, that Catholics and Puritans had many similarities in their spiritual ideals. A recent book on Samuel Rutherford rejects the claim that his mysticism was borrowed from Catholicism, John Coffey, *Politics, Religion and the British Revolutions: The Mind of Samuel Rutherford* (Cambridge: Cambridge University Press, 1997), p. 97. Theodore Dwight Bozeman, *The Precisianist Strain: Disciplinary Religion and Antinomian Backlash in Puritanism to 1638* (Chapel Hill: University of North Carolina Press, 2004), pp. 74–83, asserts the influence of Catholic devotional literature on Puritans; but his focus is on the way in which Catholic and Protestant participated alike in the devotional revival characteristic of the western Christian world in the seventeenth century and drew on a common medieval heritage in shaping emphases on religion as disciplined personal renovation.

8. Bernard McGinn, "Mysticism," in *The Oxford Encyclopedia of the Reformation*, edited by Hans Hillerbrand, 4 vols. (Oxford: Oxford University Press, 1996), vol. 3 pp. 119–24; Dennis E. Tamburello, *Union with Christ: John Calvin and the Mysticism of St. Bernard* (Louisville, Ky.: Westminster John Knox Press, 1994), pp. 2–4, 87–90, 93, 96, 103–104; Anthony Lane, *Calvin and Bernard of Clairvaux*, Studies in Reformed Theology and History (Princeton, N.J.: Princeton Theological Seminary, 1996), pp. 34, 49, also acknowledges Bernard's influence, noting that Calvin's writings were enriched by familiarity with Bernard.

9. Pinto, *Sterry*, pp. 113–14. Cf. Frederick J. Powicke, *The Cambridge Platonists, A Study* (London: J. M. Dent and Sons, 1926), p. 181, who characterizes Sterry's writings as the "Spiritual intuitions of a mystic striving for expression through an intractable mass of conventional formulae."

10. Jerald C. Brauer, "Types of Puritan Piety," *CH* 56 (March 1987): 39–58; Geoffrey F. Nuttall, "Puritan and Quaker Mysticism," *Theology* 78 (October 1975): 520,

calls attention to "a considerable corpus of Puritan mystical writing;" earlier, in *The Holy Spirit in Puritan Faith and Experience* (Oxford: Basil Blackwell, 1946, pp. 146–47), Nuttall argued that it would be surprising if there were no mysticism within Puritanism, since it was "a movement towards immediacy in communion with God." Wakefield, "Mysticism and its Puritan Types," argues that while Protestantism accepts no union with Christ beyond that offered in the gospel, there has been a Protestant mysticism of experience and expression of which many Puritan writers were exemplars. In an earlier work, *Puritan Devotion: Its Place in the Development of Christian Piety* (London: Epworth Press, 1957), pp. 103, 108, Wakefield was more guarded in claiming a Puritan mysticism. In *The Practice of Piety: Puritan Devotional Disciplines in Seventeenth-Century New England* (Chapel Hill, N. C.: University of North Carolina Press, 1982), Charles E. Hambrick-Stowe says, p. 95, "The Puritan devotional pilgrimage was a mystical journey in Christ, frequently leading to experiences of union with Him"; Janice Knight, *Orthodoxies in Massachusetts: Rereading American Puritanism* (Cambridge, Mass.: Harvard University Press, 1994), p. 2; Belden C. Lane, "Two Schools of Desire: Nature and Marriage in Seventeenth-Century Puritanism, *CH* 69 (June 2000): 373

11. N. I. Matar, "Mysticism and Sectarianism in Mid-Seventeenth Century England," *Studia Mystica* 11 (1988): 62; D. P. Walker, *The Decline of Hell: Seventeenth-Century Discussions of Eternal Torment* (Chicago: University of Chicago Press, 1964), p. 107. An older work by W. Major Scott, *Aspects of Christian Mysticism* (London: John Murray, 1907), pp. 146–63, treated Sterry as one of twelve Christian mystics about whom he wrote.

12. *ODNB*, "Sterry, Peter," *BDBR*, "Sterry, Peter," vol. 3; Pinto, *Sterry*, pp. 3–64; N. I. Matar, ed., *Peter Sterry: Select Writings*, University of Kansas Humanistic Studies (New York: Peter Lang, 1994), pp. 1–25.

13. Samuel Rogers referred to receiving such benefit from Sterry, Tom Webster, *Godly Clergy in Early Stuart England: The Caroline Puritan Movement c. 1620–1643* (Cambridge: Cambridge University Press, 1997), p. 21.

14. For Sterry's preaching before Parliament, see John F. Wilson, *Pulpit in Parliament: Puritanism during the English Civil Wars* (Princeton, N.J.: Princeton University Press, 1969), pp. 89, 92, 119.

15. *CSPD 1650*, p. 286; *CSPD 1651*, p. 65; *CSPD 1653–1654*, pp. 189, 225; *CSPD 1655*, p. 50; *CSPD 1655–1656*, pp. 52, 100, 370; Osmund Airy, ed., *Burnet's History of My Own Time*, part I, *The Reign of Charles the Second*, 2 vols. (Oxford: Clarendon Press, 1997), vol. 1, p. 148; see also Matar, *Sterry: Select Writings*, p. 6; N. I. Matar, "Peter Sterry, the Millennium, and Oliver Cromwell," *JURCHS* 2 (1982): 334, 341; Pinto, *Sterry*, pp. 35–40; Peter Sterry, *England's Deliverance from the Northern Presbytery Compared with its Deliverance from the Roman Papacy* (London, 1652).

16. N. I. Matar, "Peter Sterry and the 'Lovely Society' of West Sheen," *Notes and Queries*, n.s., 29 (February 1982): 45–46. This society consisted of Lord Lisle's family and some of their visitors, Sterry's family, and a group of pupils.

17. Richard Greaves, *Glimpses of Glory: John Bunyan and English Dissent* (Stanford, Calif.: Stanford University Press, 2002), p. 315.

18. G. Lyon Turner, *Original Records of Early Nonconformity*, vol. 1 (London: T. F. Unwin, 1911), p. 327.

19. *RB*, bk. I, part I, p. 75; Pinto, *Sterry*, pp. 60, 64–65; Matar, *Sterry: Select Writings*, pp. 24, 30 n44.

20. For the manuscripts, see Vivian de Sola Pinto, "Peter Sterry and His Unpublished Writings," *The Review of English Studies* 6 (October 1930): 385–407; N. I. Matar and P. J. Croft, "The Peter Sterry MSS at Emmanuel College, Cambridge," *Transactions of the Cambridge Bibliographical Society* 8 (1981): 42–56. Most of his manuscripts consisted of letters and treatises that had circulated within his circle of friends and pupils, Matar, *Sterry: Select Writings*, p. 9.

21. *Ath. Oxon.*, vol. 3, col. 912.

22. Matar, "Sterry, the Millennium, and Cromwell," pp. 338–39; Pinto, *Sterry*, p. 229; for Feake, see *BDBR*, vol. 1, pp. 270–71.

23. Matar, "Sterry, the Millennium, and Cromwell," pp. 338–39; Matar, "Peter Sterry and Morgan Llwyd," *JURCHS* 2 (1982): 275–79.

24. See N. I. Matar, "Peter Sterry and the Ranters," *Notes and Queries*, n.s., 29 (December 1982): 504–6.

25. Peter Sterry, *A Discourse on the Freedom of the Will* (London, 1675), sigs. a2v–a4v, b1v, d1r; Peter Sterry, *The Appearance of God to Man in the Gospel* (London, 1710), pp. 407, 409–10, 412–13. Peter Harrison, *"Religion" and the Religions in the English Enlightenment* (Cambridge: Cambridge University Press, 1990), p. 40, referred to Sterry as the most tolerant of the Cambridge Platonists. A brief treatise entitled *A Letter Found in Utopia*, published in 1675, praised Sterry as "an excellent spirit" and denounced religious disputes.

26. Owen, in an early work, *Of Toleration and the Duty of the Magistrate About Religion* (1649) maintained that only religious opinions that threatened civil order should be suppressed, but during the Restoration he was reluctant to engage in joint efforts with other Dissenters, unless they were strict Calvinists.

27. *CSPD 1655–1656*, p. 52; Cecil Roth, *A Life of Menasseh Ben Israel* (Philadelphia: Jewish Publication Society of America, 1934), p. 241.

28. Peter Sterry, *The Rise, Race and Royalty of the Kingdom of God* (London, 1683), p. 42; Matar, *Sterry: Select Writings*, p. 48; Bozeman, *Precisianist Strain*, pp. 183ff., and especially p.198, where Bozeman makes clear that such persons were "deviant insiders, mavericks of the godly movement itself;" David R. Como, *Blown by the Spirit: Puritanism and the Emergence of an Antinomian Underground in Pre-Civil-War England* (Stanford, Calif.: Stanford University Press, 2004), p. 325; Como divides the "godly" into mainstream Puritans and radical Puritans, p. 31.

29. Christopher Hill, *The Experience of Defeat: Milton and Some Contemporaries* (New York: Viking Penguin, 1984), p. 86.

30. Como, *Blown by the Spirit*, p. 44.

31. Michael P. Winship, *Making Heretics: Militant Protestantism and Free Grace in Massachusetts, 1636–1641* (Princeton, N.J.: Princeton University Press, 2002), pp. 6–7; Bozeman, *Precisianist Strain*, pp. 284–85; Como, *Blown by the Spirit*, pp. 21ff., 34–35, 39–40, 163.

32. Sterry's views on this appear in two unpublished treatises, "That the State of Wicked men after this Life is mixt of evill, and good things," Sterry MS. VI, Emmanuel College Library, Cambridge, pp. 107–17; and "An Eternity of Duration with a Beginning without any end," Ibid., pp. 118–66; Sterry MS VI, pp. 158–59; Sterry, *Freedom of the Will*, pp. 53, 213–14, 217, 220; Sterry, *Rise, Race, and Royalty*, p. 35; Walker, *Decline of Hell*, pp. 27, 104–21; Philip C. Almond, *Heaven and Hell in Enlightenment England* (Cambridge: Cambridge University Press, 1994), pp. 74–76; Allison P. Coudert, "Henry More, the Kabbalah, and the Quakers," in *Philosophy, Science, and Religion in England, 1640–1700*, edited by Richard Kroll, Richard Ashcraft, and Perez Zagorin (Cambridge: Cambridge University Press, 1992), pp. 37–38.

33. Sterry, *Freedom of the Will*, sig. dıv.

34. Peter Harrison, *"Religion" and the Religions*, pp. 55–56; Walker, *Decline of Hell*, pp. 124–26; Coudert, "Henry More, the Kabbalah, and the Quakers," pp. 42–43.

35. Jeremiah White, *The Restoration of All Things* (London, 1712), p. 201; Walker, *Decline of Hell*, p. 106.

36. J. G. A. Pocock, "Post-Puritan England and the Problem of the Enlightenment," in *Culture and Politics from Puritanism to the Enlightenment*, edited by Perez Zagorin (Berkeley: University of California Press, 1980), p. 97.

37. For the Baxter remark and its context, see Pinto, *Sterry*, pp. 221–22; Sterry, *Freedom of the Will*, pp. 220, 235; Sterry, *Appearance*, pp. 199–201, 203; Sterry MS. VII, p. 14; for Twisse see David Como, "Puritans, Predestination and the Construction of Orthodoxy in Early Seventeenth-Century England," in *Conformity and Orthodoxy in the English Church, c 1560–1660*, edited by Peter Lake and Michael Questier (Woodbridge, U. K.: Boydell Press, 2000), p. 82, where Twisse is reputed "England's most formidable defender of the doctrine of absolute predestination."

38. Bernard McGinn, *The Foundations of Mysticism: Origins to the Fifth Century* (New York: Crossroad, 1994), pp. xiii–xix.

39. Ibid., p. 5.

40. Sterry, *Appearance*, pp. 293–94, 438–39, 443; Sterry, *Freedom of the Will*, sigs. a1, c1, pp.31, 32, 81, 84ff, 93, 95, 97, 105, 154, 158, 197, 211, 219; Sterry MS I, p. 385; Sterry MS III, p. 36; Sterry MS VI, p. 119; Sterry MS I has unpaginated extracts from Plutarch, Seneca, Porphyry, and Maximus of Tyre; Matar, *Sterry: Select Writings*, p. 147. For some of Sterry's contemporaries and the Kabbalah, see Coudert, "Henry More, the Kabbalah, and the Quakers," pp. 31–67.

41. Pinto, *Sterry*, pp. 8–10, 62, emphasizes his closeness to Whichcote; Powicke, *Cambridge Platonists*, pp. 174–92, and Serge Hutin, *Henry More: Essai sur les doctrines theosophique chez les Platoniciens de Cambridge* (Hildesheim, Germany: Georg Olms, 1966), pp. 140–42, 181–82, include Sterry in the Cambridge group; Matar, *Sterry: Select Writings*, p. 13, however, notes Sterry's differences from them.

42. Nathaniel Culverwell, *An Elegant and Learned Discourse of the Light of Nature*, edited by Robert A. Greene and Hugh MacCallum (Toronto: University of Toronto Press, 1971), pp. 16, 164.

43. Charles Partee, *Calvin and Classical Philosophy* (1977; reprint, Louisville, Ky.: Westminster John Knox Press, 2005), pp.105–16.

44. The remark referred to both Sterry and John Sadler, and was made by a certain Thomas Baker, Pinto, *Sterry*, p. 10; Joseph M. Levine, "Latitudinarians, Neoplatonists, and the Ancient Wisdom," in *Philosophy, Science, and Religion in England, 1640–1700*, edited by Richard Kroll, Richard Ashcraft, and Perez Zagorin (Cambridge: Cambridge University Press, 1992), pp. 88, 103 n10; Charles Taliaferro and Alison J. Teply, eds., *Cambridge Platonist Spirituality* (New York: Paulist Press, 2004), pp. 32–33; Harold E. Toliver, *Marvell's Ironic Vision* (New Haven, Conn.: Yale University Press, 1965), p. 19.

45. Sterry MS V, p. 116.

46. Sterry, *Freedom of the Will*, pp. 198–203, 207, 229–31, 245; Walker, *Decline of Hell*, p. 109.

47. Sterry, *Rise, Race and Royalty*, p. 4. Evelyn Underhill comments that "the flowery garment of the world is for some mystics a medium of ineffable perception, a source of exalted joy, the veritable clothing of God," *Mysticism: A Study in the Nature and Development of Man's Spiritual Consciousness* (1911; reprint, New York: E. P. Dutton, 1961); Sterry MS I, pp.5–6.

48. Sterry, *Rise, Race, and Royalty*, pp. 4–8, 19; Sterry, *Freedom of the Will*, p. 121.

49. Sterry MS VII, p. 37; Sterry MS V, p. 9; Sterry, *Freedom of the Will*, p. 189.

50. Sterry, *Freedom of the Will*, pp. 202, 210. For Sterry on plenitude, see Matar, "Aristotelian Tragedy in the Theology of Peter Sterry," p. 313.

51. Margo Todd, "Seneca and the Protestant Mind: The Influence of Stoicism on Puritan Ethics," *Archiv für Reformationsgeschichte* 74 (1983): 182–99.

52. Sterry, *Rise, Race and Royalty*, p. 279.

53. Sterry, *Freedom of the Will*, pp. 30, 121; *Rise, Race, and Royalty*, p. 424; *Appearance*, p. 294; Matar, *Sterry: Select Writings*, p. 38. Cf. Underhill, *Mysticism*, p. 306; C. A. Patrides, *Premises and Motifs in Renaissance Thought and Literature* (Princeton, N.J.: Princeton University Press, 1982), pp. 45–47; David Lyle Jeffrey, "Jacob's Ladder," in *A Dictionary of Biblical Tradition in English Literature*, edited by David Lyle Jeffrey (Grand Rapids, Mich. William B. Eerdmans, 1992), pp. 388–89.

54. Sterry, *Rise, Race, and Royalty*, p. 282.

55. Sterry, *Appearance*, pp. 5, 7–8; Sterry MS VI, pp. 11–14, 17, 23–24; Peter Sterry, *The Teachings of Christ in the Soule* (London, 1648), pp. 22, 24–25; Nuttall, *Holy Spirit*, p. 37. Cf. the discussion of the editors in Culverwell , *An Elegant and Learned Discourse*, pp. xlvi–xlvii.

56. Sterry, *Teachings of Christ in the Soule*, p. 26; Peter Sterry, *The Way of God with his People in these Nations* (London, 1657), pp. 32–33; Sterry, *Appearance*, pp. 387–88.

57. N. I. Matar distinguishes Sterry from Whichcote and More, "Peter Sterry and the 'Paradise Within': A Study of the Emmanuel College Letters," *Restoration: Studies in English Literary Culture, 1660–1700* 13 (Fall 1989): 78–79; see also Taliaferro and Tepley, *Cambridge Platonist Spirituality*, p. 35.

58. Sterry MS IV, pp, 168–72; *Appearance*, p. 388; There is also a poem about the sun that has allegorical implications, MS I, pp. 5ff. For other Puritan uses of light and sun imagery, see Nuttall, *The Holy Spirit*, pp. 40–41.

59. Sterry, *Freedom of the Will*, sig. a1v-a2r; Sterry, *The Way of God*, p. 7.

60. "Letters from Peter Sterry to Morgan Lloyd at the National Library of Wales," transcribed by N. I. Matar, Emmanuel College, Cambridge MS 321.1.129, p. 13; the earlier Puritan mystic Francis Rous also referred to the soul's dark nights, *Treatises and Meditations Dedicated to the Saints, and to the Excellent throughout the three Nations* (London, 1657), p. 713.

61. Sterry MS VII, pp. 25–27, 38, 85; Sterry, *Rise, Race and Royalty*, pp. 13–15, 18–19; Sterry MS VI, p. 41; Sterry *Freedom of the Will*, pp. 213–15, 219; Matar, *Sterry: Select Writings*, pp. 201, 207, 213; Sterry, *The Comings Forth of Christ in the Power of His Death* (London, 1650), sig. A3v.

62. Sterry, *The Way of God*, p. 11; Sterry, *Freedom of the Will*, p. 213; MS VII, p. 131; Sterry, *Rise, Race, and Royalty*, pp. 152–53.

63. Sterry, *Freedom of the Will*, pp. 216, 218; Sterry, *Appearance*, p. 59.

64. Sterry, *The Clouds in Which Christ Comes* (London, 1648), pp. 25–26; Sterry MS IV, pp. 2, 54–55; Matar, *Sterry: Select Writings*, p. 39. Francis Rous also uses the image of eye salve, which he calls a gift of Christ, enabling his church to see divine and spiritual things, Francis Rous, *Treatises and Meditations*, pp. 711–12.

65. Matar, *Sterry: Select Writings*, pp. 130, 140, 220; Sterry, *Rise, Race, and Royalty*, p. 96.

66. Sterry, *Appearance*, pp. 77–78.

67. Sterry, MS V, p. 162; *Appearance*, pp. 319, 381, 463; Sterry MS III, p. 267; Matar, *Sterry: Select Writings*, pp. 38, 130. For other references to spiritual taste, see Nuttall, *Holy Spirit*, p. 39; Francis Rous, *Treatises and Meditations*, p. 718; Louis Martz discusses "the paradise within" as an Augustinian image for inner illumination, and finds this idea in poetic contemporaries of Sterry, *The Paradise Within: Studies in Vaughan, Traherne, and Milton* (New Haven, Conn.: Yale University Press, 1964).

68. Matar, *Sterry: Select Writings*, pp. 67–68.

69. Sterry, *Rise, Race and Royalty*, pp. 190, 291, 304–305; Sterry MS I, p. 6; *The Appearance of God to Man*, pp. 11, 23, 45, 75, 350; *Discourse on the Freedom of the Will*, p. 163; Sterry MS III, p. 25; Matar, *Sterry: Select Writings*, pp. 54, 63, 119, 146. Other images abound: "the Soul in the Bosom of Christ lieth, as a Pleasant Island in a Sea of Love," love is a "Golden Chaine," drawing to the "embraces of Christ," "the naked beauty" of Christ, Sterry, *Rise, Race and Royalty*, pp. 392, 409, 401. Cf. also N. I. Matar, "John Donne, Peter Sterry and the *Ars Moriendi*," *Explorations in Renaissance Culture* 17 (1991): 55–70. In a treatise begun on his own deathbed (and never finished), Sterry made reference to Donne as "a Holy Divine," Ibid., pp. 55–56. For the New England Puritan Thomas Shepard's meditations in preparation for death, see Hambrick-Stowe, *The Practice of Piety*, pp. 230–32. For sexual consummation as a kind of death in English poetry, see Arthur L. Clements, *The Poetry of Contemplation: John Donne, George Herbert, Henry Vaughan, and the Modern Period* (Albany: State University of New York Press, 1990), pp. 45–57.

70. Sterry, *Appearance*, p. 75.

71. Ainsworth commented on it in his *Annotations upon the Five Bookes of Moses, the Booke of the Psalmes, and the Song of Songs*; Mark E. Dever, *Richard Sibbes:*

Puritanism and Calvinism in Late Elizabethan and Early Stuart England (Macon, Ga.: Mercer University Press, 2000), p. 143; Johannes van den Berg, *Religious Currents and Cross-Currents: Essays on Early Modern Protestantism and the Protestant Enlightenment,* edited by Jan De Bruijn, Pieter Holtrop, and Ernestine Van Der Wall (Leiden, the Netherlands: Brill, 1999), pp. 30–31; for Rutherford, see Coffey, *Politics, Religion, and the British Revolutions,* pp. 74, 85–86; the Evelyn remark is quoted in Gordon S. Wakefield, "Mysticism and Its Puritan Types," p. 41; Nuttall, "Puritan and Quaker Mysticism," pp. 520–22; Christopher Hill remarks that "would-be poets cut their teeth" paraphrasing it, *The English Bible and the Seventeenth-Century Revolution* (London: Penguin Books, 1994), p. 338 (pp. 362–70 discuss the treatment of the book by Puritans and others). For the importance of Canticles in Christian mysticism, see Underhill, *Mysticism,* p. 137; for an older negative assessment see W. R. Inge, *Christian Mysticism* (1899; reprint, New York: Meridian Books, 1956), p. 43: "As to the Song of Solomon, its influence upon Christian Mysticism has been simply deplorable." E. Ann Matter, *The Voice of My Beloved: The Song of Songs in Western Medieval Christianity* (Philadelphia: University of Pennsylvania Press, 1990), p. 123, traces the interpretation of this biblical book as referring to the mystical marriage of the soul and God to Origen. Jean Williams, "The Puritan Quest for the Enjoyment of God: An Analysis of the Theological and Devotional Writings of Puritans in Seventeenth-century England" (Ph.D. dissertation, University of Melbourne, 1997), pp. 149–211, discusses the interpretation of the Song of Solomon in Puritan Exegesis; see also Barbara Lewalski, *Protestant Poetics and the Seventeenth-Century Religious Lyric* (Princeton, N.J.: Princeton University Press, 1979), pp. 68–69.

72. Owen's preface to Durham appeared in the second edition of *Clavis Cantici* printed in 1669.

73. Sharon Achinstein, *Literature and Dissent in Milton's England* (Cambridge: Cambridge University Press, 2003), pp. 194–200.

74. Michael , "Behold the Bridegroom Cometh! Marital Imagery in Massachusetts Preaching, 1630–1730," *Early American Literature* 27 (1992): 170–81; Matter, *The Voice of My Beloved,* p. 197 n. 33.

75. Richard Rambuss, *Closet Devotions* (Durham, N.C.: Duke University Press, 1998), pp. 1–3, 17, 96; Lane, "Two Schools of Desire," pp. 379, 401; Winship, "Behold the Bridegroom Cometh!" pp. 173, 175.

76. Sterry's verse paraphrase is found in MSS I and IV; Sterry, *Rise, Race, and Royalty,* pp. 29, 188–90.

77. Sterry, *Rise, Race, and Royalty,* pp. 309, 364.

78. Sterry MS IV, pp. 4–6, 10–11; Matar, *Sterry: Select Writings,* pp. 105–109, 119–20.

79. Nuttall, "Puritan and Quaker Mysticism," p. 527, says that "Puritans replaced the mysticism which blossomed in solitude, apart from the world, by an intense assurance of God's nearness open to ordinary men and women in their daily experiences."

80. Sterry MS IV, pp. 31, 36, 14.

81. Matar, *Sterry: Select Writings*, pp. 103, 117; MS V, pp. 54–56, 58, MS III, p.190. See N. I. Matar, "A Devotion to 'Jesus as Mother' in Restoration Puritanism," *JURCHS* 4 (1989): 304–13; Caroline Walker Bynum, *Jesus as Mother: Studies in the Spirituality of the High Middle Ages* (Berkeley: University of California Press, 1982).

82. Matar, *Sterry: Select Writings*, p. 43; for Llwyd, see Geoffrey F. Nuttall, *The Welsh Saints 1640–1660: Walter Cradock, Vavasor Powell, Morgan Llwyd* (Cardiff: University of Wales Press, 1957).

83. Sterry, *Appearance* , pp. 339–40; Sterry, *Freedom of the Will*, sigs. a1-c3, p. 41.

84. Sterry, *Freedom of the Will*, sigs. b4r-c1v, pp. 6–8.

85. Sterry, *Freedom of the Will*, sig. A1r. McGinn, *Foundations of Mysticism*, p. 4.

86. Sterry, *Freedom of the Will*, sig. C3.

87. Sterry MS V, p. 53; Sterry MS I, p. 5; Sterry, *Rise, Race and Royalty*, p. 49; Matar, *Sterry: Select Writings*, p. 169.

88. Sterry, *Appearance*, pp. 10, 338–39.

89. Sterry, *The Rise, Race and Royalty*, p. 30; *Freedom of the Will*, sig. C3.

90. Sterry, *The Spirit Convincing of Sinne* (London, 1646), p. 2; Sterry, *Appearance*, p. 17.

91. Sterry, *Appearance*, pp. 144–45.

92. Ibid., pp. 336–37.

93. Sterry, *Rise, Race, and Royalty*, pp. 201,204. For the Trinity in Christian mysticism, see Underhill, *Mysticism*, pp. 107ff., 344, 435.

94. Sterry, *Appearance*, p. 433.

95. Ibid., pp. 389–90, 428–32.

96. Sterry, *Rise, Race, and Royalty*, pp. 363, 345.

97. Matar, *Sterry: Select Writings*, pp. 44, 142.

98. Sterry, *Appearance*, pp. 438–9, 443; Sterry, *Freedom of the Will*, pp. 179, 221. For adumbrations of the Trinity in "ancient theology," see D. P. Walker, *The Ancient Theology: Studies in Christian Platonism from the Fifteenth to the Eighteenth Century* (Ithaca, N.Y.: Cornell University Press, 1972), pp. 117–21, 115–22; Pinto, *Sterry*, pp. 54, 62, 77–78.

99. Matar, *Sterry: Select Writings*, pp. 84–85, 135–36.

100. Sterry, *Freedom of the Will*, p. 93; Sterry MS IV, p. 7. Elsewhere the image is of the soul "dancing about" Christ "as the needle to the loadstone," Sterry, *Rise, Race, and Royalty*, p. 233.

101. Richard F. Lovelace, *The American Pietism of Cotton Mather* (Grand Rapids, Mich.: Christian Universities Press, 1979), pp. 188–91.

102. Sterry, *Freedom of the Will*, sigs. A2v-a3v, b1v, d1r.

103. Pinto, *Sterry*, p. 79.

104. Baxter, *Catholick Theologie*, part III, p. 108.

105. Knight, *Orthodoxies in Massachusetts*, pp. 3–4.

106. Richard Kieckhefer, "Convention and Conversion: Patterns in Late Medieval Piety," *CH* 67 (March 1998): p. 50.

107. Sterry MS III, pp. 196–97.

108. Sterry MS VII, p. 98.

109. Matar, *Sterry: Select Writings*, pp. 154ff., 177ff; Sterry, *Appearance*, pp. 282–83; Sterry, *Rise, Race, and Royalty*, p. 71; Sterry *The Teachings of Christ in the Soule*, p. 24. For the Christian allegorization of pagan lore, see Jean Seznec, *The Survival of the Pagan Gods: The Mythological Tradition and Its Place in Renaissance Humanism and Art*, translated by Barbara F. Sessions (Princeton, N.J.: Princeton University Press, 1953) and N. I. Matar, "Peter Sterry and the Puritan Defense of Ovid in Restoration England," *Studies in Philology* 88 (1991): 110–21. N. I. Matar, "Peter Sterry and the First English Poem on the Druids," *National Library of Wales Journal* 24 (Winter 1985): 222–43; Matar, "Peter Sterry and the Lovely Society," p. 45; Matar, *Sterry: Select Writings*, pp. 15–16.

110. Sterry, *Appearance*, pp. 282–83.

111. Matar, *Sterry: Select Writings*, pp. 105–109. See also Matar, "Peter Sterry and the Puritan Defense of Ovid," pp. 116–17. For the allegorization of nature and pagan subjects in painting, and its connection with ancient theology, see E. H. Gombrich, *Symbolic Images: Studies in the Art of the Renaissance* (London: Phaidon, 1975).

112. Dewey D. Wallace, Jr., "The Image of Saintliness in Puritan Hagiography," in *The Divine Drama in History and Liturgy: Essays Presented to Horton Davies on His Retirement from Princeton University* (Allison Park, Pa.: Pickwick Publications, 1984), pp. 23–43; Williams, "The Puritan Quest for the Enjoyment of God," pp. 129–34.

113. Brauer, "Types of Puritan Piety," pp, 51–56; Wakefield, *Puritan Devotion*, pp. 103–7; Wakefield, "Mysticism and its Puritan Types," pp. 38–44; Nuttall, "Puritan and Quaker Mysticism," pp. 518–31; Rupp, "A Devotion of Rapture in English Puritanism," pp. 115–31; Williams, "The Puritan Quest for the Enjoyment of God," with a focus on Sibbes and Owen, makes a strong case for the mysticism of the Puritan mainstream; Karl Reuter, "William Ames: The Leading Theologian in the Awakening of Reformed Pietism," in Matthew Nethenus, Hugo Visscher, and Karl Reuter, *William Ames*, translated by Douglas Horton (Cambridge, Mass.: Harvard Divinity School Library, 1965), p. 187; Coffey, *Politics, Religion and the British Revolutions*, pp. 82–97, treats the Scottish Rutherford alongside of English Puritans so far as theology and spiritual writing is concerned, pp. 17–18, and emphasizes his mysticism, Ibid., pp. 9, 95.

114. Rous, *Treatises and Meditations*, p. 698.

115. Nuttall, *Welsh Saints;* R. Tudur Jones, "The Heavenly Herb and the Rose of Love: The Piety of Two Welsh Puritans," in *Reformation, Conformity, and Dissent: Essays in Honour of Geoffrey Nuttall*, edited by R. Buick Knox (London: Epworth Press, 1977), pp. 154–79.

116. Rufus Jones, *Spiritual Reformers in the Sixteenth and Seventeenth Centuries* (1914; reprint, Boston: Beacon Press, 1959), pp. 239–52; Nuttall, *Holy Spirit*, p. 151, argued that Quakers, in their teaching about the Holy Spirit, carried forward a development already present in radical Puritanism.

117. Rudolf Otto perceived something of the mystical possibilities of predestination, *The Idea of the Holy*, trans. by John W. Harvey (1923; reprint, New York: Oxford University Press, 1958), pp. 88–89. D. P. Walker comments that the doctrine of predestination "corresponds closely to the psychological character of mystical experience, to its involuntary, 'given' quality," *The Decline of Hell*, p. 108.

118. William Ames, *The Marrow of Theology*, translated and edited by John D. Eusden (Durham, N.C.: Labyrinth Press, 1983), p. 251; Sterry, *Freedom of the Will*, pp. 76–77; Sterry, *Appearance*, pp.144–45; Sterry MS VII, p. 108, says that "the soul united to God alone" is "the way to perfection."

119. For Owen, Walter Cradock, and Thomas Goodwin on the union with God/ Christ, see Wakefield, "Mysticism and its Puritan Types," pp. 39, 43–44; see also Edward Polhill, *An Answer to the Discourse of Mr. William Sherlock* (London, 1675), unpaginated "to the reader."

120. Sterry, *Rise, Race and Royalty*, p. 463; Sterry, *Appearance*, pp. 75–76, 417–18; Sterry MS VII, pp. 34–35.

121. Sterry, *Rise, Race, and Royalty*, p. 200; Sterry MS IV, p. 82.

122. Sterry, *Rise, Race and Royalty*, p. 500.

123. Sterry, *Freedom of the Will*, sig. a4v, pp. 53, 213–14, 220, 235–36; *Appearance*, pp. 72, 471–74; *Rise, Race, and Royalty*, pp. 49, 78, 505–506; Matar, *Sterry: Select Writings*, p. 49; Sterry MS IV, p. 45; Sterry MS VII, p. 102. The mystical meaning of imputation in Luther is explored in Heiko Oberman, "Simul Gemitus et Raptus: Luther and Mysticism," in *The Reformation in Medieval Perspective*, edited by Steven E. Ozment (Chicago: Quadrangle Books, 1971), pp. 236–39. For the interpretation of Christ's descent into hell in English Protestant theology as Christ's suffering not triumph, see Dewey D. Wallace, Jr., "Puritan and Anglican: The Interpretation of Christ's Descent into Hell in Anglican Theology," *Archiv fur Reformationsgeschichte* 69 (1978): 260–66.

124. Sterry, *Rise, Race, and Royalty*, pp. 318–19; Sterry, *Appearance*, pp. 225, 227; Sterry MS VII, p. 18; Sterry, *Freedom of the Will*, sigs. a1-a3, b2v-b3v, c2r-c3v, pp. 40, 110, 125; Matar, *Sterry: Select Writings*, pp. 51–52. Later in New England, Cotton Mather spoke of "ravishing" spiritual experiences, Hambrick-Stowe, *The Practice of Piety*, pp. 284–86.

125. Sterry, *Appearance*, pp. 79, 224, 229, 231; Sterry, *Rise, Race, and Royalty*, pp. 186, 241; Sterry MS VII, pp. 18–19; Sterry, *Freedom of the Will*, sig. c4v, p. 53.

126. Sterry, *Rise, Race and Royalty*, p. 409; Sterry MS VII, pp. 18–19.

127. Sterry MS VI, pp. 168–78.

128. Sterry, *Appearance*, pp, 199–201, 206–207, 210–12; *The Rise, Race and Royalty*, pp. 103, 232, 365, 367; Matar, *Sterry: Select Writings*, p. 142; Williams, "The Puritan Quest for the Enjoyment of God," pp. 89–95, 116–22, 144–45.

129. Sterry, *Rise, Race, and Royalty*, p. 140.

130. For the attack on Bunyan's doctrine of imputation as Antinomian enthusiasm by Edward Fowler, later bishop of Gloucester, and on the Dissenters for hypocritical talk of "intimate communion with God" by Samuel Parker, see Dewey D. Wallace, Jr., *Puritans and Predestination: Grace in English Protestant Theology, 1525–1695* (Chapel Hill: University of North Carolina Press, 1982), pp. 165, 169. For the condemnation of Puritan piety as fanaticism, see John Spurr, *The Restoration Church of England, 1646–1689* (New Haven, Conn.: Yale University Press, 1991), pp. 263–67. For Anglican ridicule of the emotional language of Samuel Rutherford, see Coffey, *Politics, Religion, and the British Revolutions*, p. 108.

131. Sterry, *Rise, Race, and Royalty*, p. 252.

132. N. I. Matar, "Mysticism and Sectarianism in Mid-17th Century England," *Studia Mystica* 11 (1988): 55–56, 62–63; Sterry, *Rise, Race, and Royalty,* pp. 465–66; Sterry, *Appearance,* p. 54.

133. Sterry, *Freedom of the Will,* pp. 76–77; *Rise, Race and Royalty,* p. 276.

134. Sterry, *Clouds on which Christ Comes,* pp. 12–13. Walter Marshall, in *The Gospel-Mystery of Sanctification Opened in Sundry Practical Directions* (London, 1692), pp. 43–44, draws the same parallel between the soul's union with Christ and the union of the two natures in one person in Christ.

135. Matar, *Sterry: Select Writings,* p. 48. See also Matar, "Peter Sterry and the Ranters," pp. 504–506.

136. N. I. Matar, "Peter Sterry and Jacob Boehme," *Notes and Queries,* n.s., 33 (March 1986): 33–36; see B. J. Gibbons, *Gender in Mystical and Occult Thought: Behmenism and Its Development in England* (Cambridge: Cambridge University Press, 1996), p. 104, and Nigel Smith, *Perfection Proclaimed: Language and Literature in English Radical Religion, 1640–1660* (Oxford: Oxford University Press, 1989), p.185 for the translators of Boehme.

137. Pinto, *Sterry,* p. 57.

138. Matar, *Sterry: Select Writings,* pp. 45–46.

139. Matar, *Sterry: Select Writings,* p. 45; Sterry, *Freedom of the Will,* p. 213; Gibbons, *Gender in Mystical and Occult Thought,* p. 135; Nigel Smith, *Perfection Proclaimed,* p. 187; Matar, "Peter Sterry and Jacob Boehme"; Sterry, *Rise, Race, and Royalty,* p. 153; Sterry, *The Way of God,* p. 11; Sterry, *Comings Forth of Christ,* sig. a3v.

140. Nuttall, *Holy Spirit,* pp. 16–18; Rufus Jones, *Spiritual Reformers,* pp. 208–34; Smith, *Perfection Proclaimed,* pp. 186, 191; "Letters from Peter Sterry to Morgan Lloyd," Emmanuel College MS 321.1.129.

141. Gibbons, *Gender in Mystical and Occult Thought,* pp. 103–42, 163–204 give an account of English Behmenists; see also Smith, *Perfection Proclaimed,* pp. 185–225.

142. Serge Hutin, *Les Disciples Anglais de Jacob Boehme,* p. 48; Matar, "Peter Sterry and Jacob Boehme."

143. Matar, *Sterry: Select Writings,* pp. 42–46.

144. Ibid, pp. 41, 45; Sterry MS III, pp. 135–36.

145. W. R. Ward, *Early Evangelicalism: A Global Intellectual History, 1670–1789* (Cambridge: Cambridge University Press, 2006), pp. 74–75.

146. Sterry MS IV, p. 110, Sterry MS VI, p. 68.

147. See for example, *Clouds in Which Christ Comes, The Comings Forth of Christ,* and *The Teachings of Christ in the Soule.*

148. Richard Greaves, in *Deliver Us From Evil: the Radical Underground in Britain, 1660–1663* (Oxford: Oxford University Press, 1986) does not mention Sterry in his thorough explorations of radical dissenting political activity.

149. Matar, "Peter Sterry and the "Paradise Within," pp. 79–80; Robert Grant, *Gnosticism and Early Christianity,* rev. ed. (New York: Harper and Row, 1966), pp. viii, 37, 97, 118, especially emphasizes a cosmic mythological system as that into which eschatological excitement was transformed; Lorenzo Polizzotto, *The Elect Nation: The Savonarolan Movement in Florence 1494–1545* (Oxford: Clarendon Press, 1994), pp. 116, 146.

150. Matar, *Sterry: Select Writings*, p. 22.

151. Sterry, *Rise, Race, and Royalty*, pp. 89, 93.

152. Nathaniel Holmes, *The Resurrection Revealed* (London, 1653), sig. A[5]r.

153. Sterry, *The Way of God*, pp. 26, 30, 38, 41; Sterry, *The Clouds in Which Christ Comes*, pp. 6, 8, 14; Sterry, *The Comings Forth of Christ*, sig. a1-2.

154. N. H. Keeble, *Richard Baxter: Puritan Man of Letters* (Oxford: Clarendon Press, 1982), pp. 145–46.

155. Baxter, *Catholick Theologie*, bk. III, pp. 107–8.

156. Sterry, *Appearance*, unpaginated "publisher to the reader."

CHAPTER 3

1. George Eliot, *Middlemarch*, edited by Gordon S. Haight (1956; reprint, Boston: Houghton Mifflin, 1968), pp. 17–18. For hypotheses concerning the prototype of Casaubon, see Gordon S. Haight, *George Eliot: A Biography* (1968; reprint, New York: Penguin Books, 1985), pp. 563–66.

2. D. P. Walker, *The Ancient Theology* (Ithaca, N.Y.: Cornell University Press,1972), pp. 3, 144; Wayne Shumaker, *The Occult Sciences in the Renaissance* (Berkeley: University of California Press, 1972), p. 239; Peter French, *John Dee: The World of an Elizabethan Magus* (1972; reprint, New York: Dorset Press, 1989), pp. 56, 142, assumes the incompatibility of Puritanism and Hermetism; Frances A. Yates, *The Occult Philosophy in the Elizabethan Age* (London: Routledge and Kegan Paul, 1979), pp. 120, 177–79; Daniel Walker Howe notes that the Puritans found "reassurance" in that aspect of the ancient theology which taught that Plato knew Moses, "The Cambridge Platonists of Old England and the Cambridge Platonists of New England," *CH* 57 (December 1988): 472.

3. Shumaker, *Occult Sciences*, pp. 206–7; Walker, *Ancient Theology*, pp. 1–2; Brian P. Copenhaver, "Natural Magic, Hermetism, and Occultism in Early Modern Science," in *Reappraisals of the Scientific Revolution*, edited by David C. Lindberg and Robert S. Westman (Cambridge: Cambridge University Press, 1990), p. 289, prefers the terms "hermetic" and "occultist" to make the same distinction. But Ingrid Merkel and Allen G. Debus, eds., *Hermeticism and the Renaissance: Intellectual History and the Occult in Early Modern Europe* (Washington, DC: Folger Shakespeare Library, 1988), p. 8, question the usefulness of the distinction.

4. Yates, *The Occult Philosophy in the Elizabethan Age* (London: Routledge and Kegan Paul, 1979) and *The Rosicrucian Enlightenment* (Boulder, Colo.: Shambala Books, 1978).

5. Jean Seznec, *The Survival of the Pagan Gods*, translated by Barbara F. Sessions (Princeton, N.J.: Princeton University Press, 1953), pp. 12–13, 20–21, 98; Arthur B. Ferguson, *Utter Antiquity: Perceptions of Prehistory in Renaissance England* (Durham, N.C.: Duke University Press, 1993), p. 13.

6. Augustine, *Concerning The City of God Against the Pagans*, translated by Henry Bettenson (1972; reprint, Harmondsworth, U. K.: Penguin Books, 1984),

bk. VIII, chps. 11, 23–24; Frances A. Yates, *Giordano Bruno and the Hermetic Tradition* (1964; reprint, New York: Vintage Books, 1969), pp. 58, 66, 78–81, 84–86, 103.

7. Charles B. Schmitt, "Perennial Philosophy: From Agostino Steuco to Leibniz," *JHI* 27 (1966): 505–31.

8. Jerome Friedman, *The Most Ancient Testimony: Sixteenth-Century Christian-Hebraica in the Age of Renaissance Nostalgia* (Athens, Ohio: Ohio University Press, 1983), pp. 72–73, 84; D. P. Walker, *Spiritual and Demonic Magic from Ficino to Campanella* (1958; reprint, Notre Dame, Ind.: University of Notre Dame Press, 1975), pp. 90–96; Shumaker, *Occult Sciences*, pp. 182–83.

9. Howard Hotson, *Johann Heinrich Alsted, 1588–1638: Between Renaissance, Reformation, and Universal Reform* (Oxford: Clarendon Press, 2000), pp. 11, 37, 101–4, 109–10, 119–21, 123, 147, 149, 178–80.

10. Walker, *Ancient Theology*, pp. 32–33, 71–72; Phillipe de Mornay, *A Worke concerning the Trewnesse of the Christian Religion, written in French: Against Atheists, Epicures, Paynims, Jewes, Mahumetists, and other Infidels* (London, 1587), pp. 27–28, 59, 130; Yates, *Giordano Bruno*, pp. 398ff.; Anthony Grafton, *Defenders of the Text: The Traditions of Scholarship in an Age of Science, 1450–1800* (Cambridge, Mass.: Harvard University Press, 1991), pp. 79, 145–61.

11. Yates, *Giordano Bruno*, pp. 11, 184–85; John Headley, *Tommaso Campanella and the Transformation of the World* (Princeton, N.J.: Princeton University Press, 1997), pp. 17–18, 64, 319.

12. Yates, *Rosicrucian Enlightenment*, pp. 51, 99, 118–29.

13. David Stevenson, *The Origins of Freemasonry: Scotland's Century, 1590–1710* (Cambridge: Cambridge University Press, 1988), pp. 97, 232.

14. *ODNB*, "Gale, Theophilus"; Calamy,*Account*, vol. 2, p. 64; *BDBR*, "Gale, Theophilus."

15. Calamy, *Account*, vol. 2, p. 64; Calamy,*Continuation*, vol. 2, p. 97; *BDBR*, "Wharton, Philip Lord"; Gale to Lord Wharton, October 20, 1664, Letter 70, Rawlinson Mss. vol. 49, folio 255, Bodleian Library, Oxford; A. G. Mathews, "The Wharton Correspondence," *Transactions of the Congregational Historical Society* 10 (1927–1929), pp. 53–65; J. T. Cliffe, *Puritans in Conflict: The Puritan Gentry During and After the Civil Wars* (London: Routledge, 1988), pp. 43, 61, 115, 118, 130.

16. *Ath. Oxon.*, vol. 3, col. 1150; J. W. Ashley Smith, *The Birth of Modern Education: The Contribution of the Dissenting Academies, 1660–1800* (London: Independent Press, 1954), pp. 41–46; Calamy, *Account*, vol. 2, p. 66; Calamy, *Continuation*, vol. 2, p. 97; *ODNB*, " Lee, Samuel."

17. Calamy, *Account*, vol. 2, 65; Calamy, *Continuation*, vol. 2, p. 98; Norman Fiering, *Moral Philosophy at Seventeenth Century Harvard* (Chapel Hill: University of North Carolina Press, 1981), p. 280 n. 7.

18. Theophilus Gale, *The Life and Death of Thomas Tregosse, . . . and some Letters of his* (London, 1671); Gale, *The Life and Death of Mr. John Rowe* (London, 1673), sigs. A3-[A11]; Gale, *A Discourse of Christ's Coming* (London, 1673).

19. Theophilus Gale, *The Anatomie of Infidelitie* (London, 1672); it was republished in 1679 under the title *Christ's Tears for Jerusalem's Unbelief and Ruine;*

Gale, *Theophilie: Or, a Discourse of the Saints Amitie with God in Christ* (London, 1671), p. 32, passim.

20. Gale, *Theophilie*, pp. 37–43; cf. also Gale, *Anatomie of Infidelitie*, p. 174.

21. The first part of Gale's great work, *Of Philologie*, came out in 1669 and was revised in 1672; the second part of *Of Philosophie* was first published in 1670, reprinted in 1671, and published in a revised version in 1676 as *Of Barbaric and Grecanic Philosophie;* the third part appeared in 1677 as *The Vanity of Pagan Philosophies.* Part IV came out in two installments: bks. I and II in 1677 as *Of Reformed Philosophie* and bk. III in 1678 as *Of Divine Predetermination.* Each part bore the overall title of *The Court of the Gentiles.* The three "books" into which part I was subdivided were paginated separately; the other four volumes were paginated continuously. I have used the second, more complete, editions of parts I and II.

22. Theophilus Gale, *The Court of the Gentiles; or A discourse touching the original of human literature, both philologie and philosophie, from the scriptures & Jewish church*, part I, *Of Philologie*, second edition revised and enlarged (Oxford, 1672), sig. **2r.

23. Theophilus Gale, *The Court of the Gentiles: or, a discourse touching the traduction of philosophie from the Scriptures and Jewish church*, part II, *Of barbaric and grecanic philosophie*, 2nd ed. (London, 1676), pp. 71, 77, 80–81, p. 262; Theophilus Gale, *The Court of the Gentiles*, part III, *The vanity of pagan philosophie demonstrated from its causes, parts, proprieties, and effects* (London, 1677), p. 118. For Zalmoxis, see Ioan Petru Culianu and Cicerone Poghirc, "Zalmoxis," *The Encyclopedia of Religion*, 16 vols., edited by Mircea Eliade (New York: Macmillan, 1987), vol. 15, pp. 551–54.

24. Cassirer's view persists in C. A. Patrides, ed., *The Cambridge Platonists* (Cambridge, Mass.: Harvard University Press, 1970), pp. 5–6. The importance of Platonism for Puritanism has been demonstrated by Fiering, *Moral Philosophy*, pp. 246–51; Howe, "The Cambridge Platonists of Old and New England," pp. 470–74.

25.Theophilus Gale, The Court of the Gentiles, part IV, *Of Reformed Philosophie. Wherein Plato's moral, and metaphysic or prime philosophie is reduced to an useful forme and method* (London, 1677), sigs. A2-A4, Gale, Court, part III, pp. 130–36; Gale, Court, part II, pp. 271–75. Norman Fiering, Moral Philosophy, pp. 250, 280; Howe, "The Cambridge Platonists of Old and New England," p. 472.

26. Gale, *Court*, part I, bk. 1, pp.4–5.

27. Ibid., pp. 5–6.

28. Theophilus Gale, *Philosophia Generalis, In Duas Partes Disterminata* (London, 1676).

29. Gale, *Court*, part II, pp.7–11, 17–18, 20; Gale, *Court*, part I, bk. 1, pp. 14–16, 22–25, 52–59, 71–84, bk. 2, pp. 6–9, 28.

30. Gale, *Court*, part I, bk. 1, pp. 55–57, bk. 2, pp. 40, 45, 54–55; Gale, *Court*, part II, pp. 7–9, 13–14, 32, 80, 138; Yates, *Giordano Bruno*, p. 26.

31. Seznec, *Survival of the Pagan Gods*, pp. 16, 250; Gale, *Court*, part I, bk. 1, pp. 31–34, bk. 2, pp. 54–55, 72–75.

32. Gale, *Court*, part I, sig. *4, Gale, *Court*, part II, p. 7.

33. Gale, *Court*, part I, sig.*4v, bk. 1, pp. 2–12, bk. 3, p.113; Gale, *Court*, part II, pp. 90, 240.

34. Gale, *Court*, part I, bk. 1, pp. 14, 52–72; Gale, *Court*, part II, p. 7–8; Headley, *Tomasso Campanella*, p.163; cf. Guillaume Postel, who connected this point with Cabalism, William J. Bouwsma, *A Usable Past: Essays in European Cultural History* (Berkeley: University of California Press, 1990), pp. 213–14.

35. Gale, *Court*, part I, bk. 2, pp. 6–13, 28–31, 93, 100–101, 111, 117–18, 131–37.

36. Gale, *Court*, part I, bk 3, pp. 1–2, 4, 6–8, 10, 19–22, 27–28, 51, 59, 68, 87–89, 92–93, 95–97. For Gale and the poetics of Dissent, see Sharon Achinstein, *Literature and Dissent in Milton's England* (Cambridge: Cambridge University Press, 2003), pp. 184–91.

37. Gale, *Court*, part I, sig. *3; Gale, *Court*, part II, pp. 7–15, 20, 89, 145–46, 229–32, 235–36, 247–48, 251, 491–93.

38. Gale, *Court*, part II, pp. 6–15, 20–22; Gale, *Court*, part III, pp. 75–77, 116–18.

39. Gale, *Court*, part II, pp. 75–87.

40. Lewis Bayles Paton, "Sanchuniathon," *Encyclopedia of Religion and Ethics*, ed. James Hastings (New York: Charles Scribner's, 1925), vol. 11, pp.177–81; Anthony Grafton, *Joseph Scaliger: A Study in the History of Classical Scholarship*, 2 vols. (Oxford: Clarendon Press, 1983, 1993), vol. 2, p. 425; *ODNB*, "Dodwell, Henry."

41. Gale, *Court*, part I, bk. 1, pp. 22–27, 34–37, 39, 59–60; bk. 3, p. 6; Gale, *Court*, part II, pp. 46–49, 115, 124–25, 129, 237, 252, 428.

42. Stuart Piggott, *William Stukeley: An Eighteenth-Century Antiquarian*, rev. ed. (New York: Thames and Hudson, 1985), pp. 100–101.

43. Gale, *Court*, part II, sig. A2r.

44. Gale, *Court*, part II, sig. A2; Gale, *Court*, part III, sig. A2v-b1r, pp. 2, 18, 21, 25, 29, 109, 143–46; Gale, *Court*, part IV, *Reformed Philosophie*, p. 236.

45. Gale, *Court*, part IV, *Reformed Philosophie*, sigs. A2r-A4v.

46. *Ath. Oxon.*, vol. 3, col. 1149.

47. Barbara Lewalski, *Protestant Poetics and the Seventeenth-Century English Religious Lyric* (Princeton, N.J.: Princeton University Press, 1979), p. 498 n. 4; Peter J. Thuesen, ed., *Catalogues of Books, The Works of Jonathan Edwards*, vol. 26 (New Haven, Conn.: Yale University Press, 2008), p. 40.

48. Yates, *Occult Philosophy*, p. 95; Shumaker, *Occult Sciences*, pp. 238, 244; Walker, *The Ancient Theology*, pp. 31–34, 132–34; Gale, *Court*, part II, p. 95.

49. Yates, *Rosicrucian Enlightenment*, p. 119; Robert Burton, *The Anatomy of Melancholy* (New York: Tudor Publishing, 1955), passim; William Bouwsma, *The Waning of the Renaissance, 1550–1640* (New Haven, Conn.: Yale University Press, 2000), p. 162; Henry Reynolds, *Mythomystes* (Menston, Yorkshire, UK: Scolar Press, 1972), pp. 17, 21, 23, 29, 35, 39, 41, 53, 56–57, 74; Gale, *Court*, part I, bk 1, pp. 58, 64; Gale, *Court*, part II, pp. 32–36; Shumaker, *Occult Sciences*, pp. 240, 245–46; *The Prose of Sir Thomas Browne*, edited by Norman J. Endicott (Garden City, N.Y.: Doubleday, 1967), p. 294; John Milton, *Paradise Regained, The Minor Poems, and Samson Agonistes*, edited by Merritt Y. Hughes (Indianapolis, Ind.: Odyssey Press, 1937), p. 198, line 88; Johannes van den Berg, *Religious Currents and Cross-Currents: Essays on Modern Protestantism and the Protestant Enlightenment*, edited by Jan de Bruijn, Pieter Holtrop, and Ernestine van der Wall (Leiden, the Netherlands: Brill, 1999), pp. 19–23; Alan

Rudrum, ed., *The Works of Thomas Vaughan* (Oxford: Clarendon Press, 1984), pp. 102–103, 325; Walker, *Ancient Theology*, pp. 184–85; Edward, Lord Herbert, *Pagan Religion: A Translation of De religione gentilium*, edited and translated by John Anthony Butler, Medieval and Renaissance Texts and Studies (Ottawa: Dovehouse Editions, 1996), pp. 31–32, 37–38, 42–43, 274–85, 300–304.

50. Ralph Cudworth, *The True Intellectual System of the Universe* (London, 1678), pp. 319–21; Patrides, *Cambridge Platonists*, pp. 6–7; Carol L. Marks, "Thomas Traherne and Cambridge Platonism," *PMLA* 81 (December 1966): 523; Shumaker, *Occult Sciences of the Renaissance*, p. 210; Yates, *Giordano Bruno*, pp. 427–30; Henry More, *Conjectura Cabalistica. Or a conjectural Essay of Interpreting the minde of Moses, according to a Threefold Cabala* (London, 1653); Alison P. Coudert, "Henry More, the Kabbalah, and the Quakers," in *Philosophy, Science, and Religion in England, 1640–1700*, edited by Richard Kroll, Richard Ashscraft, and Perez Zagorin (Cambridge: Cambridge University Press, 1992), p. 36; Joseph M. Levine, "Latitudinarians, Neoplatonists, and the Ancient Wisdom," in *Philosophy, Science, and Religion in England, 1640–1700*, edited by Richard Kroll, Richard Ashcraft, and Perez Zagorin (Cambridge: Cambridge University Press, 1992) p. 95; Nathaniel Culverwell, *An Elegant and Learned Discourse of the Light of Nature*, edited by Robert A. Greene and Hugh MacCallum, University of Toronto Department of English Studies and Texts no. 17 (Toronto: University of Toronto Press, 1971), pp. 62–63.

51. Margaret C. Jacob, *The Newtonians and the English Revolution, 1689–1720* (Ithaca, N.Y.: Cornell University Press, 1976), pp. 218–19; Frank E. Manuel, *The Religion of Isaac Newton* (Oxford: Clarendon Press, 1974), pp. 39, 44–45; B. J. T. Dobbs, "Newton's Commentary on the Emerald Tablet of Hermes Trismegistus: Its Scientific and Theological Significance," in *Hermeticism and the Renaissance: Intellectual History and the Occult in Early Modern Europe*, edited by Ingrid Merkel and Allen G. Debus (Washington, DC: Folger Books, 1988), pp. 182–91.

52. Samuel Parker, *A Free and Impartial Censure of the Platonick Philosophie* (London, 1666), pp. 92–95, 99, 104.

53. Gale, *Court*, part I, sigs. *2r, *[4]r.

54. Gale, *Court*, part I, sig. *2.

55. Gale, *Court*, part I, sig. *2; Gale, *Court*, part II, p. 94; Gale, *Court*, part III, sig. b2.

56. Richard H. Popkin, "The Deist Challenge," in *From Persecution to Toleration: The Glorious Revolution and Religion in England*, edited by Ole Peter Grell, Jonathan I. Israel, and Nicholas Tyacke, (Oxford: Clarendon Press, 1991), pp. 196–99; Grafton, *Defenders of the Text*, p. 156.

57. E.g., Gale, *Court*, part II, pp. 71–72; Gale, *Court*, part IV, pp. 240–42.

58. Yates, *Giordano Bruno*, p. 402.

59. Gale, *Court*, part I, sig. *[4]r, bk. 1, p. 54; Gale, *Court*, part II, pp. 13, 32, 53, 94; Phillipe de Mornay, *A Worke concerning the Trewnesse of the Christian Religion*; Grafton, *Defenders of the Text*, p. 77; C. Hippeau, "Bochart (Samuel)," *Nouvelle Biographie Generale* (Paris, 1855), vol. 6: cols. 304–7; somewhat later Cotton Mather was in awe of Bochart, Thuesen, *Works of Jonathan Edwards*, vol. 26, p. 200.

60. Gale, *Court*, part I, bk. 2, p 13.

61. Gale, *Court*, part I, sigs. *2, *[4]r; Gale, *Court*, part II, p. 95.

62. John Owen, *Theologoumena Pantodapa, sive de Natura, Ortu, Progressu et Studio verae Theologiae* (Oxford, 1661), pp. 296–97.

63. Gale, *Court*, part I, sigs. *2r, *[4]r; Gale, *Court*, part II, p. 243; Sarah Hutton, "Thomas Jackson, Oxford Platonist, and William Twisse, Aristotelian," *JHI* 39 (October–December 1978): 636, 640–43; Sarah Hutton, "Edward Stillingfleet, Henry More, and the Decline of Moses Atticus: A Note on Seventeenth-Century Anglican Apologetics," in *Philosophy, Science, and Religion in England, 1640–1700*, edited by Richard Kroll, Richard Ashcraft, and Perez Zagorin (Cambridge: Cambridge University Press, 1992), pp. 68–83; Edward Stillingfleet, *Origenes Sacrae, Or A Rational Account of the Grounds of Christian Faith* (London, 1662), pp. 33–35, 429, 580; Ferguson, *Utter Antiquity*, pp. 36, 52–54.

64. Gale, *Court*, part IV, *Reformed Philosophie*, sig. A2v; Gale, *Court*, part III, p. 29; Ferguson, *Utter Antiquity*, pp. 27–28.

65. Charles Trinkaus, *In Our Image and Likeness: Humanity and Divinity in Italian Humanist Thought*, 2 vols. (Chicago: University of Chicago Press, 1970), vol. 2, pp. 736, 743–44.

66. Gale, *Court*, part I, bk. 1, pp. 55–57, bk. 2, p. 45; Gale, *Court*, part II, pp. 13–14, 30, 32; Milton, *Paradise Regained, the Minor Poems, and Samson Agonistes*, pp. 522–23 (lines 336–442).

67. Gale, *Court*, part III, pp. 56–57.

68. Gale, *Court*, part I, bk. 3, p. 65; Gale, *Court*, part II, p. 104; Gale, *Court*, part III, p. 48.

69. Gale, *Court*, part II, p. 22.

70. For Wilkins's universal scheme of knowledge, see Barbara Shapiro, *John Wilkins, 1614-1672: An Intellectual Biography* (Berkeley: University of California Press, 1969), pp, 214–21.

71. Bouwsma, *Usable Past*, pp. 120–21.

72. *BDBR*, "Wharton, Philip Lord."

73. Gale to Lord Wharton, June 11, 1662, Letter 15, Rawlinson Mss. Vol. 49, Bodleian Library, Oxford.

74. Gale, *Court*, part I, sig. **[1]v.

75. Gerald R. McDermott, *Jonathan Edwards Confronts the Gods: Christian Theology, Enlightenment Religion, and Non-Christian Faiths* (Oxford: Oxford University Press, 2000), pp. 41 n18, 92, 94, 160, 180–81, 183–84, 186–91.

76. Gale, *Court*, part I, sigs. *2r-*3r.

77. Ibid., part I, sigs. *3v-**[1]r.

78. Grafton, *Defenders of the Text*, pp. 17–19; Levine, "Latitudinarians, Neopolatonists, and the Ancient Wisdom," pp. 85–108; More, however, thought that Platonic philosophy could be traced back to Moses, Henry More, *Conjectura Cabalistica*, sigs. A3-A5, B1-B2; Cudworth, in *The True Intellectual System of the Universe*, asserted in a massive fourth chapter that in spite of their surface polytheism ancient thinkers recognized one supreme being, many even hinting at its threefold nature, pp. 192–632.

79. Gale, *Court,* part I, bk. 3, p. 114; Gale, *Court,* part II, pp. 105–107.

80. Gale, "To the Reader," *Life and Death of Rowe,* sig. A3v.

81. Fiering, *Moral Philosophy,* pp. 279–82, 289.

82. John Barker, *Strange Contrarieties: Pascal in England During the Age of Reason* (Montreal: McGill-Queen's University Press, 1975), p. 17.

83. Theophilus Gale, *The True Idea of Jansenisme, both Historick and Dogmatick* (London, 1669), p. 158.

84. Gale, *Court,* part III, p. 146; Norman Fiering asserts that Jansen was "the dominant figure in the development of Gale's thought," *Moral Philosophy,* p. 281.

85. Robin Briggs, "The Catholic Puritans: Jansenists and Rigorists in France," in *Puritans and Revolutionaries: Essays in Seventeenth-Century History presented to Christopher Hill,* edited by Donald Pennington and Keith Thomas (Oxford: Clarendon Press, 1978), 333–54; Gale, *True Idea of Jansenism,* p. 7; information on the reaction to French Jansenism in England can be found in Barker, *Strange Contrarieties.*

86. Gale, *Court,* part I, sig. **[1]r; Bouwsma, *Usable Past,* p. 257.

87. Brian G. Armstrong, *Calvinism and the Amyraut Heresy: Protestant Scholasticism and Humanism in Seventeenth-Century France* (Madison: University of Wisconsin Press, 1969); Jonathan D. Moore, *English Hypothetical Universalism: John Preston and the Softening of Reformed Theology* (Grand Rapids, Mich.: Eerdmans, 2007), p. 219; for Gale's controversy with Howe, see Dewey D. Wallace, Jr., *Puritans and Predestination: Grace in English Protestant Theology, 1525–1695* (Chapel Hill: University of North Carolina Press, 1982), pp.179–80.

88. Gale, *Court,* part III, sig. A3, p. 144; Gale, *Court,* part IV," *Reformed philosophie,* pp. 51–52; Theophilus Gale, "A Summary of the Two Covenants," preface to William Strong, *A Discourse of Two Covenants* (London, 1678), sig. A3. For the use of two covenants to maximize grace, see Michael McGiffert, "From Moses to Adam: The Making of the Covenant of Works," *SCJ* 19 (Summer 1988): 131–55.

89. Richard Popkin, "The Deist Challenge," in *From Persecution to Toleration: The Glorious Revolution and Religion in England,* edited by Ole Peter Grell, Jonathan I. Israel, and Nichlas Tyacke (Oxford: Clarendon Press, 1991), pp. 204–207.

90. Theophilus Gale, *A Discourse of Christ's Coming* (London, 1673), sig. A2; Gale, *Court,* part II, p. 419; Gale, *Court,* part III, p. 34, 108–10.

91. Gale, *Anatomie of Infidelitie,* pp. 24, 122, 143; Gale, *Court,* part IV, *Reformed Philosophie,* p. 236; Heering, *Hugo Grotius as Apologist,* pp. xix, 99.

92. Bouwsma, *Usable Past,* p. 83.

93. Walker, *Ancient Theology,* pp. 33–35, 59–62; Walker, *Spiritual and Demonic Magic,* p. 146.

94. Eugenio Garin, "Gian Francesco Pico Della Mirandola: Savonarolan Apologetics and the Critique of Ancient Thought," in *Christianity and the Renaissance: Image and Religious Imagination in the Quattrocento,* edited by Timothy Verdon and John Henderson (Syracuse, N.Y.: Syracuse University Press, 1990), p. 524; Walker, *The Ancient Theology,* pp. 42–43, 47–48; Gale, *Court,* part IV, *Reformed Philosophie,* sigs. A2v, A4r.

95. Erasmus integrated the ancient classical wisdom into his Christian philosophy without recourse to the scheme of ancient theology, Marjorie O'Rourke Boyle,

Christening Pagan Mysteries: Erasmus in Pursuit of Wisdom (Toronto: University of Toronto Press, 1981), pp. 9, 11–12, 16–17; for Calvin and natural theology, see Edward A. Dowey, Jr., *The Knowledge of God in Calvin's Theology* (New York: Columbia University Press, 1952), especially, pp. 28, 51, 56, 74; Richard A. Muller, *Post-Reformation Reformed Dogmatics: The Rise and Development of Reformed Orthodoxy, ca 1520 to ca. 1725*, vol. 1, *Prolegomena to Theology*, 2nd ed. (Grand Rapids, Mich.: Baker Academic, 2003), pp. 270–76.

96. William J. Bouwsma, *John Calvin: A Sixteenth Century Portrait* (New York: Oxford University Press, 1988), p. 103; John Calvin, *Institutes of the Christian Religion*, bk. II, 2:14–17.

97. Quoted in Bouwsma, *John Calvin*, p.115.

98. Joscelyn Godwin, *Athanasius Kircher: A Renaissance Man and the Quest for Lost Knowledge* (London: Thames and Hudson, 1979); Erik Iverson, *The Myth of Egypt and Its Hieroglyphs in European Tradition* (1961; reprint, Princeton, N.J.: Princeton University Press, 1993) pp. 94–97.

99. Walker, *Ancient Theology*, pp. 198–99, 201, 204–5, 225–26.

100. Piggott, *William Stukeley*, pp. 99–100; Gale, *Court*, part II, p. 35.

101. John C. English, "John Hutchinson's Critique of Newtonian Heterodoxy," *CH* 68 (September 1999): 561–97; Joseph J. Ellis, *The New England Mind in Transition: Samuel Johnson of Connecticut, 1696–1772* (New Haven, Conn.: Yale University Press, 1973), pp. 228–32; Friedman, *Most Ancient Testimony*, p. 20; Robert Bruce Mullin, *Episcopal Vision/American Reality: High Church Theology and Social Thought in Evangelical America* (New Haven, Conn.: Yale University Press, 1986), p. 19 n. 44.

102. Frank E. Manuel, *The Eighteenth Century Confronts the Gods* (Cambridge, Mass.: Harvard University Press, 1959), p. 4; Frank M. Turner, *The Greek Heritage in Victorian Britain* (New Haven, Conn.: Yale University Press, 1981).

CHAPTER 4

1. George Eliot, *Felix Holt, The Radical* (London: Penguin Books, 1987), p. 353.

2. Cited in Iain Murray, "Biographical Introduction," in Joseph Alleine, *An Alarm to the Unconverted* (London: Banner of Truth Trust, 1967), p. 11.

3. Norman Petit, ed., *The Life of David Brainerd, The Works of Jonathan Edwards*, vol. 7 (New Haven, Conn.: Yale University Press, 1985), p. 259. Jonathan Edwards listed it among his reading, Peter J. Thuesen, ed., *Catalogues of Books, The Works of Jonathan Edwards*, vol. 26 (New Haven, Conn.: Yale University Press, 2008), pp. 127–28.

4. Peter Sterry, *The Rise, Race, and Royalty of the Kingdom of God* (London, 1683), p. 23; Theophilus Gale, *A Discourse of Christ's Coming* (London, 1673), sigs. A3r, A4v, p. 195.

5. Baxter said he would have apostasized to unbelief had he not had an internal religious experience, cited in Debora K. Shuger, "Faith and Assurance," in *A Companion to Richard Hooker*, edited by Torrance Kirby (Leiden, the Netherlands: Brill, 2008), p. 248.

6. Iain Murray, "Biographical Introduction," p. 11.

7. Ibid.

8. Robert C. Monk, *John Wesley: His Puritan Heritage* (Nashville, Tenn.: Abingdon Press, 1966), pp.143, 262. Several of the writings of Richard Alleine were also included.

9. There were more printings of Baxter's *Call* than Alleine's *Alarm* in the seventeenth century, and this continued to be the case for the later periods.

10. Ted A. Campbell, *The Religion of the Heart* (Columbia: University of South Carolina Press, 1991), p. 102.

11. Joseph Alleine, *Christian Letters full of Spiritual Instructions, Tending to the Promoting of the Power of Godliness, both in Persons and Families* (London, 1672), p. 133.

12. Sources for his life and accounts of it are in *The Life and Death of that Excellent Minister of Christ Mr. Joseph Alleine* (London, 1672); *Ath. Oxon.*, vol. 3, cols. 819–22; Samuel Clarke, *The Lives of Eminent Persons in this Later Age*, part I (London, 1683), pp. 139–60; Calamy, *Account*, vol. 2, pp. 574–77; *CR*, "Alleine, Joseph"; Charles Stanford, *Joseph Alleine: His Companions & Times; A Memorial of "Black Bartholomew," 1662* (London, 1861); *BDBR*, "Alleine, Joseph"; *ODNB*, "Alleine, Joseph."

13. *Life and Death of Alleine*, pp. 27–28; *Ath. Oxon.*, vol. 3, col. 822; According to Stanford, *Joseph Alleine*, p. 154, these manuscripts were lost in the wreck of a vessel bound for America.

14. E.g., *Remaines of that Excellent Minister of Jesus Christ, Mr. Joseph Alleine, Being a Collection of Sundry Directions, Sermons, Sacrament-Speeches, and Letters, not heretofore Published* (London, 1674), pp. 280, 288.

15. Joseph Alleine, *A Call to Archippus, or An humble and earnest Motion to some Ejected Ministers, (by way of Letter) to take heed to their Ministry, That they Fulfil it* (London, 1664) pp. 3–6.

16. Ibid., pp. 8–10, 13, 18–19, 21.

17. Ibid., pp. 11–12.

18. Ibid., 21.

19. In the epistle "To the Reader" at the beginning of *Heaven Opened, Or A Brief and Plain Discovery of the Riches of Gods Covenant of Grace. Being the Third Part of Vindiciae Pietatis* (London, 1666), Richard Alleine, the author, refers to another as the author of the "Form of Mans Covenanting with God," and further on identifies that other as I. A., for Joseph Alleine, sig. A2r-v, p. 215; the "Form" for covenanting is on pp. 293–97.

20. Richard Alleine, *Heaven Opened*, sigs. A2r-v, A3v, pp. 215, 252.

21. Ibid., pp. 215–73; Dwight Bozeman calls attention to soliloquy, as a device appearing in Puritan spiritual diaries, in *The Precisianist Strain: Disciplinary Religion and Antinomian Backlash in Puritanism to 1638* (Chapel Hill: University of North Carolina Press, 2004), p. 107.

22. Richard Alleine, *Heaven Opened*, pp. 221, 234.

23. Ibid., p. 234.

24. *Life and Death of Alleine*, sig. A2r-v.

25. Joseph Alleine, *Christian Letters Full of Spiritual Instructions, Tending to the Promoting of the Power of Godliness, both in Persons, and Families* (London, 1672), pp. 35, 59, 80, 83, 87, 98.

26. Joseph Alleine, *A Most Familiar Explanation of the Assemblies Shorter Catechism* (London, 1674), pp. 161, 164.

27. Ibid, sig A4r.

28. *Remaines of Alleine*, sig. a[1]r-v.

29. *Ath. Oxon.*, vol. 4, cols. 13–15; Calamy, *Account*, vol. 2, pp. 580–81, Calamy, *Continuation* vol. 2, p. 731; *ODNB*, "Alleine, Richard."

30. Richard Alleine, *Cheirothesia tou Presbuterou, or a Letter to a Friend* (London, 1661), pp. 2, 3, 6, 10–11, 18, 26, 31, 52, 54, 56, 62.

31. *Life and Death of Alleine*, sig. A2v, pp. 41–42, 95; *Ath. Oxon.*, vol. 3, col. 822; *ODNB*, "Alleine, Theodosia."

32. *Ath. Oxon.*, vol. 3, col. 822.

33. *CR*, "Newton, George"; *Ath. Oxon.*, vol. 4, cols. 4–5.

34. *CR*, "Fairclough, Richard"; *Life and Death of Alleine*, p. 90; Stanford, *Joseph Alleine*, p. 363; [Richard Fairclough], *A Pastors Legacy, To his Beloved People: Being the Substance of Fourteen Farewel Sermons* (London, 1663), pp. 125, 132–33—the author is given as "a Somersetshire Minister" and the title page states that it was published "at the entreaty and charge of his Parishioners"; John Howe, *A Funeral Sermon for That Faithful and Laborious Servant of Christ, Mr. Richard Fairclough* (London, 1682).

35. *ODNB*, "Norman, John"; *CR*, "Norman, John"; Joseph Alleine, *Christian Letters*, pp.136–39; for references to "brother Norman," see Joseph Alleine, *Christian Letters*, pp.15, 31, 43 and *Remaines of Alleine*, p. 262.

36. A curious episode indicating where this group stood in relation to the Independents involved Joseph Alleine's brother Tobie, who had held the office of bailiff in Exeter. Accused of ungodliness, misbehavior, and "such like excrementitious stuff" by some in a congregation in which he and his family had participated, he blamed them in turn for Antinomianism and Independency. Seeking vindication, he went to see "Mr. Newton and my Brother Alleine" for support, which he apparently received (Tobie Alleine, *Truths Manifest*[1658]), pp. 55, 82).

37. *ODNB*, "Fairclough, Richard"; sermons printed in Samuel Annesley, *The Morning Exercise at Cripple-gate, or Several Cases of Conscience practically resolved by sundry ministers* (London, 1661) and in Nathaniel Vincent, *The Morning Exercises Against Popery* (London, 1675).

38. Howe, *A Funeral Sermon for Mr. Richard Fairclough*, pp. 1–2.

39. N. H. Keeble and Geoffrey F. Nuttall, eds., *Calendar of the Correspondence of Richard Baxter*, 2 vols. (Oxford: Clarendon Press, 1991), vol. 2, p. 101.

40. William Haller, *The Rise of Puritanism* (New York: Columbia University Press, 1938), pp. 49–82; recent studies of Greenham and Sibbes call attention to features of their life and thought that resemble this later moderate Presbyterianism, Mark E. Dever, *Richard Sibbes: Puritanism and Calvinism in Late Elizabethan and Early Stuart England* (Macon, Ga.: Mercer University Press, 2000) and Kenneth L. Parker and Eric J. Carlson, *"Practical Divinity:" The Works and Life of Revd. Richard Greenham* (Aldershot, UK: Ashgate, 1998).

41. *Life and Death of Alleine*, pp. 19, 20, 27, 53, 95.

42. Geoffrey Nuttall, *Richard Baxter* (London: Thomas Nelson and Sons, 1965), pp. 64–81; *RB*, bk. I, part I, pp. 129–30, 134, 137–38. For Baxter on controversy also see Tim Cooper, *Fear and Polemic in Seventeenth-Century England: Richard Baxter and Antinomianism* (Aldershot, UK: Ashgate, 2001), pp. 46–54. John Bunyan also sent mixed signals on controversy: claiming no desire to meddle in matters that divided "the saints," he nonetheless was "pleased" "to contend with great earnestness for the Word of faith," John Bunyan, *Grace Abounding to the Chief of Sinners*, edited by W. R. Owens (London: Penguin Books, 1987), p. 71.

43. Richard Alleine, *A Letter to a Friend*, sig A3r.

44. Richard Alleine, *A Rebuke to Backsliders, and a Spurr for Loyterers* (London, 1677), pp. 166–67.

45. Howe, *Funeral Sermon for Fairclough*, p. 42.

46. Nuttall, *Baxter*, pp. 70–73; *RB*, bk. I, part II, pp. 188–93.

47. Francis J. Bremer, *Congregational Communion: Clerical Friendship in the Anglo-American Puritan Community, 1610–1692* (Boston: Northeastern University, 1994), pp. 250–52.

48. [Fairclough], *A Pastor's Legacy*, p. 121.

49. *Life and Death of Alleine*, p. 27.

50. Ian Green, *Print and Protestantism in Early Modern England* (Oxford: Oxford University Press, 2000), p. 21.

51. J. Alleine, *Remaines of Alleine*, sig. A6v; Letters, p. 159.

52. *Life and Death of Alleine*, pp. 15, 18–19, 21.

53. In Baxter's "To the Christian Reader," introducing James Janeway's account of the life of his brother John Janeway, who also died early, *Invisibles, Realities, Demonstrated in the Holy Life an Triumphant Death of Mr. John Janeway* (London, 1673), sigs A5v-6r.

54. *Life and Death of Alleine*, pp. 46, 49.

55. *Life and Death of Alleine*, p. 56.

56. *Life and Death of Alleine*, p. 126 [mispaginated as 142].

57. *Life and Death of Alleine*, p. 62.

58. *Life and Death of Alleine*, pp. 40, 56, 112.

59. *Life and Death of Alleine*, pp. 56, 113; for Davenant on the atonement see Jonathan D. Moore, *English Hypothetical Universalism: John Preston and the Softening of Reformed Theology* (Grand Rapids, Mich.: Eerdmans, 2007), pp. 187–208; Moise Amyraux had moderated predestination and limited atonement, see Brian Armstrong, *Calvinism and the Amyraux Heresy: Protestant Scholasticism and Humanism in Seventeenth-Century France* (Madison: University of Wisconsin Press, 1969), pp. 177–221.

60. Thomas Gouge (1605–1681), son of William Gouge, an important earlier Puritan spiritual writer, though much older than Joseph Alleine, was stimulated by the latter's missionary zeal to evangelize Wales, going there in 1672, the annus mirabilis of publications concerning Joseph (*ODNB*, "Gouge, Thomas"); George Trosse, who turned to the dissenting ministry after a long spiritual struggle, was ordained to the ministry and "prayed over" in 1666 in Somersetshire by Joseph and five others

(A. W. Brink, ed., *The Life of the Reverend George Trosse, written by Himself and Published Posthumously according to his Order in* 1714 [Montreal: McGill-Queen's University Press, 1974], p. 124); Thomas Doolittle, a Baxter protégé, was known as a spiritual writer (see indexed references to Doolittle in Keeble and Nuttall, *Calendar of the Correspondence of Richard Baxter*).

61. Janeway, *Invisibles, Realities,* sig. A3v.

62. This definition is attributed to David Bebbington and cited by John Wolffe in "Anti-Catholicism in Evangelical Identity in Britain and the united States, 1830–1860," in *Evangelicalism: Comparative Studies of Popular Protestantism in North America, the British Isles, and Beyond, 1700–1990,* edited by Mark Noll, David W. Bebbington, and George A. Rawlyk (New York: Oxford University Press, 1994), 179–97, pp. 180–81.

63. Peter Iver Kaufman, in *Prayer, Despair, and Drama: Elizabethan Introspection* (Urbana: University of Illinois Press, 1996), p. 60, contrasts Calvin's worry that too much emphasis on one's own unworthiness was dangerous with the late Elizabethan preachers heightening such an emphasis.

64. Dewey D. Wallace, Jr., *The Spirituality of the Later English Puritans: An Anthology* (Macon, Ga.: Mercer University Press, 1987, pp. xi–xxiv; for Peter Lake, *Moderate Puritans and the Elizabethan Church* (Cambridge: Cambridge University Press, 1982), the imperatives of Puritan piety lay behind the Puritan desiderata of reform, pp. 3, 19, 150, 165, 279, 282; David Como refers to "mainstream Puritans" in his *Blown by the Spirit: Puritanism and the Emergence of an Antinomian Underground in Pre-Civil War England* (Stanford, Calif.: Stanford University Press, 2004), pp. 3, 28.

65. Bozeman, *The Precisianist Strain,* p. 4.

66. Ibid., pp. 14–15, 17.

67. Ibid., pp. 27, 35.

68. Ibid., p. 93.

69. Ibid., p. 131.

70. Ibid., pp. 145ff.

71. Ibid., pp. 42–43, 100, 146–47, 156

72. William Haller picked out Chaderton, Greenham, Rogers, Dod, and Sibbes as key figures in the Puritan brotherhood of preachers, *The Rise of Puritanism* (New York: Columbia University Press, 1938); Peter Lake regards Chaderton as central to the emergence of moderate Puritanism, *Moderate Puritans;* Bozeman, *The Precisianist Strain,* pp. 68–74, emphasizes the importance of Greenham, as do Parker and Carlson, *The Works and Life of Greenham;* Dever, *Richard Sibbes,* Dewey D. Wallace, Jr., "George Gifford, Puritan Propaganda and Popular Religion in Elizabethan England," *SCJ* 9 (April 1978): 27–49; Timothy Scott McGinnis, *George Gifford and the Reformation of the Common Sort: Puritan Priorities in Elizabethan Religious Life* (Kirksville, Mo: Truman State University Press, 2004); Nicholas Tyacke, "The 'Rise of Puritanism' and the Legalizing of Dissent, 1571–1719," in *From Persecution to Toleration: The Glorious Revolution and Religion in England,* edited by Ole Peter Grell, Jonathan I. Israel, and Nicholas Tyacke, (Oxford: Clarendon Press, 1991), p. 26, refers to Arthur Hildersam as an "evangelical Calvinist."

73. D. Bruce Hindmarsh, *The Evangelical Conversion Narrative: Spiritual Autobiography in Early Modern England* (Oxford: Oxford University Press, 2005), pp. 50, 105–6, 309–10; David Bebbington, *Evangelicalism in Modern Britain: A History from the 1730s to the 1980s* (London: Unwin Hyman, 1989), p. 35; Mark A. Noll, *The Rise of Evangelicalism: The Age of Edwards, Whitfield, and the Wesleys* (Downer's Grove, Ill: Intervarsity Press, 2003), pp. 54–58.

74. Dewey D. Wallace, Jr., "The Image of Saintliness in Puritan Hagiography, 1630–1700," in *The Divine Drama in History and Liturgy: Essays Presented to Horton Davies on His Retirement from Princeton University* (Allison Park, Pa: Pickwick Publications, 1984), pp. 23–43, gives examples of Puritan hagiography.

75. See, for example, Robert Kolb, *For All the Saints: Changing Perceptions of Martyrdom and Sainthood in the Lutheran Reformation* (Macon, Ga.: Mercer University Press, 1987).

76. *Life and Death of Alleine*, pp. 12–14.

77. Ibid., pp. 95, 96, 99.

78. Ibid., p. 29

79. Ibid., pp. 104–5; Richard Alleine, "To the Unconverted Reader," one of two prefatory epistles to Joseph Alleine, *An Alarme*, sigs. B4v-B5r.

80. *Life and Death of Alleine*, pp. 27–30, 43, 106, 109–10.

81. Ibid., p. 109.

82. Ibid., pp. 104–5, 107–9, 88.

83. Ibid., p. 44; the austerities and holiness of life of Gaston Jean Baptise de Renty (1611–1649) gained the attention of Protestants, perhaps because he was a married layman famous for great charity. W. R. Ward has called attention to the interest of pietists and evangelicals in some Catholic mystics and ascetics, particularly the interest of Samuel and John Wesley in de Renty, *Early Evangelicalism: A Global Intellectual History, 1670–1789* (Cambridge: Cambridge University Press, 2006), pp. 69, 120–21, 131.

84. *Life and Death of Alleine*, p. 98.

85. Ibid., p. 118.

86. Ibid., p. 96.

87. Ibid., p. 42.

88. Ibid., p. 69.

89. Ibid., pp. 43–44, 65, 89, 95, 39.

90. Ibid., pp. 69, 91, 121–22.

91. Ibid., pp. 39, 40, 41, 45, 98, 108; John Howe praised Joseph's friend Richard Fairclough for the same thing, *A Funeral Sermon for Richard Fairclough*, p. 53.

92. *Life and Death of Alleine*, p. 122–25, 101.

93. Ibid., pp. 23, 35, 96.

94. Ibid., pp. 35, 39, 122, 124.

95. Ibid., pp. 23, 39, 88, 107, 92–93.

96. George Newton, *A Sermon Preached at the Funeral of Mr. Joseph Alleine*, p. 26.

97. *Remaines of Alleine*, sigs. A1r-A7v.

98. *Life and Death of Alleine*, pp. 62–65.

99. Ibid., pp. 69–70.

100. Ibid., pp. 70, 77, 79–82.

101. Ibid p. 65.

102. Ibid., pp. 41, 80, 101, 103.

103. Parker and Carlson, *The Works and Life of Greenham*, p. 61.

104. R. Po-Chia Hsia, *Social Discipline in the Reformation: Central Europe* 1550–1750 (London, Routledge, 1989), pp. 1–2, 6–8, 184; Wietse de Boer, "Calvin and Borromeo, A Comparative Approach to Social Discipline," in *Early Modern Catholicism: Essays in Honour of John W. O'Malley, S.J.*, edited by Cathleen M. Comerford and Hilmar M. Pabel (Toronto: University of Toronto Press, 2001), pp. 85–95; Eamon Duffy, "The Long Reformation: Catholicism, Protestantism and the Multitude," in *England's Long Reformation 1500–1800*, edited by Nicholas Tyacke (London: UCL Press, 1998), p. 34.

105. *Life and Death of Alleine*, p. 104.

106. Ibid., pp. 19, 23–24.

107. Joseph Alleine, *An Alarme*, sigs. C3v-C4r.

108. George Newton, *A Sermon Preached at the Funeral of Mr. Joseph Alleine*, p. 23.

109. Ibid., pp.19–20.

110. *Life and Death of Alleine*, p. 98; "Korahism," named after Korah who led a revolt against Moses and was swallowed up by the earth (Numbers 16:1–34) was a term used to refer to those who defied godly ministers; John Norton preached a sermon entitled "Abel being Dead yet Speaketh" (1658) in which he warned New Englanders about this.

111. *Life and Death of Alleine*, p. 100.

112. Ibid., pp. 46, 49, 51, 63–64, 67, 70, 97.

113. Ibid., p. 76.

114. Ibid., pp. 66–67; Christopher Hill, "Puritans and 'the Dark Corners of the Land,' " in *Change and Continuity in Seventeenth-Century England* (Cambridge, Mass.: Harvard University Press, 1975), pp. 3–47; Duffy, "The Long Reformation," pp. 45–50.

115. *RB*, bk. I, part I, p. 131.

116. Nuttall, *Baxter*, pp. 12, 82.

117. *Life and Death of Alleine*, pp. 43, 63, 67.

118. Ibid., pp. 24–25, 66, 79, 96.

119. Ian Green, *Print and Protestantism*, pp. 292–93, unpaginated appendix 1; Keeble and Nuttall, *Calendar of the Correspondence of Richard Baxter*, vol. 1, pp. 250–51; vol. 2, pp. 200, 238–39.

120. *Life and Death of Alleine*, pp. 48, 95.

121. Mark Goldie, "The Theory of Religious Intolerance in Restoration England," in *From Persecution to Toleration: The Glorious Revolution in England*, edited by Ole Peter Grell, Jonathan I. Israel, and Nicholas Tyacke (Oxford: Clarendon Press, 1991), p. 359; for family worship see G. R. Cragg, *Puritanism in the Period of the Great Persecution, 1660–1688* (Cambridge: Cambridge University Press, 1957), pp. 136–46.

122. *Life and Death of Alleine*, pp.95, 97, 100, 123.

123. Nuttall, *Baxter*, p. 52; the Particular Baptist Benjamin Keach found himself in trouble with Church of England authorities for promoting hymns not approved by

the Church; he was also troubled by fellow Baptists who objected to congregational singing, especially if it included women, Sharon Achinstein, *Literature and Dissent in Milton's England* (Cambridge: Cambridge University Press, 2003), pp. 211, 221, 224–25, 236.

124. Paul Chang-Ha Lim,*In Pursuit of Purity, Unity, and Liberty: Richard Baxter's Puritan Ecclesiology in its Seventeenth-Century Context* (Leiden, the Netherlands: E. J. Brill, 2004), pp. 45–51.

125. *Life and Death of Alleine*, pp. 49–57.

126. Duffy, "The Long Reformation," p. 45; Ian Green, *The Christian's ABC: Catechisms and Catechizing in England, c. 1530–1740* (Oxford: Clarendon Press, 1996), passim.

127. *Life and Death of Alleine*, pp. 49–57, 63, 89–90, 95, 114–15.

128. Joseph Alleine, *An Alarme*, p. 177; *Remaines of Alleine*, p. 81; Joseph Alleine, *Christian Letters*, pp. 18, 117, 163–67; Stanford, *Joseph Alleine*, p. 371.

129. *Life and Death of Alleine*, pp. 95, 99.

130. Ibid., pp. 19–20, 40, 44, 47, 49, 51, 62, 67, 97.

131. Parker and Carlson, *The Works and Life of Greenham*, p. 68.

132. *Life and Death of Alleine*, p 90.

133. For Puritan casuistry see Keith L. Sprunger, *The Learned Doctor Ames: Dutch Backgrounds of English and American Puritanism* (Urbana: University of Illinois Press, 1972), pp. 153–82; the connection of Puritan casuistry and assurance is described in Bozeman, *The Precisianist Strain*, pp. 129–33.

134. John Norman, *Cases of Conscience Practically Resolved* (London, 1673), sigs. A2r-A5v.

135. *Life and Death of Alleine*, p. 50.

136. Joseph Alleine, *Divers Practical Cases of Conscience Satisfactorily Resolved . . . to which are Added some Counsels and Cordials* (London, 1672), title-page.

137. *Life and Death of Alleine*, p. 14; Richard Alleine, *Vindiciae Pietatis, or A Vindication of Godlinesse* (London, 1660), sig. A2v, p. 3; Richard Alleine, *Godly Fear; or the nature and Necessity of Fear* (London, 1674), p. 35.

138. [Fairclough], *A Pastor's Legacy*, p. 74.

139. *Life and Death of Alleine*, pp. 39, 40, 44, 48, 56, 68, 88–89, 96, 116.

140. Joseph Alleine, *Cases of Conscience*, pp. 45, 48; Joseph Alleine, *Christian Letters*, pp. 129–31.

141. *Life and Death of Alleine*, p. 97.

142. *Life and Death of Alleine*, p. 102.

143. E.g., Fairclough, *A Pastor's Legacy*, pp. 6–7, 70–71, 123; Richard Alleine, *Instructions about Heart Work*, 2nd ed. (London, 1684), pp. 4 13, 30, 48–51, 56, 63, 65, 142; Richard Alleine, *Godly Fear*, pp. 180–82, Richard Alleine, *A Rebuke to Backsliders*, p. 29; Cf. Eamon Duffy, "The Long Reformation," pp. 49, 55.

144. *Life and Death of Alleine*, pp. 27, 40, 44, 47, 122, 125.

145. Joseph Alleine, *Cases of Conscience*, pp. 45–46; *Remaines of Alleine*, pp. 47–59.

146. *Life and Death of Alleine*, pp. 20, 42–43, 89–90, 98.

147. Joseph Alleine, *An Alarme*, pp. 1–2, 157; Joseph Alleine, *Christian Letters*, pp. 12, 17, 62, 66; *Remaines of Alleine*, pp. 207–208.

148. Joseph Alleine, *An Alarme*, pp. 99–100, 126.

149. *Remaines of Alleine*, pp. 117, 181, 208, 209, 212–13, 219, 233, 291, 309, 317; Joseph Alleine, *Christian Letters*, pp. 33, 113.

150. Joseph Alleine, *An Alarme*, p. 21; see also *Remaines of Alleine*, 174–75 [168–69], 186.

151. David Como, *Blown by the Spirit*, pp. 188–89, notes that dissident radicals on the edge of the Puritan movement, in extolling free grace, were using a theological commonplace of the English Calvinist mainstream but misusing it in the view of the latter; Michael Winship, in *Making Heretics: Militant Protestantism and Free Grace in Massachusetts, 1636–1641* (Princeton, N.J.: Princeton University Press, 2002), p. 1, notes that in the Antinomian controversy in New England, for which he prefers the term "free grace controversy," both sides in the controversy laid claim to the phrase "free grace."

152. Joseph Alleine, *An Alarme*, pp. 25–26.

153. E. g., see D. Bruce Hindmarsh, *John Newton and the English Evangelical Tradition* (Grand Rapids, Mich.: Eerdmans, 1996), p. 157.

154. See Peter Toon, *The Emergence of Hyper-Calvinism in English Nonconformity, 1689–1765* (London: The Olive Tree, 1967).

155. *Remaines of Alleine*, pp. 228–36; see also pp. 39, 105, 129, 133, 190–93, 196, 287, 316; Joseph Alleine, *Christian Letters*, pp. 40–41; Joseph Alleine, *Cases of Conscience*, p. 33.

156. E.g., Joseph Alleine, *An Alarme*, pp. 22–23.

157. Joseph Alleine, *Christian Letters*, pp. 15, 20.

158. Joseph Alleine, *Cases of Conscience*, pp. 82–84; John von Rohr, *The Covenant of Grace in Puritan Thought* (Atlanta, Ga.: Scholars Press, 1986), pp. 9–10; for the double covenant, see Michael McGiffert, "Grace and Works: The Rise and Division of Covenant divinity in Elizabethan Puritanism," *Harvard Theological Review* 75:4 (October 1982): 463–502, and "From Moses to Adam: The Making of the Covenant of Works," *SCJ* 19 (Summer 1988): 131–55.

159. Joseph Alleine, *An Alarme*, pp. 49, 158, 163, 185, 164–69.

160. Joseph Alleine, *Cases of Conscience*, pp. 78–79; *Remaines of Alleine*, pp. 211–12.

161. Joseph Alleine, *Christian Letters*, pp. 16–20. The fourth letter in the collection is entitled "A Call to the Unconverted."

162. Much of the literature on Puritanism deals with the experience and theology of conversion. Alan Simpson's *Puritanism in Old and New England* (Chicago: University of Chicago Press, 1955) asserted the centrality of conversion in the Puritan movement; Charles Lloyd Cohen provided morphology and analysis of the concept in *God's Caress: The Psychology of Puritan Religious Experience* (Oxford: Oxford University Press, 1986); and J. Sears McGee, *The Godly Man in Stuart England: Anglicans, Puritans, and the Two Tables, 1620–1670* (New Haven, Conn.: Yale University Press, 1976) discussed "the fruits of conversion."

163. Joseph Alleine did give attention to the placement of conversion within the order of salvation, describing it, along with effectual calling and sanctification, as "a

middle link in the golden chain, fastened to election at the one end, and glorification at the other," *An Alarme*, p. 9; William Perkins's *A Golden Chaine* was a classic statement for English Calvinists in laying out the order of salvation, a way of analyzing the unfolding of grace that was one of the main organizing principles in Reformed theology and a particularly attractive one to Puritan preachers and writers, providing an apt metaphor for the process of salvation. This placement of conversion empha- sized it as a work of grace ("converting grace" is the phrase Joseph used) and as a supernatural work effected in the believer by divine power, specifically that of the Holy Spirit, *An Alarme*, pp. 43, 19–20.

164. Joseph Alleine, *An Alarme*, pp. 3, 24, 86; Joseph Alleine, *Christian Letters*, pp. 97, 142; *Remaines of Alleine*, p. 300.

165. *Remaines of Alleine*, p. 286; Joseph Alleine, *Christian Letters*, p. 90.

166. Joseph Alleine, *Christian Letters*, p. 147; *Remaines of Alleine*, p. 133; Joseph Alleine, *An Alarme*, p. 205.

167. *Remaines of Alleine*, sig.A6v; Joseph Alleine, *Cases of Conscience*, p.12; Joseph Alleine, *An Alarme*, pp. 153, 156.

168. Joseph Alleine, *Christian Letters*, pp. 14, 111.

169. Joseph Alleine, *Christian Letters*, pp. 32, 52, 66–67, 100–102. Richard Alleine had devoted a whole treatise to what he called "heart-work," *Instructions about Heart Work* (London, 1681).

170. Joseph Alleine, *Cases of Conscience*, pp. 18, 32.

171. Bozeman, *Precisianist Strain*, p. 213.

172. Joseph Alleine, *Cases of Conscience*, pp. 18–19.

173. "We are chosen through sanctification to salvation," Joseph Alleine, *An Alarme*, p. 25.

174. Ibid., p. 27.

175. Joseph Alleine, *An Alarme*, pp. 19, 24, 27, 37, 51, 56, 59f, 66; Joseph Alleine, *Cases of Conscience*, pp. 72, 74; Joseph Alleine, *Christian Letters*, pp. 63ff., 866, 93, 113.

176. *Remaines of Alleine*, p. 38; Joseph Alleine, *An Alarme*, pp. 3–5, 14.

177. For reproof, e.g., Joseph Alleine, *Cases of Conscience*, pp. 45, 47.

178. *Remaines of Alleine*, p.10; Joseph Alleine, *Christian Letters*, pp. 22, 127.

179. Joseph Alleine, *An Alarme*, pp. 37, 38; *Remaines of Alleine*, p. 269; Joseph Alleine, *Christian Letters*, p. 114; Joseph Alleine, *Cases of Conscience*, pp. 9, 11.

180. *Life and Death of Joseph Alleine*, p. 22.

181. Dewey D. Wallace, Jr., *Puritans and Predestination: Grace in English Protestant Theology, 1525–1695* (Chapel Hill: University of North Carolina Press, 1982), pp. 136–39; Tim Cooper, *Fear and Polemic in Seventeenth-Century England*, pp. 93–115, 122–38.

182. Joseph Alleine, *Christian Letters*, p. 17.

183. Ibid., p. 23; Joseph Alleine, *Cases of Conscience*, pp. 3–10.

184. Joseph Alleine, *Cases of Conscience*, pp. 3–5, 7; Joseph Alleine, *Christian Letters*, p. 74.

185. Joseph Alleine, *Christian Letters*, pp. 23, 60; Joseph Alleine, *An Alarme*, p 37; Joseph Alleine, *Cases of Conscience*, p. 9.

186. Joseph Alleine, *Cases of Conscience*, p. 57; Joseph Alleine, *Christian Letters*, p. 30; *Remaines of Alleine*, pp. 41, 57; Joseph Alleine, *An Alarme*, pp. 12, 96–97.

187. Joseph Alleine, *An Alarme*, pp. 91, 97; Joseph Alleine, *Cases of Conscience*, pp. 5, 45, 48; *Remaines of Alleine*, p. 290; Joseph Alleine, *Christian Letters*, pp. 18, 71, 81, 140–41.

188. Bozeman, *Precisianist Strain*, pp. 131–44; Michael Winship, *Free Grace Controversy*, pp. 12–27; Joel R. Beeke, *Assurance of Faith: Calvin, English Puritanism, and the Dutch Second Reformation* (New York: Peter Lang, 1991).

189. Edmund Trench, *Some Remarkable Passages in the Holy Life and Death of the late Reverend Mr. Edmund Trench; Most of them drawn out of his own Diary* (London, 1693), p. 25.

190. *Life and Death of Alleine*, p. 126 [misprinted as 142].

191. Joseph Alleine, *Cases of Conscience*, pp. 59, 70–71, 91; Joseph Alleine, *An Alarme*, p. 88; Joseph Alleine, *Christian Letters*, pp. 29, 89; *Remaines of Alleine*, sig. A6r-v, p. 27.

192. *Life and Death of Alleine*, pp. 58–61; Joseph Alleine, *A Most Familiar Explanation of the Assemblies Shorter Catechism*, pp. 161–64; Joseph Alleine, *Christian Letters*, pp. 44–46.

193. *Life and Death of Alleine*, pp. 57, 120.

194. Kaufman, *Prayer, Despair, and Drama*, p. 42; Bozeman, *Precisianist Strain*, p. 149.

195. Joseph Alleine, *Cases of Conscience*, pp. 85–86, 91–92; *Remaines of Alleine*, pp. 104, 231; Joseph Alleine, *Christian Letters*, pp. 123, 127.

196. In Richard Alleine, *Heaven Opened*, pp. 215–50.

197. U. Milo Kaufmann, in *The Pilgrim's Progress and Traditions in Puritan Meditation* (New Haven, Conn.: Yale University Press, 1966), pp. 204–205, calls attention to this habit of reading scriptural promises (and threats) as personally applicable.

198. Bebbington, *Evangelicalism in Modern Britain*, pp. 42–43.

199. Joseph Alleine, *Christian Letters*, pp. 96–98; *Remaines of Alleine*, pp. 104–105, 239.

CHAPTER 5

1. Seth Ward, *A Philosophical Essay Towards an Eviction of the Being and Attributes of God* (Oxford, 1652); Samuel Clarke, *A Discourse Concerning the Unchangeable Obligations of Natural Religion and the Truth and Certainty of the Christian Revelation* (London, 1706).

2. Hugo Grotius, *The Truth of the Christian Religion*, translated by Simon Patrick (London, 1680).

3. For the Latitudinarians, see Isabel Rivers, *Reason, Grace, and Sentiment: A Study of Religion and Ethics in England, 1660–1780*, vol. 1, *Whichcote to Wesley* (Cambridge: Cambridge University Press, 1991), pp. 25–88. For natural theology, see Ibid., pp. 66–77; Barbara J. Shapiro, *Probability and Certainty in Seventeenth-Century*

England: A Study of the Relationships Between Natural Science, Religion, History, Law, and Literature (Princeton, N.J.: Princeton University Press, 1983), pp. 82–88; Richard S. Westfall, *Science and Religion in Seventeenth-Century England* (1958, reprint, Ann Arbor: University of Michigan Press, 1973), pp. 106–45; John A. Spurr, " 'Rational Religion' in Restoration England," *JHI* 49 (October–December 1988): 571–74; for the "evidences of Christianity" see Gerard Reedy, S.J., *The Bible and Reason: Anglicans and Scripture in Late Seventeenth-Century* England (Philadelphia: University of Pennsylvania Press, 1985), pp. 46–62, and M. L. Clarke, *Paley: Evidences for the Man* (Toronto: University of Toronto Press, 1974), pp. 100–113.

4. J. M. Lloyd Thomas, "Introductory Essay," in *The Autobiography of Richard Baxter*, edited by J. M. Lloyd Thomas (London: J. M. Dent & Sons, 1931), p. xxiii.

5. Dewey D. Wallace, Jr., *Puritans and Predestination: Grace in English Protestant Theology, 1525–1695* (Chapel Hill: University of North Carolina Press, 1982), pp. 136–39; Geoffrey F. Nuttall, *Richard Baxter* (London: Thomas Nelson and Sons, 1965), p. 119; C. F. Allison, *The Rise of Moralism: The Proclamation of the Gospel from Hooker to Baxter* (London: S. P. C. K., 1966), pp. 154–64; Michael Winship, "Contesting Control of Orthodoxy Among the Godly: William Pynchon Reexamined," *William and Mary Quarterly* 3rd. ser., 54 (October 1997): 808–9.

6. Richard Baxter, *Aphorisms of Justification* (London, 1649), pp. 125–26, 289–93; Nuttall, *Baxter*, p. 121; Richard Baxter, *Richard Baxter's Penitent Confession* (London, 1691), p. 5.

7. *RB*, bk. I, part II, pp. 197–99; Baxter, *Penitent Confession*, pp. 5, 24–25; Richard Baxter, *Reasons of the Christian Religion* (London, 1667) sig. a1r, pp. 225–28, 437; Richard Baxter, *More Reasons for the Christian Religion, and no Reason Against It* (London, 1672), p. 24; William Lamont, review of Hans Boersma, *A Hot Pepper Corn: Richard Baxter's Doctrine of Justification in Its Seventeenth-Century Context of Controversy* in *JEH* 45 (October 1994): 709–11. See also Nuttall, *Baxter*, pp. 121–22 and N. H. Keeble, *Richard Baxter: Puritan Man of Letters* (Oxford: Clarendon Press, 1982) p. 72.

8. Cf. for example, Martin I. Klauber, *Between Scholasticism and Pan-Protestantism: Jean Alphonse Turretin (1671–1737) and Enlightened Orthodoxy at the Academy of Geneva* (Selinsgrove, Pa.: Susquehanna University Press, 1994), pp. 54, 58–59, 142, 165–87.

9. Robert Baillie, *The Letters and Journals of Robert Baillie*, edited by David Laing, 3 vols. (Edinburgh: Robert Ogle, 1841–42), vol. 3, p. 304; Keeble, *Baxter*, pp. 27, 42, 72; John Owen accused Baxter of Amyraldianism in *Of the Death of Christ, The Price he paid, and the Purchase he made.* (London, 1650), p. 96. For Amyraldianism, see Brian G. Armstrong, *Calvinism and the Amyraux Heresy: Protestant Scholasticism and Humanism in Seventeenth-Century France* (Madison: University of Wisconsin Press, 1969). Several members of the Westminster Assembly, including Edmund Calamy, Lazarus Seaman, Stephen Marshall, and Richard Vines had argued for a position similar or close to that of Amyraux, see Benjamin B. Warfield, *The Westminster Assembly and Its Work* (New York: Oxford University Press, 1931), pp. 130–44; *RB*, bk. I, part I, p. 125; Baxter, *Penitent Confession* (London, 1691), p. 25.

10. Nuttall, *Baxter*, p. 95.

11. Nuttall, *Baxter*, pp. 107, 112; William H. Lamont, *Richard Baxter and the Millennium* (London: Croom and Helm, 1979), pp. 162–63, 171; Richard L. Greaves, *Enemies Under His Feet: Radicals and Nonconformists in Britain, 1664–1677* (Stanford, Calif.: Stanford University Press, 1990), p. 144; William Bates, *A Funeral-Sermon for the Reverend, Holy and Excellent Divine, Mr. Richard Baxter* (London, 1692), pp. 110, 120; John Howe, *A Funeral-Sermon for that Excellent Minister of Christ, The Truly Reverend, William Bates, D.D.* (London, 1699), sig. A5, pp. 70, 97; John Howe, *A Funeral Sermon on the Decease of that worthy Gentlewoman, Mrs. Margaret Baxter* (London, 1681), sig. B1r, p. 40.

12. C. A. Haig, *John Howe* (London: Independent Press, 1961), p. 16; Craig Rose, *England in the 1690s: Revolution, Religion and War* (Oxford: Blackwell, 1999) pp. 109, 262; David P. Field, *"Rigide Calvinisme in a Softer Dresse:" The Moderate Presbyterianism of John Howe (1630–1705* (Edinburgh: Rutherford House, 2004), pp. 12–13.

13. William Bates, *The Four Last Things: Death, Judgment, Heaven Hell, Practically considered and applied, in Several Discourses* (London, 1691), pp. 367–68; Field, *Moderate Presbyterianism of Howe* (Edinburgh: Rutherford House, 2004), pp. 140–44; Wallace, *Puritans and Predestination*, pp. 179–80.

14. Richard Baxter, "A Treatise against the Dominicane doctrine of Divine Predetermination," part II, Baxter MS 61.14, vol. 18, Dr. Williams's Library, London. Baxter decided not to publish this 138 folio manuscript after he saw a work by John Humfrey that refuted Gale in what Baxter considered a plainer and briefer manner, and for which he supplied an "Epistle to the Reader," *The Middle Way of Predetermination Asserted* (London, 1679), sig. A2r-v.

15. John Howe, *The Carnality of Religious Contention in Two Sermons* (London, 1693), "Preface to the Readers," pp. i–xxxiv. See also John Howe, *The Blessednesse of the Righteous* (London, 1668), sig. A2v; Field, *"Rigide Calvinisme in a Softer Dresse,"* pp. 40–44, 52–54. For Howe's Latitudinarianism see also N. H. Keeble, *The Literary Culture of Nonconformity in Late Seventeenth-Century England* (n.p.: Leicester University Press, 1987), pp. 8, 34–35, 37, 44; Howe, *Funeral-Sermon for . . . Bates*, p. 97.

16. William Bates, *Considerations of the Existence of God, and the Immortality of the Soul*, 2nd ed., enlarged (London, 1677), p. 163; this treatise had a first edition in 1676, and when it was published again the next year printed with it was *The Divinity of the Christian Religion*, which had come out by itself earlier in 1677. The combination of the two treatises bore the title *Considerations of the Existence of God,. . . To which is now added The Divinity of the Christian Religion*. I have used the combined volume, in which the two treatises are paginated separately, but cite them under their separate titles, as each has its own title page.

17. *The Life and Death of that Excellent Minister of Christ Mr. Joseph Alleine* (London, 1672), p. 27.

18. Peter Harrison, *"Religion"and the Religions in the English Enlightenment* (Cambridge: Cambridge University Press, 1990), p. 185 n19; Baxter, *More Reasons*, p. 33; Keeble, *Baxter*, p. 31.

19. Baxter, *Reasons*, sigs. a1r-a2r, a5r.

20. Ibid., sigs. A3r, A4r, pp. 153, 205, 441, 453–54.

21. *RB*, bk. I, part I, pp. 22–23, 127–28.

22. Baxter, *More Reasons*, sig. A4, pp. 12–13, 53.

23. Baxter, *More Reasons*, sigs. A2r-A3v, pp. 79–80, 100.

24. Bates, *Considerations of the Existence of God*, sigs. A4r-A5v.

25. William Bates, *The Divinity of the Christian Religion, Proved By the Evidence of reason, and Divine Revelation* (London, 1677), sigs. B2r-B3v.

26. John Howe, *The Living Temple, or A Designed Improvement of that Notion, that a Good Man is the Temple of God,* [part I] (London, 1675), sigs. A7v-8r, pp. 4, 13–14; John Howe, *The Living Temple, or A Designed Improvement of that Notion, that a Good Man is the Temple of God,* Part II (London, 1702), pp. i–v, viii, 2–34. Part II bore the additional title *Containing Animadversions on Spinosa . . . And an account of the Destitution and Restitution of God's Temple Among Men.* Part I was not so designated until it was later reprinted with part II in 1702, and then was given the additional title *Concerning God's Existence, and his Conversableness with Man. Against Atheism and Epicurean Deism.*

27. Dr. Williams's Library MS 24.16–17 contain these lectures, much of which are devoted to natural theology and evidences of Christianity. This manuscript was eventually published in editions of Howe's collected works, apparently first in an edition by John Hunt in 1814 and later in 1827 and then 1834 in *The Works of the Reverend John Howe, M.A. . . . Complete in One Volume* (London, 1834), pp. 1049–265.

28. John Howe, "The Principles of the Oracles of God," Dr. Williams's Library MS 24.16, Dr. Williams's Library, London, pp. 8, 36.

29. Baxter, *Reasons*, pp. 491–92.

30. Howe, *Living Temple*, part I, pp. 14, 73.

31. Baxter, *Reasons*, p. 259; Richard Baxter, *The Arrogancy of Reason Against Divine Revelations* (London, 1655), p. 62; Baxter, *More Reasons*, p. 137; Bates, *Divinity of the Christian Religion*, pp. 186–88.

32. Baxter, *More Reasons*, p. 70.

33. Spurr, "'Rational Religion' in Restoration England," pp. 564, 569; Richard Ashcraft, "Latitudinarianism and Toleration: Historical Myth Versus Political History," in *Philosophy, Science, and Religion in England 1640–1700*, edited by Richard Kroll, Richard Ashcraft, and Perez Zagorin (Cambridge: Cambridge University Press, 1992), pp. 157–59; Richard Baxter et al., *The Judgment of Nonconformists, of the Interest of Reason, In Matters of Religion* (London, 1676), p. 2; N. H. Keeble and Geoffrey F. Nuttall, eds., *Calendar of the Correspondence of Richard Baxter*, 2 vols. (Oxford: Clarendon Press, 1991) vol. 2, p. 11.

34. Baxter, *Reasons*, p. 348.

35. Shapiro, *Probability and Certainty*, p. 61; Baxter, *Reasons*, pp. 115, 195, 259, 444–45.

36. Bates, *Divinity of the Christian Religion*, pp. 202–3, 207.

37. Baxter, *Reasons*, p. 259; *Correspondence of Richard Baxter*, vol. 1, p. 214.

38. Bates, *Considerations of the Existence of God*, sigs. A3–4, pp. 42–43, 50, 145, 166, 170–71, 186–93, 288–90.

39. Roland N. Stromberg, *Religious Liberalism in Eighteenth Century England* (Oxford: Oxford University Press, 1954), p. 17.

40. Baxter, *Reasons*, pp. 9, 11, 32.

41. Howe, *Living Temple*, part I, p. 16.

42. Howe, *Living Temple*, part I, pp. 141–42, 168, 170; Edmund Calamy, *Memoirs of the Late Rev'd Mr John Howe* (London, 1724); Nuttall, *Baxter*, p. 10.

43. Bates, *Divinity of the Christian Religion*, pp. 40–44; Baxter, *More Reasons*, pp. 65–67; *RB*, bk. I, part I, p. 128; the words "subjective" and "objective" are not Hooker's but Baxter's rephrasing of Hooker, and may be the first appearance of these terms in something like their modern usage, Debora K. Shuger, "Faith and Assurance," in *A Companion to Richard Hooker*, edited by Torrance Kirby (Leiden, the Netherlands: Brill, 2008), p. 249; John Wilkins, *Of the Principles and Duties of Natural Religion* (London, 1678), pp. 6–11, 31. See also Spurr, " 'Rational Religion' in Restoration England," p. 575, and Shapiro, *Probability and Certainty*, pp. 17, 28, 33–34.

44. Howe, *Living Temple*, part I, p. 2; Baxter, *Reasons*, sig. bi verso; Margo Todd, "Seneca and the Protestant Mind: The Influence of Stoicism on Puritan Ethics," *Archiv für Reformationsgeschichte* 74 (1983): 182, 184–85; for Todd's fuller discussion of the Puritan use of Erasmian humanism, see *Christian Humanism and the Puritan Social Order* (Cambridge: Cambridge University Press, 1987).

45. Bates, *Divinity of the Christian Religion*, p. 147; Field, *"Rigide Calvinisme in a Softer Dresse,"* p. 116; Baxter, *Reasons*, sig a3, p. 359. In an exchange of letters in 1663 with Joseph Glanvill, Baxter discussed the ancient theology, disagreeing with Glanvill's defense of the preexistence of souls on the basis of its being "asserted in Hermes Trismegistus" and other ancient texts, Keeble and Nuttall, *Calendar of the Correspondence of Richard Baxter*, vol. 2, pp. 37–38.

46. Isabel Rivers, *Reason, Grace and Sentiment: A Study of the Language of Religion and Ethics in England, 1660–1780*, vol. 2, *Shaftesbury to Hume* (Cambridge: Cambridge University Press, 2000), p. 4; Baxter, *Reasons*, pp. 94, 135, 141, 172, 250, 489–91.

47. Baxter, *Reasons*, pp. 489–604; Bates, *Divinity of the Christian Religion*, pp. 76–78; Bates, *Considerations of the Existence of God*, sig. A4v, pp. 51–60; Howe, *Living Temple*, part I, pp. 100–102, 253–54; D. L. Mathieu, *The Mind of William Paley* (Lincoln: University of Nebraska Press, 1976), pp. 65–66; Shapiro, *Probability and Certainty*, p. 88. For Renaissance skepticism, see Richard H. Popkin, *The History of Scepticism from Savonarola to Bayle*, rev. ed. (Oxford: Oxford University Press, 2003), especially chapters 4–5.

48. Bates, *Considerations of the Existence of God*, pp. 166, 168, 173, 186–91, 199–200, 202; Howe, *Living Temple*, part I, pp. 79–91, 94.

49. Howe, *Living Temple*, part I, pp. 50, 147; John Redwood, *Reason, Ridicule, and Religion: the Age of Enlightenment in England, 1660–1750* (Cambridge, Mass.: Harvard University Press, 1976), p. 57; Margaret C. Jacob, *The Newtonians and the English Revolution, 1689–1720* (Ithaca, N.Y.: Cornell University Press, 1976), pp. 28, 63; Johannes van den Berg, *Religious Currents and Cross-Currents: Essays on Early Modern Protestantism and the Protestant Enlightenment*, edited by Jan de Bruijn, Pieter Holtrop, and Ernestine van der Wall (Leiden, the Netherlands: Brill, 1999), p. 139; Edward

Stillingfleet, *Origines Sacrae, Or A Rational Account of the Grounds of Christian Faith* (London, 1662), p. 396.

50. Robert Crocker, *Henry More, 1614–1687: A Biography of the Cambridge Platonist* (Dordrecht, the Netherlands; Boston and London: Kluwer Academic, 2003), pp. 66–70.

51. Howe, *Living Temple*, part I, p. 92.

52. Howe, *Living Temple*, part II, pp. xiii, xx, 3–4, 34.

53. Alan P. F. Sell, "John Howe's Eclectic Theism," *JURCHS* 2 (October 1980): 188.

54. Keeble, *Literary Culture of Nonconformity*, p. 170.

55. Baxter, *More Reasons*, second part of appendix, p. 100.

56. Bates, *Considerations of the Existence of God*, pp. 106–9.

57. Baxter, *More Reasons*, p. 162.

58. Howe, *Living Temple*, part I, p. 19.

59. *RB*, bk. I, part I, p. 23.

60. Roger Morrice Historical MS 31, X, Dr. Williams's Library, London; Edward Stillingfleet, *A Letter to a Deist, in Answer to several objections Against the Truth and authority of the Scriptures* (London, 1677) sig. A3.

61. Baxter, *Reasons*, pp. 366, 371–72, 377.

62. Bates, *The Divinity of the Christian Religion*, pp. 158–59, 187–88.

63. Howe, *Living Temple*, part I, p. 78; part II, pp. 178, 417.

64. Howe, "Oracles of God," pp. 208, 216–17.

65. Baxter, *Reasons*, sigs. a3v, b1r, b3r.

66. Bates, *Considerations of the Existence of God*, sig. A4.

67. Howe, *Living Temple*, part I, sigs. A7v-A8r.

68. Baxter, *Reasons*, sigs. a3v, b1r; Bates, *Considerations of the Existence of God*, pp. 4, 118–19; Howe, *Living Temple*, part I, pp. 211, 214, 222, 224.

69. Baxter, *Reasons*, sigs. a[4]r, b3r; Bates, *Considerations of the Existence of God*, pp. 3, 98, 115; Bates, *Divinity of the Christian Religion*, p. 202; Howe, *Living Temple*, part I, pp. 214–15, 217–18, 220; Howe, "Oracles of God," p. 64.

70. Baxter, *Reasons*, sigs. a3v, b3; Bates, *Considerations of the Existence of God*, sig. A4, p. 4; William Bates, *The Danger of Prosperity: Discovered in several Sermons* (London, 1685), sig. A4.

71. Bates, *Considerations of the Existence of God*, p. 3.

72. Ibid., pp. 98–100.

73. Baxter, *Reasons*, sig. A5v; Baxter, *More Reasons*, p. 29; *RB*, bk. I, part I, p. 22.

74. Howe, *Living Temple*, part I, pp. 194, 225; *Living Temple*, part II, pp. iv–v; Bates, *Considerations of the Existence of God*, p. 3; Ernest Benson Lowrie, *The Shape of the Puritan Mind: The Thought of Samuel Willard* (New Haven, Conn.: Yale University Press, 1974), p. 48.

75. Richard Baxter, *Richard Baxter's Dying Thoughts Upon Phil I. 23* (London, 1683), p. 290.

76. Howe, *Living Temple*, part I, pp. 4, 10, 13.

77. Baxter, *More Reasons*, sig. A2v; *Reasons*, sigs. a4v, b4v; Baxter, *Arrogancy of Reason*, p. 58.

78. William Bates, *Spiritual Perfection, unfolded and Enforced* (London, 1699), sig. A4r-v.

79. Bates, *Considerations of the Existence of God*, pp. 84–92.

80. Howe, *Living Temple*, part I, pp. 19, 25; part II, p. 103; Howe, "The Oracles of God," p. 64.

81. Baxter, *More Reasons*, p. 33; for a conformist treatment of common consent, see John Wilkins, *Principles and Duties of Natural Religion*, pp. 39–61.

82. Bates, *Considerations of the Existence of God*, pp. 4, 17, 65–66, 121.

83. Baxter, *Reasons*, pp. 9–15.

84. Howe, *Living Temple*, part I, p. 32-33.

85. Baxter, *Reasons*, p. 19; Baxter, *More Reasons*, p.72; Howe, *Living Temple*, part I, pp. 30–33, 51; Howe, "Oracles of God," p. 47.

86. Baxter, *Dying Thoughts*, p. 288.

87. Bates, *Considerations of the Existence of God*, pp. 5–20, 24, 34–48, 58–59, 126.

88. Basil Willey, *The Eighteenth Century Background: Studies on the Idea of Nature in the Thought of the Period* (1940, reprint, Boston: Beacon Press, 1961), p. 27.

89. Howe, "Oracles of God," p. 56; Howe, *Living Temple*, part I, pp. 46–47, 60–64, 67, 69–70, 74, 76, 79; Thomas Doolittle, *The Young Man's Instructor* (London, 1673), p. 32.

90. Howe, *Living Temple*, part I, p. 61.

91. Shapiro, *Probability and Certainty*, p. 92; see also Shapiro, *John Wilkins*, p. 236, for the "Elegance and Beauty" of nature; Willey, *Eighteenth Century Background*, p. 40.

92. Bates, *Considerations of the Existence of God*, pp. 112–14.

93. Baxter, *Reasons*, pp. 20–25; Baxter, *More Reasons*, p. 71; Bates, *Considerations of the Existence of God*, p. 121.

94. Bates, *Considerations of the Existence of God*, p. 177; Howe, "Oracles of God," pp. 58, 255, 263, 265; Howe, *Living Temple*, part I, pp. 28–29, 34, 41, 45–46, 136, 140, 146.

95. Baxter, *Dying Thoughts*, p. 294.

96. Richard Baxter, *Of the Immortality of Mans Soul, and the Nature of it, and other Spirits* (London, 1682).

97. Bates, *Considerations of the Existence of God*, pp. 163, 167, 196, 198–99, 201, 210–17, 243; Baxter, *Reasons*, p. 120.

98. Henry More, *An Antidote against Atheisme* (London, 1653), pp. 109–11, 120–21, 123–33, 137, 164.

99. *Correspondence of Richard Baxter*, vol. 2, pp. 21, 37; Basil Willey, *Seventeenth-Century Studies* (1934; reprint, New York: Doubleday, 1955), pp. 174–205.

100. Baxter, *Reasons*, pp. 147–53.

101. Baxter, *Dying Thoughts*, p. 294.

102. *Correspondence of Richard Baxter*, vol. 2, 307.

103. Richard Baxter, *The Certainty of the World of Spirits, fully evinced by unquestionable Histories of Apparitions and Witchcrafts, Operations, Voices, etc. Proving the Immortality of Souls, the Malice and Miseries of the Devil and the Damned, and the Blessedness of the Justified* (London, 1691), sig. A4, p. 10; Baxter, *Reasons*, pp. 358–59; William M. Lamont, *Baxter and the Millennium*, p. 35.

104. Bates, *The Divinity of the Christian Religion*, pp. 3–4; Baxter, *Reasons*, sig. a3r, pp. 207, 241, 258; Howe, *Living Temple*, part I, sig. A7v, pp. 15–16; Field, "*Rigid Calvinisme in a Softer Dresse*," pp. 93–94; Nathaniel Culverwell, *An Elegant and Learned Discourse of the Light of Nature*, edited by Robert A. Greene and Hugh MacCallum (Toronto: University of Toronto Press, 1971), p. 146.

105. Field, "*Rigide Calvinisme in a Softer Dresse*," pp. 116–21, for Howe's Platonism; Bates, *Divinity of the Christian Religion*, p. 78.

106. Richard Muller, *Post-Reformation Reformed Dogmatics: The Rise and Development of Reformed Orthodoxy, ca. 1520–1725*, 4 vols. (Grand Rapids, Mich.: Baker Academic, 2003), vol. I, *Prolegomena to Theology*, 2nd ed., p. 310.

107. Baxter, *Reasons*, pp.192–97; Baxter, *More Reasons*, pp. 144–46; Dewey D. Wallace Jr., "Socinianism, Justification by Faith, and the Sources of John Locke's *The Reasonableness of Christianity*," *JHI* 45 (Jan.–March, 1984): 49–66.

108. Howe, *Living Temple*, part I, pp. 226–27.

109. Bates, *Divinity of the Christian Religion*, p. 3.

110. Bates, *Considerations of the Existence of God*, pp. 3, 91–92, 121, 137; Howe, "Oracles of God," p. 99.

111. Howe, "Oracles of God," p. 138.

112. For discussion of this and related issues, see Harrison, *"Religion" and Religions in the English Enlightenment*, and David A. Pailin, *Attitudes to Other Religions: Comparative Religion in Seventeenth and Eighteenth-Century Britain* (Manchester, UK: Manchester University Press, 1984); N. I. Matar, "Islam in Interregnum and Restoration England," *Seventeenth Century* 6 (Spring 1991): 57–71.

113. Howe, "Oracles of God," p. 145; Bates, *Divinity of the Christian Religion*, p. 10.

114. Baxter, *Reasons*, pp. 198, 457, 459.

115. Bates, *Divinity of the Christian Religion*, pp. 10–33; Baxter, *Reasons*, pp. 198–204, 363.

116. Baxter, *More Reasons*, pp. 54–55; Baxter, *Reasons*, pp. 198–204, especially p. 201.

117. Howe, "Oracles of God," p. 30.

118. Culverwell, *An Elegant and Learned Discourse*, pp. 165–66; John Wilkins, *Principles and Duties of Natural Religion*, pp. 396–97.

119. Bates, *Divinity of the Christian Religion*, pp. 45–55, 58, 72.

120. Baxter, *More Reasons*, pp. 144–47.

121. Bates, *Divinity of the Christian Religion*, p. 82.

122. Karl Barth, *The Word of God and the Word of Man* (1928; reprint, New York: Harper and Brothers, 1957); Howe, *Living Temple*, part II, p. 96.

123. Bates, *Divinity of the Christian Religion*, pp. 37–38.

124. Ibid., pp. 194–95.

125. Baxter, *More Reasons*, pp. 10–21, 158–60; *Reasons*, p. 242, 412–16.

126. Howe, *Living Temple*, part II, 95.

127. Howe, "Oracles of God," p. 103; John Owen, *Of the Divine Originall, Authority, self-evidencing Light, and Power of the Scriptures* (Oxford, 1659).

128. Daniel Whitby, *A Paraphrase and Commentary on the New Testament*, 2 vols., 2nd ed. (London, 1706), vol. I, pp. ii, v, for example, distinguished between revelation

to the apostles, in which God spoke inwardly to them, making "such a motion on their Brains, as giveth them a deep and clear Idea of that which he intended to make known to them," and revelation to Paul, in which God spoke to him as to Moses, "mouth to mouth." Others such as John in the Book of Revelation, had visions and "Angelical Discourses and Apparitions"; Howe, "Oracles of God," p. 107.

129. Howe, "Oracles of God," pp. 101, 117–18, 127, 147, 149, 151.

130. Ibid., pp. 108–9.

131. Charles Wolseley, *The Reasonableness of Scripture-Belief* (1672; reprint, Delmar, N.Y.: Scholars Facsimiles and Reprints, 1973), pp. 6–10.

132. Bates, *Divinity of the Christian Religion*, pp. 141–50, 176–78.

133. Baxter, *Reasons*, pp. 353–55.

134. Baxter, *Reasons*, pp. 259ff.,273ff., 303–305, 313–15, 381, 400–402, 423–24; Baxter, *Dying Thoughts*, p. 29; Richard Baxter, *The Unreasonableness of Infidelity* (London, 1655), pp. 19–20.

135. Bates, *Divinity of the Christian Religion*, p.185.

136. Ibid., pp.85–88, 99–100.

137. Ibid., pp. 88–101.

138. Ibid., pp. 102–15.

139. Baxter, *Reasons*, p. 420.

140. Ibid., pp. 260–65.

141. Howe, "Oracles of God," p. 116.

142. Bates, *Divinity of the Christian Religion*, pp. 116–24.

143. Ibid., pp. 127–48.

144. Ibid., p. 151.

145. Baxter, *Reasons*, 464–65; Baxter, *Unreasonableness of Infidelity*, pp. 14–15; Richard Baxter, *Catholick Theologie: Plain, Pure, Peaceable: For the Pacification of the Dogmatical Word-Warriors* (London, 1675), preface, sigs. A3-c[4].

146. John Gascoigne, *Cambridge in the Age of the Enlightenment: Science, Religion and Politics from the Restoration to the French Revolution* (Cambridge: Cambridge University Press, 1989), pp. 46, 63–64, 76–77; Spurr, *The Restoration Church of England, 1646–1689* (New Haven, Conn.: Yale University Press, 1991), pp. 223–24; Howe, *Living Temple*, part I, p. 5; Shapiro, *Wilkins*, pp. 171–75; Gerald R. Cragg, *Puritanism in the Period of the Great Persecution, 1660–1688* (Cambridge: Cambridge University Press, 1957), pp. 15–16, 250–51; Jacob, *Newtonians and the English Revolution*, pp. 48–49, 59; Edward Carpenter, *The Protestant Bishop, Being the Life of Henry Compton, 1632–1713, Bishop of London* (London: Longmans, 1956), pp. 154, 161, 265; Jonathan Israel, "William III and Toleration," in *From Persecution to Toleration: The Glorious Revolution and Religion in England*, edited by Ole Peter Grell, Jonathan I. Israel, and Nicholas Tyacke (Oxford: Clarendon Press, 1991), p.164; for the compatibility of comprehension and intolerance in the Church of England, see Mark Goldie, "The Theory of Religious Intolerance in Restoration England," in Ibid., p. 333.

147. *ODNB*, "Baxter, Richard"; Haig, *John Howe*, p. 21.

148. Edmund Calamy, *Memoirs of the Late Rev'd Mr John Howe* (London, 1724), pp. 5, 7.

149. N. H. Keeble, *The Restoration: England in the 1660s* (Oxford: Blackwell, 2002), pp. 110–13; *ODNB*, "Bates, William."

150. *Correspondence of Richard Baxter*, vol. 2, p. 21; Berg, *Religious Currents and Cross-Currents*, p. 141.

151. Paul Chang-Ha Lim, *In Pursuit of Purity, Unity, and Liberty: Richard Baxter's Puritan Ecclesiology in its Seventeenth-Century Context* (Leiden, the Netherlands: Brill, 2004), pp. 195–98.

152. Shapiro, *John Wilkins*, pp. 241–42, 319n; Wilkins, *Principles and Duties of Natural Religion*, pp. 285, 314, 330, 344, 353, 388; cf. also Isabel Rivers, "Grace, Holiness, and the Pursuit of Happiness: Bunyan and Restoration Latitudinarianism," in *John Bunyan: Conventicle and Parnassus: Tercentenary Essays*, edited by N.H. Keeble (Oxford: Clarendon Press, 1988), pp. 52–53.

153. Quoted in Berg, *Religious Currents and Cross-Currents*, pp. 142–43; Berg comments that "the accentuation of the pleasant character of the Christian Religion is one of the distinguishing marks of the Latitudinarian pastoral approach," p. 143.

154. Ward, *Philosophical Essay*, p. 5.

155. Baxter, *Reasons*, p. 457; Baxter, *More Reasons*, pp. 162–65.

156. Bates, *Divinity of the Christian Religion*, pp. 65–69, 205–6.

157. Baxter, *Reasons*, pp. 457–63; Howe, *Living Temple*, part II, 467.

158. Bates, *Divinity of the Christian Religion*, pp. 203, 222–23.

159. Wilkins, *The Principles and Duties of Natural Religion*, pp. 394–95, 397; Stillingfleet, *Origenes Sacrae*, pp. 309–10; Rogers B. Miles, *Science, Religion and Belief: The Clerical Virtuosi of the Royal Society of London, 1663–1687* (New York: Peter Lang, 1992), pp. 91, 95–99, 105–7.

160. Shapiro, *Probability and Certainty*, p. 94; see also Rivers, *Reason, Grace and Sentiment*, vol. 1, *Whichcote to Wesley*, pp. 70, 73.

161. Westfall, *Science and Religion in Seventeenth-Century England*, p. 142.

162. John Spurr, "Schism and the Restoration Church," *JEH* 41 (1990): 422.

163. Stillingfleet, *Origines Sacrae*, p. 605.

164. Howe, *Living Temple*, part II, pp. 108-16, 124–26, 129–30, 132–33, 142, 147, 150; Baxter, *Reasons*, pp. 41, 176.

165. Bates, *Divinity of the Christian Religion*, pp. 46–47. Bates did not minimize original sin, declaring in a sermon that "the corruption of Nature is not a mere privation of Holiness, as Darkness is of Light, but a contrary inherent quality, the Principle of all sinful Evils," *Spiritual Evil Unfolded and Enforced* (London, 1699), p. 4.

166. Bates, *Divinity of the Christian Religion*, pp. 50–53, 196–98, 200, 213.

167. Baxter, *Reasons*, pp. 406–408; *More Reasons*, pp. 82–87, 117–24, 161–62.

168. Howe, *Living Temple*, part II, pp. 159–62, 167, 173–74, 178–83, 189; for Howe's full discussion of the atonement, see Ibid., pp. 152–330. For redemption to be accomplished, it was necessary that God do it in this way and no other (Ibid, p. 220). Here he agreed with John Owen against William Twisse, Wallace, *Puritans and Predestination*, pp.132–33. Baxter also agreed on this point with Howe and Owen, *More Reasons*, pp. 93–94. In disputes among the Dissenters over the atonement, Howe took

a more conservatively Calvinist line than did some others, notably Daniel Williams, see Roger Thomas, *Daniel Williams, "Presbyterian Bishop,"* Friends of Dr. Williams's Library Sixteenth Lecture, 1962 (London: Dr. Williams's Trust, 1964), pp. 18–21.

169. Alan C. Clifford, *Atonement and Justification: English Evangelical Theology, 1640–1790* (Oxford: Clarendon Press, 1990), pp. 128–31.

170. Baxter, *Dying Thoughts,* p. 292; Baxter, *More Reasons,* pp. 30–31, 41, 136; Baxter, *Reasons,* pp. 279, 282, 348–50.

171. Howe, *Living Temple,* part I, sig. A8, pp. 18–19; part II, pp. 215, 339, 341, 375, 407, 409–10.

172. Bates, *Divinity of the Christian Religion,* pp. 63–64.

173. Rivers, *Reason, Grace, and Sentiment,* vol. 1, *Whichcote to Wesley,* pp. 70, 73, 82–83. John Spurr rightly cautions against pushing this point too far but nonetheless acknowledges a significant distinction between dissenting Calvinists and post-Restoration conformists in their concept of the moral life and its grounds, *Restoration Church of England,* pp. 296–311.

174. Howe, *Living Temple,* part II, p. 189.

175. Shapiro, *Probability and Certainty,* pp. 106–8.

176. For Baxter against Platonism, see Vivian de Sola Pinto, *Peter Sterry, Platonist and Puritan, 1613–1672: A Biographical and Critical Study with Passages from His Writings* (1934; reprint, New York: Greenwood Press, 1968), p. 87; for Howe and the Cambridge Platonists, see Keeble, *Literary Culture of Nonconformity,* pp. 166–67.

177. For natural theology in Calvin, see Edward A. Dowey, Jr., *The Knowledge of God in Calvin's Theology* (New York: Columbia University Press, 1952), pp. 50–86; William J. Bouwsma, *John Calvin: A Sixteenth-Century Portrait* (Oxford: Oxford University Press, 1988), pp. 73, 102–105; Calvin, *Institutes of the Christian Religion,* bk. I, chapter 4, section 2; bk. I, chapter 5, sections 1–15.

178. Richard A. Muller, *After Calvin: Studies in the Development of a Theological Tradition* (Oxford: Oxford University Press, 2003), pp. 54–55.

179. For examples of Reformed theologians elsewhere who were taking some of the same steps into a new age as were Baxter, Bates, and Howe, see Klauber, *Betweeen Reformed Scholasticism and Pan-Protestantism,* pp. 62–103; David Sorkin, "Geneva's 'Enlightened Orthodoxy': The Middle Way of Jacob Vernet (1698–1789)" *CH* 74 (June 2005): 286–305.

CHAPTER 6

1. *ODNB,* "Edwards, John."

2. Ann Hughes, "Popular Presbyterianism in the 1640s and 1650s: The Cases of Thomas Edwards and Thomas Hall," *England's Long Reformation, 1500–1800,* edited by Nicholas Tyacke (London: UCL Press, 1998), p. 243.

3. John Edwards, *Brief Remarks Upon Mr. Whiston's New Theory of the Earth. And upon an Other Gentleman's Objections Against some Passages in a Discourse of the Existence and Providence of God, Relating to the Copernican Hypothesis* (London, 1697), sig. A3, pp. 21, 23.

4. John Edwards, *Theologia Reformata: Or the body and Substance of the Christian Religion, comprised in distinct Discourses or Treatises Upon the Apostles Creed, the Lords Prayer, and the Ten Commandments*, 2 vols., continuous pagination (London, 1713).

5. A reference to Daniel Whitby, in John Edwards, *The Arminian Doctrines Condemn'd by the Holy Scriptures, By Many of the Ancient Fathers, By the Church of England, and even by the Suffrage of Right Reason* (London, 1711), sig.A2v.

6. John Edwards, *A Letter to the Reverend Lawrence Fogg, D. D. and Dean of Chester; Wherein His pretended Vindication of some passages in his new and Inconsistent Scheme of Divinity is Examined and Confuted* (London, 1715), p. 6.

7. Robert Lightfoot, *Dr. Edwards's Vindication Consider'd, In a Letter to a Friend* (London, 1710), p. 5.

8. John Edwards, *Some New Discoveries of the Uncertainty, Deficiency, and Corruptions of Human Knowledge and Learning* (London, 1714), pp. 185–95.

9. John Edwards, *A Free Discourse Concerning Truth and Error, Especially in Religion* (London, 1701), pp. 293, 342, 344.

10. Ibid., p. 159.

11. John Edwards, *Socinianism Unmask'd, A Discourse Shewing the Unreasonableness of a Late Writer's Opinion concerning the Necessity of only One Article of Christian Faith; and of his other Assertions in his late Book, Entituled, The Reasonableness of Christianity* (London, 1696), p. 103.

12. John Edwards, *The Preacher, A Discourse Shewing, what are the Particular Offices and Employments of those of that Character in the Church* (London, 1705), pp. xxxiii–xxxiv.

13. Cotton Mather, *Manductio ad Ministerium: Directions for a Candidate of the Ministry, Reproduced from the Original Edition Boston, 1726*, The Facsimile Text Society (New York: Columbia University Press, 1938), pp. 97–98; Edwards, *Some New Discoveries*, pp. 17–18.

14. John Edwards, *The Plague of the Heart* (Cambridge, 1665), sig. A2, pp. 5–7, 13–14, 17.

15. John Edwards, *A Treatise of Repentance* (London, 1718), unpaginated preface.

16. e.g., Edwards, *The Preacher*, p. iv; *The Preacher, The Second Part* (London, 1706), p.4; John Edwards, *The Time of Reformation. A Seasonable Discourse of the Effectual Means and Methods of Reforming the Lives and Manners of the whole Body of this Nation* (London, 1730) in *Remains of the late Reverend and Learned John Edwards* (London, 1731), pp. 399, 402.

17. John Edwards, *Sermons on Special occasions and Subjects* (London, 1698), sig. A6v.

18. Edwards, *The Preacher*, pp. xxvii, 163, 199, 235–38, 243, 246, 248, 256, 326, 328; Edwards, *The Time of Reformation*, p. 381.

19. Edwards, *The Preacher*, pp. 30–35.

20. Edwards's body of divinity consisted of *Veritas Redux, Evangelical Truths Restored . . . Being the First Part of the Theological Treatises, which are to compose a large Body of Christian Divinity* (London, 1707); *The Doctrine of Faith and Justification Set in a True Light . . . Being the Second Part of the Theological Treatises, which are to compose a Large Body of Divinity* (London, 1708); and *Theologia Reformata*.

21. Edwards, *Some New Discoveries*, p. 134; Edwards, *A Free Discourse*, p. 277, 304; Edwards, *The Preacher*, pp. xxv, 212.

22. Edwards, *Sermons*, sig. a2r-v; Edwards, *A Free Discourse*, p. xli; Richard A. Muller, *Post-Reformation Dogmatics: The Rise and Development of Reformed Orthodoxy, ca. 1520 to ca. 1725*, 4 vols. (Grand Rapids, Mich.: Baker Academic, 2003), vol. 3, pp. 149, 355; vol. 4, pp.138, 160, 165.

23. Edwards, *The Preacher*, pp. 20–21; John Edwards, *The Socinian Creed: Or, A Brief Account of the Professed Tenents and Doctrines of the Foreign and English Socinians* (London, 1697), pp. 63, 81.

24. John Edwards, *Some Thoughts Concerning The Several Causes and occasions of Atheism, Especially in the Present Age* (London, 1695), pp. 29, 30, 43, 58.

25. Ibid., pp. 38–39.

26. Edwards, *Socinian Creed*, sig. b2v.

27. Edwards, *Some Thoughts Concerning Atheism*, p. 41.

28. Ibid., pp. 1–3, 18, 133–34.

29. Ibid., p. 42; Edwards, *Sermons*, p. 8.

30. Edwards, *Some Thoughts Concerning Atheism*, pp. 48, 52–53.

31. Ibid., pp. 123, 130.

32. Edwards, *Some New Discoveries*, p. 18.

33. Edwards, *Some Thoughts Concerning Atheism*, pp. 100–101.

34. Ibid., pp. 124–25.

35. Ibid., pp. 85–97; Edwards, *A Free Discourse*, pp. 315–16; John Edwards, *A Demonstration of the Existence and Providence of God From the Contemplation and Study of the Visible Structure of the Greater and Lesser World, In Two Parts. The First, shewing the Excellent Contrivance of the Heavens, Earth, Sea, Etc. The Second, the Wonderful Formation of the Body of Man* (London, 1696), part I, pp. 16–18.

36. Edwards, *Some Thoughts Concerning Atheism*, pp. 80, 84; for Spinoza's challenge to traditional views of the Bible see Gerard Reedy, S. J., *The Bible and Reason: Anglicans and Scripture in Late Seventeenth-Century England* (Philadelphia: University of Pennsylvania Press, 1985), pp. 25–28.

37. Edwards, *Some Thoughts Concerning Atheism*, pp. 25, 34, 46, 67, 84, 98, 128; John Edwards, *A Brief Vindication of the Fundamentall Articles of the Christian Faith, As Also of the Clergy, Universities and Publick Schools, from Mr. Lock's Reflections upon them in his Book of Education* (London, 1697), sig. A2v; Edwards, *Arminian Doctrines Condemn'd*, p. 210; John Edwards, *A Demonstration of the Existence and Providence of God*, Part I, p. iv; John Edwards, *The Eternal and Intrinsick Reasons of Good and Evil* (Cambridge, 1699) p. 23; Edwards, *The Preacher*, pp. 6–7, 130–31.

38. Edwards, *Some Thoughts Concerning Atheism*, pp. 138–40.

39. Edwards, *Demonstration of the Existence and Providence of God*, part I, pp. vii, 6–8.

40. Ibid., Part I, pp. 15–17.

41. Ibid., Part I, pp. 143–44.

42. W. R. Ward, *Christianity Under the Ancien Regime, 1648–1789* (Cambridge: Cambridge University Press, 1999), p. 152.

43. Edwards, *Demonstration of the Existence and Providence of God*, part I, pp. 51–61, 74–94, 105–15, p. 181; Thomas Burnet, *The Theory of the Earth: Containing an Account of the Originall of the Earth, and of all the General Changes which it hath undergone*, 2nd ed. (London, 1691).

44. Ibid., Part I, pp. 117–20, 129–30, 133–34; for vegetable sermons see Stuart Piggott, *William Stukeley: An Eighteenth-Century Antiquarian*, revised and enlarged (New York: Thames and Hudson, 1985), pp. 147–49.

45. Edwards, *Demonstration of the Existence and Providence of God*, part I, pp. 187, 230, 233, 237, 240.

46. Ibid., part II, pp. 2–3, 6–7, 19,22–24, 28–41, 56, 65–66, 129.; for circulation of the blood see also Edwards, *Some Thoughts Concerning Atheism*, p. 97.

47. John Edwards, *Cometomantia. A Discourse of Comets* (London, 1684), pp. 1–3, 11, 23, 52, 61, 67, 77–80, 104, 113, 118–21, 150, 157; Peter Harrison, *Protestantism, the Bible, and Science* (Cambridge: Cambridge University Press, 1998), pp. 181–82.

48. Edwards, *Demonstration of the Existence and Providence of God*, Part I, pp. 153–54; Edwards, *Cometomantia*, pp. 81–82.

49. Edwards, *Brief Remarks upon Mr. Whiston's New Theory of the Earth*, sig. A3, pp. 1–3, 8, 19, 21, 23, 26.

50. Edwards, *Some New Discoveries*, pp. 68, 74; Edwards, *Some Thoughts Concerning Atheism*, p. 93.

51. Edwards, *Some New Discoveries*, pp. 75–76; John Edwards, *Some Brief Critical Remarks on Dr. Clarke's Last Papers* (London, 1714), p.37; John Gascoigne, *Cambridge in the Age of the Enlightenment: Science, Religion and Politics from the Restoration to the French Revolution* (Cambridge: Cambridge University Press, 1989), pp. 169–70.

52. Edwards, *Some Thoughts Concerning Atheism*, p. 136; Edwards, *Sermons*, p. 434; Edwards, *The Preacher*, p. 46; Edwards, *Socinian Creed*, p. 125.

53. John Edwards, *A Discourse Concerning the Authority, Stile, and Perfection of the Books of the Old and New-Testament* (London, 1693), pp. 4, 44–45, 61–62, 88–89, 101, 268–69; *Theologia Reformata* I, pp. 182–83. In 1692 Edwards published two books dealing with the interpretation of problematic texts, *An Enquiry into Four Remarkable Texts of the New Testament which Contain Difficulty in them, with a Probable Resolution of Them* (Cambridge, 1692) and *A Farther Enquiry into Several Remarkable Texts of the Old and New Testament which contain Some Difficulty in them with a Probable Resolution of them* (London, 1692).

54. John Edwards, *Polupoikilos Sophia. A Compleat History or Survey of all the Dispensations and Methods of Religion, From the beginning of the World to the Consummation of all Things . . . against the Cavils of the Deists*, 2 vols. with continuous pagination (London, 1699), vol. 1, pp. 534, 536–37, 567; vol. 2, p. 637.

55. Edwards, *A Free Discourse*, p. xli.

56. Edwards, *Sermons*, pp. 9–12, 14, 18.

57. Edwards, *A Free Discourse*, pp. 1–11, 16, 18–19, 22, 27–29, 33–34, 36–39, 43, 61; Edwards, *Cometomantia*, p. 14.

58. Edwards, *A Free Discourse*, pp. 70, 73, 77, 92.

59. Ibid., pp. 94, 96, 102–103.

60. Edwards, *Sermons*, p. 433.

61. Edwards, *A Free Discourse*, pp. 123, 125–27, 135–37; Edwards, *Polupoikilos Sophia. A Compleat History of Religion*, vol. 1, p. 536.

62. Edwards, *The Eternal and Intrinsick Reasons of Good and Evil*, p. 18.

63. Edwards, *A Free Discourse*, pp. 67–69.

64. Ibid., p. 70; Edwards, *Some New Discoveries*, p. 1.

65. Edwards, *A Brief Vindication*, pp. 39, 44; Edwards, *Socinian Creed*, sig. A1v; Edwards, *A Free Discourse*, pp. 302–303; Edwards, *Doctrine of Faith*, pp. 67–68; Edwards, *Veritas Redux*, p. 479; Edwards, *The Preacher*, p. 47; Edwards, *The Preacher the Second Part*, p. 147; Edwards, *Sermons*, pp. 328–29, 342, 347, 352–55, 358, 361–67, 375, 381, 426. In the preface to *An Enquiry into Four Remarkable Texts of the New Testament*, sigs. A1-2, Edwards says that God "Wisely ordered" that there should be mysteries so that the sacred text would be given greater reverence and beget humility in interpreters. "If all places were easy, this Book would be liable to Contempt, and there would be no room left for our Diligent Search and Enquiry." Some places are plain and clear to "ordinary capacities" while other portions exercise the learned.

66. For discussion of "mysteries" in this period, see Reedy, *The Bible and Reason*, pp. 17–18, 22, 34, 101–102, 125–26, 134–35; Jan W. Wojcik, *Robert Boyle and the Limits of Reason* (Cambridge: Cambridge University Press, 1977), pp. 27–28, 36,40, 216.

67. R. D. Stock, *The Holy and the Demonic from Sir Thomas Browne to William Blake* (Princeton, N.J.: Princeton University Press, 1982), pp. 26–36); A. Keith Walker, *William Law: His Life and Thought* (London: SPCK, 1973), pp. 76–78, 80; William Law answered Deism in *The Case of Reason, or Natural Religion, fairly and fully stated, in answer to a book entitled Christianity as Old as the Creation* (London, 1731).

68. Edwards, *A Free Discourse*, pp. 275–86.

69. Edwards, *Sermons*, pp. 331–33; Peter Harrison, *'Religion' and the Religions in the English Enlightenment* (Cambridge: Cambridge University Press, 1990), pp. 87, 145.

70. Edwards, *A Free Discourse*, pp. 252–55.

71. John Edwards, *The Preacher. The Third Part. Containing Farther Rules and Advices, For The Right Discharging of the Sacred Office of Preaching* (London, 1707), pp. 45, 49, 57.

72. Edwards, *Sermons*, pp. 377, 426; Edwards, *A Free Discourse*, p. 66.

73. John Edwards, *Some Animadversions on Dr. Clark's Scripture-Doctrine (as he stiles it) of the Trinity* (London, 1712), p. 3.

74. When Edwards wrote *Socinianism Unmask'd* as a refutation of *The Reasonableness of Christianity* he did not know Locke was the author, but he understood it to reject the doctrine of the Trinity (pp. 4, 11); by the time he wrote *The Socinian Creed* (1697) he knew Locke was the author and also attacked other writings he considered Socinian. It was probably against these books of Edwards that Stephen Nye authored the anonymous *The Agreement of the Unitarians, with the Catholick Church. Being Also, A Full Answer to the Infamations of Mr. Edwards and the Needless Exceptions, of My Lords the Bishops of Chichester, Worcester, and Sarum* (n.p. , 1697). Against Edwards and the bishops this treatise emphasized that neither scripture nor the earliest fathers upheld the Trinity. H. John McLachlan, *Socinianism in*

Seventeenth-Century England (Oxford: Oxford University Press, 1951), p. 323, has identified Nye, a Church of England incumbent, and one of the first to use the term "Unitarian," as the likely author of the tract. That same year Edwards published *A Brief Vindication of the Fundamentall Articles of the Christian Faith* (London, 1697) to defend the doctrine of the Trinity against "a nameless Socinian," presumably Nye.

75. John Edwards, *A Supplement to the Animadversions on Dr. Clarke's Scripture-Doctrine of the Trinity* (London, 1713); *Some Brief Critical Remarks on Dr. Clarke's Last Papers* (London, 1714), pp. 6, 34–35, 37.

76. Edwards, *Some Animadversions on Dr. Clarke*, p. 4; Edwards, *Socinian Creed*, pp. 135–36; Edwards, *Socinianism Unmasked*, p. 104; Edwards, *Brief Vindication of the Fundamentall Articles*, pp. 40, 44; Edwards, *Sermons*, p. 361; Edwards, *The Preacher*, p.46; Wojcik, *Robert Boyle*, pp. 40, 46, 58; Isabel Rivers, *Reason, Grace and Sentiment: A Study of the Language of Religion and Ethics in England, 1660–1780*, vol. 2, *Shaftesbury to Hume* (Cambridge: Cambridge University Press, 2000), p. 61.

77. Edwards, *Veritas Redux*, p. 494.

78. Edwards, *Letter to Fogg*, p. 31, elsewhere Edwards says that Sanderson was Calvinist "as to the main," Edwards, *The Arminian Doctrines*, pp. 235–36, 244; Jeffrey Jeremiah, "Edward Reynolds (1599–1676): Pride of the Presbyterian Party" (unpublished dissertation, George Washington University, 1992); *ODNB*, "Morley, George"; Peter Lake, "Serving God and the Times: The Calvinist Conformity of Robert Sanderson," *Journal of British Studies* 27 (April 1988): 81–116.

79. *ODNB*, "Conant, John."

80. Alan Macfarlane, *The Family Life of Ralph Josselin: A Seventeenth-Century Clergyman* (New York: Norton, 1970), p. 193; John Spurr, "From Puritanism to Dissent, 1660–1700," in *The Culture of English Protestantism, 1560–1700*, edited by Christopher Durston and Jacqueline Eales (New York: St. Martin's Press, 1996), p. 240.

81. Stephen Hampton, *Anti-Arminians: The Anglican Reformed Tradition from Charles II to George I* (Oxford: Oxford University Press, 2008).

82. Edwards, *Some Thoughts Concerning Atheism*, sig. A3v; Edwards, *A Free Discourse*, p. xli; "An Answer to Pilate's Question, What is Truth? A Sermon Preach'd before King Charles II at Newmarket," in Edwards, *Sermons*, pp. 1–28.

83. *Cometomantia* (1684) was dedicated to Seth Ward, bishop of Salisbury; *A Discourse concerning the Authority, Stile, and Perfection of the Books of the Old and new Testament* (1693) was dedicated to Simon Patrick, bishop of Ely, as was *A Farther Enquiry into Several Remarkable Texts of the Old and New Testament* (1692); *The Socinian Creed* (1697) was dedicated to Edward Stillingfleet, bishop of Worcester; and two works, *A Demonstration of the Existence and Providence of God* (1696) and *Some Thoughts Concerning Atheism* (1695) were dedicated to the archbishop of Canterbury, Thomas Tenison; *The Preacher*, p. v, and *Arminian Doctrines*, 218–19, criticized Tillotson.

84. Edwards, *Brief Vindication of the Fundamentall Articles*, p. 109.

85. Edwards, *Socinianism Unmasked*, p. 13.

86. Unpaginated list at the end of Edwards, *The Preacher*; Edwards, *Some Thoughts Concerning Atheism*, p. 104.

87. Edwards, *The Preacher*, p. xii.

88. Edwards, *The Preacher, The Third Part*, p. 128.

89. Edwards, *The Preacher*, p. xix; John Edwards, *One Nation and One King. A Discourse on Ezek. Xxxvii.22. Ocassion'd by the Happy Union of England and Scotland*, (London, 1707), pp. 9–12.

90. Edwards, *Brief Vindication of the Fundamentall Articles*, sig. A4r; *Supplement to the Animadversions*, pp. 67ff.; Edwards, *Socinian Creed*, p. 167.

91. Edwards, *The Preacher, The Second Part*, pp. ix–x; Pasi Ihalainen, *Protestant Nations Redefined: Changing Perceptions of National Identity in the Rhetoric of the English, Dutch and Swedish Public Churches, 1685–1772* (Leiden, the Netherlands: Brill, 2005), pp. 179–83.

92. Edwards, *Sermons*, pp. 92, 114.

93. Edwards, *The Preacher*, p. 254.

94. Scott H. Hendrix, "Deparentifying the Fathers: The Reformers and Patristic Authority," in *Auctoritas Patrum: Zur Rezeption der Kirchenvater im 15 und 16 Jahrhundert*, edited by Leif Grane, Alfred Schindler, and Markus Wriedt (Mainz, Germany: Verlag Philipp Von Zabern, 1993), pp. 55–68; Joseph C. McLelland, *The Visible Words of God: A Study in the Theology of Peter Martyr* (London: Oliver and Boyd, 1957), pp. 267–71; Johannes Van Oort, "John Calvin and the Church Fathers," in Backus, *Reception*, vol. 2, pp. 665–66, 671–75, 678; Irena Backus, "Ulrich Zwingli, Martin Bucer, and the Church Fathers," in Backus, *Reception*, vol. 2, pp. 644, 654, 657–58; Bruce Gordon, "Heinrich Bullinger," in *The Reformation Theologians*, edited by Carter Lindbert (Oxford: Blackwell, 2002), p. 178.

95. Jean-Louis Quantin, "The Fathers in Seventeenth-Century Anglican Theology," in Backus, *Reception*, vol. 2, pp. 990–91.

96. Richard A. Muller, *After Calvin: Studies in the Development of a Theological Tradition* (Oxford: Oxford University Press, 2003), p. 74; E. P. Meijering, "The Fathers and Calvinist Orthodoxy: Systematic theology," in Backus, *Reception*, vol. 2, pp. 867–87.

97. S. L. Greenslade, *The English Reformers and the Fathers of the Church* (Oxford: Clarendon Press, 1960), pp. 10, 14, 19; Mark Vesey, "English Translations of the Latin Fathers, 1517–1611," in Backus, *Reception*, vol. 2, pp. 777–78.

98. Irena Backus, "The Fathers and Calvinist Orthodoxy: Patristic Scholarship," in Backus, *Reception*, vol. 2, pp. 839–40.

99. John C. English, "The Duration of the Primitive Church: An Issue for Seventeenth and Eighteenth Century Anglicans," *Anglican and Episcopal History* 73 (March 2004): 35–51.

100. William P. Haugaard, "Renaissance Patristic Scholarship and Theology in Sixteenth-Century England," *SCJ* 10 (fall 1979): 37–60; Leslie W. Garnard, "The Use of the Patristic Tradition in the Late Seventeenth and Early Eighteenth Centuries," in *Scripture, Tradition and Reason: A Study in the Criteria of Christian Doctrine, Essays in Honour of Richard P. C. Hanson*, edited by Richard Bauckham and Benjamin Drewery (Edinburgh: T. and T. Clark, 1988), pp. 174–78; Quantin, "The Fathers in Seventeenth Century Anglican Theology," in Backus, *Reception*, vol. 2, p. 987; Gunther Thomann,

"John Ernest Grabe (1660–1711): Lutheran Syncretist and Patristic Scholar," *JEH* 43 (July 1992): 414–27.

101. Gasciogne, *Cambridge in the Enlightenment*, p. 57.

102. D. W. Dockrill, "The Fathers and the Theology of the Cambridge Platonists," *Studia Patristica* 17 (1982): 427–39.

103. John K. Luoma, "Who Owns the Fathers? Hooker and Cartwright on the Authority of the Primitive Church," *SCJ* 8:3 (1977): pp. 45–60.

104. Anthony Milton, *Catholic and Reformed: The Roman and Protestant Churches in English Protestant Thought, 1600–1640* (Cambridge: Cambridge University Press, 1995), pp. 273–76.

105. John Edwards, *Patrologia, Or A Discourse Concerning the Primitive Fathers and Antient Writers of the Christian Church* (London, 1730), in John Edwards, *The Remains of the late Reverend and Learned John Edwards, D.D.* (London, 1730), pp. 112–14.

106. Correspondence to and from Dodwell, in Bodleian MS Cherry 23, folios 229–49; Mark Goldie, "The Theory of Intolerance in Restoration England," in *From Persecution to Toleration: The Glorious Revolution in England*, edited by Ole Peter Grell, Jonathan I. Israel, and Nicholas Tyacke (Oxford: Clarendon Press, 1991), pp. 335, 350; Edwards, *Divine Perfection Vindicated*, p. 30; Edwards, *Some New Discoveries*, pp. 142–43; Edwards, *A Supplement to the Animadversions*, sig. A2v; Edwards, *Patrologia*, pp. 15, 122.

107. D. W. Dockrill, "The Authority of the Fathers in the Great Trinitarian Debates of the Sixteen Nineties," *Studia Patristica* 18:5 (1990):337–38.

108. Richard Muller, *After Calvin*, p. 60.

109. Edwards, *Theologia Reformata*. vol. 1, pp. v–viii; Quantin, "The Fathers in Seventeenth Century Anglican Theology," pp. 992–94; *ODNB*, "Reeve, William."

110. Edwards, *Free Discourse*, pp. 59, 63, 141, 150, 189–91, 205–207, 235, 240, 244–46.

111. Edwards, *Patrologia*, pp. 3–6, 9, 24, 47, 49.

112. Daniel Whitby, *A Treatise of Traditions*, part I (London, 1688), pp. xviii–xxiv.

113. Edwards, *Free Discourse*, pp. 171, 190, 196; in the same treatise however, Edwards faults an excessive regard for the moderns: not every "little Pamphlet" they produce is to be preferred to earlier authors, and one should beware of a love of "novelty," p. 175.

114. Ian Breward, ed., *The Works of William Perkins*, vol. 3 of Courtenay Library of Reformation Classics (Appleford, UK: Sutton Courtenay Press, 1970), pp. 52–53.

115. Margaret C. Jacob, *The Newtonians and the English Revolution, 1689–1720* (Ithaca, N.Y.: Cornell University Press, 1976), pp. 78–70; Barbara J. Shapiro, *Probability and Certainty in Seventeenth-Century England* (Princeton, N.J.: Princeton University Press, 1983), pp. 122–23; for the battle of the books (ancients versus moderns), see Preserved Smith, *The Enlightenment, 1687–1776* (1934; Reprint, New York: Collier Books, 1962), pp. 204–208; Peter Gay, *The Enlightenment: An Interpretation*,vol. 2,*The Science of Freedom* (New York: Alfred Knopf, 1969), pp. 124–25; Robert Nisbet, *History of the Idea of Progress* (New York: Basic Books, 1980), pp. 151–56; and Richard Foster Jones, *Ancients and Moderns: A Study of the Background*

of the Battle of the Books, (St. Louis, Mo.: Washington University Studies, New Series, Language and Literature 6, 1936), especially chapter 6, "The Revolt from Aristotle and the Ancients," pp. 124–53; in a sermon welcoming George I, John Edwards emphasized modern improvements: unreasonable complainers "over-valued" the past, but in the present all learning is much advanced, for example, in history, navigation, architecture, music, chemistry, mathematics, and "all Natural and Mechanical philosophy," *How to Judge Aright of Former and Present Times, Occasion'd By the Late Happy Accession of King George to the British Throne* (London, 1714), pp. 8, 11, 36.

116. Edwards, *Patrologia,* pp. 22, 57, 65, 75, 140–43, 111, 119; Edwards, *Some Thoughts Concerning Atheism,* p. 96; Edwards did, however, accept the authenticity of the correspondence between Abgar and Jesus, *Discourse Concerning the Authority, Stile, and Perfection of the Books of the Old and New-Testament,* pp. 348–50.

117. Edwards, *Patrologia,* pp. 116–17, 134.

118. John Edwards, *The Doctrines Controverted between Papists and Protestants Particularly and Distinctly Considered* (London, 1724) p. iv.

119. Edwards, *Patrologia,* pp. 119, 128.

120. Ibid., p. 114; *Arminian Doctrines,* pp. 105, 107–109; Edwards, *Some New Discoveries,* pp. 109–11; Edwards, *Veritas Redux,* p. 535.

121. Edwards, *Some New Discoveries,* p. 111.

122. Anthony N. S. Lane, *John Calvin: Student of the Church Fathers* (Grand Rapids, Mich.: Baker Books, 1990), pp. 27–29, 40–41; Van Oort, "John Calvin and the Church Fathers," vol. 2, pp. 697–99.

123. John Edwards, *The Time of Reformation. A Seasonable Discourse of the Effectual Means and Methods of Reforming the Lives and Manners of the Whole Body of this Nation* (London, 1730), in *Remains of Edwards,* pp. 410–12, 417, 421.

124. John Edwards, *A Discourse of Episcopacy: Wherein this Question is resolved, Whether in the Primitive Times there was a Distinct Order of Bishops different from that of Presbyters* (London, 1730) in *Remains of Edwards,* pp. 176, 180–82, 189, 236–37, 256–62, 270; An earlier hint of his views appeared in *The Preacher,* p. xxviii, where Edwards cited Jerome on the identity of elders and bishops. For competing claims for Hooker and his legacy, see Michael Brydon, *The Evolving Reputation of Richard Hooker: An Examination of Responses 1600–1714* (Oxford: Oxford University Press, 2006), especially chapters 4–6, and p. 142 for Baxter's assertion that Hooker would have supported reduced episcopacy.

125. Edwards, *Sermons,* pp. 248–49, 251–52.

126. John Edwards, *Great Things done by God for Our Ancestors, and Us of this Island* (London, 1710), title page, p. 17; James Sharpe, *Remember, Remember: A Cultural History of Guy Fawkes Day* (Cambridge, Mass.: Harvard University Press, 2005), pp. 109–11.

127. Edwards, *How to Judge Aright of Former and Present Times,* pp. 8, 11, 37, 39–40.

128. Edwards, *Sermons,* pp. 37–38.

129. John Edwards, *A Resolution of the Query Wherein the Doctrine of Non-Resistance and Passive Obedience is to be understood without any Limitation and Restriction* (London, 1730) in *Remains of Edwards,* pp. 446–47.

130. Edwards, *Some New Discoveries*, p. 64.

131. Edwards, *Arminian Doctrines*, pp. 214–15.

132. Edwards, *One Nation, One King*, p. 10; Edwards, *Some Brief Critical Remarks*, p. 35.

133. Edwards, *The Preacher*, p. viii.

134. *ODNB*, "Conant, John."

135. Edwards, *The Doctrine of Faith*, p. 313.

136. Edwards, *Doctrines Controverted*, pp. 51–52

137. Ibid., p. 49.

138. Milton, *Catholic and Reformed*, pp. 435, 446.

139. Edwards, *Arminian Doctrines*, p. 108; Edwards, *The Preacher*, p. xvii; *The Preacher, The Third Part*, pp. vi–vii, 271; Edwards, *Veritas Redux*, pp. xix, 513–33, 535; Edwards, *Theologia Reformata*, vol. 2, pp. iii–iv.

140. Edwards, *Free Discourse*, pp. 424–27; Edwards, *Some New Discoveries*, pp. 117–19; Edwards, *Arminian Doctrines*, pp. 107, 112.

141. The book by Burnet to which Edwards objected was *Exposition of the XXXIX Articles* (London, 1699); Edwards, *A Discourse Concerning Truth and Error*, pp. 424–30; Burnet's elastic view of what the articles meant brought forth many opponents, Stephen Hampton, *Anti-Arminians*, pp. 28–31.

142. Edwards, *Arminian Doctrines*, p. 110.

143. Ibid., p. 109.

144. Ibid., pp. 110–11; Edwards, *Veritas Redux*, pp. 535–58.

145. Brydon, *Evolving Reputation of Richard Hooker*, p. 188; Edwards, *Veritas Redux*, p. 539; Edwards, *The Doctrine of Faith*, pp. 313–14.

146. Edwards, *Doctrines Controverted*, pp. 69–73; Edwards, *The Preacher, The Second Part*, pp. 159–61.

147. Burke W. Griggs presents evidence of some churchmen, including Burnet, objecting to John Walker's project of calling attention to Interregnum sufferings of the clergy since they thought much of the blame was Laud's, "Remembering the Puritan Past: John Walker and Anglican Memories of the English Civil War," in *Protestant Identities: Religion, Society, and Self-Fashioning in Post-Reformation England*, edited by Muriel C. McClendon, Joseph P. Ward, and Michael MacDonald (Stanford, Calif.: Stanford University Press, 1999), p. 168.

148. *Richard Baxter's Confession of his Faith* (London, 1655), p. 27; Baxter contrasted the old Reformed Church of England with the Laudians, *RB*, part II, p.149.

149. Edwards, *Arminian Doctrines*, p. 114.

150. Daniel Whitby, *A Discourse Concerning: I. The true Import of the Words Election and Reprobation . . . II. The extent of Christ's Redemption. III. The grace of God . . . IV. The liberty of the will . . . V. The perseverance or defectibility of the Saints* (London, 1710), pp. i–iv, vi–vii, ix, xv, 359–61; Wallace, *Puritans and Predestination*, pp. 124–25; Edwards, *The Arminian Doctrines*, pp. 2–13.

151. Edwards, *Letter to the Reverend Lawrence Fogg*, pp. 8–9, 15.

152. Edwards, *Arminian Doctrines*, pp. 3–8, 20–24.

153. Ibid., sig. A2r, pp. 16, 108–11, 114, 236.

154. Ibid., pp. 11–12, 97.

155. Edwards, *Free Discourse*, p.400; Edwards, *Doctrines Controverted*, pp. 74–75; for the importance of the pope as the Antichrist to many English Protestants see Christopher Hill, *Antichrist in Seventeenth Century England* (London: Oxford University Press, 1971).

156. John Edwards, *A Brief Confutation of these Two False and Dangerous Positions; Namely, I. That the Church of Rome is a true Church, and consequently that Salvation may be attained in it. II That the Ministers of the Gospel are True and Proper priests, and have their True and Proper Sacrifice and Altar now on Earth* (London, 1730) in *Remains of Edwards*, pp. 290, 294, 310; extensive anti-Roman polemic also appeared in his *Doctrines Controverted*, pp. 281, 284–90, 294, 303, 310–12, 323–26, 328–31.

157. Edwards, *Patrologia*, p. 15.

158. John Edwards, *Great Things done by God for our Ancestors, and Us of this Island. A sermon Preach'd before the University of Cambridge . . . Being appointed a Day of Thanksgiving for the Deliverance from the Intended Bloody Massacre by Gunpowder, and for the Happy Arrival of King William* (London, 1710), pp. 12–17; the university press at Cambridge refused to print his sermon but the dedication to Edward, earl of Orford, a member of the privy council, got it published in London, sigs A2–A3.

159. Edwards, *Veritas Redux*, pp. 510–11; *The Preacher*, unpaginated list of recommended books; see also *The Preacher, The Second Part*, p. xxv.

160. Edwards, *Arminian Doctrines*, p. 28.

161. Ibid., pp. 218–19; Edwards, *The Preacher, The Second Part*, p. v.; Robert Lightfoot, *Remarks upon some Passages in Dr. Edwards's Preacher, Discovering his False Reasonings and Unjust Reflection Upon his Brethren the Clergy* (London, 1709), pp. 25–27, 37–39; Robert Lightfoot, *Dr. Edwards's Vindication consider'd, In a Letter to a Friend. Wherein the late Archbishop Tillotson and Others are more fully Vindicated from his Unjust Reflections* (London, 1710), pp. 15–16, 37, which responded to Edwards's *The Divine Perfections Vindicated* (London, 1710).

162. Edwards, *Arminian Doctrines*, pp. 218–19; Edwards, *A Letter to the Reverend Lawrence Fogg*, pp. 27–28.

163. Edwards, *The Preacher*, pp. iii–iv, xxi–xxii, xxxvii, 72–76, 163, 326, 328.

164. Edwards, *Arminian Doctrines*, p. 28.

165. Edwards, *Socinianism Unmask'd*, p. 96; Edwards, *Free Discourse*, p. 302.

166. Edwards *Veritas Redux*, p. 494.

167. Edwards, *Some Thoughts Concerning Atheism*, p. 113.

168. Edwards, *Socinianism Unmasked*, p. 44.

169. Ibid., p. 4.

170. Edwards, *Brief Vindication of the Fundamentall Articles*, sigs. A2v-A3r.

171. Edwards, *Socinian Creed*, sigs. b2v, b5r; pp. 38, 63, 81. See also Edwards, *Brief Vindication of the Fundamentall Articles*, pp. 110, 116–17.

172. Edwards, *Some Thoughts Concerning Atheism*, pp. 104–105.

173. Edwards, *Arminian Doctrines*, p. xi.

174. Jonathan Israel, *Enlightenment Contested: Philosophy, Modernity, and the Emancipation of Man, 1670–1752* (Oxford: Oxford University Press, 2006), pp. 117–18, 121–22.

175. Edwards, *Theologia Reformata*, I, p. iii.

176. Joseph Alleine, *Remaines*, sig. A3v; David P. Field, *"Rigide Calvinisme in a Softer Dresse:" The Moderate Presbyterianism of John Howe (1630–1705)* (Edinburgh: Rutherford House, 2004), p. 115; Theophilus Gale, *The Court of the Gentiles, Part IV . . . Book 3. Of Divine Predetermination . . . With a Vindication of Calvinists* (London, 1678); Richard Baxter, "To the Christian Reader," in Thomas Hotchkis, *An Exercitation Concerning the Nature of Forgiveness of Sin* (London 1655), sig. B[7]r-v.

177. Milton, *Catholic and Reformed*, pp. 407–408.

178. Hampton, *Anti-Arminians*, pp. 9–21.

179. Edwards, *Doctrine of Faith*, p. 399; *Doctrines Controverted*, p. 37; *Veritas Redux*, pp. 510–13; *Arminian Doctrines*, pp. 108–10, 113.

180. Edwards, *The Preacher, The Third Part*, pp. 128, 223; Edwards, *Arminian Doctrines*, p. 115; Edwards named many of the Church of England opponents of Calvinism, such as Peter Heylyn, John Bramhall, and Samuel Parker, and included among them Jonathan Swift, whom he only knew as the author of *The Tale of A Tub*, "said to be a clergyman," Edwards, *The Preacher, The Second Part*, pp. xvi–xvii.

181. Edwards, *Arminian Doctrines*, sig. A2r.

182. Ibid., p. 236.

183. Edwards, *Arminian Doctrines*, p. 122; Edwards, *The Preacher, The Third Part*, pp. xviii–xix.

184. Edwards, *Arminian Doctrines*, pp. 14–16, 120–21; Edwards, *Some New Discoveries*, p. v; Edwards, *Sermons*, p. 18, in a sermon on "What is Truth" preached before King Charles II; Edwards, *The Preacher, The Second Part*, p. 10.

185. Edwards, *Veritas Redux*, pp. 160–71; see also Edwards, *Some New Discoveries*, pp. 134–35.

186. Edwards, *Veritas Redux*, pp. 237–46.

187. John Locke, *The Reasonableness of Christianity as delivered in the Scriptures*, edited by John C. Higgins-Biddle, The Clarendon Edition of the Works of John Locke (Oxford: Clarendon Press, 1999), pp. 3, 170; for the revival of Crispianism see Dewey D. Wallace, Jr., "Socinianism, Justification by Faith, and the Sources of John Locke's *The Reasonableness of Christianity*," *JHI* 45 (January–March, 1984): 51–55; Michael R. Watts, *The Dissenters: From the Reformation to the French Revolution* (Oxford: Clarendon Press, 1978), pp. 289–97.

188. [John Edwards], *Crispianism Unmask'd;Or, A Discovery of the Several Erroneous Assertions, and Pernicious Doctrines Maintain'd in Dr. Crisp's Sermons. Occasion'd by the Reprinting of those Discourses* (London, 1693), pp. 2–3, 18, 38, 34, 47, 52–53, 59, 65; *A Plea for the Late Accurate and Excellent Mr. Baxter, and those that speak of the Suffering of Christ as he does. In Answer to Mr. Lobb's insinuated charge of Socinianism Against 'em, in his late Appeal to the Bishop of Worcester, and Dr. Edwards* (London,1699) has sometimes been attributed to John Edwards, but the Dr. Edwards mentioned in the title is the English Jonathan Edwards, a conformist High Churchman and anti-Socinian author.

189. Edwards, *Veritas Redux*, pp. xxvii–xxviii; Edwards, *Theologia Reformata*, p. v; Edwards, *Divine Perfections*, p. 29; Samuel Taylor Coleridge, *Notes on English Divines*, edited by Derwent Coleridge, 2 vols. (London, 1853), vol. 2, p. 38; Augustus Toplady, as

a Church of England Calvinist later in the eighteenth century, refined Edwards's argument about rebellion: it was, he said, Puritans, not Calvinists, who killed the King, as the horror of Archbishop Ussher at the act demonstrated, *Historic Proof of the Doctrinal Calvinism of the Church of England* (London, 1793), pp. 350–51.

190. Peter Heylyn, *Aerius Redivivus, or the History of the Presbyterians* (Oxford, 1670), sig A2v, pp. 23, 25; Calvin was defended against Heylyn's attack by James Harrington in his *The Stumbling-Block of Disobedience and Rebellion Cunningly imputed by P. H. unto Calvin, removed in a Letter to the said P. H.* (n.p., 1658).

191. Edwards, *Free Discourse*, p. 159; Edwards, *Veritas Redux*, p. xx.

192. Edwards, *Theologia Reformata*, I, p. 393; Theophilus Gale, *The Court of the Gentiles: or A Discourse touching the Original of human Literature, Both Philologie and Philosophie, from the Scriptures and Jewish Church. Part I. Of Philologie*, second edition revised and enlarged (Oxford, 1672), bk. 2, pp. 48–49; Dewey D. Wallace, Jr., "Puritan and Anglican: The Interpretation of Christ's Descent Into Hell in Elizabethan Theology," *Archiv fur Reformationsgeschichte* 69 (1978): 280–84.

193. Edwards, *Free Discourse*, p. 326; Edwards, *Doctrine of Faith*, p. 240; Edwards, *The Preacher, The Third Part*, p. 296. While Calvin is not as clear as later Reformed theologians on this point, Edwards seems mistaken on this matter about Calvin (communication with Richard A. Muller, June 9, 2008).

194. Jonathan Edwards knew John Edwards's writings, Peter J. Thuesen, ed., *Catalogues of Books, The Works of Jonathan Edwards* 26 (New Haven, Conn.: Yale University Press, 2008), pp. 130, 142, 174; George Whitfield commented that what John Edwards wrote on the divine decrees, except for one point, was "unanswerable," George Whitefield, *A Letter to the Reverend Mr. John Wesley: in Answer to Sermon, Entituled, Free-Grace* (London, 1741), p. 6; other eighteenth-century evangelical Calvinists citing him were Thomas Bowman, *A Review of the Doctrines of the Reformation, with an Account of the several Deviations to the present general Departure from them* (Norwich, 1768), p. 127; [Augustus Toplady], *The Church of England Vindicated from the charge of Arminianism . . . By a Presbyter of the Church of England* (London, 1769), cites Edwards (pp. 21–22, 56, 76), calling him "The great and famous Dr. John Edwards," one of Cambridge University's "brightest ornaments (p. 50); B. W. Young, *Religion and Enlightenment in Eighteenth-Century England: Theological Debate from Locke to Burke* (Oxford: Clarendon Press, 1998), p. 77, remarks that John Edwards was a hero to Toplady.

CONCLUSION

1. Lynn Hunt, Margaret C. Jacob, and Wijnand Mijnhardt, *The Book That Changed Europe: Picart & Bernard's Religious Ceremonies of the World* (Cambridge, Mass.: Belknap Press of Harvard University Press, 2010), p. 288.

2. Peter Berger, *The Heretical Imperative: Contemporary Possibilities of Religious Affirmation* (Garden City, N.J.: Anchor Press/Doubleday, 1979), pp. 52–53.

Bibliography

MANUSCRIPT SOURCES

Baxter, Richard. "A Treatise Against the Dominicane Doctrine of Divine Predetermination." Baxter MS 61.14. Vol. 18. Dr. Williams's Library, London.

Dodwell, Henry. Correspondence. Cherry MS 23, folios 229–49. Bodleian Library, Oxford.

Gale, Theophilus. Letters to Philip Lord Wharton. Rawlinson MSS. Vol. 49, letters 15, 31. Bodleian Library, Oxford.

Howe, John. "The Principles of the Oracles of God." Dr. Williams's Library MS 24.16. Dr. Williams's Library, London.

Jolly MS, folio 8. Dr. Williams's Library, London.

Roger Morrice Historical MS 31, X. Dr. Williams's Library, London.

Sterry, Peter. "Letters from Peter Sterry to Morgan Lloyd at the National Library of Wales." Transcribed by N. Matar. Emmanuel College MS 321.1.129. Cambridge.

Sterry, Peter. Peter Sterry MSS I–VII. Emmanuel College Library, Cambridge.

PRIMARY SOURCES

Airy, Osmund, ed. *Burnet's History of My Own Time*. Part I. *The Reign of Charles II*. 2 vols. Oxford: Clarendon Press, 1897.

Alleine, Joseph. *An Alarme to Unconverted Sinners*. London, 1675.

———. *A Call to Archippus, or An humble and earnest Motion to some Ejected Ministers*. London, 1664.

———. *Christian Letters Full of Spiritual Instructions, Tending to the Promoting of the Power of Godliness*. London, 1672.

———. *Divers Practical Cases of Conscience Satisfactorily Resolved*. London, 1672.

———. *A Most Familiar Explanation of the Assemblies Shorter Catechism*. London, 1674.

———. *Remaines of that Excellent Minister of Jesus Christ, Mr. Joseph Alleine*. London, 1674.

Alleine, Richard. *Cheirothesia tou Presbuterou, or a Letter to a Friend*. London, 1661.

———. *Godly Fear; or the Nature and Necessity of Fear*. London, 1674.

———. *Heaven Opened, Or A Brief and Plain Discovery of the Riches of Gods Covenant of Grace*. London, 1666.

———. *Instructions about Heart Work*. London, 1681.

———. *A Rebuke to Backsliders and a Spurr for Loyterers*. London, 1677.

———. *Vindiciae Pietatis, or A Vindication of Godlinesse*. London, 1660.

Alleine, Tobie. *Truths Manifest*. 1658.

Ames, William. *The Marrow of Theology*. Edited by John Dykstra Eusden. Durham, N.C.: Labyrinth Press, 1968.

Annesley, Samuel, ed. *The Morning Exercise at Cripple-gate, or Several Cases of Conscience practically resolved by sundry ministers*. London, 1661.

Ascham, Roger. *The Schoolmaster 1570*. Edited by Lawrence V. Ryan. Charlottesville: Published for the Folger Shakespeare Library by the University Press of Virginia, 1967.

Augustine, St. *Concerning the City of God Against the Pagans*. Translated by Henry Bettenson. 1972; reprint, Harmondsworth, UK: Penguin Books, 1972.

Bacon, Francis. *Essays, Advancement of Learning, New Atlantis, and Other Pieces*. Edited by Richard Foster Jones. New York: Odyssey Press, 1937.

Bates, William. *Considerations of the Existence of God, and the Immortality of the Soul*. London, 1677.

———. *The Danger of Prosperity: Discovered in Several Sermons*. London, 1685.

———. *The Divinity of the Christian Religion, Proved By the Evidence of Reason, and Divine Revelation*. London, 1677.

———. *The Four Last Things: Death, Judgment, Heaven, Hell, Practically considered and applied, in Several Discourses*. London, 1691.

———. *A Funeral-Sermon for the Reverend, Holy and Excellent Divine, Mr. Richard Baxter*. London, 1692.

———. *Spiritual Perfection Unfolded and Enforced*. London, 1699.

Baxter, Richard. *Aphorisms of Justification*. London, 1649.

———. *The Arrogancy of Reason Against Divine Revelations*. London, 1655.

———. *Catholick Theologie Plain, Pure, Peaceable: For the Pacification of Dogmatical Word-Warriours*. London, 1675.

———. *The Certainty of the World of Spirits, fully evinced by unquestionable Histories of Apparitions and Witchcrafts, Operations, Voices*. London, 1691.

———. *The Judgment of Nonconformists, of the Interest of Reason, In Matters of Religion*. London, 1676.

———. *More Reasons for the Christian Religion, and no Reason Against It*. London, 1672.

————. *Of the Immortality of Mans Soul, and the Nature of it, and other Spirits.* London, 1682.

————. *Reasons of the Christian Religion.* London, 1667.

————. *Richard Baxter's Confession of his Faith.* London, 1655.

————. *Richard Baxter's Dying Thoughts Upon Phil I. 23.* London, 1683.

————. *Richard Baxter's Penitent Confession.* London, 1691.

————. *The Unreasonableness of Infidelity.* London, 1655.

Bowman, Thomas. *A Review of the Doctrines of the Reformation.* Norwich, 1768.

Bradstreet, Anne. *The Complete Works of Anne Bradstreet.* Edited by Joseph R. McElrath, Jr., and Allan P. Robb. Boston: Twayne Publishers, 1981.

Breward, Ian, ed. *The Works of William Perkins.* Abingdon, UK: Sutton Courtenay Press, 1970.

Bunyan, John. *A Defence of the Doctrine of Justification, etc. Miscellaneous Works of John Bunyan.* Vol. 4. Edited by T. L. Underwood. Oxford: Clarendon Press, 1989.

————. *Grace Abounding to the Chief of Sinners.* Edited by W. R. Owens. London: Penguin Books, 1987.

————. *Pilgrim's Progress.* Edited by W. R. Owens. Oxford: Oxford University Press, 2003.

————. *Some Gospel Truths Opened, A Vindication of Some Gospel Truths Opened, A Few Sighs from Hell, Miscellaneous Works of John Bunyan.* Vol. 1. Edited by T. L. Underwood. Oxford: Clarendon Press, 1980.

Burnet, Gilbert. *Exposition of the XXXIX Articles.* London, 1699.

Burton, Robert. *The Anatomy of Melancholy.* Edited by Floyd Dell and Paul Jordan-Smith. New York: Tudor Publishing, 1955.

Butler, Samuel. *Hudibras in Three Parts.* London, 1684.

Calamy, Edmund. *Memoirs of the Late Rev'd. Mr. John Howe.* London, 1724.

Calvin, John. *Institutes of the Christian Religion.* 2 vols. Edited by John T. McNeill and translated by Ford Lewis Battles. Philadelphia: Westminster Press, 1960.

Cane, John Vincent. *Fiat Lux, A General Conduct to a right understanding in the great Combustions and Broils about Religion here in England.* London, 1662.

Clarke, Samuel (1599-1682). *The Lives of Eminent Persons in this Later Age.* Part I. London, 1683.

Clarke, Samuel (1675-1729). *A Discourse Concerning the Unchangeable Obligations of Natural Religion and the Truth and Certainty of the Christian Revelation.* London, 1706.

Cudworth, Ralph. *The True Intellectual System of the Universe.* London, 1678.

Culverwell, Nathaniel. *An Elegant and Learned Discourse of the Light of Nature.* Edited by Robert A. Greene and Hugh MacCallum. Toronto: University of Toronto Press, 1971.

Doolittle, Thomas. *The Young Man's Instructor.* London, 1673.

Dryden, John. *Selected Works.* Edited by William Frost. San Francisco: Rinehart, 1971.

Edwards, John. *The Arminian Doctrines Condemn'd by the Holy Scriptures, By Many of the Ancient Fathers, By the Church of England, And even by the Suffrage of Right Reason.* London, 1711.

————. *A Brief Confutation of these Two False and Dangerous Positions; Namely, I. That the Church of Rome is a True Church, and consequently that Salvation may be attained in it. II. That the Ministers of the Gospel are True and Proper Priests and have* their *True and Proper Sacrifice and Altar now on Earth*. London, 1730. In *Remains of the late Reverend and Learned John Edwards*. London, 1731.

————. *Brief Remarks upon Mr. Whiston's New Theory of the Earth And upon an Other Gentleman's Objections Against Some Passages in a Discourse of the Existence and Providence of God, Relating to the Copernican Hypothesis*. London, 1697.

————. *A Brief Vindication of the Fundamentall Articles of the Christian Faith, As Also of the Clergy, Universities and Publick Schools, from Mr. Lock's Reflections upon them in his Book of Education*. London, 1697.

————. *Cometomantia: A Discourse of Comets*. London, 1684.

————. *Crispianism Unmask'd; Or, A Discovery of the Several Erroneous Assertions, and Pernicious Doctrines Maintain'd in Dr. Crisp's Sermons, Occasion'd by the Reprinting of those Discourses*. London, 1693.

————. *A Demonstration of the Existence and Providence of God, From the Contemplation and Study of the Visible Structure of the Greater and Lesser World. In Two Parts. The First, shewing the Excellent Contrivance of the Heavens, Earth, Sea, Etc. The Second, the Wonderful Formation of the Body of Man*. London, 1696.

————. *A Discourse Concerning the Authority, Stile, and perfection of the Books of the Old and New-Testament*. London, 1693.

————. *A Discourse of Episcopacy: Wherein this Question is resolved, Whether in the Primitive Times there was a Distinct Order of Bishops different from that of Presbyters*. London, 1730. In *Remains of the late Reverend and Learned John Edwards*. London, 1731.

————. *The Divine Perfections Vindicated*. London, 1710.

————. *The Doctrine of Faith and Justification Set in a True Light. . . . Being the Second Part of the Theological Treatises, which are to compose a Large Body of Divinity*. London, 1708.

————. *The Doctrines Controverted between Papists and Protestants Particularly and Distinctly Considered*. London, 1724.

————. *An Enquiry into Four Remarkable Texts of the New Testament which Contain Difficulty in them, with a Probable Resolution of Them*. Cambridge, 1692.

————. *The Eternal and Intrinsick Reasons of Good and Evil*. Cambridge, 1699.

————. *A Farther Enquiry into Several Remarkable Texts of the Old and New Testament which contain Some Difficulty in them with a Probable Resolution of them*. London, 1692.

————. *A Free Discourse Concerning Truth and Error, Especially in Religion*. London, 1701.

————. *Great Things done by God for Our Ancestors, and Us of this Island. A Sermon Preach'd before the University of Cambridge . . . Being appointed a Day of Thanksgiving for the Deliverance from the Intended Bloody Massacre by Gunpowder and for the Happy Arrival of King William*. London, 1710.

————. *How to Judge Aright of Former and Present Times Occasion'd By the Late Happy Accession of King George to the British Throne*. London, 1714.

————. *A Letter to the Reverend Lawrence Fogg, D.D. and Dean of Chester; Wherein His Pretended Vindication of some passages in his new and Inconsistent Scheme of Divinity is Examined and Confuted*. London, 1715.

———. *One Nation and One King. A Discourse on Ezek. Xxxvii.22. Occasion'd by the Happy Union of England and Scotland.* London, 1707.

———. *Patrologia: Or A Discourse Concerning the Primitive Fathers and Antient Writers of the Christian Church.* London, 1730. In *Remains of the late Reverend and Learned John Edwards.* London, 1731.

———. *The Plague of the Heart.* Cambridge, 1665.

———. *Polupoikilos Sophia. A Compleat History or Survey of All the Dispensations and Methods of Religion, From the beginning of the World to the Consummation of all Things ... against the Cavils of the Deists.* 2 vols. London, 1699.

———. *The Preacher. A Discourse Shewing, what are the Particular Offices and Employments of those of that Character in the Church.* London, 1705.

———. *The Preacher. The Second Part.* London, 1706.

———. *The Preacher. The Third Part. Containing Farther Rules and Advices, For the Right Discharging of the Sacred Office of Preaching.* London, 1707.

———. *A Resolution of the Query, Whether The Doctrine of Non-Resistance and Passive Obedience is to be understood without any Limitation and Restriction.* London, 1730. In *Remains of the late Reverend and Learned John Edwards.* London, 1731.

———. *Sermons on Special occasions and Subjects.* London, 1698.

———. *The Socinian Creed: Or, A Brief Account of the Professed Tenents and Doctrines of the Foreign and English Socinians.* London, 1697.

———. *Socinianism Unmask'd, A Discourse Shewing the Unreasonableness of a Late Writer's Opinion concerning the Necessity of only One Article of Christian Faith; and of his other Assertions in his late Book, Entituled, The Reasonableness of Christianity.* London, 1696.

———. *Some Animadversions on Dr. Clarke's Scripture-Doctrine (as he stiles it) of the Trinity.* London, 1712.

———. *Some Brief Critical Remarks on Dr. Clarke's Last Papers.* London, 1714.

———. *Some Brief Observations and Reflections on Mr. Whiston's late Writings, Falsely Entitul'd Primitive Christianity.* London, 1712.

———. *Some New Discoveries of the Uncertainty, Deficiency, and Corruptions of Human Knowledge and Learning.* London, 1714.

———. *Some Thoughts Concerning The Several Causes and occasions of Atheism, Especially in the Present Age.* London, 1695.

———. *A Supplement to the Animadversions on Dr. Clarke's Scripture-Doctrine of the Trinity.* London, 1713.

———. *Theologia Reformata: Or the body and substance of the Christian Religion, Comprised in distinct Discourses or Treatises Upon the Apostles Creed, the Lords prayer, and the Ten Commandments.* 2 vols. London, 1713.

———. *The Time of Reformation. A Seasonable Discourse of the Effectual Means and Methods of Reforming the Lives and Manners of the whole Body of this Nation.* London, 1730. In *Remains of the late Reverend and Learned John Edwards.* London, 1731.

———. *A Treatise of Repentance.* London, 1718.

———. *Veritas Redux. Evangelical Truths Restored . . . Being the First Part of the Theological Treatises, which are to compose a large Body of Christian Divinity.* London, 1707.

Eliot, George. *Felix Holt, The Radical.* Edited by Peter Coveney. 1972. Reprint, London: Penguin Books, 1987.

———. *Middlemarch.* Edited by Gordon S. Haight. 1956, Reprint, Boston: Houghton Mifflin, 1968.

[Ellis, Clement]. *The Vanity of Scoffing.* London, 1674.

Endicott, Norman J., ed. *The Prose of Sir Thomas Browne.* Garden City, N.Y.: Doubleday, 1967.

Eyre, William. *Justification Without Conditions.* London, 1653.

Fairclough, Richard. *A Pastors Legacy, to his Beloved People: Being the Substance of Fourteen Farewel Sermons.* London, 1663.

Fotherby, Martin. *Atheomastix: clearing foure Truthes, Against Atheists and Infidels.* London, 1622.

Gale, Theophilus. *The Anatomie of Infidelitie.* London, 1672.

———. *The Court of the Gentiles: or A Discourse touching the Original of Human Literature, Both Philologie and Philosophie, from the Scriptures & Jewish Church. Part I. Of Philologie.* Second edition revised and enlarged. Oxford, 1672.

———. *The Court of the Gentiles: or A Discourse touching the Traduction of Philosophie from the Scriptures and Jewish Church. Part II. Of Barbaric and Grecanic Philosophie.* 2nd ed. enlarged. London, 1676.

———. *The Court of the Gentiles. Part III. The Vanity of Pagan Philosophie.* London, 1677.

———. *The Court of the Gentiles. Part IV. Of Reformed Philosophie.* London, 1677.

———. *The Court of the Gentiles. Part IV . . . Book 3. Of Divine Predetermination . . . With a Vindication of Calvinists.* London, 1678.

———. *A Discourse of Christ's Coming.* London, 1673.

———. *The Life and Death of Mr. John Rowe.* London, 1673.

———. *The Life and Death of Thomas Tregosse . . . and some Letters of his.* London, 1671.

———. *Philosophia Generalis, In Duas Partes Disterminata.* London, 1676.

———. "A Summary of the Two Covenants." Preface to William Strong, *A Discourse of Two Covenants.* London, 1678.

———. *Theophilie: Or, a Discourse of the Saints Amitie with God in Christ.* London, 1671.

———. *The True Idea of Jansenisme, both Historick and Dogmatick.* London, 1669.

Glanvill, Joseph. *Some Discourses, Sermons, and Remains of the Reverend Mr. Jos. Glanvill.* London, 1681.

Grotius, Hugo. *The Truth of the Christian Religion.* Translated by Simon Patrick. London, 1680.

Harrington, James. *The Stumbling-Block of Disobedience and Rebellion Cunningly imputed by P. H. unto Calvin, removed in a letter to the said P. H.* No place, 1658.

Herbert, Edward, Lord. *De Veritate.* Translated by Meyrick H. Carre. Bristol, UK: J. W. Arrowsmith, 1937.

———. *Pagan Religion: A Translation of De religione gentilium.* Edited by John Anthony Butler. Medieval and Renaissance Texts and Studies. Ottowa: Dovehouse Editions, 1996.

Heylyn, Peter. *Aerius Redivivus, or the History of the Presbyterians.* Oxford, 1670.

Holmes, Nathaniel. *The Resurrection Revealed.* London, 1653.

Hotchkis, Thomas. *An Exercitation Concerning the Nature of Forgivenesse of Sin.* London, 1655.

[Howard, Robert]. *History of Religion Written by a person of Quality.* London, 1694.

Howe, John. *The Blessedness of the Righteous Discoursed from Psal. 17, 15.* London, 1668.

————. *The Carnality of Religious Contention in Two Sermons.* London, 1693.

————. *A Funeral-Sermon for that Excellent Minister of Christ, The Truly Reverend, William Bates, D.D.* London, 1699.

————. *A Funeral Sermon for That Faithful and Laborious Servant of Christ, Mr. Richard Fairclough.* London, 1682.

————. *A Funeral Sermon on the Decease of that worthy Gentlewoman, Mrs. Margaret Baxter.* London, 1681.

————. *The Living Temple, or a Designed Improvement of that Notion, a Good Man is the Temple of God.* Part I. London, 1675.

————. *The Living Temple,* Part II, *Containing Animadversions on Spinosa, and an Account of the Destitution and Restitution of God's Temple among Men.* London, 1702.

————. *The Works of the Reverend John Howe, M.A., . . . Complete in One Volume.* London, 1834.

Humfrey, John. *The Middle Way of Predetermination Asserted.* London, 1679.

Janeway, James. *Invisibles, Realities, Demonstrated in the Holy Life and Triumphant Death of Mr. John Janeway.* London, 1673.

Jollie, Thomas. *A Vindication of the Surey Demoniack.* London, 1698.

Keach, Benjamin. *The Travels of True Godliness, From the Beginning of the World to this present Day: in an apt and Pleasant Allegory.* London, 1684.

————. *A Trumpet Blown in Zion: or An Alarm in God's Holy Mountain.* London, 1694.

Keeble, N. H., and Nuttall, Geoffrey F., eds. *Calendar of the Correspondence of Richard Baxter.* 2 vols. Oxford: Clarendon Press, 1991.

Laing, David, ed. *The Letters and Journals of Robert Baillie.* 3 vols. Edinburgh: Robert Ogle, 1841-42.

Law, William. *The Case of Reason, or Natural Religion, fairly and fully stated, in answer to a book entitled Christianity as Old as the Creation.* London, 1731.

Lee, Samuel, *Orbis Miraculum, or The Temple of Solomon.* London, 1659.

The Life and Death of that Excellent Minister of Christ Mr. Joseph Alleine. London, 1672.

Lightfoot, Robert. *Dr. Edwards's Vindication Consider'd, In a Letter to a Friend.* London, 1710.

————. *Remarks upon some passages in Dr. Edwards's Preacher, Discovering his False Reasonings and Unjust Reflection Upon his Brethren the Clergy.* London, 1709.

Locke, John. *An Essay Concerning Human Understanding.* 2 vols. Edited by Alexander Campbell Fraser. New York: Dover Publications, 1959.

————. *The Reasonableness of Christianity as delivered in the Scriptures.* Edited by John C. Higgins-Biddle. The Clarendon Edition of the Works of John Locke. Oxford: Clarendon Press, 1999.

Marshall, Walter. *The Gospel-Mystery of Sanctification.* London, 1692.

Matar, N. I., ed. *Peter Sterry: Select Writings.* University of Kansas Humanistic Studies. New York: Peter Lang, 1994.

Mather, Cotton. *Manductio ad Ministerium: Directions for a Candidate of the Ministry,
Reproduced from the Original Edition Boston, 1726*. The Facsimile Text Society. New
York: Columbia University Press, 1938.

Milton, John. *Paradise Lost*. Edited by Merritt Y. Hughes. New York: Odyssey Press, 1935.

———. *Paradise Regained, The Minor Poems, and Samson Agonistes*. Edited by Merritt
Y. Hughes. Indianapolis, Ind.: Odyssey Press, 1937.

———. *The Works of John Milton*. Vol. 6, *English Political Tracts*. Edited by William
Haller and Frank Allen Patterson. New York: Columbia University Press, 1932.

More, Henry. *An Antidote against Atheisme*. London, 1653.

———. *Conjectura Cabalistica. Or a conjectural Essay of interpreting the Minde of Moses,
according to a Threefold Cabala*. London, 1653.

———. *Enthusiasmus Triumphatus*. 1662. Facsimile Reprint, William Andrews Clark
Memorial Library Publication Number 118. Los Angeles, 1966.

Mornay, Phillipe de. *A Work Concerning the Trewnesse of the Christian Religion*.
Translated by Philip Sidney. London, 1587.

Newton, George. *A Sermon Preached at the Funeral of Mr. Joseph Alleine*. London, 1672.

Norman, John. *Cases of Conscience Practically Resolved*. London, 1673.

Norton, John. *Abel Being Dead yet Speaketh: A Biography of John Cotton*. Facsimile
Reproduction with an Introduction by Edward J. Gallagher. Delmar, N.Y.:
Scholars' Facsimiles & Reprints, 1978.

Nye, Stephen. *The Agreement of the Unitarians, with the Catholick Church*. No place, 1697.

Owen, John. *Animadversions on a Treatise Entitled Fiat Lux*. In *The Works of John Owen*,
edited by W. H. Goold. Vol. 14, pp. 2–172. London, 1851.

———. *Of the Death of Christ, the Price he paid, and the Purchase he made*. London, 1650.

———. *Of the Divine Originall, Authority, self-evidencing Light and Power of the
Scriptures*. Oxford, 1659.

———. *Of Toleration and the Duty of the Magistrate About Religion*. London, 1649.

———. *Theologoumena Pantodapa, sive de natura, Ortu, Progressu et Studio verae
Theologiae*. London, 1661.

———. *Vindication of the Animadversion on Fiat Lux*. In *The Works of John Owen*,
edited by W. H. Goold. Vol. 14, pp. 174–480. London, 1851.

Parker, Samuel. *A Free and Impartial Censure of the Platonick Philosophie*. London, 1666.

Petit, Norman, ed. *The Life of David Brainerd. The Works of Jonathan Edwards*. Vol. 7.
New Haven, Conn.: Yale University Press, 1985.

*A Plea for the Late Accurate and Excellent Mr. Baxter, and those that speak of the Suffering
of Christ as he does. In Answer to Mr. Lobb's insinuated charge of Socinianism Against
'em, in his late Appeal to the Bishop of Worcester, and Dr. Edwards*. London, 1699.

Polhill, Edward. *An Answer to the Discourse of Mr. William Sherlock*. London, 1675.

Reynolds, Henry. *Mythomystes*. 1632. Reprint, Menston, Yorkshire, UK: Scolars
Press, 1972.

Rous, Francis. *Treatises and Meditations Dedicated to the Saints, and to the Excellent
throughout the three Nations*. London, 1657.

Rudrum, Alan, ed. *The Works of Thomas Vaughan*. Oxford: Clarendon Press, 1984.

Smith, Henry. *Gods Arrow Against Atheists*. London, 1604.

[Stephens, William]. *An Account of the Growth of Deism in England*. 1696. Facsimile Reprint, William Andrews Clark Memorial Library Publication Number 261. Los Angeles, 1990.

Sterry, Peter. *The Appearance of God to Man in the Gospel*. London, 1710.

——. *The Clouds in Which Christ Comes*. London, 1648.

——. *The Comings Forth of Christ in the Power of his Death*. London, 1650.

——. *A Discourse on the Freedom of the Will*. London, 1675.

——. *England's Deliverance from the Northern Presbytery Compared with its Deliverance from the Roman Papacy*. London, 1652.

——. *The Rise, Race, and Royalty of the Kingdom of God*. London, 1683.

——. *The Spirit Convincing of Sinne*. London, 1646.

——. *The Teachings of Christ in the Soule*. London, 1648.

——. *The Way of God with his People in these Nations*. London, 1657.

Stillingfleet, Edward. *A Letter to a Deist, in answer to several Objections Against the Truth and Authority of the Scriptures*. London, 1677.

——. *Origenes Sacrae, Or A Rational Account of the Grounds of Christian Faith*. London, 1662.

Taylor, Zachary. *Popery, Superstition, Ignorance and Knavery confess'd and fully proved upon the Surey Dissenters*. London, 1699.

——. *Popery, Superstition, Ignorance and Knavery very fully proved upon the Dissenters*. London, 1698.

Thuesen, Peter J., ed. *Catalogues of Books. The Works of Jonathan Edwards*. Vol. 26. New Haven, Conn.: Yale University Press, 2008.

Toland, John. *Christianity Not Mysterious, Or a Treatise Shewing, That there is nothing in the Gospel Contrary to Reason, nor Above it: and that no Christian Doctrine can be properly call'd a Mystery*. London, 1696.

Toplady, Augustus. *The Church of England Vindicated from the charge of Arminianism*. London, 1769.

——. *Historic Proof of the Doctrinal Calvinism of the Church of England*. London, 1793.

Tourneur, Cyril. *The Atheist's Tragedie: or the Honest Man's Revenge*. London, 1611.

Travers, Walter. *An Answer to a Supplicatorie Epistle of G. T.* London, 1583.

Trench, Edmund. *Some Remarkable Passages in the Holy Life and Death of the late Reverend Mr. Edmund Trench; Most of them drawn out of his own Diary*. London, 1693.

Trosse, George. *The Life of the Reverend Mr. George Trosse, Written by himself, and Published Posthumously According to his Order in 1714*. Edited by A. W. Brink. Montreal and London: McGill-Queens's University Press, 1974.

Turner, G. Lyon, ed. *Original Records of Early Nonconformity*. Vol. 1. London: T. F. Unwin, 1911.

Vincent, Nathaniel, ed. *The Morning Exercises Against Popery*. London, 1675.

Ward, Seth. *A Philosophical Essay Towards an Eviction of the Being and Attributes of God*. Oxford, 1652.

Whitby, Daniel. *A Discourse Concerning: I. The true Import of the Words Election and Reprobation . . . II. The extent of Christ's Redemption. III. The grace of God . . . IV. The liberty of the will . . . V. The Perseverance or defectibility of the Saints*. London, 1710.

————. *A Paraphrase and Commentary on the New Testament.* 2 vols. 2nd ed.
London, 1706.

————. *A Treatise of Traditions.* Part I. London, 1688.

White, Jeremiah. *The Restoration of All Things.* London, 1712.

Whitefield, George. *A Letter to the Reverend Mr. John Wesley: in Answer to a Sermon, Entituled, Free-Grace.* London, 1741.

Wilkins, John. *Of the Principles and Duties of Natural Religion.* London, 1678.

Wolseley, Charles. *The Reasonableness of Scripture Belief.* 1672. Reprint, Delmar, N.Y.: Scholars Facsimiles and Reprints, 1973.

SECONDARY SOURCES

Achinstein, Sharon. *Literature and Dissent in Milton's England.* Cambridge: Cambridge University Press, 2003.

Allison, C. F. *The Rise of Moralism: The Proclamation of the Gospel from Hooker to Baxter.* London: S.P.C.K., 1966.

Almond, Philip C. *Heaven and Hell in Enlightenment England.* Cambridge: Cambridge University Press, 1994.

Armstrong, Bryan G. *Calvinism and the Amyraux Heresy: Protestant Scholasticism and Humanism in Seventeenth-Century France.* Madison: University of Wisconsin Press, 1969.

Ashcraft, Richard. "Latitudinarianism and Toleration: Historical Myth Versus Political History." In *Philosophy, Science, and Religion in England, 1640–1700,* edited by Richard Kroll, Richard Ashcraft, and Perez Zagorin, pp. 151–77. Cambridge: Cambridge University Press, 1992.

Atkin, Nicholas, and Frank Tallett. *Priests, Prelates and People: A History of European Catholicism Since 1750.* Oxford: Oxford University Press, 2003.

Aylmer, G. E. "Unbelief in Seventeenth-Century England." In *Puritans and Revolutionaries: Essays in Seventeenth-Century History Presented to Christopher Hill,* edited by Donald Pennington and Keith Thomas, pp. 22–46. Oxford: Clarendon Press, 1978.

Backus, Irena. "The Fathers and Calvinist Orthodoxy." In Backus, *Reception.* Vol. 2, pp. 839–65.

————. "Ulrich Zwingli, Martin Bucer, and the Church Fathers." In Backus, *Reception.* Vol. 2, pp. 628–60.

Baker, J. W. *Heinrich Bullinger and the Covenant: The Other Reformed Tradition.* Athens, Ohio: Ohio University Press, 1980.

Barker, John. *Strange Contrarieties: Pascal in England During the Age of Reason.* Montreal: McGill-Queen's University Press, 1975.

Barth, Karl. *The Word of God and the Word of Man.* 1928. Reprint, New York: Harper and Brothers, 1957.

Bebbington, David. *Evangelicalism in Modern Britain: A History from the 1730s to the 1980s.* London: Unwin Hyman, 1989.

Becker, Carl L. *The Heavenly City of the Eighteenth-Century Philosophers.* New Haven, Conn.: Yale University Press, 1932.

Beeke, Joel. *Assurance of Faith: Calvin, English Puritanism, and the Dutch Second Reformation*. New York: Peter Lang, 1991.

Benedict, Philip. *Christ's Churches Purely Reformed: A Social History of Calvinism*. New Haven, Conn.: Yale University Press, 2002.

———. *The Faith and Fortunes of France's Huguenots, 1600–1685*. Aldershot, UK: Ashgate, 2001.

Berg, Johannes van den. *Religious Currents and Cross-Currents: Essays on Early Modern Protestantism and the Protestant Enlightenment*. Edited by Jan de Bruijn, Pieter Holtrop, and Ernestine van der Wall. Leiden, the Netherlands: Brill, 1999.

Berger, Peter. *The Heretical Imperative: Contemporary Possibilities of Religious Affirmation*. Garden City, N.J.: Anchor Press/Doubleday, 1979.

Berman, David. *A History of Atheism in Britain: From Hobbes to Russell*. London: Croom and Helm, 1988.

Bethell, S. L. *The Cultural Revolution of the Seventeenth Century*. London: Dennis Dobson, 1951.

Boer, Wietse de. "Calvin and Borromeo, A Comparative Approach to Social Discipline." In *Early Modern Catholicism: Essays in Honour of John W. O'Malley, S. J.*, edited by Cathleen M. Comerford and Hilmar M. Pabel, pp. 85–95. Toronto: University of Toronto Press, 2001.

Bolam, C. G., Jeremy Goring, H. L. Short, and Roger Thomas. *The English Presbyterians: From Elizabethan Puritansim to Modern Unitarianism*. Boston: Beacon Press, 1968.

Bouwsma, William J. *John Calvin: A Sixteenth-Century Portrait*. Oxford: Oxford University Press, 1988.

———. *A Usable Past: Essays in European Cultural History*. Berkeley: University of California Press, 1990.

———. *The Waning of the Renaissance, 1550–1640*. New Haven, Conn.: Yale University Press, 2000.

Bouyer, Louis. *Orthodox, Protestant, and Anglican Spirituality*. London: Burns and Oates, 1969.

Boyle, Marjorie O'Rourke. *Christening Pagan Mysteries: Erasmus in Pursuit of Wisdom*. Toronto: University of Toronto Press, 1981.

Bozeman, Dwight. "Forum: Neglected Resources in Scholarship." *Religion and American Life: A Journal of Interpretation* 7 (Winter 1997): 14–20.

———. *The Precisianist Strain: Disciplinary Religion & Antinomian Backlash in Puritanism to 1638*. Chapel Hill: University of North Carolina Press, 2004.

Brauer, Jerald C. "Types of Puritan Piety." *CH* 56 (March 1987): 39–58.

Brautigan, Dwight. "Prelates and Politics: Uses of 'Puritan,' 1625–40." In *Puritanism and Its Discontents*, edited by Laura Lunger Knoppers, pp. 49–66. Newark, Del.: University of Delaware Press, 2003.

Bredvold, Louis I. *The Intellectual Milieu of John Dryden*. Ann Arbor: University of Michigan Press, 1934.

Bremer, Francis. *Congregational Communion: Clerical Friendship in the Anglo-American Puritan Community, 1610–1692*. Boston: Northeastern University Press, 1994.

Briggs, Robin. "The Catholic Puritans: Jansenists and Rigorists in France." In *Puritans and Revolutionaries: Essays in Seventeenth-Century History presented to Christopher Hill*, edited by Donald Pennington and Keith Thomas, pp. 333–54. Oxford: Clarendon Press, 1978.

Brydon, Michael. *The Evolving Reputation of Richard Hooker: An Examination of Responses, 1600–1714*. Oxford: Oxford University Press, 2006.

Buckley, Michael J., S. J. *At the Origins of Modern Atheism*. New Haven, Conn.: Yale University Press, 1987.

Burkert, Walter. *Greek Religion*. Cambridge, Mass.: Harvard University Press, 1985.

Bynum, Caroline Walker. *Jesus as Mother: Studies in the Spirituality of the High Middle Ages*. Berkeley: University of California Press, 1982.

Campbell, Ted A. *The Religion of the Heart*. Columbia: University of South Carolina Press, 1991.

Carpenter, Edward. *The Protestant Bishop, Being the Life and Times of Henry Compton, 1632–1713, Bishop of London*. London: Longmans, 1956.

Cerny, Gerard. *Theology, Politics and Letters at the Crossroads of European Civilization: Jacques Basnage and the Baylean Huguenot Refugees in the Dutch Republic*. Dordrecht, the Netherlands: Martin Nijhoff, 1987.

Champion, J. A. I. *The Pillars of Priestcraft Shaken: The Church of England and Its Enemies, 1660–1730*. Cambridge: Cambridge University Press, 1992.

Chappell, Warren. *A Short History of the Printed Word*. New York: Dorset Press, 1970.

Clark, J. C. D. *English Society, 1688–1832*. Cambridge: Cambridge University Press, 1985.

———. *The Language of Liberty 1660–1832*. Cambridge: Cambridge University Press, 1994.

Clarke, M. L. *Paley: Evidences for the Man*. Toronto: University of Toronto Press, 1974.

Clebsch, William A. *England's Earliest Protestants, 1520–1535*. New Haven, Conn.: Yale University Press, 1964.

Clements, Arthur L. *The Poetry of Contemplation: John Donne, George Herbert, Henry Vaughan, and the Modern Period*. Albany: State University of New York Press, 1990.

Cliffe, J. T. *Puritans in Conflict: The Puritan Gentry During and After the Civil Wars*. London: Routledge, 1988.

Clifford, Alan C. *Atonement and Justification: English Evangelical Theology, 1640–1790, An Evaluation*. Oxford: Clarendon Press, 1990.

Coady, C. A. J. "The Socinian Connection—Further Thoughts on the Religion of Hobbes." *Religious Studies* 22 (June 1986): 277–80.

Coffey, John. *Politics, Religion and the British Revolutions: The Mind of Samuel Rutherford*. Cambridge: Cambridge University Press, 1997.

Cohen, Charles Lloyd. *God's Caress: The Psychology of Puritan Religious Experience*. Oxford: Oxford University Press, 1986.

Cohen, I. Bernard, ed. *Puritanism and the Rise of Modern Science: The Merton Thesis*. New Brunswick, N.J.: Rutgers University Press, 1990.

Coleridge, Samuel Taylor. *Notes on English Divines*. Edited by Derwent Coleridge. 2 vols. London, 1853.

Colgar, Anne. *Impolite Learning: Conduct and Continuity in the Republic of Letters, 1680–1750*. New Haven, Conn.: Yale University Press, 1995.

Collinson, Patrick. "England and International Calvinism." In *International Calvinism, 1541–1715*, edited by Menna Prestwich, pp. 197–224. Oxford: Clarendon Press, 1985.

———. *The Religion of Protestants: The Church in English Society, 1559–1625*. Oxford: Oxford University Press, 1982.

Como, David R. *Blown by the Spirit: Puritanism and the Emergence of an Antinomian Underground in Pre-Civil-War England*. Stanford, Calif.: Stanford University Press, 2004.

———. "Puritans, Predestination and the Construction of Orthodoxy in Early Seventeenth-Century England." In *Conformity and Orthodoxy in the English Church, c 1560–1660*, edited by Peter Lake and Michael Questier, pp. 34–87. Woodbridge, UK: Boydell Press, 2000.

Cooper, Tim. *Fear and Polemic in Seventeenth-Century England: Richard Baxter and Antinomianism*. Aldershot, UK: Ashgate, 2001.

Copenhaver, Brian P. "Natural Magic, Hermetism, and Occultism in Early Modern Science." In *Reappraisals of the Scientific Revolution*, edited by David C. Lindberg and Robert S. Westman, pp. 260–301. Cambridge: Cambridge University Press, 1990.

Coudert, Allison P. "Henry More, the Kabbalah, and the Quakers." In *Philosophy, Science, and Religion in England, 1640–1700*, edited by Richard Kroll, Richard Ashcraft, and Perez Zagorin, pp. 31–67. Cambridge: Cambridge University Press, 1992.

Cragg, Gerald R. *The Cambridge Platonists*. Oxford: Oxford University Press, 1968.

———. *From Puritanism to the Age of Reason: A Study of Changes in Religious Thought Within the Church of England, 1660–1700*. Cambridge: Cambridge University Press, 1950.

———. *Puritanism in the Period of the Great Persecution, 1660–1688*. Cambridge: Cambridge University Press, 1957.

Crocker, Robert. *Henry More, 1614–1687: A Biography of the Cambridge Platonist*. Dordrecht,Boston, and London: Kluwer Academic, 2003.

Culianu, Ioan Petru, and Cicerone Poghirc. "Zalmoxis." In *The Encyclopedia of Religion*. Edited by Mircea Eliade. 16 vols.; vol. 15, pp. 551-54. New York: MacMillan, 1987.

Dale, R. W. *History of English Congregationalism*. London: Hodder and Stoughton, 1907.

Damrosch, Leopold, Jr. "Hobbes as Reformation Theologian: Implications of the Free-Will Controversy." *Journal of the History of Ideas* 40 (July–September 1979): 339–52.

Davie, Donald. *A Gathered Church: The Literature of the English Dissenting Interest, 1700–1930*. New York: Oxford University Press, 1978.

DeKrey, Gary S. "Reformation in the Restoration Crisis, 1679–1682." In *Religion, Literature, and Politics in Post-Reformation England, 1540–1688*, edited by Donna, B. Hamilton and Richard Strier, pp. 231–52. Cambridge: Cambridge University Press, 1996.

Dever, Mark E. *Richard Sibbes: Puritansim and Calvinism in Late Elizabethan and Early Stuart England*. Macon, Ga.: Mercer University Press, 2000.

Dobbs, B. J. T. "Newton's Commentary on the Emerald Tablet of Hermes Trismegistus: Its Scientific and Theological Significance." In *Hermeticism and the Renaissance: Intellectual History and the Occult in Early Modern Europe*, edited by Ingrid Merkel and Allen G. Debus, pp. 182–91. Washington, D.C.: Folger Shakespeare Library, 1988.

Dockrill, D. W. "The Authority of the Fathers in the Great Trinitarian Debates of the Sixteen Nineties." *Studia Patristica* 18 (1990): 335–47.

———. "The Fathers and the Theology of the Cambridge Platonists." *Studia Patristica* 17 (1982): 427–39.

Donnelly, John Patrick. *Calvinism and Scholasticism in Vermigli's Doctrine of Man and Grace*. Leiden, the Netherlands: E. J. Brill, 1976.

Dowey, Edward A., Jr. *The Knowledge of God in Calvin's Theology*. New York: Columbia University Press, 1952.

Duffy, Eamon. "The Long Reformation: Catholicism, Protestantism, and the Multitude." In *England's Long Reformation 1500–1800*, edited by Nicholas Tyacke, pp. 33–69. London: UCL Press, 1998.

Duke, Alastair, Gilian Lewis, and Andrew Pettegree, eds. *Calvinism in Europe, 1540–1620*. Cambridge: Cambridge University Press, 1994.

Eisenstein, Elizabeth. *The Printing Press as an Agent of Change*. 2 vols. in 1. London: Cambridge University Press, 1979.

Ellis, Joseph J. *The New England Mind in Transition: Samuel Johnson of Connecticut, 1696–1772*. New Haven, Conn.: Yale University Press, 1973.

English, John C. "The Duration of the Primitive Church: An Issue for Seventeenth and Eighteenth-Century Anglicans." *Anglican and Episcopal History* 73 (March 2004): 35–51.

———. "John Hutchinson's Critique of Newtonian Orthodoxy." *CH* 68 (September 1999): 561–97.

Febvre, Lucien. *The Problem of Unbelief in the Sixteenth Century: The Religion of Rabelais*. Translated by Beatrice Gottlieb. Cambridge, Mass.: Harvard University Press, 1982.

Ferguson, Arthur B. *Utter Antiquity: Perceptions of Prehistory in Renaissance England*. Durham, N.C: Duke University Press, 1993.

Ferrell, Lorrie Anne. *Government by Polemic: James I, The King's Preachers, and the Rhetoric of Conformity, 1603–1625*. Stanford, Calif.: Stanford University Press, 1998.

Field, David P. *"Rigide Calvinisme in a Softer Dresse:" The Moderate Presbyterianism of John Howe (1630–1705)*. Edinburgh: Rutherford House, 2004.

Fiering, Norman. *Moral Philosophy at Seventeenth-Century Harvard*. Chapel Hill: University of North Carolina Press, 1981.

Frei, Hans. *The Eclipse of Biblical Narrative: A Study in Eighteenth and Nineteenth Century Hermeneutics*. New Haven, Conn.: Yale University Press, 1974.

French, Peter. *John Dee: The World of an Elizabethan Magus*. 1972. Reprint, New York: Dorset Press, 1989.

Friedman, Jerome. *The Most Ancient Testimony: Sixteenth-Century Christian Hebraica in the Age of Renaissance Nostalgia.* Athens, Ohio: Ohio University Press, 1983.

Furey, Constance. *Erasmus, Contarini, and the Religious Republic of Letters.* Cambridge: Cambridge University Press, 2006.

Gardiner, Samuel. *History of the Commonwealth and Protectorate, 1649–1656.* Vol. 2. London: Longmans, 1903.

Garin, Eugenio. "Gian Francesco Pico Della Mirandola: Savonarolan Apologetics and the Critque of Ancient Thought." In *Christianity and the Renaissance: Image and Religious Imagination in the Quattrocento,* edited by Timothy Verdon and John Henderson, pp. 522–32. Syracuse, N.Y.: Syracuse University Press, 1990.

Garnard, Leslie W. "The Use of the Patristic Tradition in the late Seventeenth and Early Eighteenth Centuries." In *Scripture, Tradition, and Reason: A Study in the Criteria of Christian Doctrine, Essays in Honour of Richard P. C. Hanson,* edited by Richard Bauckham and Benjamin Drewery, pp. 174–203. Edinburgh: T and T Clark, 1988.

Gascoigne, John. *Cambridge in the Age of Enlightenment:Science, Religion, and Politics from the Restoration to the French Revolution.* Cambridge: Cambridge University Press, 1989.

Gay, Peter. *The Enlightenment: An Interpretation.* Vol. 1, *The Rise of Modern Paganism.* New York: Alfred Knopf, 1967. Vol. 2, *The Science of Freedom.* New York: Alfred Knopf, 1969.

Gerrish, B. A. *Grace and Gratitude: The Eucharistic Theology of John Calvin.* Minneapolis, Minn.: Fortress Press, 1993.

Gibbons, B. J. *Gender in Mystical and Occult Thought: Behmenism and Its Development in England.* Cambridge: Cambridge University Press, 1966.

Gibson, William. *The Church of England, 1688–1832.* London and New York: Routledge, 2001.

Gillespie, Charles Coulton. *Genesis and Geology: The Impact of Scientific Discoveries Upon Religious Beliefs in the Decades Before Darwin.* 1951. Reprint New York: Harper and Row, 1959.

Glover, Willis B. "God and Thomas Hobbes." *CH* 29 (September 1960): 275–97.

Godwin, Joscelyn. *Athanasius Kircher: A Renaissance Man and the Quest for Lost Knowledge.* London: Thames and Hudson, 1979.

Goldie, Mark. "Danby, the Bishops and the Whigs." In *The Politics of Religion in Restoration England,* edited by Tim Harris, Paul Seaward, and Mark Goldie, pp. 75–106. Oxford: Basil Blackwell, 1990.

———. "The Theory of Religious Intolerance in Restoration England." In *From Persecution to Toleration: The Glorious Revolution in England,* edited by Ole Peter Grell, Jonathan I. Israel, and Nicholas Tyacke, pp. 331–68. Oxford: Clarendon Press, 1991.

Gombrich, E. H. *Symbolic Images: Studies in the Art of the Renaissance.* London: Phaidon, 1975.

Gordon, Bruce. "Heinrich Bullinger." In *The Reformation Theologians,* edited by Carter Lindberg, pp. 170–83. Oxford: Blackwell, 2002.

Grafton, Anthony. *Defenders of the Text: The Tradition of Scholarship in an Age of Science, 1450–1800.* Cambridge: Harvard University Press, 1991.

———. *Joseph Scaliger: A Study in the History of Classical Scholarship.* 2 vols. Oxford: Clarendon Press, 1983, 1993.

Grant, Robert. *Gnosticism and Early Christianity.* Rev. ed. New York: Harper and Row, 1966.

Greaves, Richard. *Deliver Us From Evil: The Radical Underground in Britain, 1660–1663.* New York: Oxford University Press, 1986.

———. *Enemies Under His Feet: Radicals and Nonconformists in Britain, 1664–1677.* Stanford, Calif.: Stanford University Press, 1990.

———. *Glimpses of Glory: John Bunyan and English Dissent.* Stanford, Calif.: Stanford University Press, 2002.

———. *Secrets of the Kingdom: British Radicals from the Popish Plot to the Revolution of 1688–1689.* Stanford, Calif.: Stanford University Press, 1992.

Green, Ian. *The Christian's ABC: Catechisms and Catechizing in England, c. 1530–1740.* Oxford: Clarendon Press, 1996.

———. *Print and Protestantism in Early Modern England.* Oxford: Oxford University Press, 2000.

Greenslade, S. L. *The English Reformers and the Fathers of the Church.* Oxford: Oxford University Press, 1960.

Griffin, Martin I. J., Jr. *Latitudinarianism in the Seventeenth-Century Church of England.* Leiden, the Netherlands: Brill, 1992.

Griggs, Burke W. "Remembering the Puritan Past: John Walker and Anglican Memories of the English Civil War." In *Protestant Identities: Religion, Society and Self-Fashioning in Post-Reformation England,* edited by Muriel McClendon, Joseph P. Ward, and Michael MacDonald, pp. 158–91. Stanford, Calif.: Stanford University Press, 1999.

Haig, C. A. *John Howe.* London: Independent Press, 1961.

Haight, Gordon. *George Eliot: A Biography.* 1968. Reprint, New York: Penguin Books, 1985.

Hall, Basil. "Calvin Against the Calvinists." In *John Calvin: A Collection of Distinguished Essays,* edited by Gervase E. Duffield, pp. 19–37. Grand Rapids, Mich.: Eerdmans, 1966.

Haller, William. *The Rise of Puritanism.* New York: Columbia University Press, 1938.

Hambrick-Stowe, Charles E. *The Practice of Piety: Puritan Devotional Disciplines in Seventeenth-Century New England.* Chapel Hill: University of North Carolina Press, 1982.

Hampton, Stephen. *Anti-Arminians: The Anglican Reformed Tradition from Charles II to George I.* Oxford: Oxford University Press, 2008.

Harnack, Adolf. *History of Dogma.* Translated by Neil Buchanan. 7 vols. in 4. 1896–99. Reprint, New York: Dover Publications, 1961.

Harris, Tim. "Introduction: Revising the Restoration." In *The Politics of Religion in Restoration England,* edited by Tim Harris, Paul Seaward, and Mark Goldie, pp. 1–28. Oxford: Basil Blackwell, 1990.

Harrison, Peter. *Protestantism, the Bible, and Science*. Cambridge: Cambridge University Press, 1998.

———. *"Religion" and the Religions in the English Enlightenment*. Cambridge: Cambridge University Press, 1990.

Haugaard, William P. "Renaissance Patristic Scholarship and Theology in Sixteenth-Century England." *SCJ* 10 (Fall 1979): 37–60.

Hazard, Paul. *The European Mind: 1685–1715*. Translated by J. Lewis May. 1952. Reprint, Cleveland, Ohio: World Publishing, 1963.

Headley, John. *Tommaso Campanella and the Transformation of the World*. Princeton, N.J.: Princeton University Press, 1997.

Heering, J. P. *Hugo Grotius as Apologist for the Christian Religion: A Study of His Work De Veritate Religionis Christianae*. Leiden, the Netherlands: Brill, 2004.

Hendrix, Scott H. "Deparentifying the Fathers: The Reformers and Patristic Authority." In *Auctoritas Patrum: Zur Rezeption der Kirchenvater im 15 und 16 Jahrhundert*, edited by Leif Grane, Alfred Schindler, and Markus Wriedt, pp. 55–68. Mainz, Germany: Verlag Philipp Von Zabern, 1993.

Hill, Christopher. *Antichrist in Seventeenth-Century England*. London: Oxford University Press, 1971.

———. *Change and Continuity in Seventeenth-Century England*. Cambridge, Mass.: Harvard University Press, 1975.

———. *The English Bible and the Seventeenth-Century Revolution*. London: Penguin Books, 1994.

———. *The Experience of Defeat: Milton and Some Contemporaries*. New York: Viking Penguin, 1984.

———. *A Tinker and a Poor Man: John Bunyan and His Church, 1628–1688*. New York: Norton, 1988.

Hindmarsh, D. Bruce. *The Evangelical Conversion Narrative: Spiritual Autobiography in Early Modern England*. Oxford: Oxford University Press, 2005.

———. *John Newton and the English Evangelical Tradition*. Grand Rapids, Mich.: Eerdmans, 1996.

Hippeau, C. "Bochart (Samuel)," *Nouvelle Biographie Generale*. Vol. 6: cols. 304-7. Paris, 1855.

Holmes, Geoffrey. *Politics, Religion and Society in England, 1679–1742*. London: Hambledon Press, 1986.

Hotson, Howard. *Johann Heinrich Alsted, 1588–1638: Between Renaissance, Reformation, and Universal Reform*. Oxford: Clarendon Press, 2000.

Howe, Daniel Walker. "The Cambridge Platonists of Old England and the Cambridge Platonists of New England." *CH* 57 (December 1988): 470–85.

———. "The Decline of Calvinism: An Approach to its Study." *Studies in Society and History* 14 (June 1942): 306–27.

Hsia, R. Po-Chia. *Social Discipline in the Reformation: Central Europe 1550–1750*. London and New York: Routledge, 1989.

Hudson, Elizabeth. "The Catholic Challenge to Puritan Piety, 1580–1620." *Catholic Historical Review* 77 (January 1991): 1–20.

Hughes, Ann. "Popular Presbyterianism in the 1640s and 1650s: The Cases of Thomas Edwards and Thomas Hall." In *England's Long Reformation, 1500–1800,* edited by Nicholas Tyacke, pp. 235–59. London: UCL Press, 1998.

Hunt, Lynn, Margaret C. Jacob, and Wijnand Mijnhardt. *The Book That Changed Europe: Picart and Bernard's Religious Ceremonies of the World.* Cambridge, Mass.: Belknap Press of Harvard University Press, 2010.

Hunter, Michael. "The Problem of Atheism in Early Modern England." *Transactions of the Royal Historical Society,* 5th ser., 35 (1985): 135–57.

Hutin, Serge. *Les Disciples Anglais de Jacob Boehme aux XVIIe et XVIIIe siecles.* Paris: Editions Denoel, 1960.

———. *Henry More: Essai sur les doctrines theosophique chez les Platoniciens de Cambridge.* Hildesheim, Germany: Georg Olms, 1966.

Hutton, Sarah. "Edward Stillingfleet, Henry More, and the Decline of Moses Atticus: A Note on Seventeenth-Century Anglican Apologetics." In *Philosophy, Science, and Religion in England, 1640–1700,* edited by Richard Kroll, Richard Ashcraft, and Perez Zagorin, pp. 68–83. Cambridge: Cambridge University Press, 1992.

———. "Thomas Jackson, Oxford Platonist, and William Twisse, Aristotelian." *JHI* 39 (October–December 1978): 635–52.

Ihalainen, Pasi. *Protestant Nations Redefined: Changing Perceptions of National Identity in the Rhetoric of the English, Dutch, and Swedish Churches, 1685–1772.* Leiden, the Netherlands: Brill, 2005.

Inge, W. R. *Christian Mysticism.* 1899. Reprint, New York: Meridian Books, 1956.

Israel, Jonathan I. *The Dutch Republic: Its Rise, Greatness, and Fall 1477–1806.* Oxford: Clarendon Press, 1995.

———. *Enlightenment Contested: Philosophy, Modernity, and the Emancipation of Man, 1670–1752.* Oxford: Oxford University Press, 2006.

———. *Radical Enlightenment: Philosophy and the Making of Modernity, 1650–1750.* Oxford: Oxford University Press, 2001.

———. "William III and Toleration." In *From Persecution to Toleration: The Glorious Revolution and Religion in England,* edited by Ole Peter Grell, Jonathan I. Israel, and Nicholas Tyacke, pp. 129–70. Oxford: Clarendon Press, 1991.

Iverson, Erik. *The Myth of Egypt and Its Hieroglyphs in European Tradition.* 1961. Reprint, Princeton, N.J.: Princeton University Press, 1993.

Jacob, James R. *Henry Stubbe, Radical Protestantism and the Early Enlightenment.* Cambridge: Cambridge University Press, 1983.

Jacob, Margaret. *The Newtonians and the English Revolution, 1689–1720.* Ithaca, N.Y.: Cornell University Press, 1976.

Jeffrey, David Lyle. "Jacob's Ladder." In *A Dictionary of Biblical Tradition in English Literature,* edited by David Lyle Jeffrey, pp. 388-90. Grand Rapids, Mich.: William B. Eerdmans, 1992.

Jeremiah, Jeffrey. "Edward Reynolds (1599–1676): 'Pride of the Presbyterian Party.' " Ph.D. Dissertation, George Washington University, 1992.

Jones, Norman. *The English Reformation: Religion and Cultural Adaptation.* Oxford: Blackwell, 2002.

Jones, R. Tudur. "The Heavenly Herb and the Rose of Love: The Piety of Two Welsh Puritans." In *Reformation, Conformity, and Dissent: Essays in Honour of Geoffrey Nuttall,* edited by R. Buick Knox, pp. 154-79. London: Epworth Press, 1977.

Jones, Richard Foster. *Ancients and Moderns: A Study of the Background of the Battle of the Books.* St. Louis, Mo.: Washington University Studies, New Series, Language and Literature 6, 1936.

Jones, Rufus M. *Mysticism and Democracy in the English Commonwealth.* Cambridge, Mass.: Harvard University Press, 1932.

———. *Spiritual Reformers in the Sixteenth and Seventeenth Centuries.* 1914. Reprint, Boston: Beacon Press, 1959.

Kaufman, Peter Iver. *Prayer, Despair, and Drama: Elizabethan Introspection.* Urbana: University of Illinois Press, 1996.

Kaufmann, U. Milo. *The Pilgrim's Progress and Traditions in Puritan Meditation.* New Haven, Conn.: Yale University Press, 1966.

Keeble, N. H. *The Literary Culture of Nonconformity in Later Seventeenth-Century England.* No place: Leicester University Press, 1987.

———. *The Restoration: England in the 1660s.* Oxford: Blackwell, 2002.

———. *Richard Baxter: Puritan Man of Letters.* Oxford: Clarendon Press, 1982.

Kieckhefer, Richard. "Convention and Conversion: Patterns in Late Medieval Piety." *CH* 67 (March 1998): 32–51.

Klauber, Martin I. *Between Scholasticism and Pan-Protestantism: Jean Alphonse Turretin (1671–1737) and Enlightened Orthodoxy at the Academy of Geneva.* Selinsgrove, Pa.: Susquehanna University Press, 1994.

Knight, Janice. *Orthodoxies in Massachusetts: Rereading American Puritanism.* Cambridge, Mass.: Harvard University Press, 1994.

Kolb, Robert. *For All the Saints: Changing Perceptions of Martyrdom and Sainthood in the Lutheran Reformation.* Macon, Ga.: Mercer University Press, 1987.

Labrousee, Elisabeth. *Bayle.* Translated by Denys Potts. Oxford: Oxford University Press, 1983.

Lake, Peter. "Defining Puritanism—Again?" In *Puritanism: Transatlantic Perspectives on a Seventeenth-Century Anglo-American Faith,* edited by Francis J. Bremer, pp. 3–29. Boston: Massachusetts Historical Society, 1993.

———. *Moderate Puritans and the Elizabethan Church.* Cambridge: Cambridge University Press, 1982.

———. "Serving God and the Times: The Calvinist Conformity of Robert Sanderson." *Journal of British Studies* 27 (April 1988): 81–116.

Lamont, William. *Puritanism and Historical Controversy.* London: UCL Press, 1996.

———. "Review of Hans Boersma, *A Hot Pepper Corn: Richard Baxter's Doctrine of Justification.*" *JEH* 45 (October 1994): 709–11.

———. *Richard Baxter and the Millennium.* London: Croom and Helm, 1979.

Lane, Anthony. *Calvin and Bernard of Clairvaux.* Studies in Reformed Theology and History, n.s., 1. Princeton, N.J.: Princeton Theological Seminary, 1996.

———. *John Calvin: Student of the Church Fathers.* Grand Rapids, Mich.: Baker Books, 1990.

Lane, Belden C. "Two Schools of Desire: Nature and Marriage in Seventeenth-Century Puritanism." *CH* 69 (June 2000): 372–402.

LeGoff, Jacques. *The Birth of Purgatory.* Translated by Arthur Goldhammer. Chicago: University of Chicago Press, 1984.

Levine, Joseph M. "Latitudinarians, Neoplatonists, and the Ancient Wisdom." In *Philosophy, Science, and Religion in England 1640–1700,* edited by Richard Kroll, Richard Ashcraft, and Perez Zagorin, pp. 85–108. Cambridge: Cambridge University Press, 1992.

Lewalski, Barbara. *Protestant Poetics and the Seventeenth-Century Religious Lyric.* Princeton, N.J.: Princeton University Press, 1979.

Lim, Paul Chang-Ha. *In Pursuit of Purity, Unity, and Liberty: Richard Baxter's Puritan Ecclesiology in Its Seventeenth-Century Context.* Leiden, the Netherlands: E. J. Brill, 2004.

Lovelace, Richard F. *The American Pietism of Cotton Mather: Origins of American Evangelicalism.* Grand Rapids, Mich.: Christian University Press, 1979.

———. "The Anatomy of Puritan Piety: English Puritan Devotional Literature, 1600–1640." In *Christian Spirituality: Post-Reformation and Modern,* edited by Louis Dupre and Don E. Saliers, pp. 294–323. New York: Crossroads, 1991.

Lowrie, Ernest Benson. *The Shape of the Puritan Mind: The Thought of Samuel Willard.* New Haven, Conn.: Yale University Press, 1974.

Luoma, John K. "Who Owns the Fathers? Hooker and Cartwright on the Authority of the Primitive Church." *SCJ* 8:3 (Fall 1977): 45–60.

Luther, Martin. *Three Treatises.* 2nd rev.ed. Philadelphia: Fortress Press, 1970.

MacCulloch, Diarmaid. *The Later Reformation in England, 1547–1603.* 2nd ed. New York: Palgrave, 2001.

———. "Richard Hooker's Reputation." *English Historical Review* 117 (September 2002): 773–812.

———. *Thomas Cranmer: A Life.* New Haven, Conn.: Yale University Press, 1996.

Macfarlane, Alan. *The Family Life of Ralph Josselin: A Seventeenth-Century Clergyman.* New York: Norton, 1970.

Maltby, Judith. *Prayer Book and People in Elizabethan and Early Stuart England.* Cambridge: Cambridge University Press, 1998.

Manuel, Frank E. *The Eighteenth Century Confronts the Gods.* Cambridge, Mass.: Harvard University Press, 1959.

———. *The Religion of Isaac Newton.* Oxford: Clarendon Press, 1974.

Marks, Carol L. "Thomas Traherne and Cambridge Platonism." *PMLA* 81 (December 1966): 521–34.

Martz, Louis L. *The Paradise Within: Studies in Vaughan, Traherne, and Milton.* New Haven, Conn.: Yale University Press, 1964.

———. *The Poetry of Meditation: A Study in English Religious Literature of the Seventeenth Century.* New Haven, Conn.: Yale University Press, 1954.

Matar, N. I. "Aristotelian Tragedy in the Theology of Peter Sterry." *Journal of Literature and Theology* 6 (December 1992): 310–19.

————. "A Devotion to 'Jesus as Mother' in Restoration Puritanism." *JURCHS* 4 (1989): 304–13.

————. "John Donne, Peter Sterry and the *Ars Moriendi.*" *Explorations in Renaissance Culture* 17 (1991): 55–70.

————. "Mysticism and Sectarianism in Mid-Seventeenth Century England." *Studia Mystica* 11 (1988): 55–65.

————. "Peter Sterry and the First English Poem on the Druids." *National Library of Wales Journal* 24 (Winter 1985): 222–243.

————."Peter Sterry and Jacob Boehme." *Notes and Queries*, n.s., 33 (March, 1986): 33-36.

————. "Peter Sterry and the 'Lovely Society' of West Sheen." *Notes and Queries*, n.s., 29 (February 1982): 45–46.

————. "Peter Sterry, the Millennium, and Oliver Cromwell." *JURCHS* 2 (1982): 334–43.

————. "Peter Sterry and Morgan Llwyd." *JURCHS* 2 (1982): 275–79.

————. "Peter Sterry and the 'Paradise Within': A Study of the Emmanuel College Letters." *Restoration: Studies in English Literary Culture, 1660–1700* 13 (Fall 1989):76–84.

————. "Peter Sterry and the Puritan Defense of Ovid in Restoration England." *Studies in Philology* 88 (1991): 110–21.

————. "Peter Sterry and the Ranters." *Notes and Queries*, n.s., 29 (December 1982: 504–6).

Matar, N. I., and P. J. Croft. "The Peter Sterry MSS at Emmanuel College, Cambridge." *Transactions of the Cambridge Bibliographical Society* 8 (1981): 42–56.

Mathews, A. G. "The Wharton Correspondence." *Transactions of the Congregational Historical Society* 10 (1927–1929): 53–65.

Mathieu, D. L. *The Mind of William Paley.* Lincoln: University of Nebraska Press, 1976.

Matter, E. Ann. *The Voice of My Beloved: The Song of Songs in Western Medieval Christianity.* Philadelphia: University of Pennsylvania Press, 1990.

May, Henry F. *The Enlightenment in America.* New York: Oxford University Press, 1976.

McDermott, Gerald R. *Jonathan Edwards Confronts the Gods: Christian Theology, Enlightenment Religion, and Non-Christian Faiths.* Oxford: Oxford University Press, 2000.

McGee, J. Sears. *The Godly Man in Stuart England: Anglicans, Puritans, and the Two Tables, 1620–1670.* New Haven, Conn.: Yale University Press, 1976.

McGiffert, Michael. "From Moses to Adam: The Making of the Covenant of Works." *SCJ* 19 (Summer 1988): 131–56.

————. "Grace and Works: The Rise and Division of Covenant Divinity in Elizabethan Puritanism." *Harvard Theological Review* 75:4 (1982): 463–502.

————. "The Perkinsian Moment of Federal Theology." *Calvin Theological Journal* 29 (1994): 117–48.

McGinn, Bernard. *The Foundations of Mysticism: Origins to the Fifth Century.* New York: Crossroad, 1994.

————. "Mysticism." In *The Oxford Encyclopedia of the Reformation*, edited by Hans Hillerbrand. 4 vols. Vol. 3, pp. 119-24. New York and Oxford: Oxford University Press, 1996.

McGinnis, Scott. *George Gifford and the Reformation of the Common Sort: Puritan Priorities in Elizabethan Religious Life* (Kirksville, Mo: Truman State University Press, 2004.

McGrath, Alister. *A Life of John Calvin.* Oxford: Basil Blackwell, 1990.

McKim, Donald K. *Ramism in William Perkins.* New York: Peter Lang, 1987.

McLachlan, H. John. *Socinianism in Seventeenth-Century England.* Oxford: Oxford University Press, 1951.

McLelland, Joseph C. *The Visible Words of God: A Study in the Theology of Peter Martyr.* London: Oliver and Boyd, 1957.

Meijering, E. P. "The Fathers and Calvinist Orthodoxy: Systematic Theology." In Backus, *Reception.* Vol. 2, pp. 867–87.

Merkel, Ingrid, and Allen G. Debus, eds. *Hermeticism and the Renaissance: Intellectual History and the Occult in Early Modern Europe.* Washington, D.C.: Folger Shakespeare Library, 1988.

Miles, Rogers. *Science, Religion, and Belief: The Clerical Virtuosi of the Royal Society of London, 1663–1687.* New York: Peter Lang, 1992.

Milton, Anthony. *Catholic and Reformed: The Roman and Protestant Churches in English Protestant Thought 1600–1640.* Cambridge: Cambridge University Press, 1995.

Monk, Robert C. *John Wesley: His Puritan Heritage.* Nashville, Tenn.: Abingdon Press, 1966.

Moore, Jonathan D. *English Hypothetical Universalism: John Preston and the Softening of Reformed Theology.* Grand Rapids, Mich.: Eerdmans, 2007.

Muller, Richard A. *After Calvin: Studies in the Development of a Theological Tradition.* Oxford: Oxford University Press, 2003.

———. *Post-Reformation Reformed Dogmatics: The Rise and Development of Reformed Orthodoxy, ca. 1520-ca. 1725.* 4 vols. 2nd ed.. Grand Rapids, Mich.: Baker Academic, 2003.

———. *The Unaccommodated Calvin: Studies in the Foundation of a Theological Tradition.* Oxford: Oxford University Press, 2000.

Mullin, Robert Bruce. *Episcopal Vision/American Reality: High Church Theology and Social Thought in Evangelical America.* New Haven, Conn.: Yale University Press, 1986.

Murray, Iain. "Biographical Introduction." In Joseph Alleine, *An Alarm to the Unconverted,* pp. 7–12. London: Banner of Truth Trust, 1967.

Nauert, Charles G., Jr. *Humanism and the Culture of Renaissance Europe.* Cambridge: Cambridge University Press, 1995.

Nisbet, Robert. *History of the Idea of Progress.* New York: Basic Books, 1980.

Noll, Mark A. *The Rise of Evangelicalism: The Age of Edwards, Whitfield, and the Wesleys.* Downer's Grove, Ill.: Intervarsity Press, 2003.

Null, Ashley. *Thomas Cranmer's Doctrine of Repentance.* Oxford: Clarendon Press, 1994.

Nuttall, Geoffrey. *The Holy Spirit in Puritan Faith and Experience.* Oxford: Basil Blackwell, 1946.

———. "Puritan and Quaker Mysticism." *Theology* 78 (October 1975): 518–31.

———. *Richard Baxter.* London: Thomas Nelson and Sons, 1965.

———. *The Welsh Saints, 1640–1660.* Cardiff: University of Wales Press, 1957.

———. *Visible Saints: The Congregational Way.* Oxford: Basil Blackwell, 1957.

Oberman, Heiko. "Simul Gemitus et Raptus: Luther and Mysticism." In *The Reformation in Medieval Perspective,* edited by Steven E. Ozment, pp. 219–251. Chicago: Quadrangle Books, 1971.

Ogg, David. *England in the Reign of Charles II.* 2 vols. 2nd ed. Cambridge: Cambridge University Press, 1956.

Otto, Rudolf. *The Idea of the Holy.* Translated by John W. Harvey. 1923. Reprint, New York: Oxford University Press, 1958.

Pailin, David A. *Attitudes to Other Religions: Comparative Religion in Seventeenth and Eighteenth-Century Britain.* Manchester, UK: Manchester University Press, 1984.

Parker, Kenneth L., and Eric J. Carlson. *"Practical Divinity:" The Works and Life of Revd Richard Greenham.* Aldershot, UK: Ashgate, 1998.

Parnham, David. *Sir Henry Vane, Theologian: A Study in Seventeenth-Century Religious and Political Discourse.* Madison, N. J., 1997.

Partee, Charles. *Calvin and Classical Philosophy.* 1977. Reprint, Louisville, Ky.: Westminster John Knox, 2005.

Paton, Lewis Bayles. "Sanchuniathon." In *Encyclopedia of Religion and Ethics.* Edited by James Hastings. 13 vols.; vol. 11, pp. 177–81. New York: Charles Scribner's Sons, 1925.

Patrides, C. A., ed. *The Cambridge Platonists.* Cambridge, Mass.: Harvard University Press, 1970.

———. *Premises and Motifs in Renaissance Thought and Literature.* Princeton, N.J.: Princeton University Press, 1982.

Piggot, Stuart. *William Stukeley: An Eighteenth-Century Antiquarian.* Rev. ed. New York: Thames and Hudson, 1985.

Pinto, Vivian de Sola. "Peter Sterry and His Unpublished Writings." *The Review of English Studies* 6 (October 1930): 385–407.

Pinto, Vivian de Sola. *Peter Sterry, Platonist and Puritan, 1613–1672: A Biographical and Critical Study with Passages Selected from His Writings.* 1934. Reprint, New York: Greenwood Press, 1968.

Pococke, J. G. A. "Post-Puritan England and the Problem of the Enlightenment." In *Culture and Politics From Puritanism to the Enlightenment,* edited by Perez Zagorin, pp. 91–111. Berkeley: University of California Press, 1980.

———. "Thomas Hobbes: Atheist or Enthusiast? His Place in a Restoration Debate." *History of Political Thought* 11 (Winter 1990): 737–49.

Polizzotto, Lorenzo. *The Elect Nation: The Savonarolan Movement in Florence 1494–1545.* Oxford: Clarendon Press, 1994.

Popkin, Richard. "The Deist Challenge." In *From Persecution to Toleration: The Glorious Revolution and Religion in England,* edited by Ole Peter Grell, Jonathan I. Israel, and Nicholas Tyacke, pp. 195–215. Oxford: Clarendon Press, 1991.

———. *The History of Scepticism from Savonarola to Bayle.* Rev. ed. Oxford: Oxford University Press, 2003.

Porter, Roy. "The Enlightenment in England." In *The Enlightenment in National Context*, edited by Roy Porter and Mikulas Teich, pp. 1–18. Cambridge: Cambridge University Press, 1981.

Powicke, Frederick J. *The Cambridge Platonists, A Study*. London: J. M. Dent and Sons, 1926.

Prestwich, Menna, ed. *International Calvinism 1541–1715*. Oxford: Clarendon Press, 1985.

Quantin, Jean Louis. "The Fathers in Seventeenth-Century Anglican Theology." In Backus, *Reception*. Vol. 2, pp. 987–1008.

Rambuss, Richard. *Closet Devotions*. Durham, N.C.: Duke University Press, 1998.

Ramsbottom, John D. "Presbyterians and 'Partial Conformity' in the Restoration Church of England." *JEH* 43 (1992): 249–70.

Redwood, John. *Reason, Ridicule and Religion: The Age of Enlightenment in England, 1660–1750*. Cambridge, Mass.: Harvard University Press, 1976.

Reedy, Gerard, S. J. *The Bible and Reason: Anglicans and Scripture in Late Seventeenth-Century England*. Philadelphia: University of Pennsylvania Press, 1985.

Rehnman, Sebastian. *Divine Discourse: The Theological Methodology of John Owen*. Grand Rapids, Mich.: Baker Academic, 2002.

Reuter, Karl. "William Ames: The Leading Theologian in the Awakening of Reformed Pietism." In Matthew Nethenius, Hugo Visscher, and Karl Reuter, *William Ames*. Translated by Douglas Horton. Cambridge, Mass.: Harvard Divinity School Library, 1965.

Ritschl, Albrecht. *Three Essays*. Translated by Philip Hefner. Philadelphia: Fortress Press, 1972.

Rivers, Isabel. "Grace, Holiness, and the Pursuit of Happiness: Bunyan and Restoration Latitudinarianism." In *John Bunyan: Conventicle and Parnassus: Tercentenary Essays*, edited by N. H. Keeble, pp. 45–69. Oxford: Clarendon Press, 1988.

———. *Reason, Grace and Sentiment: A Study of the Language of Religion and Ethics in England 1660–1780*. Vol. 1, *Whichcote to Wesley*. Vol. 2, *Shaftesbury to Hume*. Cambridge: Cambridge University Press, 1991, 2000.

Rose, Craig. *England in the 1690s: Revolution, Religion and War*. Oxford: Blackwell, 1999.

Roth, Cecil. *A Life of Menasseh Ben Israel*. Philadelphia: Jewish Publication Society of America, 1934.

Rupp, Gordon. "A Devotion of Rapture in English Puritanism." In *Reformation, Conformity, and Dissent: Essays in Honour of Geoffrey Nuttall*, edited by R. Buick Knox, pp. 115–31. London: Epworth Press, 1977.

Sandberg, Karl C. *At the Crossroads of Faith and Reason: An Essay on Pierre Bayle*. Tucson: University of Arizona Press, 1966.

Schmitt, Charles B. "Perennial Philosophy: From Agostino Steuco to Leibniz." *JHI* 27 (1966): 505–31.

Scott, W. Major. *Aspects of Christian Mysticism*. London: John Murray, 1907.

Sell, Alan P. F. "John Howe's Eclectic Theism." *JURCHS* 2 (October 1980): 187–93.

Seznec, Jean. *The Survival of the Pagan Gods: The Mythological Tradition and its Place in Renaissance Humanism and Art.* Translated by Barbara F. Sessions. Princeton, N.J.: Princeton University Press, 1953.

Shapiro, Barbara J. *John Wilkins, 1614–1672: An Intellectual Biography.* Berkeley: University of California Press, 1969.

———. *Probability and Certainty in Seventeenth-Century England: A Study of the Relationships Between Natural Science, Religion, History, Law, and Literature.* Princeton, N.J.: Princeton University Press, 1983.

Sharpe, James. *Remember, Remember: A Cultural History of Guy Fawkes Day.* Cambridge: Cambridge University Press, 2005.

Sheehan, Jonathan. *The Enlightenment Bible.* Princeton, N.J.: Princeton University Press, 2005.

Shuger, Debora K. "Faith and Assurance." In *A Companion to Richard Hooker,* edited by Torrance Kirby, pp. 221–50. Leiden, the Netherlands: Brill, 2008.

Shumaker, Wayne. *The Occult Sciences in the Renaissance.* Berkeley: University of California Press, 1972.

Simpson, Alan. *Puritanism in Old and New England.* Chicago: University of Chicago Press, 1955.

Smith, J. W. Ashley. *The Birth of Modern Education: The Contribution of the Dissenting Academies 1660–1800.* London: Independent Press, 1954.

Smith, Nigel. *Perfection Proclaimed: Language and Literature in English Radical Religion, 1640–1660.* Oxford: Oxford University Press, 1989.

Smith, Preserved. *The Enlightenment, 1687–1776.* 1934. Reprint, New York: Collier Books, 1962.

Sommerville, C. John. *Popular Religion in Restoration England.* Gainesville: University of Florida Press, 1977.

———. *The Secularization of Early Modern England: From Religious Culture to Religious Faith.* Oxford: Oxford University Press, 1992.

Sorkin, David. "Geneva's 'Enlightened Orthodoxy:' The Middle Way of Jacob Vernet (1698–1789)." *CH* 74 (June 2005): 286–305.

Spalding, James C., and Brass, Maynard F. "Reduced Episcopacy as a Means to Unify the Church of England, 1640–1662." *CH* 30 (December 1961): 414–32.

Spellman, W. M. *The Latitudinarians and the Church of England, 1660–1700.* Athens, Ga.: University of Georgia Press, 1993.

Sprunger, Keith L. "Ames, Ramus, and the Method of Puritan Theology." *Harvard Theological Review* 59 (April 1966): 133–51.

———. *The Learned Doctor Ames: Dutch Backgrounds of English and American Puritanism.* Urbana: University of Illinois Press, 1972.

Spurr, John. *England in the 1670s: 'This Masquerading Age.'* Oxford: Blackwell, 2000.

———. "From Puritanism to Dissent, 1660–1700." In *The Culture of English Puritanism, 1560–1700,* edited by Christopher Durston and Jacqueline Eales, pp. 234–65. New York: St. Martin's Press, 1996.

———. " 'Rational' Religion in Restoration England." *JHI* 49 (October–December 1988): 563–85.

————. *The Restoration Church of England, 1646–1689.* New Haven, Conn.: Yale University Press, 1991.

————. "Schism and the Restoration Church." *JEH* 41 (July 1991): 408–24.

Stanford, Charles. *Joseph Alleine: His Companions & Times; A Memorial of "Black Bartholomew," 1662.* London, 1861.

Steinberg, S. H. *Five Hundred Years of Printing.* 2nd ed. Baltimore, Md.: Penguin Books, 1961.

Stevenson, David. *The Origins of Freemasonry: Scotland's Century, 1590–1710.* Cambridge: Cambridge University Press, 1988.

Stock, R. D. *The Holy and the Demonic from Sir Thomas Browne to William Blake.* Princeton, N.J.: Princeton University Press, 1982.

Stromberg, Roland N. *Religious Liberalism in Eighteenth-Century England.* Oxford: Oxford University Press, 1954.

Taliaferro, Charles, and Alison J. Teply, eds. *Cambridge Platonist Spirituality.* New York: Paulist Press, 2004.

Tamburello, Dennis E. *Union with Christ: John Calvin and the Mysticism of St. Bernard.* Louisville, Ky.: Westminster John Knox Press, 1994.

Thomann, Gunther. "John Ernest Grabe (1660–1711): Lutheran Syncretist and Patristic Scholar." *JEH* 43 (July, 1992): 414–27.

Thomas, J. M. Lloyd. "Introductory Essay." In *The Autobiography of Richard Baxter,* edited by J. M. Lloyd Thomas. London: J. M. Dent and Sons, 1931.

Thomas, Roger. *Daniel Williams, "Presbyterian Bishop."* Friends of Dr. Williams's Library Sixteenth Lecture. London: Dr. Williams's Trust, 1964.

————. "Partners in Nonconformity." In *The English Presbyterians: From Elizabethan Puritanism to Modern Unitarianism,* edited by C. G. Bolam, Jeremy Goring, H. L. Short, and Roger Thomas, pp. 93–112. Boston: Beacon Press, 1968.

Todd, Margo. *Christian Humanism and the Puritan Social Order.* Cambridge: Cambridge University Press, 1987.

————. "Seneca and the Protestant Mind: The Influence of Stoicism on Puritan Ethics." *Archiv fur Reformationsgeschichte* 74 (1983): 182–99.

Toliver, Harold E. *Marvell's Ironic Vision.* New Haven, Conn.: Yale University Press, 1965.

Toon, Peter. *The Emergence of Hyper-Calvinism in English Nonconformity, 1689–1765.* London: Olive Tree, 1967.

Trevor-Roper, Hugh. *From Counter-Reformation to Glorious Revolution.* Chicago: University of Chicago Press, 1992.

Trinkaus, Charles. *In Our Image and Likeness: Humanity and Divinity in Italian Humanist Thought.* 2 vols. Chicago: University of Chicago Press, 1970.

Troeltsch, Ernst. *The Social Teachings of the Christian Churches.* Translated by Olive Wyon. 2 vols. 1931. Reprint, New York: Harper and Brothers, 1960.

Trueman, Carl R. *The Claims of Truth: John Owen's Trinitarian Theology.* Carlisle, UK: Paternoster Press, 1998.

————. *Luther's Legacy" Salvation and English Reformers, 1525–1556.* Oxford: Clarendon Press, 1994.

Tuck, Richard. "The Christian Atheism of Thomas Hobbes." In *Atheism from the Reformation to the Enlightenment*, edited by Michael Hunter and David Wootton, pp. 111–30. Oxford: Clarendon Press, 1992.

Turk, F. A. "Charles Morton: His Place in the Historical Development of British Science in the Seventeenth Century." *Journal of the Royal Institution of Cornwall*, n.s., 4 (1961–1964): 353–63.

Turner, Frank M. *The Greek Heritage in Victorian Britain*. New Haven, Conn.: Yale University Press, 1981.

Tyacke, Nicholas. *Anti-Calvinists: The Rise of English Arminianism*. Oxford: Oxford University Press, 1987.

———. "The 'Rise of Puritanism' and the Legalizing of Dissent, 1571–1719." In *From Persecution to Toleration: The Glorious Revolution and Religion in England*, edited by Ole Peter Grell, Jonathan I. Israel, and Nicholas Tyacke, pp. 17–49. Oxford: Clarendon Press, 1991.

Underhill, Evelyn. *Mysticism: A Study in the Nature and Development of Man's Spiritual Consciousness*. 1911. Reprint, New York: E. P. Dutton, 1961.

Underwood, T. L. *Primitivism, Radicalism, and the Lamb's War*. Oxford: Oxford University Press, 1997.

Van Oort, Johannes. "John Calvin and the Church Fathers." In Backus, *Reception*. Vol. 2, pp. 661–700.

Vesey, Mark. "English Translations of the Latin Fathers, 1517–1611." In Backus, *Reception*. Vol. 2, pp. 775–835.

von Rohr, John. *The Covenant of Grace in Puritan Thought*. Atlanta, Ga.: Scholars Press, 1986.

Wakefield, Gordon. "Mysticism and Its Puritan Types." *London Quarterly and Holborn Review*, 6th ser., 35 (January 1966): 34–45.

———. *Puritan Devotion: Its Place in the Development of Christian Piety*. London: Epworth Press, 1957.

Walker, A. Keith. *William Law: His Life and Thought*. London: SPCK, 1973.

Walker, D. P. *The Ancient Theology: Studies in Christian Platonism from the Fifteenth to the Eighteenth Century*. Ithaca, N.Y.: Cornell University Press, 1972.

———. *The Decline of Hell: Seventeenth-Century Discussions of Eternal Torment*. Chicago: University of Chicago Press, 1964.

———. *Spiritual and Demonic Magic from Ficino to Campanella*. 1958. Reprint, Notre Dame, Ind.: University of Notre Dame Press, 1976,

Wallace, Dewey D., Jr. "George Gifford, Puritan Propaganda, and Popular Religion in Elizabethan England." *Sixteenth Century Journal* 9 (April 1978): 27–49.

———. "The Image of Saintliness in Puritan Hagiography." In *The Divine Drama in History and Liturgy: Essays Presented to Horton Davies on His Retirement from Princeton University*, edited by John E. Booty, pp. 23–43. Allison Park, Pa.: Pickwick Publications, 1984.

———. "Puritan and Anglican: The Interpretation of Christ's Descent Into Hell in Elizabethan Theology." *Archiv für Reformationsgeschichte* 69 (1978): 248–87.

————. *Puritans and Predestination: Grace in English Protestant Theology, 1525–1695.* Chapel Hill: University of North Carolina Press, 1982.

————. "Socinianism, Justification by Faith, and the Sources of John Locke's *The Reasonableness of Christianity.*" *JHI* 45 (January–March, 1984): 49–66.

————. *The Spirituality of the Later English Puritans: An Anthology.* Macon, Ga.: Mercer University Press, 1987.

Ward, W. R. *Christianity Under the Ancien Regime, 1648–1789.* Cambridge: Cambridge University Press, 1999.

————. *Early Evangelicalism: A Global Intellectual History, 1670–1789.* Cambridge: Cambridge University Press, 2006.

Warfield, Benjamin. *The Westminster Assembly and Its Work.* New York: Oxford University Press, 1931.

Watkins, E. I. *Poets and Mystics.* London: Sheed and Ward, 1953.

Watts, Michael R. *The Dissenters: From the Reformation to the French Revolution.* Oxford: Clarendon Press, 1978.

Weber, Max. *The Protestant Ethic and the Spirit of Capitalism.* New York: Charles Scribner's, 1958.

Webster, Tom. *Godly Clergy in Early Stuart England: The Caroline Puritan Movement c. 1620–1643.* Cambridge: Cambridge University Press, 1997.

Weir, David A. *The Origins of the Federal Theology in Sixteenth-Century Reformation Thought.* Oxford: Clarendon Press, 1980.

Westaway, Jonathan, and Richard D. Harrison. "The 'Surey Demoniack:' Defining Protestantism in 1690s Lancashire." In *Unity and Diversity in the Church: Papers Read at the 1994 Summer Meeting and the 1995 Winter Meeting of the Ecclesiastial History Society,* edited by R. N. Swanson, pp. 263–82. Cambridge, Mass.: Blackwell, 1996.

Westfall, Richard S. *Science and Religion in Seventeenth-Century England.* 1958. Reprint, Ann Arbor: University of Michigan Press, 1973.

White, B. R. *The English Baptists of the Seventeenth Century.* London: Baptist Historical Society, 1983.

————. "The Twilight of Puritanism in the Years Before and after 1688." In *From Persecution to Toleration: The Glorious Revolution and Religion in England,* edited by Ole Peter Grell, Jonathan I. Israel, and Nicholas Tyacke, pp. 306–30. Oxford: Clarendon Press, 1991.

Willen, Diane. "Communion of the Saints: Spiritual Reciprocity and the Godly Community in Early Modern England." *Albion* 27 (1995): 19–41.

Willey, Basil. *The Eighteenth-Century Background: Studies on the Idea of Nature in the Thought of the Period.* 1940. Reprint, Boston: Beacon Press, 1961.

————. *Seventeenth-Century Studies.* 1934. Reprint, New York: Doubleday, 1955.

Williams, Jean. "The Puritan Quest for the Enjoyment of God: An Analysis of the Theological and Devotional Writings of Puritans in Seventeenth-Century England." Ph.D. dissertation, University of Melbourne, 1997.

Wills, John E., Jr. *1688: A Global History.* New York: Norton, 2001.

Wilson, John F. *Pulpit in Parliament: Puritanism during the English Civil Wars, 1640–1648.* Princeton, N. J.: Princeton University Press, 1969.

Winship, Michael. "Behold the Bridegroom Cometh! Marital Imagery in
    Massachusetts Preaching, 1630–1730." *Early American Literature* 27 (1992):
    170–81.
———. "Contesting Control Among the Godly: William Pynchon Reexamined."
    William and Mary Quarterly 3rd ser., 54 (October 1997): 795–822.
———. *Making Heretics: Militant Protestantism and Free Grace in Massachusetts,
    1636–1641.* Princeton, N.J.: Princeton University Press, 2002.
———. *Seers of God: Puritan Providentialism in the Restoration and Early Enlightenment.*
    Baltimore, Md.: Johns Hopkins Press, 1996.
Wojcik, Jan W. *Robert Boyle and the Limits of Reason.* Cambridge: Cambridge
    University Press, 1997.
Wolffe, John. "Anti-Catholicism in Evangelical Identity." In *Evangelicalism:
    Comparative Studies of Popular Protestantism in North America, The British Isles, and
    Beyond, 1700–1990,* edited by Mark A. Noll, David W. Bebbington, and George A.
    Rawlyk, pp. 179–97. New York: Oxford University Press, 1994.
Wootton, David. "New Histories of Atheism." In *Atheism from the Reformation to the
    Enlightenment,* edited by Michael Hunter and David Wootton, pp. 13–54. Oxford:
    Clarendon Press, 1978.
Yates, Francis A. *Giordano Bruno and the Hermetic Tradition.* 1964. Reprint, New York:
    Vintage Books, 1969.
———. *The Occult Philosophy in the Elizabethan Age.* London: Routledge and Kegan
    Paul, 1979.
———. *The Rosicrucian Enlightenment.* Boulder, Colo.: Shambala Books, 1978.
Young, B. W. *Religion and Enlightenment in Eighteenth-Century England: Theological
    Debate from Locke to Burke.* Oxford: Clarendon Press, 1998.

Index

Clarke, Samuel, Puritan
    hagiographer, 143
Clarke, Samuel, Church of England
    theologian, 48, 221, 226, 231
Clement of Alexandria, 81, 97, 192,
    210, 225
Climacus, John, 61
Cocceius, Johannes, 5
Coffey, John, 263n7
Coleridge, Samuel Taylor, 239
Collinson, Patrick, 10
comets, 214
Como, David R., 56, 265n28,
    266n37, 289n151
Conant, John, 23, 222, 231
confessionalization, 18–19
Congregationalists, see Independents
Conventicle Act, 22
conversion, 127, 134, 136, 139, 162, 166
Cooper, William, 154
Copernicus, and Copernican
    Astronomy, 214–15
Cotton, John, 73
Covenant, 112–13, 126, 159–60
Cradock, Walter, 74
Cragg, Gerald R., 4, 28
Cranmer, Thomas, 13, 131, 229
Crisp, Tobias, 5, 238–39
Cromwell, Oliver, 54, 56
Cudworth, Ralph, 59, 113, 168, 179,
    197, 217
    on ancient theology, 103, 110,
        279n78
    on atheism, 45, 47
Culverwell, Nathaniel, 35, 59, 103, 110,
    190, 192
Cyprian, 133

Daillé, Jean. 225, 227–28
Davenant, John, 138
Davenport, John, 73
Davie, Donald, 9
Defoe, Daniel, 27

Deism, Deists, 30, 36–38, 180–81, 194,
    215–16, 260n132
DeKrey, Gary S., 253n39
Democritus, 29, 35, 46, 178–79
Derham, William, 185–86
Descartes, 29, 179, 187, 213–14
    and atheism, 44, 46
    and Cambridge Platonists, 32
    John Edwards on, 245
    on reason, 32
    See also Cartesianism
Descent of Christ into hell, 239–40
Diagoras, 46
Diodati, Charles, 105
Diodati, Giovanni, 105
Diogenes Laertes, 94
Dionysios the Areopagite, 220
Dionysios of Halicarnassus, 207
Dissenters, 20–27, 125, 171, 175–76, 180,
    197–98, 225, 231, 254nn48–49
dissenting academies, 27, 32, 93
Dod, John, 134, 141
Doddridge, Philip, 141
Dodwell, Henry, 224, 226
Dolittle, Thomas, 27, 152, 186
Domincans, 239
Donne, John, 67, 71, 268n69
Dort, Synod of, 13, 138, 233, 238, 240
Drayton, Michael, 102
Druids, 54, 90, 95, 100, 118, 220
Dryden, John, 37
Duffy, Eamon, 149, 151
Dugdale, Richard, 40
Duns Scotus, 17
D'Urfe, Honore, 54, 73
Durham, James, 67

Eckhart, Meister, 58
Edward VI, King, 13
Edwards, John, 6–7, 95, 141, 240–42,
    308nn113, 115
    as "affectionate divine," 208–09
    on allegory, 220